Donated by...

The

Jost-Ore

To Olive Hopkin
(Nottingham '69)
and the memory
of Dorothy Brett
(Taos '75)

LADY CHATTERLEY

The Making of the Novel

Also from Unwin Hyman

THE SHORT SEASON BETWEEN TWO SILENCES
The Mystical and the Political in the Novels of Virginia Woolf
Madeline Moore

POUND'S CANTOS
Peter Makin

THE ART OF FAILURE: CONRAD'S FICTION
Suresh Raval

BACKGROUNDS FOR JOYCE'S DUBLINERS
Donald T. Torchiana

LADY CHATTERLEY

The Making of the Novel

Derek Britton
Department of English Language
University of Edinburgh

London
UNWIN HYMAN
Boston   Sydney   Wellington

Published by the Academic Division of
Unwin Hyman Ltd
15/17 Broadwick Street, London W1V 1FP, UK

Allen & Unwin Inc.,
8 Winchester Place, Winchester, Mass. 01890, USA

Allen & Unwin (Australia) Ltd,
8 Napier Street, North Sydney, NSW 2060, Australia

Allen & Unwin (New Zealand) Ltd in association with
the Port Nicholson Press Ltd,
60 Cambridge Terrace, Wellington, New Zealand

First published in 1988

British Library Cataloguing in Publication Data

Britton, Derek
　　Lady Chatterley: the making of the novel.
1. Lawrence, D. H. Lady Chatterley's lover
I. Title
823'.912　　PR6023.A93L2
ISBN 0-04-800075-2

Library of Congress Cataloging-in-Publication Data

Britton, Derek.
　　Lady Chatterley: the making of the novel.
Bibliography: p.
Includes index.
1. Lawrence, D. H. (David Herbert), 1885–1930.
Lady Chatterly's lover. I. Title.
PR6023.A93.L3127　1988　　923'.912　　87–13069
ISBN 0-04-800075-2 (alk. paper)

Typeset in 10 on 12 point Garamond by Computape (Pickering) Ltd
and printed in Great Britain by
Billing & Sons Ltd, Worcester

Contents

Acknowledgements

Researching the material for this book was an immensely enjoyable task. It was a pleasure to acquaint myself better with the works and character of D. H. Lawrence, to read the works of my predecessors in the field of Lawrentian studies, to tramp the woodland paths of the Lawrence country and visit some of the country houses and estates of my native Derbyshire, and to meet or correspond with the very many kind and engaging personalities who responded to my requests for help.

Out of the large general debt which I owe to all those whose works are referred to in this book I should like to cite in particular my grateful dependence on Edward Nehls's *D. H. Lawrence: A Composite Biography*, on the writings of Keith Sagar (especially his *D. H. Lawrence: A Calendar of his Works* and his article on 'Lawrence and the Wilkinsons'), on Michael Squires's *The Creation of 'Lady Chatterley's Lover'*, and on the work of the editors of *The Letters of D. H. Lawrence*. James Boulton, the general editor of these volumes of letters, and Michael Black of the Cambridge University Press generously allowed me to examine and refer to in paraphrase the unpublished letters of D. H. Lawrence; and Professor Boulton was kind enough to give me the use of his room at Birmingham University Library, where I had access to copies of all Lawrence's extant correspondence. I have also benefited from the scholarship and editorial skills of Professor James C. Cowan, who kindly agreed to read my first draft. To all these I owe my warmest thanks, as I do also the University of Edinburgh for assistance towards typing and travel expenses.

For invaluable information and warm hospitality I am especially grateful to Mrs Olive Hopkin, Mrs Margaret Needham and Mr Reresby Sitwell. I should also like to thank the following for the help or encouragement they gave at various stages in the preparation of this book: Keith Ashfield, Virginia Barnes, Constance Britton, T. B. B. Bingham, Jane Harris-Matthews, Gordon Hill, Pamela Kettle, George Leslie, J. MacKerracher, Martin Pope and Jane Thompson. My thanks are due, too, to my family – to my wife

Patricia for her patience, support and judicious criticism, to my daughter Rosalind for her companionship on walks in Eastwood and to my daughter Niamh for her contagious zest.

I am grateful to Laurence Pollinger and the Estate of Mrs Frieda Lawrence Ravagli and also to Cambridge University Press and Viking Penguin, Inc. for permission to quote from the published writings of D. H. Lawrence and Frieda Lawrence; to the University of Wisconsin Press for permission to quote from Edward Nehls, *D. H. Lawrence: A Composite Biography*, copyright © 1957, 1958, 1959 the Regents of The University of Wisconsin; to Chatto & Windus Ltd and to Harper & Row, Publishers, Inc. for permission to quote from Grover Smith (ed.) *The Letters of Aldous Huxley*, copyright © 1969 Laura Huxley and Grover Smith, and also from Aldous Huxley, *Two or Three Graces*, copyright 1926, renewed 1953 by Aldous Huxley; to Churchill Livingstone, Medical Publishers, for permission to quote from John Bancroft, *Human Sexuality and its Problems*; to Nottinghamshire County Council, Local Studies Library for permission to quote from a transcript of a conversation between David Gerard and Charles Leeming; to A. D. Peters & Co. Ltd for permission to quote from Sean Hignett, *Brett: From Bloomsbury to New Mexico*, published by Hodder & Stoughton Ltd.

Abbreviations

Ada: A. Lawrence, and G. Stuart Gelder, *Young Lorenzo: Early Life of D. H. Lawrence* (London: Secker, 1932).

Adventures: G. Orioli, *Adventures of a Bookseller* (London: Chatto & Windus, 1938).

Aldington: R. Aldington, *Life for Life's Sake* (London: Cassell, 1968).

Brett: D. Brett, *Lawrence and Brett: A Friendship* (London: Secker, 1933).

Brett III: p. III of the Epilogue to D. Brett, *Lawrence and Brett: A Friendship*, ed. J. Manchester (Santa Fe, N. Mex.: Sunstone Press, 1974).

Brew: E. Brewster, and A. Brewster, *D. H. Lawrence: Reminiscences and Correspondence* (London: Secker, 1934).

Brown: C. Brown, *Contacts* (London: Cassell, 1935).

Bynner: W. Bynner, *Journey with Genius* (London: Nevill, 1953).

Calendar: K. Sagar, *D. H. Lawrence: A Calendar of His Works* (Manchester: Manchester University Press, 1979).

Carswell: C. Carswell, *The Savage Pilgrimage* (London: Secker, 1932).

Cent: D. H. Lawrence, *The Centaur Letters* (Austin, Tex.: Humanities Research Center, University of Texas at Austin, 1970).

Cerf: B. Cerf, 'Trade winds', *Saturday Review of Literature*, vol. 35, no. 13 (29 March 1952), pp. 6–8.

CL: H. T. Moore (ed.), *The Collected Letters of D. H. Lawrence* (London: Heinemann, 1962).

Daleski: H. M. Daleski, *The Forked Flame: A Study of D. H. Lawrence* (London: Faber, 1965).

Delany: P. Delany, *D. H. Lawrence's Nightmare* (Hassocks, Sussex: Harvester, 1979).

Delavenay: E. Delavenay, 'Les trois amants de Lady Chatterley', *Etudes Anglaises*, vol. 29 (1976), pp. 46–63.

DHLR: *D. H. Lawrence Review*.

EC: D. H. Lawrence, *The Escaped Cock*, ed. G. M. Lacy (Los Angeles, Cal.: Black Sparrow Press, 1973).

Echo: D. Garnett, *The Golden Echo* (London: Chatto & Windus, 1953).

Edith: E. Sitwell, *Taken Care Of* (London: Hutchinson, 1965).

EKA: Eastwood and Kimberley Advertiser.

Ellman: R. Ellmann *James Joyce* (London: Oxford University Press, 1959).

EP: D. H. Lawrence, *Etruscan Places* (Harmondsworth: Penguin, 1950).

Farjeon: E. Farjeon, *Nuts and May* (London: Collins, 1926).

FLC: D. H. Lawrence, *The First Lady Chatterley* (Harmondsworth: Penguin, 1973).

Flowers: D. Garnett, *Flowers of the Forest* (London: Chatto & Windus, 1955).

Frieda: F. Lawrence, *Frieda Lawrence: The Memoirs and Correspondence*, ed. E. W. Tedlock (London: Heinemann, 1961).

Gill: S. Gill, 'The composite world: two versions of *Lady Chatterley's lover*', *Essays in Criticism*, vol. 21, no. 4 (1971), pp. 347–64.

Gossip: B., Lady Glenavy, *Today We Will Only Gossip* (London: Constable, 1964).

Gransden: K. W. Gransden, 'Rananim: D. H. Lawrence's letters to S. S. Koteliansky', *Twentieth Century*, vol. 159 (January 1956), pp. 22–32.

Griffin: A. R. Griffin, *Mining in the East Midlands 1550–1947* (London: Cass, 1981).

Hignett: S. Hignett, *Brett: From Bloomsbury to New Mexico: A Biography* (London: Hodder & Stoughton, 1984).

Hinz: E. J. Hinz, 'Pornography, novel, mythic narrative: the three versions of *Lady Chatterley's Lover*', *Modernist Studies*, vol. 3 (1979), pp. 35–47.

Holloway: M. Holloway, *Norman Douglas* (London: Secker & Warburg, 1976).

Hux: A. Huxley (ed.), *The Letters of D. H. Lawrence* (London: Heinemann, 1932).

Irv: P. Irvine and A. Kiley (eds), 'D. H. Lawrence and Frieda Lawrence: Letters to Dorothy Brett', *D. H. Lawrence Review*, vol. 9 (Spring 1976), pp. 1–116.

Jackson: D. Jackson, 'Literary allusions in *Lady Chatterley's Lover*', in M. Squires and D. Jackson (eds), *D. H. Lawrence's 'Lady': A New Look at 'Lady Chatterley's Lover'* (Athens, Ga: University of Georgia Press, 1986), pp. 172–80.

JTLJ: D. H. Lawrence, *John Thomas and Lady Jane* (Harmondsworth: Penguin, 1973).

Lacy: G. M. Lacy and L. Vasey, *A Calendar of the Letters of D. H. Lawrence*, 2 vols (Austin, Tex.: Humanities Research Center, University of Texas at Austin, 1976).

'Lady': M. Squires and D. Jackson (eds), *D. H. Lawrence's 'Lady': A New Look at 'Lady Chatterley's Lover'* (Athens, Ga: University of Georgia Press, 1985).

LAH: D. H. Lawrence, *Love Among the Haystacks and Other Stories* (Harmondsworth: Penguin, 1960).

LCL: D. H. Lawrence, *Lady Chatterley's Lover* (Harmondsworth: Penguin, 1960).

Lea: F. A. Lea, *Life of John Middleton Murry* (London: Methuen, 1959).

Let 1, 2 and *3*: J. T. Boulton, A. Robertson and G. J. Zytaruk (eds), *The Letters of D. H. Lawrence*, Vols 1–3 (Cambridge: Cambridge University Press, 1979–84).

Life: K. Sagar, *The Life of D. H. Lawrence* (London: Eyre Methuen, 1980).

Lloyd: T. O. Lloyd, *Empire to Welfare State: English History 1906–1967* (Oxford: Oxford University Press, 1970).

Looking Back: N. Douglas, *Looking Back: An Autobiographical Excursion* (London: Chatto & Windus, 1934).

Luhan: M. Luhan, *Lorenzo in Taos* (London: Secker, 1933).

Mackenzie V: C. M. Mackenzie, *My Life and Times: Octave Five, 1915–1923* (London: Chatto & Windus, 1966).

Mackenzie VI: C. M. Mackenzie, *My Life and Times: Octave Six, 1923–1930* (London: Chatto & Windus, 1967).

Mohr: M. Mohr (ed.), 'The unpublished letters of D. H. Lawrence to Max Mohr', *T'ien Hsia Monthly*, vol. 1 (1935), pp. 21–36, 166–79.

More Than: F. Mackenzie, *More Than I Should* (London: Collins, 1940).

Murry: J. M. Murry, *Reminiscences of D. H. Lawrence* (London: Cape, 1933).

Musical Chairs: C. Gray, *Musical Chairs or Between Two Stools* (London: Home & Van Thal, 1948).

Nehls 1, 2 and 3: E. Nehls (ed.), *D. H. Lawrence: A Composite Biography*, Vols 1–3 (Wisconsin: University of Wisconsin Press, 1957–9).

Neville: G. H. Neville, *A Memoir of D. H. Lawrence*, (Cambridge: Cambridge University Press, 1981).

NG: *Nottingham Guardian*.

NJ: *Nottingham Journal*.

'*Not I*': F. Lawrence, '*Not I, But the Wind . . .*' (London: Heinemann, 1935).

Ober: W. B. Ober, *Boswell's Clap and Other Essays: Medical Analyses of Literary Men's Afflictions* (Carbondale and Edwardsville, Ill.: Southern Illinois University Press, 1979), 'Lady Chatterley's what?', pp. 89–117.

Osbert: O. Sitwell, *Penny Foolish* (London: Macmillan, 1935).

Pearson: J. Pearson, *Façades: Edith, Osbert and Sacheverell Sitwell* (London: Macmillan, 1978).

Ph: D. H. Lawrence, *Phoenix: The Posthumous Papers of D. H. Lawrence*, ed. E. D. McDonald (London: Heinemann, 1936).

Ph 2: D. H. Lawrence, *Phoenix II*, ed. W. Roberts and H. T. Moore (London: Heinemann, 1968).

PL: H. T. Moore, *The Priest of Love* (London: Heinemann, 1974).

Poems: V. de Sola Pinto and W. Roberts (eds), *The Complete Poems of D. H. Lawrence* (London: Heinemann, 1964).

Point: A. Huxley, *Point Counter Point: A Novel* (London: Chatto & Windus, 1928).

Portrait: R. Aldington, *Portrait of a Genius, But . . .* (London: Heinemann, 1950).

Pugh: B. Pugh, 'Locations in D. H. Lawrence', in K. Sagar (ed.), *A D. H. Lawrence Handbook* (Manchester: Manchester University Press, 1982), pp. 239–64.

Rainbow: D. H. Lawrence, *The Rainbow* (Harmondsworth: Penguin, 1981).

Sanders: S. Sanders, *D. H. Lawrence: The World of the Major Novels* (London: Vision, 1973).

Sec: M. Secker, (ed.), *Letters from D. H. Lawrence to Martin Secker* (priv. publ., 1970).

Sklar: K. Sagar and S. Sklar, 'Major productions of Lawrence's plays', in K. Sagar (ed.), *A D. H. Lawrence Handbook* (Manchester: Manchester University Press, 1982), pp. 283–328.

SL: D. H. Lawrence, *Sons and Lovers* (Harmondsworth: Penguin, 1948).

Smith: G. Smith (ed.), *Letters of Aldous Huxley* (London: Chatto & Windus, 1969).

Spencer: R. Spencer, *D. H. Lawrence* (London: Woolf, 1981).

Spilka: M. Spilka, 'Lawrence versus Peeperkorn on abdication; or what happens to a pagan vitalist when the juice runs out?', in R. B. Partlow Jr and H. T. Moore (eds), *D. H. Lawrence: The Man Who Lived* (Carbondale and Edwardsville, Ill.: Southern Illinois University Press, 1981), pp. 105–20, 274–6 (notes).

Squires: M. Squires, *The Creation of Lady Chatterley's Lover* (Baltimore and London: Johns Hopkins University Press, 1983).

Strickland: G. Strickland, 'The first "Lady Chatterley's Lover"', *Encounter*, vol. 36 (January 1971), pp. 44–52.

VG: D. H. Lawrence, *The Virgin and the Gipsy* (Harmondsworth; Penguin, 1950).

Widmer: K. Widmer, 'The pertinence of modern pastoral: the three versions of *Lady Chatterley's Lover*', *Studies in the Novel*, vol. 5 (1973), pp. 298–313.

Wilk: K. Sagar, 'Lawrence and the Wilkinsons', *Review of English Literature*, vol. 3, no. 4 (October 1963).

WL: D. H. Lawrence, *Women in Love*, eds D. Farmer, L. Vasey and J. Worthen (Cambridge: Cambridge University Press, 1987).

WP: D. H. Lawrence, *The White Peacock*, ed. A. Robertson (Cambridge: Cambridge University Press, 1983).

WWRA: D. H. Lawrence, *The Woman Who Rode Away and Other Stories*, (Harmondsworth: Penguin, 1950).

Zyt: G. Zytaruk (ed.), *The Quest for Rananim: D. H. Lawrence's Letter to S. S. Koteliansky* (Montreal and London: McGill–Queen's University Press, 1970).

LADY CHATTERLEY

The Making of the Novel

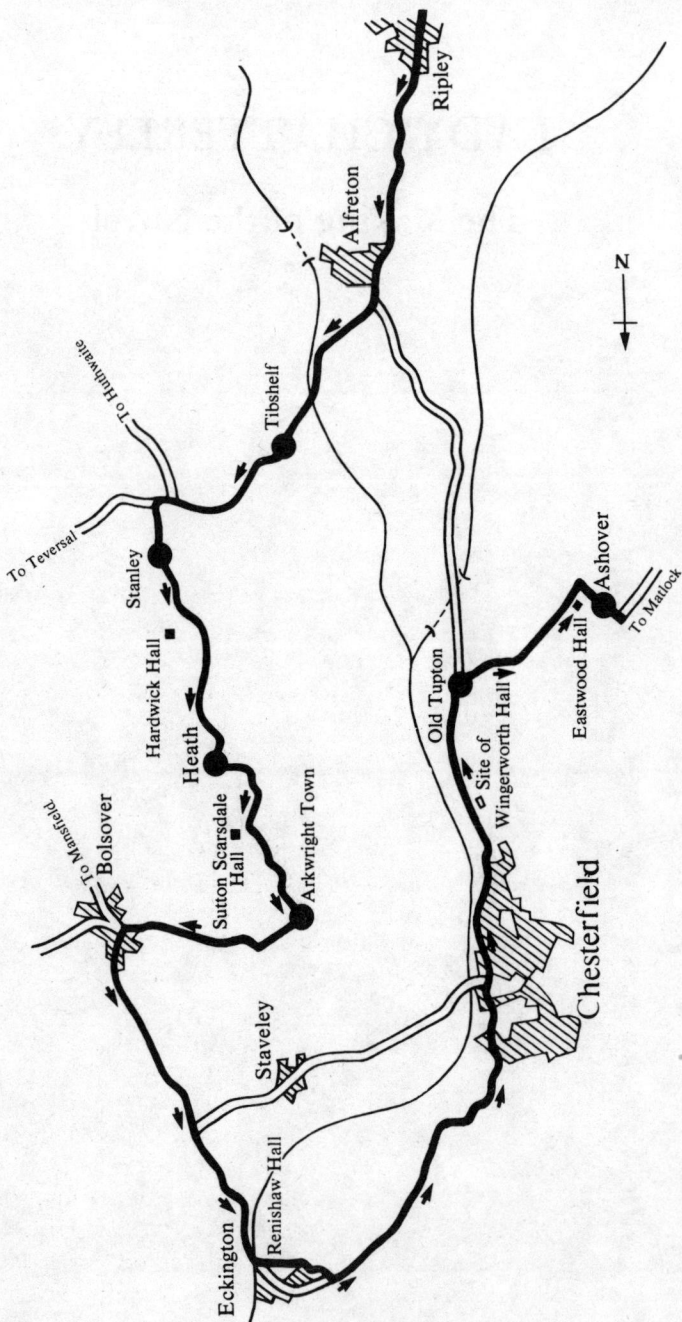

Conjectured Route of Lawrence's Drive Through Derbyshire 15th September 1926

N

Ripley
Alfreton
To Hulthwaite
Tibshelf
To Teversal
Stanley
Hardwick Hall
Heath
Sutton Scarsdale Hall
Arkwright Town
To Mansfield
Bolsover
Staveley
Renishaw Hall
Eckington
Chesterfield
Site of Wingerworth Hall
Old Tupton
Eastwood Hall
Ashover
To Matlock

miles
0   2

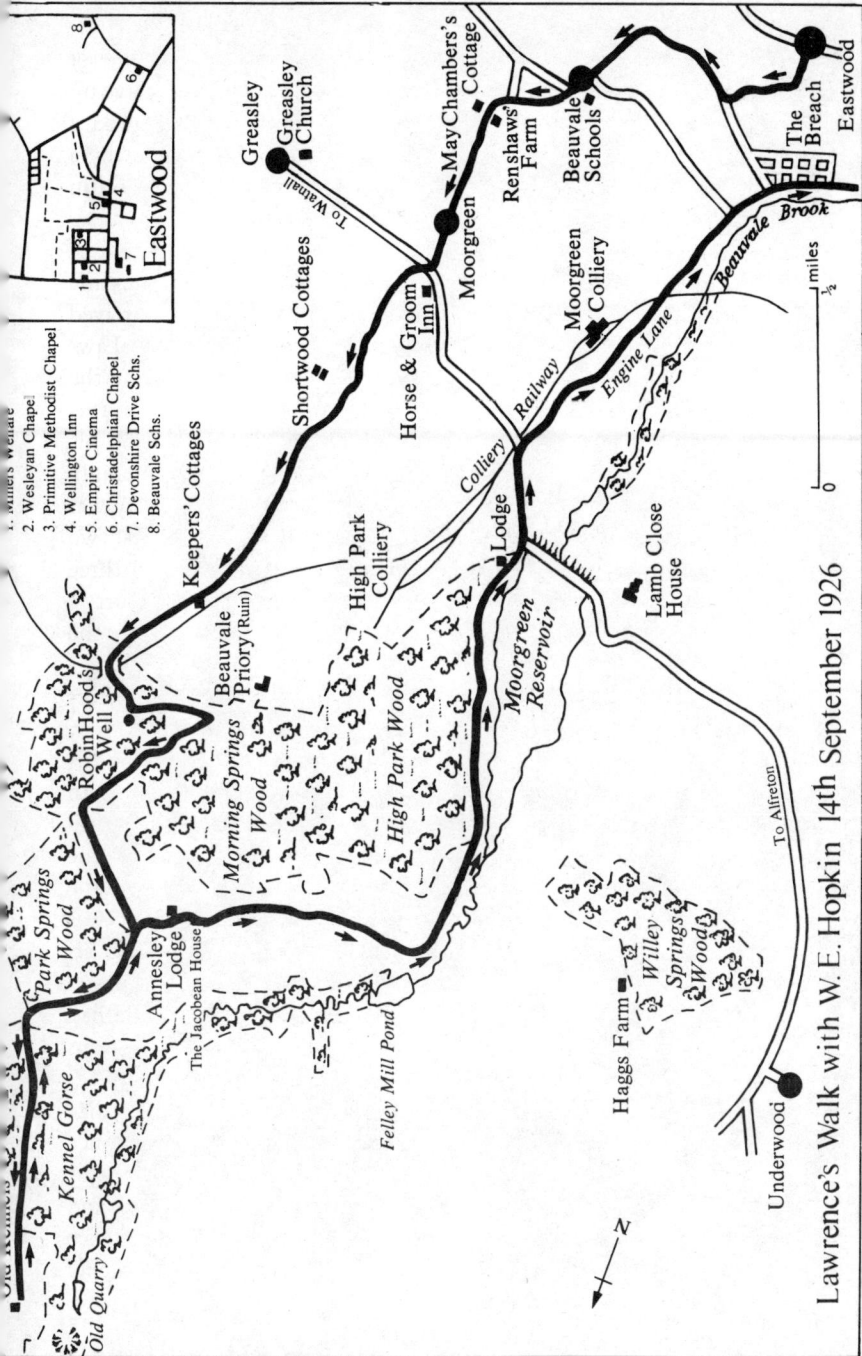

Lawrence's Walk with W.E. Hopkin 14th September 1926

Eastwood

1. Miners Welfare
2. Wesleyan Chapel
3. Primitive Methodist Chapel
4. Wellington Inn
5. Empire Cinema
6. Christadelphian Chapel
7. Devonshire Drive Schs.
8. Beauvale Schs.

Greasley
Greasley Church

To Watnall

Shortwood Cottages

Horse & Groom Inn

Moorgreen

May Chambers's Cottage

Renshaws' Farm

Beauvale Schools

The Breach
Eastwood

Beauvale Brook

Moorgreen Colliery

Keepers' Cottages

Colliery Railway

Engine Lane

Lodge

Lamb Close House

Moorgreen Reservoir

High Park Colliery

High Park Wood

Beauvale Priory (Ruin)

Morning Springs Wood

Robin Hood's Well

Park Springs Wood

Annesley Lodge

The Jacobean House

Felley Mill Pond

Kennel Gorse

Old Quarry

Haggs Farm

Willey Springs Wood

Underwood

To Alfreton

N

0   ½ miles

1

11 September 1925:
Prospects and Retrospects

On 11 September 1925, D. H. Lawrence reached the age of 40. The day was passed on a train that was ploughing its way eastwards through the dreary landscapes of the American prairies towards Chicago, from where Lawrence was to travel on to New York, to embark a week later for England and the Old World. Judged by the timing of his rail journey, Lawrence saw the day itself as undeserving of any special celebration; but the uncharacteristic proclamations of his age in writings of the ensuing year or so suggest that he attached some significance to his entry into the fifth decade of life. As a marker of the onset of middle age it seems to have evoked in Lawrence responses which differed from those of others only to the extent that the frailty of his health gave greater potency to the dispiriting recognition of how quickly the years had passed and of what little of life remained. It was for Lawrence, as for other men, an age for taking stock of one's life and career and for decisions regarding new directions in the future. Since he was accustomed to approach every phase of his life as a crossroads, this was not a novel experience for him, but it was made no easier by the fact that he was by nature irresolute except in obstinacy, and changeable except in his constant passion for life.

His first impulses, developed when he settled in Italy in November 1925, were towards cultivating a more carefree, softer and more acquiescent approach to life. This habit of 'insouciance' was to be adopted in relations with himself: 'I don't take myself seriously, except between 8.0 and 10.0 a.m., and at the stroke of midnight' (*CL* 875f.); and it was to apply to relations with others: 'I do think one ought, if one can, to remove the fight . . . from the field of one's personal relationships' (*CL* 915). It was to be extended also to his work. The world was not 'going to change very radically, not for all the telling of all men put together' (*Ph* 117). Hence, there seemed no

1

reason why he should bring himself to a state of nervous and physical exhaustion writing of dreams of spiritual and social renewal that would never bear fruit: 'No, no! I'm forty, and I want, in a good sense, to enjoy my life. Saying my say and seeing other people sup it up doesn't amount to a hill o'beans, as far as I go. I want to waste no time over it' (*CL* 876).

Within a year of Lawrence's first formulation of the doctrine of insouciance – by the end of November 1926 – this acquiescent approach to life had come to be threatened by a mood of rebellion and angry disillusionment, accompanied by feelings of lonely isolation and alienation from his fellow men. In some of its symptoms, notably the spirit of revolt against the established institutions of society, this mood marked a reversion to feelings he had experienced in the summer of 1925.[1] He took to calling this phase in the emotional life of the male 'the change of life', and in attributing its origins to physiological factors he appears to have been the first inventor of the myth of the male menopause. In a letter to his artist friend, Earl Brewster, who was also suffering the emotional upheavals of confrontation with middle age, Lawrence wrote:

> You and I are at the *âge dangereuse* for men: when the whole rhythm of the psyche changes: when one no longer has an easy flow outwards: and when one rebels at a good many things. It is as well to know the thing is physiological: though that doesn't nullify the psychological reality. One resents bitterly a certain swindle about modern life, and especially a sex swindle. One is swindled out of one's proper sex life, a great deal.
>
> (*CL* 967)

The swindle to which Lawrence referred was very probably the loss of sexual potency which afflicted him in his fortieth year.[2]

For several months, during which the mood of disenchanted revulsion with the modern world intensified, Lawrence struggled successfully to combat the temptation towards bitterness by clinging with patient optimism to the belief that the 'revolt of the angels' (*CL* 974) raging inside him was menopausal and therefore transient. But by November 1927 Lawrence had good reason to suppose that what he had to face up to was not a change of life, but an imminent passing from life. Prolonged ill-health without promise of remission bred mental instability, which declared itself in largely irrational feelings of persecution; and Lawrence finally turned to bitter rage as the only remedy against the torpor of despair.

The three different versions of *Lady Chatterley* seem faithfully to reflect the chronology of Lawrence's changing moods, as attested in the letters of the period 1926–8. The original draft, *The First Lady Chatterley*, was begun in October 1926, during the time of Lawrence's insouciance, whose spirit may be detected in the mellow tone of the narrative voice, in the lack of 'fight' in the relationship between Constance and the gamekeeper, and in the somewhat nonchalant attitude of the author towards his characters and their situation which allows for scenes of high comedy. Where, principally, this version of the novel runs counter to the doctrine of insouciance is in the author's revived sense of a mission to change society.

The writing of the second version, *John Thomas and Lady Jane*, probably between December 1926 and February 1927, coincided with the beginning of the time when the easy passivity of insouciance came to be challenged by a resurgence of pugnacity that had grown out of feelings of isolation and alienation from humanity. In May 1927, three months after completing his second draft of the novel, Lawrence wrote to Earl Brewster: 'We have been repressed and too "spiritual" all our lives: and too much insisted on the sympathetic flow, without a balance of the combative. Now the hour-glass turns over' (*CL* 974). *John Thomas and Lady Jane* seems to express this counterpoint of disparate emotions and conflicting inclinations: it combines, in happy equipoise, a controlled, unembittered anger in the treatment of the modern, man-made world of Wragby Hall and the surrounding mining settlements with, on the other hand, tender, lyrical, somewhat wistful qualities that are especially associated with the depiction of the ancient, natural world of Wragby woods and with the expression of Lawrence's vision of a society in which man may exist in harmony with himself, with womankind and with created nature.

When Lawrence began the final version of the novel, *Lady Chatterley's Lover*, in late November 1927, most of the sand had sifted from the compartment of the hour-glass which represented Lawrence's 'feminine' aspect – that part of his personality which was delicate, spiritual and responsive to the power and beauty of the living world. The fight had become paramount, and the lyrical qualities of the preceding drafts were largely and apparently wilfully deleted. What had been a tender, lyrical evocation of the mystery of the phallus became an acerbic, rather arid polemic against contemporary English society and the prudish, middle-class, money-grabbing values which had shaped it. It is the work of a man who, like his hero, Mellors the gamekeeper, has few beliefs left to hang on to: all that remains is the precious illusion that through warm-heartedness a man and a woman may together find redress from the swindle of modern sex and attain a wholeness and harmony which might see them through the coming social débâcle.

In periods of remission from ill-health Lawrence could regard his turning 40 with a special sense of personal triumph. Fifteen years earlier, after Lawrence's first novel, *The White Peacock*, had been accepted for publication, Ford Madox Hueffer had written to Lawrence's mother prophesying: 'By the time he is forty he will be riding in his carriage.' At this, so Lawrence had been told, his mother sighed gloomily, 'Ay, if he lives to be forty!' He *had* lived to be 40, and since he had several times managed to wriggle free when death fingered him, there was every reason for him to suppose that he would continue to resist for a good while yet:

> So there's one in the eye for that sighing remark. I was always weak in health, but my life was strong. Why had they all made up their minds that I was to die? Perhaps they thought I was too good to live. Well, in that case they were had!
>
> *(Ph 2 260)*

Lawrence seems to have attached some weight to Hueffer's prophecy. He detested great wealth and would often sincerely protest that too much money would have destroyed him as an artist. Nonetheless, one suspects, from the frequency with which he drew unfavourable comparisons between his own income and those of other writers, that he would have liked to see Hueffer's prediction of riches modestly fulfilled. It would have been a token of his stature as a writer, and it would have conferred the security, independence and freedom of action that had always eluded him. Still, at 40 he was for the first time in his life reasonably well-off, with a couple of thousand dollars in the bank and more thousands owed to him; and he could contemplate with wry cheerfulness his possession of two horses and a light buggy that served him for a coach and pair 'on a little ranch (also my own, or my wife's through me) away on the western slope of the Rocky Mountains' *(Ph 2 260)*.

Two days before his fortieth birthday, Lawrence had shuttered the Kiowa Ranch in New Mexico and arranged for his manuscripts and some of his few possessions to be stored for his return the following spring. Though he was unaware of the fact at the time, a chapter in his life had closed. His period of sampling life in remote parts of the globe was at an end. Despite hankerings after the ranch which grew stronger as time passed, he was to spend his remaining years in Europe. Only Frieda Lawrence had any specific knowledge of how few those years would be.

Just after completing *The Plumed Serpent* in Mexico in January 1925 Lawrence had almost been brought to the grave by an illness which he attributed to a combined bout of malaria, influenza and typhoid. Probably these were in reality fevers associated with the advanced state of tuberculosis which was subsequently diagnosed by specialists in Mexico City. Lawrence was told of his condition, but the medical prognosis was withheld from him: he had at best two years to live.

Lawrence's approach to the threat of consumption was to refuse to acknowledge the existence of the tubercle within him. Throughout the remainder of his short life – he died in Vence, France, in March 1930 – he never named the disease in his correspondence or, so far as is known, in conversation. As he showed later, when he knew he was dying, this was not because he was fearful of death. Perhaps the idea of bodily purity being defiled by disease was too repellent for him to accept. As far as Lawrence was concerned, the root of his ill-health lay in the bronchitis that had afflicted him since the age of 2. Even in 1930, when he recognized that death was near, he replied to a friend's suggestion that he should be visited by an English specialist in tubercular disease: 'I simply don't want to talk about *lungs* when the trouble is bronchials' (Zyt 392). In one respect he was right to see his troublesome 'bronchs' as a major threat to his life: while his lungs remained weakened by disease there was a grave danger that any cold which developed into bronchitis or pneumonia might lead to death by asphyxiation.

Wintering on the isolated ranch, 8,000 feet up in the Rockies, was impossible for a man in Lawrence's condition. But there were other factors which called for Lawrence's departure. He felt in need of a change from the tension and materialism he associated with life in America and was nostalgically attracted to England and Europe. Frieda, too, was pressing for a return to Europe so that she could see her son and two daughters by Ernest Weekley and visit her mother, the Baroness von Richthofen, in Germany. Moreover, both Lawrences were anxious to escape the presence of Dorothy Brett, who was prevailed upon to remain behind in New Mexico.

Brett, as she was known to her friends, was the only disciple who had followed Lawrence's summons to found a colony of artists and writers in America. She herself was a painter, who had trained at the Slade School in London. Through the friendship she had made there with Mark Gertler she had got to know Lawrence, Katherine Mansfield and Mansfield's husband, the editor and critic John Middleton Murry, who became her lover after his wife's death. She was afflicted by severe deafness which seems to have had its roots in juvenile hysteria,[3] and she could hear only imperfectly with the aid of an ear-trumpet.

Brett was a shy, gauche, submissive woman whose innocent charm and passive ways made her attractive to Lawrence. He had brought her to New Mexico so that she might act as a buffer between him and Frieda, with whom he could no longer live in harmony. But Brett was disposed to play quite a different role. As S. S. Koteliansky, the erstwhile mutual friend of Lawrence and Brett, had predicted at the outset, Brett's aim was to win Lawrence for herself.[4] It may have been revenge which, together with Lawrence's attractiveness to women, inspired her purpose: she could be forgiven for believing that her relationship with Murry had been brought to an end through the intervention of Frieda, who had an affair with Murry, apparently unconsummated, in the last months of 1923.

On the ranch, and later in Mexico, Frieda found herself cut out of conversations and activities, and she was driven more to supreme irritation than sexual jealousy by the tender intimacies of the curate and spinster relationship that developed between Lawrence and Brett. In the aftermath of scenes with Frieda, Lawrence (on occasion in rage but more often with weary exasperation) would take her part against Brett, who was eventually banished from the ranch to a cabin at a neighbouring ranch. Though Brett, nothing daunted, continued to ride daily up to the ranch to see Lawrence, her expulsion meant the break-up of the cell from which he yet hoped might emerge 'Rananim', the name he chose for the Utopian colony that was to set a pattern for living which would revolutionize society.[5] In a letter of January 1926, almost exactly eleven years from the time when his ideas for Rananim had first taken shape, he was obliged to tell Koteliansky, one of the first movers of the community scheme: 'That *Rananim* of ours, it has sunk out of sight' (Zyt 276).

The demise of the Rananim ideal marked a turning-point in Lawrence's life and ideology. His view of the world was largely egocentric, the direction of his thoughts often being governed by how circumstances affected him personally. Communal life having proved, not for the first time, to be a failure, it was henceforth Lawrence's destiny to spend much of his time alone with Frieda, with whom he would have to find new means of living at ease. Perhaps, then, it was a response to his own situation that eventually brought him to the point of view expressed in *Lady Chatterley*, where the vision of a proper harmony between man and woman replaces the community ideal of 'the completeness of us all as one' (*Let 2* 271) as the instrument of change in the consciousness and structure of society.

The message of Lawrence's last novel is a more emphatic reiteration of a belief expounded many years earlier, when his attention had likewise been focused on his relationship with Frieda. It had been stated in a letter of 1913, which appears to suggest that such a view was the covert burden of *Sons and Lovers*: 'Pray to your Gods for me that *Sons and Lovers* shall succeed. People *should* begin to take me seriously now. And I do so break my heart over England when I read the *New Machiavelli*.[6] And I am so sure that only through a readjustment between men and women, and making free and healthy of the sex, will she get out of the present atrophy' (*Let 1* 544).

Lawrence's ambition to write a bawdy romance dated back at least as far as 1912, when he and Frieda had first become acquainted;[7] and since his interest in human sexuality was informed by a deep moral puritanism, it may have been that already, in that early period, Lawrence conceived of a novel such as *Lady Chatterley* was intended to be – one which in a pure and honest treatment of sex would cleanse sexuality of its associations with shame and smut. For Lawrence the only valid and morally acceptable sexual responses were physical and instinctive. Thought and fantasy, which he associated with masturbatory impulses, were regarded as impure and, by virtue of their taint of onanism, anti-sexual because true sex could only be expressed in consummation. Any literary treatment of sex which seemed to Lawrence to have been designed to titivate the mind he therefore adjudged dirty and dishonest; and his desire to write openly and honestly of sexual relations appears to have been strengthened by his reactions to books whose accounts of sexual acts smacked of prurience. Among such works of erotic literature Lawrence's *bêtes noires*, against which he was often heard to fulminate, were the picaresque memoirs of Casanova[8] and James Joyce's *Ulysses*.

Lawrence first read a volume of Casanova's memoirs in 1913 and may subsequently have read other volumes. In 1921 he wrote to a friend:

> I tried Casanova, but he smells. One can be immoral if one likes, but one must not be a creeping, itching, fingering, inferior being, led on chiefly by a dirty sniffing kind of curiosity, without pride or clearness of soul . . . But I will treat the battered volumes as gingerly as such *crotte* deserves.
>
> (*CL* 662)

Future events would lend some irony to these observations. The friend to whom he was writing – the possessor, it seems, of the 'battered volumes' of Casanova, since he wrote from the flat in Florence which she had loaned him – was Nelly Morrison, who, in 1927, having begun typing Lawrence's MS of *Lady Chatterley's Lover*, was so repelled by its contents that she abandoned the task, accusing Lawrence of pandering to pornographic tastes.

Lawrence read *Ulysses* in 1920, when it appeared in serial form in *The Little Review*. He found it entirely distasteful and was especially revolted by Molly Bloom's speech at the end of the novel: ' "This *Ulysses* muck is more disgusting than Casanova", he proclaimed. "I must show it can be done without muck." ' These remarks were addressed to the novelist Compton Mackenzie, who later came to wonder whether *Lady Chatterley* might have been conceived in that moment.[9]

The return to the theme of love in *Lady Chatterley* was accompanied by Lawrence's abandonment of the preoccupation with power that had characterized his last three novels – *Aaron's Rod*, *Kangaroo* and *The Plumed Serpent*. Disillusionment with the pursuit of the Rananim ideal may have been one factor which made for the rejection of the quasi-fascism associated with his dreams of power, which were of the establishment of a natural aristocracy of charismatic heroes who would lead the people back to the ways of an ancient, darker and more 'civilized' past. Another factor in Lawrence's loss of faith in the creed of *The Plumed Serpent* may have been his experience in Italy of the realities of life under fascist rule, which he found unpalatable, though apparently for no ideological reason other than his dislike of systems. While it may not be true, as Compton Mackenzie once claimed, that Lawrence's disenchantment with fascism began when a fascist policeman stood on his big toe when he was watching a procession in Florence,[10] it was nevertheless a personal sense of discomfort in the atmosphere of nervous irritability generated by fascism which seems to have most profoundly coloured his view of Mussolini's regime.

By the autumn of 1926, when Lawrence wrote 'Return to Bestwood', 'true democracy' had replaced rule by natural aristocracy in Lawrence's political *credo*. What precisely he meant by the term is not clearly defined, and there are some aspects of the democracy to which Lawrence aspired which would appal every humane democrat. Nevertheless, it is plain that Lawrence had abandoned much of the pernicious ideology of *The Plumed Serpent* and had returned, briefly, to his youthful sympathies with the socialist movement. 'Return to Bestwood' heralds the major themes of *Lady Chatterley* in its gospel of tenderness and warm human contact as the keys to individual and social redemption. The essay (and the shift in political opinions which it expresses) had been inspired by the miners' strike of 1926, the effects of which on the mining community of his native Eastwood Lawrence witnessed in September of that year. This return to the North Midlands and Lawrence's response to the social, architectural and natural landscapes of the region proved influential, to an extent unparalleled by all other experiences, in determining the genesis of *Lady Chatterley*.

2

'The Old, Young Insouciance'

Lawrence arrived in England on 30 September 1925 and established a base in London at Garland's Hotel, an old favourite of his, which was remembered in *Lady Chatterley's Lover* as 'Hartland's', 'a little hotel off Pall Mall' (*LCL* 284, 265), where Constance Chatterley stayed. The nostalgia that Lawrence had felt for his native country quickly gave way to the gloom which habitually overtook him on reaching English shores. 'You were quite right', he told Brett, 'not to come to England; it's much worse than when I was here last time, almost gruesome . . . There's no *life* in anybody' (*CL* 858). The letter reported a weekend in 'damp and dismal Bucks.', where Lawrence stayed with the writer Catherine Carswell, the only member of his old circle whose friendship he still valued, and then went on to visit his publisher, Martin Secker, at Iver.

A return to his home regions for a fortnight intensified Lawrence's mood of estrangement and left him prostrate with depression, aggravated by the ill-health he suffered in the smoke and damp of the industrial North Midlands. 'The weather's awful and we simply hate it up here' (*PL* 516), Lawrence wrote from Nottingham, where he stayed with his sister, Emily King, before moving to Ripley, Derbyshire, to spend a week with Ada Clarke, his younger sister.

The first couple of days at Ada's were spent touring in the Clarkes' new car. 'Been motoring all over my well-known Derbyshire', Lawrence told Martin Secker. 'But I can't look on the body of my past. The spirit seems to have flown' (Sec 65). These excursions appear to have contributed to the fictional car journey of the Saywell girls in *The Virgin and the Gipsy*, written in January 1926.[1] And it was possibly on a drive towards scenes from Lawrence's past – to the Cromford area, where he had lived in 1918 – that Lawrence found or rediscovered 'The Bridge House' near Cromford Church, which became a model for the Saywells' vicarage.[2] In September of the following year another tour of Derbyshire with the Clarkes would provide similar material for *Lady Chatterley* – a source for Connie

Chatterley's car journey from Tevershall to Uthwaite and one of the models for the Chatterleys' Wragby Hall.

The Lawrences returned from the Midlands to a flat in Gower Street, London, let to them by Catherine Carswell's brother. Only one week remained before their departure for Germany, and during this time Lawrence led a busy, though generally quiet, social life, which included separate meetings with two once-intimate friends and confidants – Lady Cynthia Asquith and John Middleton Murry – neither of whom were to see him again. Both friendships dated from July 1913, the period of Lawrence's elation at the critics' responses to *Sons and Lovers*, and both were of crucial significance in the time of Lawrence's descent into the nightmare abyss of the war years of 1914–18. His relations with these two friends had much in common: each had represented ideals of physical beauty and spiritual companionship to which he turned in retreat from the bitter conflicts with Frieda in the wartime period; both had pliant natures and minds that were immature and impressionable, seeming ripe for implantation with Lawrence's doctrines; and each friendship had ultimately proved disappointing, though in Murry's case Lawrence's disillusion had been far greater and more galling.

Lady Cynthia Asquith was the daughter of the Earl of Wemyss and the wife of Herbert Asquith, son of the former Prime Minister. From the time of their first meeting to Lawrence's leaving England in 1919 she and Lawrence had shared a close platonic union that rested on mutual admiration and the gratification of emotional needs that were unfulfilled in marriage.[3] Lawrence's appeal lay in his zest, his humour and the sympathetic intimacy which he brought to relationships with women. In Lady Cynthia's eyes Lawrence was a Pentecostal spirit of fire who, in the war years especially, brought consolation and spiritual uplift to a woman whose personality and home life denied her other close human relationships. Her husband had inherited from the Asquiths an intense reserve which was deepened by his experience in the trenches, leaving him withdrawn and shut-in upon himself when he came home; at a further remove from communication was her son, John, whose disturbing behaviour showed all the symptoms of autism.

If circumstances had permitted, Lawrence might have fallen in love with Cynthia Asquith, for whom he felt a strong physical and emotional desire. He came to find in her company a repose denied to him by his strife with Frieda, whom for a while she displaced as his source of inspiration. Lady Cynthia had a delicacy and grace of manner and appearance, and a personality which in one aspect matched the unconventional, ethereal quality of her beauty. Lawrence applied himself to cultivating that part of her which was spiritual, idealistic and in revolt against established moral and social codes. But at times Lady Cynthia allowed her other self – worldly, conventional and loyal to her own class – to rule her, causing Lawrence to be angered by her surrender to 'that which [was] merely temporal and foul and external' (*Let 3* 118). Ultimately he was obliged, after their meeting in London in 1925, to acknowledge that Lady Cynthia 'belonged finally, fatally to her own class'.[4]

Lunch with Herbert and Cynthia Asquith proved an unsatisfactory reunion which left Lawrence with a 'sense of failure' (*CL* 863) and with the impression that he had angered Lady Cynthia in some way.[5] Perhaps the situation at luncheon resembled that of the melancholy formal dinner party in the story 'Glad Ghosts', where Mark Morier (Lawrence), ill-at-ease, and chattering recklessly after too many glasses of burgundy, finds himself unable to regain with his hostess, Lady Carlotta Lathkill (Cynthia Asquith), their former 'curious, abstract intimacy that went very deep' (*WWRA* 164). 'Glad Ghosts', written in December 1925 at Lady Cynthia's request, was originally destined for an anthology of ghost stories that she intended to publish. But the story, a ghostly fantasy of wish-fulfilment, evolved in a way that made it quite inappropriate for Lady Cynthia's anthology, as Lawrence came to realize. Morier, by his sympathetic presence, invites the return of the family ghost, the female crocus-spirit of spring rejuvenation and fertility. The ghost transforms and enriches the lives of everyone in the house that night, and by granting to Carlotta and Morier a night of physical love in spirit form she enables them to find at last the perfect union which their respective situations have denied them.

'Perhaps', Lawrence wrote of Morier and Lady Carlotta in 'Glad Ghosts', 'in modern people, only after long suffering and defeat, can the naked intuition break free between woman and man' (*WWRA* 184). In *Lady Chatterley* the union of the gamekeeper and Lady Constance occurs in identical circumstances; and some superficial aspects of the background of Cynthia Asquith connect with Constance Chatterley. Lady Cynthia was married, like Constance in the last two versions of the novel, when she was 23 and her husband 29; her Scottish ancestry may have been borrowed for Constance Chatterley, and the rakish past of her father could have been transferred to Sir Malcolm Reid, the father of Constance; her maiden name, Charteris, might have suggested the Eastwood name, Chatterley; and her husband's elder brother, like Sir Clifford's in *Lady Chatterley's Lover*, had been killed in action in 1916.[6] Moreover, in an earlier story, 'The Thimble' (later revised as 'The Ladybird'), Lawrence had drawn on Cynthia Asquith for a character in a situation rather similar to that of Constance: in these stories she figured as a young wife whose husband had left to fight in France shortly after their marriage, and later came home wounded and numbed in spirit.

One or two features of the characters of the three Constances in the successive versions of the novel also resemble traits that Lawrence discerned in Cynthia Asquith, such as the poise, the gentle repose and popularity as a hostess of the first Constance, the stoicism and hard frozen interior of her successor, and the inability to make contact with anyone or anything of the third of the line of Constances. It might appear that there is a case for supposing that in *Lady Chatterley* Lawrence once again made love to Cynthia Asquith in the spirit; but Lady Cynthia was not the only or even the principal contributor to the portrait of Constance Chatterley, who is, in any case, essentially a dream woman, who in the totality of her character and behaviour bears no close resemblance to any actual person.

John Middleton Murry, whom Lawrence met on the eve of his departure for Germany, was also destined to make contributions to characters in *Lady Chatterley*. He was handsome, powerfully built, gifted with outstanding critical sensibilities, impulsively enthusiastic and speciously warm in his lack of the emotional restraint which disappointed Lawrence in many of those he met in the literary circles of the time. Lawrence seems to have hoped to find with him that close, supportive comradeship with a physically stronger man of morally 'wicked' temperament that he had enjoyed in the Eastwood days with his philandering contemporary, George Neville.

Lawrence's early hopes for a partnership with Murry were also encouraged by a false perception of himself in Murry and an unwarranted faith in Murry's capacity to become a second, greater Lawrence. Murry, as Lawrence later disdainfully acknowledged, was essentially a man of straw. Weak, timorous and neurotically self-absorbed, he was in no way qualified to be a reliable ally in Lawrence's tempestuous dealings with the world. Murry felt a genuine affection and awe for Lawrence which he wished to be reciprocated. But this only served to complicate a relationship whose history was one of recurrent rifts, most of them occasioned by Murry's failure to live up to Lawrence's expectations.[7] Their meeting in London followed a break in correspondence of some eight months, brought about by a bitter letter of rejection from Lawrence after he had received maudlin letters written in Murry's self-pitying, martyred vein.

In the Lawrence–Murry friendship there was a strong element of rivalry, which had come to a head in the last months of 1923, the time of the Lawrences' estrangement and separation, when Frieda arrived alone in London and formed a romantic liaison with Murry.[8] Lawrence, sometimes complaisant in his attitudes towards Frieda and the men she chose, did not feel any necessity to break with Murry on this issue.[9] But he was hurt and murderously angry, and later took his revenge in three short stories – 'The Border-Line', 'The Last Laugh' and 'Jimmy and the Desperate Woman'. In each of them Murry was depicted as a foolish and inadequate figure, bested and in the first two stories done to death by the spirit of Lawrence.[10] And for all three Lawrence had cruelly drawn on embarrassing moments in Murry's recent life – his train journey to Germany with Frieda, a flight into the arms of a prostitute after Brett had accepted his offer of marriage, and a crazy dash to Lawrence's Midlands in pursuit of a Mansfield poetess with whom he had become smitten after reading her verses.[11]

By 1925 Lawrence had little respect for Jack Murry, and on his return to England he had meted out some cavalier treatment in studiously neglecting to suggest arrangements for their meeting until the very last moment. When, finally, they met at the Lawrences' London flat, the two men temperately confronted the ideological issues which now divided them, chief among which was Murry's recent adoption of Christianity in the course of writing his *Life of Jesus*. Lawrence, to whom this seemed only a 'sloppy and nasty' reflex of Murry's sentimentality (*CL* 858), upheld the view he had expressed in a recent letter: 'Must you really write about Jesus? Jesus becomes more and more *unsympatisch* to me, the longer I live: crosses and nails and tears and all that stuff: I think he showed us into a nice *cul de sac*' (*CL* 861). On the matter of Jesus, Murry was for once uncompromising. He felt he had impressed Lawrence on this occasion and that he had proved himself 'at least his equal and perhaps more than his equal'. He had always feared that Lawrence had the power to destroy him; now he was satisfied that Lawrence no longer had any power over him at all.[12]

After all had been said, there existed between them, according to Murry, 'a twilight cool' in which he and Lawrence felt deeply 'the pain of the old affection'.[13] But a reconciliation of sorts had been achieved; and Murry was invited to bring his new wife (Violet le Maistre) and young child to Italy to stay with the Lawrences. Murry accepted without reckoning on the difficulty of transporting a baby and a pregnant woman of delicate health across Europe. Partly as a result of his failure to honour this commitment, he and Lawrence were not to meet when Lawrence returned to England for the last time in the summer of 1926. There were no farewells when they parted company. Ten minutes before Murry was due to leave for the station, Lawrence went out to buy fruit for him to take back to his home in Dorset. If Lawrence had not returned by the time Murry was due to leave, he was to drive towards the shop in the taxi and meet Lawrence as he walked back to the flat. In a way that epitomizes the history of their relationship, Murry's taxi took a different route from the one Lawrence had taken, and they missed each other.

On the day Murry returned to Dorset the Lawrences, too, left London *en route* for Germany to visit Frieda's mother in Baden-Baden before travelling on via Switzerland to Italy, where they planned to spend the winter.

By the last week in November Lawrence and Frieda had found a villa on the Riviera coast at the village of Spotorno, recommended to them by Martin Secker's wife, Rina, whose parents (the Capelleros) lived there. Spotorno was a simple Italian village, with nothing especially picturesque about it; and to Lawrence, who preferred 'the frayed edges' of the world (*CL* 866) to places of trim or romantic beauty, it was congenial enough, though his preferences had been for a house in Capri or Sicily where he could expect milder winter weather.

The letting of the house in Spotorno had been arranged through the owner's husband, the Tenente Angelo Ravagli, an officer in the Italian Bersaglieri regiment. Since the day of his appointed meeting with the Lawrences was the birthday of the Queen of Italy, he was obliged to turn out in full dress uniform. Frieda took instantly to the dapper little figure in cockfeather plumes, whose person she found 'almost as nice as the feathers' (Irv 59). He became a regular Sunday visitor to the Lawrence household; and at some time, probably during the Lawrences' stay in Spotorno, Frieda took him as her lover. They continued to meet occasionally after the Lawrences moved, and after Lawrence's death they set up house together at the ranch in New

Mexico. In 1950 Ravagli became Frieda's third husband, and when she died he returned to Italy to his former wife, who was then living in the house she had let to Lawrence and Frieda in 1925.

The Villa Bernarda was a pleasant old house of three storeys, pink-coloured and perched on a hillside overlooking the village and the Bay of Noli; its large gardens, planted with vines, olive groves and almond trees, climbed up to the ruins of an old castle, beyond which lay wild hills dotted with umbrella pines. Here Lawrence settled contentedly into reacquainting himself with the experience of life in Italy:

> The sun shines, the eternal Mediterranean is blue and young, the last leaves are falling from the vines in the garden. The peasant people are nice. I've got my little stock of red and white wine – from the garden of this house – we eat fried chicken and pasta and smell rosemary and basilica in the cooking once more – and somebody's always roasting coffee – and the oranges are already yellow on the orange trees. It's Italy, the same forever.
>
> (*Life* 195)

In Spotorno Lawrence slipped out of the hide of tensions and anxieties that had gripped him for many years. He 'let the tight coils inside . . . come slack' (*Ph* 118) and rediscovered in himself and in the life around him the quality of insouciance, a youthful, carefree 'sort of bubbling-in of life' (*Ph* 118) that he had earlier come to associate with Italy during his stay of 1919–22. In the short essay 'Europe v. America', probably composed shortly after moving into the Villa Bernarda, Lawrence argued that life had been squeezed out of American civilization under the grip of care, while Europe, with all its imperfections, still preserved 'the old, young insouciance' (*Ph* 118) which was the clue to life and faith. In this mood he began to shy away from the prospect of returning to the ranch in the spring.

Relaxation and contentment bred in Lawrence inclinations towards indolence and escapism. Already, in October, he had declared a preference for a winter of writing reviews and a disinclination towards creative work on books of his own.[14] And in Spotorno he felt the temptation, which persisted up to the time when he began *Lady Chatterley*, to abandon serious work altogether. Having regained the habit of insouciance he had no wish to lose it in the emotional intensity of the act of writing, which for Lawrence meant a stressful process of engaging his innermost personal feelings. He thought, as he was later to do when writing *Lady Chatterley's Lover*, of his namesake T. E. Lawrence, with whose 'unsatisfactory mysticism' and 'conceit of self-abasement' (*LCL* 294) he was altogether out of sympathy. Lawrence of Arabia had recently abandoned name, rank and glory to enlist in the ranks as Private Shaw; and though the humility of the act held no appeal for Lawrence, the idea of escaping responsibility and casting off one's past identity seemed worth entertaining playfully: 'I feel at present I should love to throw my pen in the sea for ever, and call myself Abinadab Straw, no more D. H. L. walk under the heavens nor books appear in his name. Ah, if one were rich enough!' (*CL* 870).

Despite the temptation to lethargy, Lawrence produced in the month of December three short stories – 'Smile', 'Sun' and 'Glad Ghosts' – which between them amounted to some 25,000 words. 'Smile' was another of Lawrence's satires of Murry, who figured as a serious-minded Englishman, grown dead to feeling and beauty, who travelled to an Italian convent to the death-bed of his capricious, obstinate wife, Ophelia (Katherine Mansfield). Though the choice of subject was a tasteless one, Lawrence handled it with delicacy and with a more gentle humour than he employed in the earlier Murry stories.

By the time the story was completed, Lawrence had written three letters to Murry since their encounter in London, and the fact that he maintained a correspondence, in which he continued to refer to the possibility of Murry joining him in Italy, shows the measure of reconciliation that had been effected between them. The brevity of the letters, however, and the general matter-of-factness of their contents, suggest that Murry was still low in the hierarchy of Lawrence's friends and that Lawrence wished to distance himself from him. His contempt for Murry's sentimentality had not been diminished by reading a copy of his *Keats and Shakespeare*, sent to him by Vere Collins of the Oxford University Press:

> Murry's *Keats* was quite good . . . but oh heaven, so die-away – the text might be: Oh lap up Shakespeare till you've cleaned the dish, and you may hope to swoon in raptures and die an early but beautiful death at 25.
>
> I'm sick to death of this maudlin twaddle and England's rotten with it. Why doesn't somebody finally and loudly say Shit! to it all!
>
> (*CL* 865)

In a letter of early January to Harold Mason of the Centaur Bookshop Lawrence wrote: 'I do thank heaven for the sun, it's the love of God to me, any day' (*Cent* 26). The short story 'Sun', arguably the finest Lawrence had produced for many years, is a paean to his divine benefactor. In it, a jovial, godly sun, phallic in the naked splendour of its rising above the line of the sea, penetrates the body and being of an angry, frustrated woman who, like Lawrence, had journeyed from New York to the Mediterranean to find herself healed of her tensions and brought to new life under the sun's beneficence. In her state of ripened sensuality she longs to conceive a child by a peasant worker, created in the image of the sun, whose pride, shyness and flame-like procreative qualities he shares. The story prefigures *Lady Chatterley* in aspects of its plot, and the peasant figure – lone, independent, vital, a natural aristocrat, feral in his quicksilver movements and in his instincts – bears a close resemblance to the gamekeeper, which results from the fact that each portrays Lawrence as he liked to see himself.[15]

'Sun' had been written under the inspiration of days of brilliant sunshine and warmth that accompanied the move to the Villa Bernarda; but though the weather continued generally sunny, there were spells when the coast was raked by rough, chilling winds. Lawrence went down with a chest-cold and was laid up in bed when Frieda's daughter, Barbara Weekley, arrived to spend a few days with her mother in the second week of December.

The remorse Lawrence felt for the harm he had done the Weekley children in eloping with their mother did not dispose him to feel affection for Frieda's daughters, whom he disliked for their middle-class ways – their 'suburban bounce and *suffisance*' (*CL* 863). Frieda maintained that he was jealous of them, and it may have been true that his attitude was coloured by resentful memories of times when Frieda's anguish over the loss of her children had been one of the major sources of their marital problems.

The cold Lawrence was suffering from when 'Barby' Weekley arrived excluded him from the happy intimacy between her and Frieda, confining him to a bed in the sitting-room, from where he listened to their talk through the open door to the kitchen. Next morning Barby awakened to the sound of loud bumps from the room above. Frieda had stung Lawrence with a remark that heightened his fear of being isolated: now that Barby was with her he was to stop interfering and keep out of their relationship. A fight had ensued, and Barby, hastening to intervene, found Lawrence sullen and pale with anger and Frieda in tears with a scratch on her neck. Later in the week, after another argument, Lawrence flung a glass of wine in Frieda's face while her daughter looked on.[16]

It is hard to find in the Lawrence given to such brutalized behaviour an attractive figure. Though he recognized that their violence to each other was degrading, and was generally the more deeply and lastingly affected than was Frieda, he appears to have felt that to punish physically a wayward wife was a duty which the role of the male imposed upon him. A few months later he complained wearily to Dorothy Brett of how humiliating it was to beat a woman, as though in doing so he reluctantly obeyed some externally imposed obligation.[17]

The physical violence of Lawrence's relations with Frieda was echoed in the gamekeeper's history of his marriage to his estranged wife, Bertha Coutts, in *Lady Chatterley's Lover*: 'She sort of let things go, didn't give me a proper dinner when I came home from work, and if I said anything, flew out at me. And I flew back, hammer and tongs. She flung a cup at me and I took her by the scruff of the neck and squeezed the life out of her' (*LCL* 210). Other aspects of the Mellors–Coutts marriage seem also to have been modelled on that of Lawrence and Frieda, for they tally with parts of the known history of their relations: Mellors's denunciation of Bertha's character and behaviour – lazy, spoiled by her husband, wilful and insolent, despising her husband for his subservience in waiting upon her, yet also resentful of his bossiness, from which she sought escape by sleeping in a separate room – smacks of the author's personal complaint against his own lot in marriage. If, too, the acerbity with which Mellors decries his wife's 'brutal' behaviour in lovemaking derives its force from authorial experience, it would seem that the theatre of the Lawrences' war for supremacy was extended to the marriage-bed, and that in some moods Lawrence thought of marriage to Frieda as a disappointment in the sphere of sexual as well as social relations.

It seems reasonable to ask, as Barby did after the wine-throwing affair, whether Lawrence really cared for Frieda at all. His response to a question he considered impertinent was deliberately shallow – hadn't he just shown caring enough by helping her mother with her rotten painting?[18] And in a life of constant attentiveness to Frieda's needs he had, it is true, shown a devoted solicitude. But the real gauge of the depth of his feelings for Frieda was the extent of his dependence on her presence. Though he experienced bouts of weariness with the strife between them, and was frequently impatient with her behaviour, he was never bored by her company which was as necessary to his existence, so Aldous Huxley once observed, as 'the liver in one's belly, or one's spinal marrow'. 'I have seen him', he wrote, 'on two occasions rise from what I thought was his death-bed, when Frieda, who had been away, came back after a short absence. The mysteries of human relationships are impenetrably obscure.'[19]

It was this life-giving attribute of Frieda's, communicated through the impulsive gusto of her own appetite for living, that made her an indispensable companion to Lawrence and ensured that, however impossibly wayward and stupid her behaviour not infrequently was, she remained without serious rival during their life together. Her portrait as Cynthia, the fallen wife of the vicar in *The Virgin and the Gipsy*, begun in late December or early January, captures the appeal of her vitality and hints that Lawrence's fascination was sustained by a mildly masochistic reverence for the aura of uncertainty, threatening and yet stimulating, that attended her. The value of her presence to Lawrence is defined in terms of the reactions of Cynthia's children to her departure:

> She had made a great glow, a flow of life, like a swift and dangerous sun in the home, forever coming and going. They always associated her presence with brightness, but also with danger; with glamour, but with fearful selfishness.
> Now the glamour was gone ... The danger of instability, the peculiarly *dangerous* sort of selfishness, like lions and tigers, was also gone. There was now a complete stability, in which one could perish safely.
>
> (*VG* 173f.)

During Barby's visit there had, at least, been no constant quarrelling, and Frieda reported to Brett that the three of them had been happy together. Exchanges of confidences between Lawrence and Barby had established a degree of intimacy, and from these conversations and others Lawrence was able to build a picture of the Weekley household that provided him with the family background of the vicar and his daughters in *The Virgin and the Gipsy*. But Lawrence had not yet warmed to Barby in the way that he was to do on her subsequent visits. 'Those children of F's are duds' (*CL* 870) he told Brett in a letter written shortly after Barby's departure.

At about the time of Barby's first visit, Martin Secker, 'a nice, gentle soul, without a thrill', arrived in Spotorno to join his wife, whom Lawrence described as 'a living block of discontent' (Irv 59). In letters he complained that the Seckers were dull company, but perhaps by virtue of their dullness they were at least easy to be with, and Secker's lack of aggression seems to have made for a harmonious relationship between publisher and author, whom Secker frequently visited and went walking with during his month's stay in Spotorno.

On Christmas Day Barby arrived again – 'nicer this time' (CL 873) in Lawrence's opinion – and joined the Lawrences, Seckers and Capelleros for Christmas dinner at the local inn, the Albergo Ligure. Balmy, spring-like weather came to the Riviera shortly before the Christmas period and continued well into the New Year, making it possible for Lawrence to spend most of the daylight hours out of doors. His general health seemed outwardly better than it had been for years. There had been nothing irritating in the way of news from the outside world to test his new-found spirit of effervescent tranquillity, which was buoyed up by what on the whole seems to have been a period of calm in relations with Frieda, who had been happy since reaching Spotorno and was now the more content and fulfilled for having regained a mother's role. 1925, which had threatened disaster for Lawrence with his near-fatal illness in Mexico and the detection of malignant disease, drew to its close in what seemed the most propitious of circumstances.

3

Jack Strangeways

In early January came a letter from Murry, Lawrence's response to which set in train the growth of a fierce mutual antagonism which brought to absolute extinction a relationship that over the years had passed through several false deaths. In Murry's view of events it was Lawrence who was the first to take umbrage and whose unreasonableness began the rift. Murry had promised to visit Lawrence with his wife and child when they had met in London, and in December he had written restating his intention to come to Italy. It was only afterwards that he decided he should take the precaution of consulting the family doctor concerning his wife's fitness to travel. Because of her pregnancy and poor health the doctor would in no way countenance the journey, and Murry was obliged to tell Lawrence that they would not be coming after all. According to Murry, Lawrence wrote 'a furious letter' in reply.[1] No letter that is transparently of that character exists, and Harry T. Moore concluded, or was told by Murry, that the letter had been lost.[2] But Murry's narrative in his *Reminiscences of D. H. Lawrence*, together with the evidence of Lawrence's correspondence with others at that period, leaves little doubt that Murry misconstrued as 'furious' the extant letter of 4 January 1926. This letter, quoted in full below, is indisputably intemperate and patronizingly offensive, but it is difficult to see behind it emotion which greatly exceeds irritation.

Murry's letter announcing the cancellation of his visit had been written in a despondent vein which, judging by Lawrence's reactions to such letters in the past, would have caused Lawrence as much or more irritation than Murry's breaking a promise that had only recently been reaffirmed. Murry's anxieties seem to have centred on his wife's health in pregnancy and on the future of *The Adelphi* magazine, of which he was editor. In his letter he proposed that it should be written jointly by him and Lawrence, or, if Lawrence was unwilling, entirely by himself. The motives behind the suggestion of a joint Lawrence–Murry venture, recreating their collaboration on the short-lived magazine *The Signature* in the old days, are not clear. Perhaps Murry entertained rash hopes that the ginger Lawrence would add to *The Adelphi* might boost its declining sales. Alternatively, the offer could have been intended to placate the anger he expected in Lawrence when he learned that he was backing out of the visit to Spotorno. Whatever the reasons behind the proposal to collaborate on *The Adelphi*, it held no appeal for Lawrence, and instead of declining with polite thanks he wrote as follows:

Dear Jack: *A la guerre comme à la guerre!* Make up your mind to change your ways, and call the baby Benvenuto.

My dear Jack, *it's no good!* All you can do now, sanely, is to leave off. *A la vie comme à la vie.* What a man has got to say, is never more than relatively important. To kill yourself, like Keats, for what you've got to say, is to mix the eggshell in with the omelette. That's Keats' poems to me. The very excess of beauty is the eggshell between one's teeth.

Carino, basta! Carito, déjà, déjà, la canzon, cheto! Cheto, cheto! Zitto, zitto, zitto! Basta la mòssa.

In short, shut up. Throw the *Adelphi* to the devil, throw your own self after it, say goodbye to J. M. M. *Filius Meus, Salvatore di Nessuno se non di se stesso*, and my dear fellow – *give it up!*

As for your humble, he says his say in bits, and pitches it as far from him as he can. And even then it's sometimes a boomerang.

Ach! du lieber Augustin, Augustin, Augustin – I don't care a straw who publishes me and who doesn't, nor where nor how, nor when nor why. I'll contrive, if I can, to get enough money to live on. But I don't take myself seriously, except between 8.0 and 10 a.m., and at the stroke of midnight. At other seasons, my say, like any butterfly, may settle where it likes: on the lily of the field or the horsetod in the road: or nowhere. It has departed from me.

My dear chap, people don't want the one-man show of you alone, nor the Punch and Judy show of you and me. Why, oh why, try to ram yourself down people's throats? Offer them a tasty tit-bit, and if they give you five quid, have a drink on it.

No, no! I'm forty and I want, in a good sense, to enjoy my life. Saying my say and seeing other people sup it up doesn't amount to a hill o'beans, as far as I go. I want to waste no time over it. That's why I have an agent. I want my own life to live. 'This is my body, keep your hands off!'

Earn a bit of money journalistically, and kick your heels. You've perhaps got J. M. M. on the brain even more seriously than J. C. Don't you remember we used to talk about having a little ship? The Mediterranean is glittering blue today. Bah, that one should be a mountain of mere words! Heave-O! my boy! get out of it!

(*CL* 875f.)

23

Essentially, Lawrence was endeavouring, condescendingly and with somewhat manic levity, to impart to Murry the hang-it-all and quasi-hedonistic values of the doctrine of insouciance; and the overall intention of the letter seems not to have been malevolent, despite the jeering tone and the implicit want of respect for the addressee. Lawrence had always been sceptical about Murry's visit, and news of his withdrawal would have come as no great surprise to him. Nevertheless, his exasperation is transparent, and the fact that he was also piqued can reasonably be inferred from his silence on the matter of Murry's decision to back out. There is, too, a bizarre quality to the letter, especially in the opening paragraphs with their macaronic juxtaposition of English, French, German, Latin, and frenetic exclamatory sentences in Italian, whose message, as Lawrence pointed out, is 'Shut up!'. Behind the letter was clearly an extremely complex reaction which Murry, who was in the habit of scrutinizing Lawrence's letters very carefully for their subliminal import, chose to diagnose as fury.

Lawrence, on reflection, must himself have realized that he had gone too far, for a few days later he wrote another letter which restated, in sober and sympathetic tones, the content of his letter of 4 January. But by then it was too late to repair the damage, and since Lawrence's pride had been too great to append an apology for the preceding letter, Murry remained unappeased. Indeed, the changed tone of this following letter seems merely to have confirmed in him the view that Lawrence's behaviour had become wholly irrational.

In Murry's history of their friendship Lawrence was cast as the thwarted lover whose unreasoning demands proved impossible to meet, and it was in this light that he interpreted Lawrence's letters of January 1926. According to Murry, Lawrence was so alarmingly dependent on his (Murry's) person that the denial of his presence provoked a wild, paranoid rage which suspected deliberate fiction in the excuses Murry offered.[3] By contrast, Murry presented himself as entirely reasonable and temperate. Lawrence's first January letter struck him as 'a bitter denunciation', phrased 'in frenzied terms', but though it left him feeling 'sore', he had reached a stage at which he 'was beyond caring'.[4] The truth of the matter was that the effect of the letter on Murry's neurotically insecure ego was shattering: it left him with feelings of nausea that persisted for weeks afterwards.[5] Obsessed with Lawrence, and, contrary to his claims in *Reminiscences*, still very much in awe of him, he needed tokens of Lawrence's affection and respect. This jeering letter seemed to deny him both. On their last meeting he had convinced himself that he was more than a match for Lawrence and that Lawrence's power to destroy him had evaporated. His reactions to Lawrence's letter must have revealed to him how ill-founded those convictions were.

To add to Murry's wounds there arrived, within a few days of the letter, a copy of Lawrence's essay anthology, *Reflections on the Death of a Porcupine*. Lawrence's letter had implied that Murry's editorship of *The Adelphi* was an ineffectual waste of time. Now, prefacing the essay 'The Crown', first published in *The Signature*, he found scornful comments on the periodical which he and Lawrence had jointly written in 1915 in the heyday of their friendship: 'To me the venture meant nothing real: a little escapade. I can't believe in "doing things" like that. In a great issue like the war, there was nothing to be "done", in Murry's sense. There is still nothing to be "done" ' (*Ph 2* 364). In the following paragraph Lawrence had written: 'Personally, little magazines mean nothing to me . . . I have no hankering after quick response, nor the effusive, semi-intimate back-chat of literary communion.'

In the past Murry might have taken blows like these lying down; but he now had sufficient self-assurance to answer Lawrence in kind, and so he wrote back denouncing Lawrence. In his *Reminiscences* there is no reference to this letter. Lawrence, at the time of these paroxysms in the expiration of their friendship, is depicted as subject to constant, inexplicable changes of mood. In reality Murry's own behaviour was the more unaccountably variable.

On receiving Murry's letter of denunciation, Lawrence told Koteliansky ('Kot') that Murry had written to him 'with more spite and impudence than I have yet had from him . . . which makes me imagine he must be nearing the end of his tether' (Zyt 278). Within a week Lawrence received another letter from Murry begging a favour of him. Lawrence summed up his reactions to this extraordinary shift of tack in a letter to Brett:

Murry . . . wrote me impertinently about the *Porcupine*, that I was a professional heel-kicker, lucky I'm not a professional behind-kicker. Now he adds insult to injury, asking if I will allow him to print the essay on power, gratis, and various other things, gratis, in the *Adelphi*, 'as the gift of one man to another' . . . He's an incorrigible worm![6]

The difference between the genuine fury which Lawrence now felt, and the irritation which inspired his 4 January letter, is pointed up by the cool brevity of his reply to Murry's request:

> I would rather you didn't publish my things in the *Adelphi*. As man to man, if ever we were man to man, you and I, I would give them to you willingly. But as writer to writer, I feel it is a sort of self-betrayal. Surely you realise the complete incompatibility of my say with your say. Say your say, *caro*! – and let me say mine. But for heaven's sake, don't let us pretend to mix them.
>
> (*CL* 883)

Murry wrote back asking Lawrence to define his position (which seems to have been made clear enough), and asking whether he meant that he was not to publish the two pieces – a review of *Saïd the Fisherman* and a short poem, 'Creative Evolution' – which he had already received from Lawrence or his agent. Lawrence replied agreeing to their publication and restating the opinions of his preceding letter, adding for good measure: 'I can't go between the yellow covers of the *Adelphi* without taking on a tinge of yellow which is all right in itself, but not my colour for me' (*CL* 886).

When he came to write *Reminiscences of D. H. Lawrence*, Murry had expunged from memory any recollection of his own angry letter, which had been the principal cause of Lawrence's rift with him. He was convinced, then, that Lawrence's behaviour could only be explained by reference to the cancelled visit to Spotorno; and it is not unlikely that in 1926 his capacity for self-delusion and the extent of his isolation in the world of his imagination were such that, even then, he failed to perceive the true reason for Lawrence's hostility. Having convinced himself of the unreasonableness of Lawrence's attitude and behaviour, he found it that much easier to accept the coldness between them. He therefore wrote to Lawrence, telling him that if their 'co-operation was to depend upon such intensely personal happenings, it was manifestly not a real co-operation at all: merely an empty pretence which it was better for both . . . to have done with.'[7]

Lawrence never read this letter. It arrived while he was away from Spotorno, in late February or March; and Frieda tore it up. However, he learned something of its contents when he returned in April, and resolved not to reply. Instead he chose a more oblique means of getting in the last blow. Murry was in possession of essays from Lawrence's *Mornings in Mexico* anthology. One of them had already appeared in the December 1926 issue of *The Adelphi*, and Murry had since written claiming he could not afford the cost of publishing the essays. Lawrence wrote to Nancy Pearn, the girl at the Curtis Brown agency responsible for placing magazine articles, wondering whether payment had been received for the essay that had appeared, and asking her to seek the return of the other two essays Murry held.[8] It was hardly in the agency's interest to summon the return of articles that had been accepted, especially since Murry had acted quite blamelessly in the matter; and it was probably at Nancy Pearn's request that Murry contacted Lawrence to ask, somewhat unctuously and patronizingly, what all the fuss was about. A fortnight later he had a brief but temperate reply. This was towards the end of May 1926. In July Lawrence set him a postcard, honouring an earlier promise to let him know when he expected to reach England that summer. He had even begun to entertain thoughts, not perhaps very serious ones, of visiting Murry: 'Shall we', he suggested to Kote-liansky, 'go down to Murry's Dorset together? – and see his second baby, son and heir, another John Middleton, ye Gods!' (Zyt 289). If he meant it at all, it was probably as a malicious ploy: since 'Kot' and Murry had been enemies since 1924, and Murry was jealous of Lawrence's affection for Kot, their arrival together would have caused their host some considerable discomfiture. By the time he was almost due to travel to England, Lawrence had ceased to toy with the idea. He would not see Murry, he told Brett: 'He is too much, or too little, for me' (*CL* 929).

'Pour moi vous n'existez pas, mon cher' (*CL* 886) – this was the position Lawrence felt he had taken with regard to Murry by February 1926. But rancorous thoughts of Murry persisted for at least a year afterwards, and may have been fuelled by his review of *The Plumed Serpent* as a 'disappointing' book, one that suggested Lawrence had 'lost faith in his own imagination'.[9] However, this review had been followed, in the editorial of the next issue, by a very handsome compensation in the form of a tribute to Lawrence as 'the most significant writer we have'.[10]

Lawrence's ill-feeling towards Murry found its most overt expression in one of the last of his vindictive, satirical caricatures of Murry, which appears in *John Thomas and Lady Jane*. Here Murry, appropriately bearing the name Jack Strangeways, is one of a small group of relatives and friends who spend Christmas with the Chatterleys at Wragby. Strangeways is accompanied by his wife, Olive, whose sharp, sarcastic wit, demonic spirit and promiscuous ways reveal that she was created with Katherine Mansfield in mind. Murry is portrayed much as he was in the short stories of 1924 and 1925 – 'good looking' and not ungifted, but rather a fool. That the affair between Murry and Frieda may have continued to rankle with Lawrence can be supposed from the narrator's comments on Strangeways, whose immaturity and inadequacy are most apparent in his dealings with women:

> He terribly wanted to make women *feel* for him: but he rather overdid it . . . And he seemed so convinced that the woman must, simply must feel tremendously for *him*, his appeal, and what he was saying, that most women laughed at him a little spitefully.
> So it was with Constance . . . Nevertheless he followed her about . . . like a persistent little boy dogging his mother. He was not little at all. He was big, and good-looking in the romantic style, like a young Siegfried already a bit too fat and vapid. Yet he, too, had his own peculiar intelligence, a certain insight into things, though it was the insight of a rather timid child who wished things could be made 'safe'.
>
> (*JTLJ* 61)

There is also a cruelly percipient summary of the history of the relationship between Murry and Katherine Mansfield, both of whom are described as 'second-rate':

> She picked up a lover where she could. But invariably she found him terribly unsatisfactory, and invariably she returned to her tension with Jack. That seemed to her the only thing in her life: the tight string that tied her to Jack, and made her spend most of her time strangling his soul, while he, equally canny at the game, had tight strings round all her limbs and pulled them till he paralysed her. A great deal of it was mutual torment! And that was the most real thing she had in her life. She felt herself like an embodied demon.
>
> (*JTLJ* 72f.)

When, in the final version, Jack and Olive Strangeways visit Wragby, they arrive shorn of the attributes which associated them with the Murrys, and are presented merely as characterless voices in a desultory conversation on the subject of test-tube babies. By that period there was good reason for Lawrence to show more charity towards his old adversary: earlier in the year, as Lawrence had no doubt learned from correspondents in England, Violet Murry, like Katherine before her, had been diagnosed as a consumptive.

28

The original draft of the novel, *The First Lady Chatterley*, is not without its Murry-figure. Lawrence's portrait of Sir Clifford began by being loosely based, in terms of bare outline and background, though not in character, on Thomas Philip Barber, one of the owners of the Barber, Walker Colliery Company in Lawrence's home town of Eastwood. It was not the first time he had used Barber in his fiction, for he had also appeared in *Women in Love* as the model for Gerald Crich, the coal-owner's son, whose physical appearance resembles that of the first of Lawrence's Sir Cliffords. Lawrence had no personal acquaintance with Barber, and for the character of Gerald Crich he had drawn extensively on Murry. Precedent may therefore have led Lawrence to think of Murry for the Barber-figure in *The First Lady Chatterley*. There was also a motive for the choice of Murry as Sir Clifford in the grudge Lawrence bore him over his relationship with Frieda. In a novel in which two men representing different worlds and different states of consciousness contend for possession of a woman, it was perhaps almost inevitable that, as in 'The Border Line', Lawrence should have thoughts of Murry when shaping the character of the loser in the struggle.

The Clifford of *The First Lady Chatterley* is in no sense a caricature of Murry, but it could be said of Clifford, as Harry T. Moore observed of Gerald Crich, that he stands for the kind of man Lawrence discerned in Murry, who was admirably qualified, in terms of Lawrence's view of him, for Clifford's role as the anti-type to the Lawrentian hero. Inwardly a much softer man than the Cliffords who succeed him, and for the greater part of the novel less repellent than his successors, the Sir Clifford of *The First Lady Chatterley* resembles Murry in these respects: he is 'an abstract man', 'who had already died to everything except nervous appreciation or irritation', a Platonist with 'the soul of the earnest seeker after truth', and a mystic 'deeply concerned with the question of immortality' (*FLC* 21, 55, 35); he has a Murryish tendency to succumb to bouts of self-pity and self-reproach; and he fits Lawrence's conception of Murry as a man drawn towards subservient, self-annihilatory worship of the female, a tendency which, when fully embraced towards the end of the novel, serves to alienate Constance for ever.

It was in letters to Murry in January 1926 that Lawrence first declared the anti-nominal views which went hand in hand with his dissatisfaction with the writer's profession, and which also, in rather incongruous fashion, became one of the motifs of *Lady Chatterley*.

'Bah, that one should be a mountain of mere words' was one of the imprecations which concluded his 4 January letter to Murry, and he echoed that sentiment at the close of the letter which followed. In *The First Lady Chatterley* Clifford is the target, as Murry is implicitly in the letters, of Lawrence's contempt for words, expressed through Connie's irritation with literary allusions which were abstract in that they were at a remove from the concrete, physical existence of the object of beauty to which they referred. Clifford's mental response to words is more potent than the response of his senses to the beauty of the physical world:

> ' "Thou still unravished bride of quietness" ', he said, looking with emotion at the wind-flowers and violets in his hand. 'Spring flowers always make me think of that', he said, 'far more than a Grecian urn. Don't they you?'
>
> 'Yes!' she said, vaguely. Then she added, 'But why ravished? It's such a violent word! If bees come, or little insects, I don't think they feel ravished, do you? I mean, the flowers.'
>
> 'Maybe not', he said. 'They're quaint, aren't they? – The nodding violet! – Do you know, I don't think we should care half so much for flowers if it weren't for the lovely things the poets have said about them.'
>
> She stopped suddenly. Was it true? It was only half true. The things poets said had indeed opened doors, strange little doors to the flowers, through which one could go. But once passed through the poet's gate, the flowers were more flowerily unspoken than ever.
>
> (*FLC* 46)

If there is any definite clue that Lawrence specifically had Murry in mind when he first created Clifford, it may lie in Clifford's quoting from Keats and Shakespeare ('the nodding violet').[11] This might be seen as an allusion, perhaps made quite unconsciously, to Murry's *Keats and Shakespeare*.

While one friendship dating from pre-war days was in the process of dissolution, another had begun to revive after a hostile silence of some eighteen months. S. S. Koteliansky, 'Kot', was a Jewish Russian emigré whom Lawrence had first got to know on a walking tour of the Lake District in August 1914, during which they had come down from the fells to learn that war had been declared. Leonard Woolf, who knew both men, wrote of their first meeting: 'Kot's passionate approval of what he thought good, particularly in people, his intense hatred of what he thought bad, the directness and vehemence of his speech, his inability to tell a lie – all this appealed to Lawrence, and they became very fond of each other.'[12] That two men so volatile and candid in their relations with others should have found a lasting friendship was remarkable, and inevitably their relationship was not without its troughs, which more often than not seem to have resulted from hurt feelings on Kot's side rather than Lawrence's. He was a passionate admirer of Lawrence's gifts, which he considered the finest and rarest of the age; and he regarded Lawrence's person with an affection which seemed to some to amount to adoration. Frieda, who was one of that number, had from an early period in their acquaintance been alienated by Kot's blunt outspokenness, and perhaps also by his devotion to Lawrence. To her he was the most inimical of all Lawrence's male friends.

The rift between Lawrence and Kot coincided with Lawrence's return to America in 1924. There had been a quarrel shortly before Lawrence sailed, though Lawrence appears to have been untouched by it, for he wrote warmly to Kot soon after he docked in New York. However, there was no further letter from Lawrence until December 1925; and when Lawrence had returned to London in the autumn of that year, he had made no attempt to contact Kot. Though this break in communication could have been brought about by Kot's being too deeply offended to reply to Lawrence, Kot himself seems to have believed he was the victim of malicious gossip, and his anger with Brett when she arrived in London in November 1925 could mean that she was one of the suspects.[13]

When they resumed their correspondence in December 1925, Lawrence tried to reassure Kot that no one had spoken ill of him, but he was a good deal less convincing on that matter than he was in the expression of a continuing warm regard. The friendship had come to life again, and they continued to correspond regularly until the time of Lawrence's death. Kot had never been much enamoured of Murry, and towards the end of 1924 had broken with him completely when, as business manager of *The Adelphi*, he took exception to Murry transforming the journal into a one-man concern. In the past Kot had been the vessel into which Lawrence poured his invective against Murry. When the quarrel with Murry began in January 1926, Kot resumed this customary role, which he now shared with Brett.

4

'Chapter of Dismalnesses'[1]

The warm spell which began with the turn of the year lasted until the end of the third week of January 1926. Taking advantage of the opportunity to write, as he preferred to, in the open air, Lawrence dashed off *The Virgin and the Gipsy* at an average rate of some 2,000 words a day. By the 21st of the month the novella was ready to be posted to London for typing and for Secker's assessment. What Lawrence's publisher thought of this disappointingly inconsequential and ill-constructed piece is not known; but after Secker returned the MS Lawrence set it aside and apparently gave no more heed to it, for he made no further reference to *The Virgin and the Gipsy* in his correspondence. The work did not appear in print in Lawrence's lifetime. It was first published without the author's final revision by Orioli in Florence in 1930, shortly after Lawrence's death.

The Virgin and the Gipsy was the last work of any considerable length that Lawrence produced before the autumn of 1926, when he began work on *Lady Chatterley*, with which *The Virgin and the Gipsy* shows a number of significant affinities. Both works share the theme of erotic renewal and embody the same story-pattern in the attraction of a well-born lady to a man of low degree; each has the device of the two sisters (Yvette and Lucille in *The Virgin and the Gipsy* and Constance and Hilda in *Lady Chatterley*); there is a degree of correspondence in character-type between the would-be-kindly but fundamentally base and oppressive rector and Sir Clifford, and between the sage man of the world, Major Eastwood, and Brigadier Tommy Dukes of the last two versions of *Lady Chatterley*; and there are close similarities in behaviour and background between the gipsy and the gamekeeper.

It would appear that in the winter of 1925/6 Lawrence's creative imagination was preoccupied with a number of the themes, situations, character-types and narrative devices that were later to be drawn on in the writing of *Lady Chatterley*. 'Sun' and 'Glad Ghosts' also prefigure *Lady Chatterley* in a number of their features; and with

The Virgin and the Gipsy they form a trio of works, written consecutively within the space of a few weeks, which taken together make a strong case for supposing that this stage in Lawrence's writing career marked a distinct prelude to the *Lady Chatterley* period.

All three stories concern the regeneration into bodily awareness of a 'modern' woman whose sexuality has been wounded or repressed; and in each of the stories a silent flame of desire is lit between the woman and an outsider of lower social status – a solitary, vital, somewhat mysterious, Pan-like figure whose sexual magnetism derives largely from the direct relationship he enjoys with the elemental powers of the cosmos. In the physical sexuality which he exudes he contrasts with the men in the social sphere of the heroine, who as followers of the mental life have become bodily dead. 'Sun' and 'Glad Ghosts' share with *Lady Chatterley* the motif of the child conceived out of wedlock through the union of the lady and the 'sans-culotte', but in 'Sun' this is merely a wish on the woman's part that is never fulfilled, and in 'Glad Ghosts' it is achieved through union of the spirit, not of the flesh. 'Glad Ghosts' and *The Virgin and the Gipsy* open, like *Lady Chatterley*, with a picture of the stifling, sterile world within a gloomy country-house in Derbyshire; and they conclude, like *Lady Chatterley's Lover*, with a letter bringing news of one of the parted 'lovers' to the other.

Thematically, 'Glad Ghosts' comes closest of the three stories to *Lady Chatterley* in that the general renewal of those present in the Lathkills's house is achieved through recognition of the importance of touch and warmth of feeling in relations between men and women. However, though class difference is explored in the relationship between Morier and Lady Carlotta, the theme of 'tenderness' does not carry the socio-political significance which it bears with varying degrees of emphasis in the three versions of *Lady Chatterley*: there is no overt suggestion that through warm human contacts the class divisions of society may be healed. It is the absence of this message from the stories belonging to the Spotorno period which chiefly distinguishes them from *Lady Chatterley*, which owes its splicing of the themes of erotic renewal and societal reunification to Lawrence's shocked encounter with the despair and class hatred engendered by the imminent collapse of the miners' strike in the Nottinghamshire and Derbyshire area in September 1926.[2]

The first weeks of January were especially lively ones in the Lawrence household, which was usually buzzing with activity on some creative or practical project. Lawrence worked in the mornings on the completion of *The Virgin and the Gipsy* and at other times was rarely seen without a Russian dictionary in his hands: he had half a mind to visit Russia in the spring and had therefore set about acquiring the rudiments of the language. Meanwhile, Frieda was working excitedly at her German translation of Lawrence's play *David*. Barby, thrilled by the atmosphere of intellectual and artistic endeavour, began producing some very successful landscapes which, in turn, excited the interest of Frieda and Lawrence in painting. In his youth Lawrence had shown some skill in copying pictures and had received a little training in art; he had also observed Brett's technique with oils in New Mexico and occasionally added figures to her landscapes. In Spotorno Lawrence worked with Barby on a couple of paintings and was well pleased with the results. This period marked the beginning of an interest in painting as an alternative means of expressing himself, which developed in tandem with his disenchant-ment with words and with the demands of writing.

The last ten days of the month put an end to outdoor activities. In the garden and on the hillsides the blossoming almond trees announced the arrival of a Mediterranean spring to the accom-paniment of a forbidding spell of cold weather and pouring rain which lasted for three weeks. 'January is always a hard month to climb through' (*CL* 884), Lawrence told Brett, thinking in particular of his experiences in Mexico in the preceding year; and though the month passed with no sign of ill-health, the first days of February found him at a low ebb – the first symptom, perhaps, of the illness that followed shortly afterwards.

Other factors combined with the onset of illness to leave Lawrence feeling down. On 23 January, almost a year after its completion in Mexico, *The Plumed Serpent* appeared, and received 'a rather feeble review' (*CL* 885) in *The Times Literary Supplement*. This was the first real test of his self-schooling in not taking the world seriously. He regarded *The Plumed Serpent* as the most important of all his novels and had described it as dearer to him than any of his other works. Though he had written in similar vein of other major novels, he had a special reason for his attachment to *The Plumed Serpent* in that he completed it on the day he went down with the illness from which he very nearly died in Mexico. Like many authors he was fearful of publication, but Lawrence's dread of his most cherished works going out into the world surpassed that of most of his fellows. What he feared was more than professional failure. His novels were the embodiments, not only of passionately-held convictions which he wished to be accepted and propagated, but of his whole psyche. A hostile review therefore constituted for him a humiliating personal rejection that was reminiscent of his experiences in Eastwood as a boy.

'Nobody will like it', he had prophesied of *The Plumed Serpent* in a letter to Edward McDonald;[3] and having donned the armour of pessimism, as he not infrequently did before publication of a novel, he perhaps felt himself better equipped to face reviews which might confirm his prediction. When *The Times Literary Supplement* review appeared, he referred to it in a letter to Brett without anger or disappointment. But in the days that followed, its effect began to tell on him. In early January he had told McDonald: 'So long as the sun shines ... we don't give a cent for the world' (*CL* 881). Now, trapped inside the fireless villa by the vile weather, it was harder to keep spleenful thoughts of the world at bay. In a letter of 1 February to Harold Mason, Lawrence wrote bitterly of the reception accorded *The Plumed Serpent*: 'I could weep over THAT book, I do so hate it's [*sic*] being published and going into the tuppenny hands of the tuppenny public. Small private editions are really *much* more to my taste. Odi profanum vulgum [*sic*] – though it's not the vulgus, it's literatus literatibus' (*Cent* 27)'. One advantage of the private edition, of course, as Lawrence had once remarked to Secker, was that it was not necessary to distribute review copies.

The reviews of *The Plumed Serpent* were almost universally unfavourable, and the effect of this rejection was to intensify Lawrence's dissatisfaction with the writer's profession, especially in regard to the writing of novels. At the end of his letter to Mason he declared a hope that he would never write another serious novel, and in a letter written on the same day to Secker, warning him not to expect a book from him in the autumn, he wrote: 'I feel at the moment I will never write another word' (Sec 70).

This attitude survived until October 1926, when he began work on the first draft of *Lady Chatterley*; and an abiding, casual lack of interest in publication determined that he would approach the task of producing a finished version of the novel with no great urgency, with the result that three years elapsed between the completion of *The Plumed Serpent* and his finishing the final draft of his next novel. The only comparable gap in the past had been between *Women in Love* and

The Lost Girl, when depression, persecution and the unwillingness of publishers to accept *Women in Love* had brought about a rather longer interval between the completion of successive novels.

The effects of adverse reviews of *The Plumed Serpent* caused Lawrence more than wounded pride and disappointment: what grieved him most was the poor return he received in plaudits and expected in cash for an investment of intense effort that had almost put an end to him. Though in February he told Knopf, his publisher in America, that the price he had paid had been worth it,[4] he later came to doubt whether the rewards of novel-writing justified the demands on his energy and health. In July 1926 he wrote to Secker: 'Why do any more books? There are so many, and such a small demand for what there are. So why add to the burden, and waste one's vitality over it. Because it costs one a lot of blood' (Sec 74).

When counting the personal cost of *The Plumed Serpent* Lawrence had reason, given his belief that illnesses could be brought on by chagrin, to believe that he had twice paid dearly for the novel. In early February, little more than a year after his Mexico illness, Lawrence fell victim to an attack of influenza accompanied by a bout of haemorrhaging. For some ten or eleven days he was confined to bed, too feeble to get up and constrained by doctor's advice to lie still. When, on 11 February, he was able for the first time to write a couple of letters, he reported to his American friend Earl Brewster that he was 'rather downcast' (*CL* 888). No doubt similarly under-stated was his observation that Frieda was 'cross'. On the previous day his sister Ada had arrived with a friend, Lizzie Booth, for a fortnight's stay with the Lawrences. She was very distressed by the condition in which she found her brother, and for the first days of her holiday she seems to have given him all her attention, never stepping out of the house for a moment. It would not be surprising if, having like her brother inherited Lydia Lawrence's passion for tidiness and good order, she was aghast at the state of affairs at the Villa Bernarda. Frieda was ill-qualified to act the part of sick-nurse and inexperienced in running a household: the added burden of guests must have taxed to the utmost her limited competence in either role.[5] Ada, who shared the Lawrentian managerial instinct, seems quickly to have endeavoured to take charge of the care of her brother, thereby exciting Frieda's intolerance of any attempt to subject her to the will of others.

Added to Frieda's indignation over interference in her domestic affairs was an irrational resentment of the relationship between Lawrence and Ada. It was now her turn to feel excluded, as Lawrence had when Barby arrived, from the intimacies of blood-relations; and she regarded with jealous suspicion any show of brotherly affection.[6] Later she rationalized and tried to objectify her behaviour within a theory of psychotherapy. It was not jealousy or dislike of Ada, she claimed in her autobiography, which prompted her hostility: it was because her presence threatened to lure Lawrence back into a sad past which he had fought hard to exorcise and from which it was therapeutically necessary for him to dissociate himself.[7] The idea that Ada was a baleful influence may have come originally from Lawrence. Of a later visit from Ada in 1929, Lawrence wrote: 'I am fond of her, but she fills me with tortures of angry depression. I feel all those Midlands behind her, with their sort of despair' (Hux 786).

Outside the Villa Bernarda the rains continued to pour down. Within, the climate also soon turned extremely ugly, as the ailing, bedridden Lawrence became the focus of a struggle for domination between two women of powerful will and volatile temperament. During one angry exchange Ada, who had from the first disapproved of Lawrence's association with Frieda, told her that she hated her from the bottom of her heart; and on another occasion Frieda went to Lawrence's room to find the door locked against her: Ada had walked off with the key. The conspiracy evident in this incident suggests that Lawrence, sick as he was, was not entirely a passive victim of events or an impartial witness to them.

Two days after Ada's arrival Frieda's elder daughter, Elsa, reached Spotorno, accompanied by Barby. It had been decided that the two girls should stay at the inn, watched over by a Mrs Seaman whom Ernest Weekley had sent to act as *duenna*. Because of the enmity that had arisen before Elsa's arrival, the two families divided almost immediately into hostile camps, and shortly after her daughters had taken up residence at the Albergo Ligure Frieda angrily packed her bags and joined them. Her story of Ada's visit has it that Lawrence timed the arrival of his sister to coincide with that of Elsa and Barby in order to counterbalance the presence of her family.[8] Aldington, in his malevolent biography of Lawrence, was probably right to see in Frieda's remark the implication that the feuding which ensued was due in large measure to petty-minded jealousy on Lawrence's part. But her claim was not strictly true. Lawrence might conceivably have argued that he had a right to entertain Ada for a while if Frieda was to have her daughters with her for several weeks; but their arrival within a couple of days of each other came about through Elsa's change of plan: Ada's visit had been scheduled for February at a time when Elsa was expected at Christmas.[9]

Lawrence chose to see himself as a disinterested bystander innocently caught up in a faction-fight between womenfolk, and as soon as he was up and able to totter about he began hatching plans for escape:

> I feel absolutely swamped out, must go away by myself for a bit, or I shall give up the ghost ... Somehow everything feels in a great muddle, with daughters that are by no means mine, and a sister who doesn't see eye to eye with F. What a trial families are![10]

Lawrence's major problem was actually in his relations with Frieda. His complicity in the affair of the locked bedroom, the only act of his which Frieda believed had ever caused her any serious hurt, had placed such an emotional ice-field between them that a separation had become necessary. When, before he was fully recovered, he departed with Ada for a long-planned excursion to Monte Carlo, he was left in no doubt that his return would not be welcomed.

After a short stay in Monte Carlo – 'Wonderful weather, romantic place to look at, but one gets awfully sick of it. It's rather common and come-down' (Irv 62) – Lawrence moved on to Nice, where Ada and her friend were to begin the return journey to England. After seeing them off on the train, Lawrence spent an afternoon sitting on the beach contemplating his next move. The debilitating effects of his illness had put an end to hopes of carrying out any of the several plans for challenging expeditions to new places that he had dreamed up for the spring. What he needed now was somewhere peaceful to rest up, lick his wounds and work out what to do with a marriage that had broken down as completely as when he and Frieda had separated in 1923. He thought first of a visit to Florence, to be preceded, perhaps, by a short stay to gather strength for the journey at Bormes-les-Mimosas, a quiet village with a good hotel in the hills above Le Lavandou, just down the coast from Nice. In the end he settled on an immediate and exacting two-day journey next morning to Capri. For a sick man, 'tired of straining with the world' (*CL* 892), Capri was a good place to head for. It offered, besides its beauty and promise of healing sunshine, the company of several friends from the past. Principal amongst these were the Brewsters, his American friends, and Brett, who had followed the Lawrences from America to Italy and had been living on the island for some four months, quietly willing Lawrence to honour a promise to visit her. That her wish was now granted was probably due for the most part to the fact that in her Lawrence could be sure of finding soothing, restorative companionship and a sympathetic listener to all his marital woes. But Lawrence may also have hoped that their coming together would serve to annoy Frieda and perhaps evoke a spark of jealousy that would be a sign of some residue of feeling for him.

Once out of Brett's company, after they left the ranch, Frieda had warmed to her again, and for a while they had corresponded gaily and exchanged gifts. After Christmas the letter-writing had ceased on Frieda's side, though all seemed well on 2 February, when Lawrence told Brett that he might visit Capri with Frieda in March. But on the 11th, mid-way through his attack of influenza, Lawrence wrote: 'I doubt if we shall ever see comfortable days together. Frieda declares an implacable intention of never seeing you again and never speaking to you if she does see you – and I say nothing. Don't you say anything either, it only makes scenes: which is ridiculous' (*CL* 887). It seems, from a reference in the following letter to 'another rumpus' (*CL* 891) when his sister came, that there had been a row about Brett not long before the arrival of Ada, who may have been to some extent a victim of the sourness that followed.

The quarrel between Frieda and Brett was almost certainly connected with the affair of the typewriter. Brett had been acting as Lawrence's typist and had been loaned his typewriter for that purpose. Frieda wanted her daughter Elsa to have the machine so that she could type out Frieda's German translation of *David* for her when she visited Spotorno. When Lawrence wrote on 2 February, asking for the return of the typewriter,[11] Brett decided that she was the victim of a plot on Frieda's part: the typing she was doing for Lawrence demanded a frequent exchange of letters; and Brett reasoned that Frieda's aim was to curtail this correspondence by eliminating its cause with the removal of the typewriter.[12]

Advised by telegram of Lawrence's impending arrival in Capri, Brett was waiting to greet him near the landing-stage with Harwood, the Brewsters' daughter; and together they drove by carriage up the hill to her parents' villa, the Quattro Venti, where Brett had arranged for him to stay. The Brewsters were in the process of packing all their belongings for a voyage to India, which they were to embark on within the fortnight. The amount of time they could give to entertaining Lawrence was limited, and Brett was often left in the happy position of having Lawrence to herself for much of the day, strolling with him along the many cliff paths through the olive woods, or on the sands of the Marina Piccola. The steep slopes of the mountainous island made even a short walk difficult for Lawrence. He was still very feeble and had difficulty in drawing breath when the going became hard: 'Sometimes', he confessed, 'I feel so weak. I feel like a white geranium in a pot.'[13]

On their walks Lawrence and Brett would occasionally call on friends Lawrence had made in the time he spent on the island in the winter of 1919–20: John Ellingham Brooks, the 'character' of the British colony, an amiable old lotus-eating scholar and poet; and Compton Mackenzie's wife, Faith, now living much of her life apart from her husband, who was away on Jethou, one of the small Channel Islands that he had leased from the British Government. Faith Mackenzie – grown a slightly pathetic figure, Lawrence thought, trying to cover up her sadness with an outward show of gaiety – was Lawrence's companion over dinner at a restaurant one evening. Beguiled by the wine and Lawrence's sympathetic charm, she talked too freely and trustingly of her personal life and of 'Monty', her husband: next year, to her annoyance, she found sketches of herself and her husband in 'Two Blue Birds' and of Monty in 'The Man Who Loved Islands'. What most offended her, it would seem, was not simply that in 'Two Blue Birds' her appearance had been lent to an unreliable, 'incompetent and extravagant' adulteress (*WWRA* 15), but that what Lawrence had written showed an obvious debt to the confidences she had trusted Lawrence with that night on Capri.[14]

It was a treacherous act by one of literature's scavengers, always on the look-out for a story-line, a scene or a character that he could put to use; and in his exploitation of friends and acquaintances in this way he showed a selfish disregard for the feelings of his 'victims' that was either ruthless or thoughtlessly naïve. Sometimes his motive was malicious devilment, but this was not the case with 'Two Blue Birds' which owed its inspiration to a sympathetic analogy that he sensed between his own domestic situation and the Mackenzies' marriage. The opening sentence of the story – 'There was a woman who loved her husband, but she could not live with him' (*WWRA* 11) – in fact reproduces almost word for word a comparison he drew between Frieda and Faith Mackenzie in a letter he wrote to Ada shortly after he

left Capri;[15] and the precise chronological history of the marriage of
the writer Cameron Gee and his nameless spouse, 'married for the last
dozen years, and couldn't live together for the last three or four'
(*WWRA* 12), belongs to the Lawrences. It was of Frieda that he was
mainly thinking, when he wrote of the 'gallant affairs' (*WWRA* 13)
with which the author's wife amused herself while her complaisant
husband was away; and Mrs Gee's unreliability and her incompetence
and extravagance suggest a grafting of traits of Frieda's on to the
portrait of Faith Mackenzie. Likewise, the woman's contempt for the
chaste, exploitive relationship between her husband and his slavishly
selfless, adoring secretary mirrors Frieda's attitude towards Lawrence
and Brett.

In 1920, when he first heard of Compton Mackenzie's acquiring
the lease on the islands of Herm and Jethou, Lawrence had ribbed
him about it, promising: 'I shall write a skit on you one day.
There will be a Lady of the Lake in it. And a rare to-do between
the pair' (*Let 3* 594). He carried out this threat, using the further
information he had picked up from Faith, in 'The Man Who Loved
Islands'. Many of the people who recognized themselves in Lawrence's fiction seem to have imagined that what appeared on paper
was Lawrence's view of their real selves. Compton Mackenzie, more
perceptive in this regard, defined Lawrence's methods of composing the characters of his fiction thus: 'He had a trick of describing
a person's setting or background vividly, and then putting into the
setting an ectoplasm entirely of his own creation'.[16] Part of the
mould for the character would derive from the principal model;
other parts might be the traits or attributes of some secondary
source among Lawrence's circle of acquaintances – often someone in
whom he perceived some association with his major source. In the
case of 'The Man Who Loved Islands' this second person had been a
mutual friend of Lawrence and Mackenzie, another hedonistic Scot
with an English public-school background and an ironic wit, who
was a lover of islands and natural history – the writer Norman
Douglas. On reaching Florence in April 1926, Lawrence was
mistakenly informed that Douglas had been working for some time
on 'The Flowers of the Greek Anthology'.[17] When Lawrence wrote
'The Man Who Loved Islands' in June, he had Cathcart working
for years on his islands at an anthology of the flora mentioned in
classical sources, giving his author the very considerable botanical
expertise that was one of Douglas's attributes.[18]

Compton Mackenzie also realized that the ectoplasms that Law-rence fashioned owed a great deal to his habit of projecting himself into the characters of his fiction.[19] The writer who longed to escape from the civilized world to create a perfect, self-contained Utopian community which ultimately brought him only disillusionment was Lawrence himself. As in 'Two Blue Birds' he had woven into the narrative feelings and experiences from his own life, including the material which supplied grounds for the legal action Mackenzie threatened after he read 'The Man Who Loved Islands'. Lawrence's promise of an island love-match with a Lady of the Lake had been fulfilled, on a diminished scale, in the form of a squalid, passionless affair between the writer and the 33-year-old spinster daughter of his housekeeper: it was substantially based on the unhappy outcome of Lawrence's relationship with Brett.

On Capri, Brett's chances of weaning Lawrence away from Frieda were enhanced by the arrival of harsh, unfeeling letters from Spotorno, which did nothing to alleviate the bitterness he felt towards Frieda or the despairing weariness that overcame him when he surveyed his marriage. He confessed to Brett that life with Frieda had become unbearable and that he could stand it no longer; it was sapping his energy and making him ill. At the same time he was unable to reach any firm resolve as to what to do. Brett, convinced that the only answer was a break with Frieda, but doubting whether he had the courage and strength to leave her, tried to steer him in that direction. When Lawrence spoke of a longing for freedom, she reminded him, with comically innocent candour, that he was free at the moment and ought to make hay while the sun shone.[20] Brett's hopes of acquiring Lawrence for herself may have been raised, as her biographer, Sean Hignett, suggests, by reading the MS of 'Glad Ghosts'. Lawrence had created Carlotta Fell by conflating aspects of Brett's biography with those of Cynthia Asquith; and Brett, seeing herself in the character, may have assumed that the union Lawrence yearned for was with her.[21]

When Lawrence had been with the Brewsters for a week and a half, it became time for them to leave for India. At the same time Lawrence and Brett also left the island for Amalfi on the mainland, to seek out Millicent Beveridge, a Scottish artist who had painted Lawrence's portrait in Sicily in 1921. She was travelling with her fellow-artist, Mabel Harrison, and Lawrence finally made contact with them at Ravello, in the hills just above Amalfi. The hotel where they were staying was full, but Lawrence and Brett were found rooms in a vacant cottage in the village.

Lawrence's walks with her on the steep, rocky footpaths of Ravello and Amalfi in the few days they spent in the area were worked into the second of the three parts of 'The Man Who Loved Islands'; and so, too, were the depressing consequences of their finding themselves alone together in the cottage, though in the story failure occurs only on an emotional level:

> She was so quiet, so wistful. But he sensed in her a persistency which made him uneasy. She said she was so happy: really happy. She followed him quietly, like a shadow, on the rocky track where there was never room for two people to walk side by side. He went first, and could feel her there, immediately behind him, following so submissively, gloating on him from behind.
>
> It was a kind of pity for her which made him become her lover: though he never realized the extent of the power she had gained over him, and how *she* willed it. But the moment he had fallen, a jangling feeling came upon him, that it was all wrong. He felt a nervous dislike of her. He had not wanted it. And it seemed to him, as far as her physical self went, she had not wanted it either. It was just her will. He went away, and climbed at the risk of his neck down to a ledge near the sea. There he sat for hours, gazing all jangled at the sea, and saying miserably to himself: 'We didn't want it. We didn't really want it.'
>
> It was the automatism of sex that had caught him again . . . He thought he had come through, to a new stillness of desirelessness. Perhaps beyond that there was a new fresh delicacy of desire, an unentered frail communion of two people meeting on untrodden ground.
>
> (*LAH* 13)

Nevertheless, that evening, driven by his sympathy and her mute will, Cathcart asks Flora once more to make love, which they do after she has been assured that Cathcart will not hate her for it afterwards. It is hatred of himself and a sense of humiliation that Cathcart is left with, following this second and equally unsatisfying attempt to enter into the delicate 'frail communion' to which he aspires.

Towards the end of her life Brett gave her own version of these episodes, which she had excluded from the original edition of *Lawrence and Brett*: one evening, while Lawrence and she were staying at the cottage in Ravello, Lawrence entered Brett's room in his dressing-gown and declared that he had no belief in any relationship in which physical relations played no part:

I was frightened as well as excited. He got into my bed, he turned and kissed me. I can still feel the softness of his beard, still feel the tension, the overwhelming desire to be adequate, I was passionately eager to be successful, but I had no idea what to do, nothing happened. Suddenly Lawrence got up, said 'It's no good', and stalked out of the room. I was devastated, helpless, bewildered. All the next day Lawrence was a bit glum. Nothing was said, I was too tense and nervous to say anything, if I had known what to say. Then that night he walked into my room and said, 'Let's try again'. So again he got into my bed. So there we lay. I felt desperate; all the love I had for him, all the closeness to him spiritually, the passionate desire to give what I felt I should be giving, was frustrated by fear and not knowing what to do. I tried to be warm and loving and female, he was I think struggling to be successfully male; it was a horrible failure. Nothing happened until he got up and stalked out of the room turning on me and saying, 'Your pubes are wrong', which left me ashamed, bewildered, miserable. After hours of self-torment, misery, I slept.[22]

This was strange behaviour for a man of genuinely puritanical views, who, though he championed sensuality, held against promiscuous sexual behaviour. Perhaps it could be squared with his known character and professed beliefs if, as may have been the case, making love to Brett was meant as a step towards establishing a permanent relationship that would replace the failed partnership with Frieda. More extraordinary, and inconsistent with more deeply held Lawrentian doctrines, was the coldly cerebral manner in which he initiated their experiment. The advocate of passionate, instinctive sexual encounter entered Brett's room with a proposal whose words made plain that behind it lay a decision of the intellect, not the impulses of the libido. This was the principal among several reasons for the failure of Lawrence and Brett in their tense endeavours to achieve consummation, a reason that was perhaps acknowledged in 'The Man Who Loved Islands' when he wrote of the coming together of Cathcart and Flora as 'an act of will' (*LAH* 114); though it is not clear whether the phrase is to apply to each of them, or only Flora, whose silent will has been paramount elsewhere in the story.

The will behind Lawrence's wish that he and Brett should become lovers could perhaps be seen as a collective one that also involved Frieda, whose power over Lawrence's actions was being exerted, albeit at an unconscious level, even in his intended adultery. In Mexico she had scorned the spiritual, curate and spinster relationship of Lawrence and Brett, and had even told Brett that she resented the fact that they did not make love to each other. Lawrence must have heard this same line from Frieda, because immediately after the altercation between her and Frieda, Brett had a letter from Lawrence which echoed Frieda's words, making it known to her that any friendship between man and woman must engage both the sensual and the spiritual halves of their personalities, and stating that her kind of one-sided friendship betrayed the essential man that he was.[23]

Pity was the emotion which incited Cathcart to heed the tacit commands of Flora and became her lover; and the emotional trigger of womanly pathos (albeit in this case inspiring compassion rather than pity) similarly stirs the gamekeeper to action in his first seduction of Constance Chatterley. It is as if the pathos of the woman bestows on the male the sense of superior power which confirms his virility and thus gives him the confidence to act. Quite possibly it was the same for Lawrence himself, who, at the time when he tried to become Brett's lover, had little cause for self-confidence in his virility where sexual functioning was concerned. By 1926 he had, according to Frieda, become completely incapable of achieving potency within their relationship; and he may have felt that through Brett, who was gentle, submissive and pitiable where Frieda was intimidating, aggressive and arrogant, he might find his potency restored.

The absolute impotence of Lawrence's last years may have been the final stage in a gradual decline in sexual capacity that afflicted him for much of his married life. Cecil Gray, Frieda's lover in the period of 1917–18, wrote in his memoirs that he was certain that Lawrence was 'not very far removed' from impotence.[24] And in *Aaron's Rod*, completed in 1921, Lawrence described the renascence of Aaron Sisson's desire after a long period of sexual apathy with imagery and rhetoric of such force as to suggest that the episode was of deeply personal significance.[25]

Clinical studies of potency disorders of this type, characterized by a progressive and accelerated falling-off in sexual potency over a period of years, suggest that the origins of the condition typically lie in a combination of psychogenic and constitutional factors, with the latter often exerting a dominant influence. It may have been that Lawrence's decline in potency had similar joint causes. Whether the major determinant was constitutional or psychogenic is impossible to tell.

Diseases which cause generalized metabolic disturbance frequently have the effect of diminishing sexual desires and responses, and it is thus very likely that the advance of tuberculosis, which Lawrence may have contracted as early as 1913, contributed significantly to the development of Lawrence's potency disorder.[26] Identifying possible psychogenic causes is a more speculative matter. In the sentiments, behaviour and histories of the gamekeepers in the three versions of *Lady Chatterley* there are suggestions of a number of psychological factors which might potentially have contributed to the development of sexual problems. Lawrence identified closely with the keepers and he invested them, especially those of the second and third versions, with a great deal of his own thought and experience. Could the sexual psychology of the keepers be identical with that of their creator? Plainly this is not a question that can be answered with any certainty. But it seems reasonable to suspect autobiographical sources where correspondences can be adduced either with opinions expressed elsewhere by Lawrence or with what is known of Lawrence's personal life.

An authoritative work on human sexuality suggests that the anxiety which underlies many sexual problems falls into two general types in the male – 'fear of failure' and 'fear of success':

> Fear of sexual failure or rejection by a sexual partner is usually associated with lack of self-confidence or low self-esteem, or uncertainty about one's gender identity, sexual attractiveness or sexual competence. For such an individual, rejection or failure may be less likely with certain kinds of partner . . .
>
> Fear of success is the fear of the actual sexual encounter, perhaps stemming from guilt about sexual enjoyment or fear of its consequences, learnt during childhood and perhaps reinforced by a sexually repressive environment. More specifically, guilt or anxiety about the sexuality of one's relationship with the opposite sex parent may be involved – the so-called Oedipus complex which plays such a central part in psychoanalytic theory. If for some reason the boy learnt to be threatened by the sexual implications of his relationship with his mother, he may avoid sexual relationships that bear any similarity – e.g. with a similar type of woman, or which involve love. He may even avoid heterosexual relationships altogether.[27]

Parkin and Mellors seem to show symptoms of both types of anxiety: 'fear of success' in the dread of woman's controlling power and in phobias of female genitalia;[28] and 'fear of failure' in their obsession with the optimal environment for sexual pleasure, and in the anxiety and sense of inferiority associated with Parkin's shame at the effeminacy of his nature.

Fear, mistrust and even hatred of women, wilful women most especially, are features of the gamekeeper's character in each version of the novel. In the first two versions fear of women is specifically attributed to the influence of a domineering mother, who in *John Thomas and Lady Jane* is the cause, not only of hatred of the female, but of hatred of sexuality: 'She [Connie] realised that it was the soul of his phallus ... that had been wounded all his life, wounded through his mother and his step-father from the beginning of his days, and whose wound gaped with the pain and hatred of sex' (*JTLJ* 237). This is Connie's interpretation of the cause of the unresolved conflicts of thought and desire in Parkin: 'His desire for sex intercourse, and his hatred of sex! His desire for woman, and his hatred of women!' In the gamekeeper, as perhaps in Lawrence, fear of women's social dominion has been extended to the sexual sphere. Mellors in *Lady Chatterley's Lover* dreads the controlling influence of an active partner striving for clitoral orgasm after the man is spent: then the vagina becomes an instrument of a man's humiliation and torture, a fearsome, tearing 'beak'. If Compton Mackenzie is to be believed, there could have been an autobiographical source for this fear in Lawrence's relationship with Frieda, with whom he was unable to achieve simultaneous orgasm.[29]

True sex, the optimal condition for successful arousal and fulfil-ment, is for Parkin in the first two versions of the novel, as it is for Cathcart in 'The Man Who Loved Islands', a meeting of passions that are tender, frail, delicate, peaceful, and silent. It is the expression of the truly feminine qualities that Lawrence found lacking in modern womanhood. The ideal partner for the keeper of *The First Lady Chatterley*, 'the burning flicker of his hope' is one 'with a gentle, warm soul and a warm, soft desirous body' (*FLC* 120). In the final version emphasis on the frail delicacy of sexual communion is rejected, perhaps as too 'feminine' a desire in the keeper, who is tailored to fit the new authorial stance of aggressive masculinity: his ideal is correspondingly more earthily robust – 'fucking with a warm heart' (*LCL* 215) is what Mellors believes in.

None of the keepers has found his ideals or desires gratified in his wife. Mellors, who is given wider sexual experience than his predecessors, has found satisfaction with no one. He cites an acrimonious catalogue of the punishments inflicted upon his sexuality by the three principal women of his past life, who represent three different types of deviation from true sexuality and seem to be based on five women with whom Lawrence had significant relationships. The first of Mellors's women would appear to have been created out of a conflation of Jessie Chambers and Louie Burrows; the second is manifestly Helen Corke; and the third, Bertha Coutts, perhaps combines features of Frieda with those of Alice Dax, the Eastwood chemist's wife who is said to have initiated Lawrence's experience of sex.[30]

Judged by the personalities of his gamekeepers, Lawrence had extremely rigid and particular views on the proper nature and behaviour of his partner in sex. Such views appear to be compatible with the generally obsessional and inflexible aspects of his character. Mellors remarks to Connie: 'I could never fool myself. I knew what I wanted with a woman and I could never say I'd got it when I hadn't' (*LCL* 213). Whether Lawrence consistently knew what he wanted is open to question. The ideals expressed in *Lady Chatterley* are not easily reconcilable with the view he sometimes held, in which conflict with a fiercely arrogant, dangerous woman was regarded as inspirational and life-giving. Perhaps he expected such a woman, Frieda, to undergo a change of personality in bed. One suspects that what Lawrence truly desired was an unattainable sexual union that transcended bodily congress. It seems almost as if he catches himself out in an unacceptable but sincere drift of thought when in *The First Lady Chatterley* Connie finds herself thinking of a man and a woman wrapped together as 'a kind of prison'. She immediately corrects herself: 'No, not a prison! If one thought in that way it was really a prison to have a body at all. If one wanted to be so tremendously free one must evaporate into nothingness' (*FLC* 120). If, like Lawrence and his gamekeepers and like Tommy Dukes in *John Thomas and Lady Jane*, one is fearful of touching and being touched, the body must seem an inconvenient obstacle to the meeting of desires; and it may be symptomatic of a wish to escape the encumbrances of the flesh that Lawrence's metaphors for desire and for the ideal sexual encounter tend to overlap in their suggestion of the incorporeal: in *John Thomas and Lady Jane*, for example, desire is a 'flame', like true sexual communion, which is 'a soothing flame of peace' (*JTLJ* 94). The sexual intercourse of two spirits which takes place in 'Glad Ghosts' might possibly have constituted for Lawrence the most desirable kind of sexual encounter; and Cecil Gray may well have been not far from the mark when he described Lawrence's 'sexual potentialities' as 'exclusively cerebral':[31] Lawrence, as we shall see later, was inclined towards a similar view of himself, which he expressed in his satirical self-portrait as Tommy Dukes.

The frailty of Lawrence's ego, his fears of ridicule and rejection and his anxieties about his virility are consciously laid bare in the character of Parkin in *John Thomas and Lady Jane*. Personal and sexual humiliation in his marriage to Bertha Coutts have killed all desire in Parkin, leaving him with a profound and lasting sense of shame, and a determination never again to involve himself with a woman. His affair with Connie brings new life, but the fear of being rebuffed and humiliated remains. Connie must not abuse his dependence on her and must grant him at least the illusion of superiority: 'Let me be mysen, an' let me feel as if tha wor littler than me! Dunna ma'e me feel sma', and *down*! – else I canna stop wi' thee' (*JTLJ* 334). The measure of trust established between Connie and Parkin allows him, as here in a moment of dejection, to relax and let drop the façade of aggressive virility to reveal 'the maimed human being' (*JTLJ* 94) of the inner man, who considers himself to be as 'handicapped' (*JTLJ* 334) emotionally as Clifford is physically. At the root of this handicap is shame at the effeminacy of his nature. His mother had often told him he was only half a man, and he is ready to acknowledge that this may be true: 'If I've got too much of a woman in me, I have, an' I'd better abide by it' (*JTLJ* 332). But the sense of his womanliness remains unacceptably humiliating to him, while at the same time he rejects conventional masculine behaviour.

The conversation between Connie and Parkin at this point may reflect an interior dialogue in which Lawrence, who from childhood had often been considered effeminate in his ways, struggles to come to terms with his 'feminine' traits and to learn to regard them as assets to his personality and the source of his talents. It could be, however, that the dialogue is not an imaginary one, but a remembered conversation with Frieda: while Bertha Coutts may embody that aspect of Frieda that was hard, bullying and arrogant, it may equally be the case that Connie is, in part, the Frieda who was warm, generous, untouched by neurosis, accepting and understanding. Connie counsels self-acceptance to Parkin. There is no reason why he should not be different from other men; his shame for his feminine qualities is an 'implied insult to womanhood' (*JTLJ* 333) and his striving to be more manly is self-destructive; if his sensitivity is womanly, then he should be proud to possess it and grateful that through it he has a 'gift of life' (*JTLJ* 333) that is rarely found in other men. 'Tha's cured me' (*JTLJ* 338), says Parkin, when they part. Through the reassurance of a woman whom he can trust he has learnt to value himself for what he is and to see himself as no less of a man for having womanly qualities.

There is a suggestion here of a Lawrence who was groping towards new directions in his thought and writing through reconciliation with himself and through an awareness of the overcompensation that lay behind the exaggeratedly male posturings of the heroes and the narrative voice of his novels. As it was, this new awareness proved ephemeral. The appalling haemorrhages of July 1927 left him an invalid whose realization that an early death might now be inescapable made him bitterly angry, unbalanced and determined on a fight to the last gasp, in which he could not appear vulnerably 'feminine'. In a reworking of the conversation in *John Thomas and Lady Jane* in which the keeper reflects on his misfit character, Lawrence has Mellors in the final version of the novel specifically deny what Parkin had confessed: 'They used to say I had too much of the woman in me. But it's not that' (*LCL* 289). Mellors's problems are externally caused. They stem from the fact that he has always stood against 'the bossy impudence' of established authority because he hates 'the impudence of money, and . . . of class'. He has also been the victim of the bossy impudence of wilful women, for whom he feels a deadly hatred. Reflecting on his wife, Bertha, he proclaims, with no suggestion of comic hyperbole, that 'when a woman gets absolutely possessed by her own will, her own will set against everything, then it's fearful, and she should be shot at last' (*LCL* 293). The revulsion inspired by this pronouncement is not allayed by Lawrence's attempt to reconcile such an opinion with the tenderness that Mellors advocates: 'The tenderest thing you could do for them, perhaps, would be to give them death . . . Death ought to be sweet to them' (*LCL* 293f.).

Was it hatred of women and conquest of the female through degradation that Lawrence expressed in the notorious scene of anal intercourse, an act briefly hinted at in *The Rainbow* and *Women in Love*,[32] and first introduced in *Lady Chatterley* in the second version of the novel?[33] This is what William Ober has suggested,[34] and it is a charge not easy to refute. The keeper's mood before the couple retire is, in both *John Thomas and Lady Jane* and *Lady Chatterley's Lover*, one of anger. It is not directed towards Connie but towards her sister, Hilda, who has just left the cottage, having shown on her visit all the arrogance and wilfulness of modern womanhood, and clear signs of the 'impudence of class'. But the insults received from Hilda seem to demand satisfaction, and Connie would appear to be made the victim of a revenge on womankind in general. Only in *Lady Chatterley's Lover*, however, are the sado-masochistic implications of the act and the reduction of woman to a mere object made explicit: 'She had to be a passive, consenting thing, like a slave, a physical slave' (*LCL* 258). However liberating in function the act may be in freeing her from all repressions in sensuality by breaking the shameful taboo, there can be no getting round the fact that the impulse behind it is a displaced sadistic anger that seeks to subjugate and depersonalize.[35]

The act is an expression of contempt, not solely because it involves contact with a distasteful bodily organ, but because it unsexes a woman by making her femaleness redundant: she is used as one male might use another. Some have seen in Lawrence's inclusion of a scene of anal intercourse the expression of his latent homosexuality.[36] An alternative explanation might be that since Parkin and Mellors have specific and different phobias about female genitalia, which may have been Lawrence's, a sexual encounter with a woman that avoided vaginal contact might have been regarded as less threatening and more pleasurable. But by the same token, if the phobias were Lawrence's and symptomatic of a general fear of woman, it could be argued that such fears could well have made for a predilection for safer encounters with partners of the same sex. Thus, for Lawrence, it might have been that a major psychogenic factor in his potency disorder was a repressed primary sexual preference for men.

If Lawrence identified fully with the views and experiences he attributes to Rupert Birkin, then he acknowledged homosexual preferences in 'Prologue', the first chapter of the original draft of *Women in Love*: 'All the time, he recognised that, although he was always drawn to women . . . yet it was for men that he felt the hot, flushing, roused attraction which a man is supposed to feel for the other sex' (*WL* 501). A remark once made to Compton Mackenzie might also be interpreted as a statement of preference for homosexual love, though due allowance must be made for the possibility of hyperbole and romanticization of adolescence on Lawrence's part. Mackenzie, writing some forty years after the event, recalled that Lawrence had once declared: 'I believe that the nearest I've ever come

51

to perfect love was with a young coal-miner when I was about sixteen'.[37] Delany was inclined to accept the report as genuine, but believed it to be imperfectly remembered: the miner, he thought, was more likely to have been a young farmer, Alan Chambers, the brother of Jessie.[38] But it seems that at 14 or 15 Lawrence *did* have a homoerotic relationship with a miner of roughly his own age, who lived near the Lawrences' home in Walker Street. This miner, in middle age, told his story to a young man, Frank Lyons, who subsequently became the vicar of Annesley, near Eastwood.

In his book, *The Hills of Annesley*,[39] Lyons recalled how he had been introduced to this man, referred to as 'Tom' in his narrative, after expressing an interest in Lawrence. Tom in the early 1930s had grown into a prematurely aged and brutish vulgarian who evidently relished the effect which his stories of Lawrence's adolescent sexual behaviour had on a demure and unworldly youth. As Lyons appreciated, all Tom's tales of Lawrence could have been a fabricated leg-pull, and he was disinclined to lend them any credence until years later he read what Lawrence had said to Mackenzie.

According to Tom, Lawrence was in the habit of calling round to see him in the evenings while he was in the bath-tub in front of the fire, washing away the pit-dust. One evening Tom's mother, who usually went out after preparing his bath, came home early to find the young Lawrence kneeling on the floor, biting her son's buttocks. When told that he ought to get down on his knees and beg his Maker's forgiveness, Lawrence archly replied: 'I'll ask Tom's pardon if he wants me to.' The response, true to the character and manner of the later Lawrence, seems to validate a story which both accords with and gives a special explanation for the obsession with the scene of the working man bathing that is a recurrent feature of Lawrence's novels.

It seems, on the face of it, somewhat paradoxical that Lawrence should have embarked on his most explicitly sexual and phallic novel in the same year that he faced the likelihood of the loss of desire as an enduring fact in his life. Yet it would seem that there was a causal connection between the two events. At a subconscious level the writing of *Lady Chatterley* might be explained within the framework of the psychoanalytical tradition as an act of displacement, a demonstration to the world through his writing of a vigorous sensuality to which he could no longer give bodily expression. His writings furnished him, as far as the general public was concerned, with a priapic image which may have pleased him rather more than he acknowledged; and he was most certainly aware, when he decided to write for publication, that *Lady Chatterley* would create a sensation which would associate the proud phallus with D. H. Lawrence for as long as his name was remembered. The pictures which he painted while working on *Lady Chatterley* might be seen in a similar light, as a sort of surrogate exhibitionism. To Earl Brewster he wrote of the paintings: 'I . . . put a phallus, a lingam you call it, in each one of my pictures somewhere. And I paint no picture that won't shock people's castrated social spirituality' (*CL* 967).

A more certain connection between the loss of desire and the writing of *Lady Chatterley* lies in the therapeutic purpose of the book. It was intended both as self-therapy for the author through the act of writing and as therapeutic instruction for its readership: by profiting from the lessons and teachings of the novel, Lawrence's readers might further the work of preserving future generations of men from the sexual apathy which Lawrence thought he shared with many of the men of his time.

Self-therapy had been an important function of *Sons and Lovers*. In a well-known letter to Arthur McLeod, his former colleague at the Davidson Road School, Croydon, he had written: 'One sheds one's sicknesses in books – repeats and presents again one's emotions, to be master of them' (*Let 2* 90). The same intention could be imputed to several of the succeeding novels. But in none since *Sons and Lovers* is self-psychotherapy so powerful a determinant in shaping the content of the novel as in *Lady Chatterley*, which arguably is as much concerned with impotence and sexual apathy as with the fulfilment of desire. Possibly the self-therapy was intended to achieve a number of personal aims. First amongst these was probably the intention of trying to come to terms with and accept without self-sympathy the fact that his loss of potency might be permanent. A second aim, related to the first, may have been to help Lawrence to keep alive, as Parkin did, 'the burning flicker of his hope' for the return of desire. A third possible objective may have been to effect a cure of his potency disorder by setting down on paper, principally in relation to the gamekeepers, the fears and fetishes which could have been the psychogenic causes of his ailment.

Impotence in *Lady Chatterley* is not the lot of Clifford alone. In each version of the novel three of the principal male figures have suffered impotence, or a loss of desire which implies a period of lost potency. They face their lot in different ways: Clifford turns to self-sympathy and to displacement in the pursuit of success in writing (in the last two versions); the gamekeepers keep alive their hopes and remain attuned to the phallic consciousness in that they never lose their vital relationship with the cosmos; Duncan Forbes of the first version and Tommy Dukes in the last two versions cynically and bravely accept their condition.

In each version of *Lady Chatterley* Lawrence uses the device, employed earlier in *Aaron's Rod*, of a Janus-like division of his personality into two selves. One represents the natural, animal, phallic man; the other is a satirical caricature of himself as cerebral man. This latter figure is the public, cosmopolitan, man-of-the-world Lawrence, self-confident to the point of cockiness, racy in his speech-style, regaling his audiences in a rather patronizing manner with *bons mots* and outrageous pronouncements: in *Aaron's Rod* this character is Rawdon Lilly. The other Lawrence-figure is the private, retiring, sentient, somewhat insecure provincial of humble origins – Aaron Sisson in *Aaron's Rod*, the keeper in *Lady Chatterley*. Probably the choice of the self-dividing device in *Lady Chatterley* was first determined, as in *Aaron's Rod*, by the practical need for a character to express authorial views which the proletarian hero was incapable of articulating. In the final version of *Lady Chatterley*, where the keeper has been transformed into an eloquent, educated man, the functional necessity for another Lawrence-figure is diminished, but not entirely redundant, because Mellors tends to inhabit the realm of intuitive responses rather than the world of ideas.

Lawrence's keepers have each experienced the extinction of desire in their past lives and have found renewal through meeting Connie. The cerebral Lawrence-figures have experienced the same death, but live in no hope of resurrection. In The *First Lady Chatterley* it is Duncan Forbes, the artist, who constitutes the Lawrentian mouthpiece and object of self-satire:

> 'And the grasshopper shall be a burden, and desire shall fail!' I saw that quotation somewhere. I think it's fine. Not only the grasshopper is a burden, everything is a burden that is not oneself. Anything that is not myself is a burden to me. And desire *has* failed, thank God, so the little grain of sand is completely on its own along with all the other grains of sand.
>
> (*FLC* 214)

This is one way in which to face impotence; to accept cynically through a rationalization which makes the best of a bad lot. In one of the set of 'Tortoise' poems written in 1920 Lawrence had written of the adolescent 'crucifixion' (*Poems* 361) into sex and the 'complex manifold involvedness' (*Poems* 361) with woman that followed from it. Having lost desire one could escape back to the freedom of isolation of the pre-pubertal stage. But this refuge in individualism is not presented as a laudable aim in *The First Lady Chatterley* – the grain of sand is an image of the barrenness of modern egotism which isolates the individual from everything, and which is one of the fundamental causes of modern social ills.

In *John Thomas and Lady Jane* and *Lady Chatterley's Lover* Lawrence the preacher is represented by Tommy Dukes, one of a group of Clifford's friends who provide a sort of symposium on human sexuality. In *Lady Chatterley's Lover*, Tommy Dukes's contempt for the mental life and the sterile systemic formulae it produces is entirely Lawrentian, as also is his unsentimental rejection of love and his belief in bodily awareness. Like Lawrence he has a problem as preacher of the new gospel of the resurrection of the body in that he is incapable, he confesses, of bridging the gap between thought and action. Intellectually, he believes 'in having a good heart, a chirpy penis, a lively intelligence and the courage to say "shit!" in front of a lady' (*LCL* 41). When assured by a young admirer that he has all these attributes, he replies, with roaring laughter: 'You angel boy! If only I had! If only I had! No; my heart's as numb as a potato, my penis droops and never lifts its head up, I dare rather cut him clean off than say "shit!" in front of my mother or my aunt . . . and I'm not really intelligent, I'm only a "mental-lifer".' Lawrence's diagnosis, then, of himself, as of modern man, was that his upbringing and education to an essentially cerebral, intellectual life had diminished his emotional, sensory and sexual responses.

The Dukes of *John Thomas and Lady Jane* is less explicit in the matter of his sexual adequacy, but he is equally critical of his incapacity to live up to the doctrines he advocates. Dukes's remedy for modern social ills is the establishment of a democracy of touch – the restoration of warm human contact between individuals. But, like Lawrence, whose adopted slogan 'Noli me tangere' is debunked, he is himself afraid of touch. When Connie chides him with this he replies: 'I don't belong to the democracy of touch myself: I only prognosticate it '(*JTLJ* 68). Dukes regards himself as beyond hope of attaining the new life. Through him Lawrence declares the task of salvation that he had taken upon himself. His role is to preserve future generations from the living death which he and his contemporaries have experienced:

> What does it matter if we go through the rest of our lives with sore, untouchable bodies, and the incessant *noli me tangere!* in our mouths? We have done the worst bit. And those that come after, even if they aren't my children, will be able to make the ascent on to a new earth. By which I mean have new bodies, with new good blood in them, born for a new epoch of mankind. Surely that's heaven on earth! It would be to me! though I shall never experience it. But I believe I've made a bit of a way for it, and I'll go on trying.
>
> (*JTLJ* 70)

Frieda remarked that Lawrence put a great deal of himself into Clifford Chatterley.[40] The 'self' was not his personality, as in the cases of the keepers and Forbes and Dukes, but his personal experience. He was himself, in some sense, an invalid, and he had lived through the sleepless nights of physical pain that afflicted Clifford. Like Clifford of *The First Lady Chatterley* he had felt in the woodlands 'the thrill of life', 'a peculiar triumph over doom and death', though he had never sensed, nor would have wished to, the triumph 'over life itself' (*FLC* 19) that Clifford rejoiced in. He had faced impotence and his wife's infidelity and would seem to have taken a complaisant view of Frieda's behaviour, as Clifford did of Connie's. But Clifford and Lawrence are only superficially alike in this regard. Clifford does the right thing in quite the wrong way or for the wrong reasons. The approaches of the three successive Cliffords to this situation illustrate admirably the evolution of the character from a sympathetic, credible personality to a negative stereotype. The first Clifford advises Connie to take a lover 'bravely' but also 'glibly' (*FLC* 21): he treats the matter as a hypothetical case and does not face up to the reality of his suggestion. His successor in *John Thomas and Lady Jane* makes the same proposal only after promptings from Connie's father; he cannot do so without uttering self-pitying remarks, and offers Connie her freedom only because he believes the life of the body is entirely superficial. The third Clifford is entirely selfish in his suggestion that Connie should take a lover: his motives are dynastic – Wragby must have an heir.

Clifford represents, perhaps, temptations into which Lawrence feared he might fall. When, after they parted , Brett sent Lawrence from Capri a wretchedly miserable, self-pitying letter, Lawrence replied:

The greatest virtue in life is real courage, that knows how to face facts and live beyond them. Don't be Murryish, pitying yourself and caving in. It's despicable. I should have thought after a dose of that fellow, you'd have too much desire to be different from him, to follow his sloppy self-indulgent melancholics, absolutely despicable ... My God, did you learn *nothing* from Murry, of how NOT to behave?

(CL 894)

Clifford is, perhaps, especially John Middleton Murry in these respects. He does not know 'how to face facts and live beyond them'. Like Murry he is an object lesson in how not to behave when faced with adversity.

Relations between Brett and Lawrence after their failure in love-making seem to have passed into an awkward phase with Lawrence in a fearsome rage and each of them sunk in feelings of self-reproach and inadequacy. Lawrence proclaimed that he could not possibly remain in Ravello any longer, but was dissuaded from leaving by Brett, who reminded him that he owed it to Millie Beveridge and Mabel Harrison to stay: they had built all their holiday arrangements around him. It was therefore decided that Brett should return to Capri until the arrival of her quota papers for entry into the United States.[41] On 16 March Brett took the steamer from Amalfi, and with a sense of foreboding watched Lawrence's carriage as it disappeared from view round a bend in the road to Ravello. There was a vague plan that they might meet up again in Florence, which Lawrence was to visit with Millie Beveridge and Mabel Harison at the end of the month. Brett duly set out to meet him and booked into the Pensione Lucchesi, where Lawrence usually stayed when visiting the city. Lawrence, however, was living in grand style at the Hotel Washington, and Brett failed to run him to ground. He had no wish to meet Brett again for a good while, and later, as Brett pressed hard for the chance to see him, he had to spell this out for her in a letter from Spotorno.[42]

If Lawrence was now weary of fawning, earnest female companionship, he must have found a diverting change in the company of Millie Beveridge. She was a plump, genial, rather conservative Scotswoman in her mid-50s; she had a somewhat intimidating strength of character and independence of mind; and she was endowed with a keen sense of the ridiculous and a sardonic wit.[43] Lawrence thought her 'nice and intelligent' (Zyt 317). After Brett left for Capri, Lawrence spent a fortnight with Miss Beveridge and Mabel

Harrison. From Ravello they wove their way northwards through Italy, visiting Rome, Perugia, Assisi, Florence and Ravenna, where he fell ill and had to rest for two days before they could move on to Milan. Few of the cities attracted Lawrence: Rome was wet and overcast; Florence was overcrowded; Assisi was 'too museumish' (*CL* 907); and the mosaics of the churches of Ravenna seemed unnaturally stylized. But in Perugia, one of the twelve *lucomonie*, the principalities of the vanished Etruscan race, Lawrence found a lively, naturalistic art and the remnants of a culture which excited him a good deal. Etruscan civilization became a subject which occupied him for the next year and more, and which he kept returning to in his mind for two and a half years.

In the bronzes of the civic museum and in the tombs of the ancient necropolis he rediscovered an enthusiasm for the Etruscans and a fascination with the mystery of their civilization that dated back to the time of his last stay in Italy. Probably it was visits to the museums of Florence and its suburb Fiesole, an ancient Etruscan hill citadel, that first stirred Lawrence to ponder the enigma of the Etruscan soul and to probe the mystery of the serene, disturbingly sensual smiles on the faces of the statues. In 1921 Lawrence had written to Catherine Carswell, shortly after a visit she paid to Perugia, asking her: '*What* then was the secret of the Etruscans, which you saw written so plainly in the place you went to?' (*CL* 668). What he saw himself of the necropolis at Perugia suggested to him that the key to an understanding of Etruscan civilization lay in the *cippi*, the stone pillars which stood outside the tombs, which seemed obviously to represent the sacred lingam of a culture that was vital and insouciant by virtue of its phallic consciousness.

Lawrence had read and bought for himself some years back the Everyman edition of George Dennis's *The Cities and Cemeteries of Etruria*, the standard work in English. After visiting Perugia he decided that his next major work would be a small-scale, popular, modern successor to this book, which like Dennis's would be part travel-book, part scholarly study of Etruscan civilization. As it was first conceived the book (eventually published half-complete and posthumously as *Etruscan Places*) was to deal exclusively with sites in Umbria; and Lawrence intended to spend two months researching his subject there after the lease on the Villa Bernarda expired in April.

Lawrence returned to Spotorno on Easter Saturday. The most recent letters from Frieda had been milder in tone than those he received in Capri; and Lawrence had come to find humour in the situation, sending her a drawing of Jonah and the whale bearing the caption 'Who is going to swallow whom?' ('*Not I*' 169). Frieda, however, was still unsure whether she would have Lawrence back; and it was only through the cajolings of her daughters that she arrived at the station to greet him, dressed, like Elsa and Barby, in her best outfit.

Lawrence was impressed by their efforts to welcome him: 'For the moment I am the Easter-lamb' (*CL* 894), he told Frieda's mother. But there was still a residue of anger fermenting within him;[44] and relations between him and Frieda remained tense, so that after a week at Spotorno, Lawrence was writing to Mabel Luhan: 'Lord, what a life! It's pouring with rain, and I'm feeling weary to death of struggling with Frieda' (*CL* 900). When the Lawrences took their leave of Spotorno on 20 April for a few days in Florence, there was a possibility that thereafter they would go their separate ways – Frieda to Baden-Baden with the girls to stay with the baroness, and Lawrence to Umbria to gather material on the Etruscans. There was no definite plan for Frieda to join Lawrence afterwards.

5

The Villa Mirenda

Two days after leaving Spotorno, having broken their journey to explore Pisa, the Lawrences reached Florence. Lawrence hated it. They were greeted on arrival by chill, drenching rains that fell relentlessly for almost a week. The ill-tempered bustle of the city intensified his world-weariness and his desire to cut himself off for ever from 'the dreariness and mechanism of man' (*CL* 905). He wanted 'the world from the inside, not the outside' (*CL* 905), he told Earl Brewster, and he longed for some spot where he could lead an anchoretical life of quiet contemplation, shared perhaps with one or two kindred spirits. He could not entirely go along with Earl's leanings towards the Buddhist faith – desire and anger seemed to him to be gifts from God which ought not to be extinguished – but he found himself more and more drawn towards Brewster's position:

> I am convinced that every man needs a bho tree of some sort in his life. What ails us is, we have cut down all our bho trees. How long it takes a new one to grow, I don't know: probably many years. In a generation one can hack down forests of them. Still, here and there in the world a solitary bho tree must be standing: 'where two or three of ye have met together.' And I'm going to sit right down under one, to be American about it, when I come across one.
>
> (*CL* 905)

He might well join the Brewsters, he promised, if they happened to find 'a bit of bho-tree-shade' in their monastery on the slopes of the Himalayas. But by autumn the Brewsters, dissatisfied with India and drained by illness, were about to return to Europe, and Lawrence had already discovered tranquil isolation and fulfilment in the shade of an umbrella pine-tree among the hills outside Florence.

Among Lawrence's old friends in Florence there were a number of entertaining characters who could be relied upon to enliven Elsa and Barby's stay in the city. They were introduced to Reggie Turner, proclaimed by his friend Max Beerbohm to be 'the wittiest man in the world', whose stalwart friendship with Oscar Wilde at the time of his troubles had brought him the reward of a treasure-chest of Wildean anecdotes. According to Barby they also met Norman Douglas,[1] presumably just before he set off for Greece and through some intermediary other than Lawrence, who was not at the time on speaking terms with him. And it cannot have been long after their arrival before Lawrence took the girls down the Lungarno Corsini to the bookshop whose glass door bore in gold letters the name of Pino Orioli. Orioli had been born the seventh child of a sausage-maker, had trained as a barber's assistant, and on occasion had turned to street-singing to keep body and soul together – an unlikely prelude to his subsequent career in the antiquarian book-trade. He had acquired his expertise in this field in the course of a long stay in London, where he eventually opened a shop in Museum Street. It was during his period in England, at the time of the First World War, that he first met Lawrence while visiting some friends in Zennor, Cornwall, where the Lawrences were living. A short, roly-poly man with dancing eyes behind round, owlish spectacles, Orioli was warm-hearted, generous and lively, a gossipy raconteur with a decidedly Rabelaisian bent.[2] He was universally loved by his acquaintances, who found in him, as Lawrence was to do, an amusing companion and a loyal friend.

Orioli later played a vital role in the production of *Lady Chatterley's Lover*, as Lawrence's extremely competent and energetic assistant in the publication of the book; and he seems also to have been instrumental in finding for Lawrence the beautiful retreat where the novel was composed – the Villa Mirenda in the hamlet of San Polo Mosciano, about seven miles south of Florence. Perhaps Orioli had heard of the villa from Arthur Wilkinson, an Englishman who rented the Villa Poggi on a neighbouring hill-top. After being introduced to Wilkinson Lawrence was invited to lunch and a viewing of the Mirenda on the following Sunday.

The push towards acquiring a villa near Florence had come from Frieda. Since their arrival in the city Lawrence and she had completely revised their earlier plans of action in a way that suggests a reconciliation between them. Frieda now had no wish to go to Germany without Lawrence, who did not want to leave Italy. She evidently drew the line at following Lawrence to Perugia, where they would know no one; and a Tuscan house not far from Florence offered a suitable compromise between Lawrence's wish for seclusion and Frieda's insistence that they should live more with other people.

When, after Frieda's daughters had been despatched to England, there came the first fine, bright day since their arrival, the Lawrences took a trip into the countryside for an early preview of the Mirenda, making what was to become a familiar journey for them over the next two years. The first stage was a half-hour tram-ride which began at the Via dei Pecori near the Duomo and ended, after passing through the mean streets of the suburb of Scandicci, at Ponte Vingone on the edge of the hills. Next came a one-and-a-half-mile walk along a narrow, rutted lane that meandered gently upwards through open, hilly country, past vineyards, olive orchards and fields of grain. The Tuscan countryside was at its loveliest, with the green wheat standing lush in the fields and everywhere bright with flowers. At the spot where two cypresses stood 'close together as two fingers' (Nehls 3 203) their road branched left and dipped down into a valley, revealing the picturesque view of the Mirenda standing on a small hill above a silvery grey sea of olives, with peasant houses and the small church of San Polo Mosciano clustering behind it among cypress trees. The Mirenda was an imposing building, handsome, though rather gaunt, after the manner of the Tuscan villa, with a plain, box-like exterior. It was said to date from the time of the Medicis, when Florentine merchants built such houses as retreats from urban life, where they could enjoy bucolic surroundings and perhaps, like Cosimo de Medici the Elder, ease their minds while tending the vines on their estates for hours on end.

The Mirenda stood in 'absolutely unspoiled country, one family of English neighbours, and then never another *forestière*, ever', with 'farms on little green hills, and pine woods fringing the ridges' (*CL* 912). From its northerly aspect the villa looked out over the valley of the Arno, with distant views of the foothills of the Apennines, and beyond them, visible on a clear day, the mountains. To the south were prospects of the wooded hills and beyond them again the Apennines in the far distance. All around the house was a deep quiet, broken only by calls and snatches of song from the birds or from the peasant labourers working in the fields, or by the sound of water being drawn from the well.[3]

Lawrence had acquiesced in Frieda's idea of renting a villa in Tuscany, but had no great enthusiasm for it. But the sight of the Mirenda and its pristine setting in sunshine captivated both of them; and Lawrence wrote off to Arthur Wilkinson telling him that they would almost certainly decide to take the villa when they arrived on Sunday to look over the house and meet the *padrone*,[4] Raul Mirenda, a cavalry officer who lived in Florence and used the lower half of the villa as a holiday residence.

The conveniences of the typical Tuscan villa of the 1920s had been little improved since Renaissance times. At the Mirenda there was no running water, lighting was by oil-lamp and cooking had to be done over a charcoal fire in the kitchen; the six large interconnecting rooms of the apartment, each curtainless and uncarpeted, were 'big and rather bare – with red brick floors: spacious, rather nice, and very still' (*CL* 920). This monastic simplicity was ideally suited to Lawrence's ascetic tastes, though the 'five sticks of furniture' (*CL* 909), which was all the apartment contained, made for a comfortlessness that was excessive even by Lawrence's spartan standards. After agreeing to take the Mirenda for a year at a paltry rent of £25 the Lawrences set about adding a few simple pieces that would lend a little more ease and comfort to their suite – a couple of straw-covered armchairs, a small rustic table, a book-case; and in the autumn a piano was hired from Florence for Frieda's use.

One precious and, in Italian houses, rare commodity which the upper half of the Mirenda possessed was a tiled stove in the large sitting-room, the *salotto*. This would mean that in the winter, which would be a good deal more severe than on the Riviera, the Lawrences would not have to huddle together in the warmth of the kitchen, as they had in Spotorno, but could bask in heat that had not originally been intended for human ease, but for the silk-worms that the Mirendas had bred there before the war.

Off the *salotto*, facing south, was a small balcony which became one of Lawrence's favourite places to sit. It looked out over the part of the gardens set aside for their use – a wide green lawn shaded by two large chestnut trees, then in full flower, whose branches canopied the balcony above. Just beyond the garden was a grove of aspens of a 'lovely, feathery pinky colour' (Wilk 73) in their spring foliage, a reminder, perhaps, of the aspens in New Mexico on the ranch which he still dreamed of and whose call he felt strongly. But, despite Brett's persistent badgering that he should return, he remained obdurate in his aversion to America.

It was Lawrence's good fortune, during the two years he rented the Villa Mirenda, to have contact with three families – the Wilkinsons,

Huxleys and Brewsters – who were sufficiently self-assured and integrated in their collective personalities, and who set a high enough value on the tonic vitality Lawrence could generate, as to be able to take a sympathetic and often mildly amused view of the absurd or bigoted extremes of his obstreperous moods and of the sometimes irksome aspects of his social behaviour. Of greatest worth to Lawrence was the extraordinary Wilkinson family, comprising Arthur, his Scots wife Lillian and their two adolescent children, Frances and William. Lunch with the Wilkinsons on the day the Lawrences viewed the Mirenda, was the first of some four score 'formal' visits exchanged between the families, in addition to innumerable casual encounters and a succession of walks and picnics taken together in the woods and hills around the villas. In the years of comparative seclusion at the Villa Mirenda, when interaction with others was mainly through the medium of correspondence, contact with the Wilkinsons provided Lawrence and Frieda with their only regular and continuous social relationship. Happily for Lawrence's biographers, their meetings were fully documented in the entertaining family journals which Arthur and Lillian Wilkinson jointly kept up at that period.

Lawrence was amused by the Wilkinsons' arty-crafty appearance and excited by their zestful, bohemian lifestyle. Shortly after meeting them he wrote to his niece, Peggy:

> We have one family of English neighbours who would send you into fits if you saw them: he's got the wildest red beard, sticking out all round – and wife and daughter and son, all with sandals and knapsacks. But they're jolly and very clever: paint, and play guitar and things. They used to have a very fine puppet show, puppets they made themselves, and play plays they wrote themselves, going with a caravan and giving shows in all the villages in England. Rather fun! I want to bring the caravan and puppets here, and I'll go with them and bang the drum.
>
> (*CL* 909)

Lawrence, for all his doctrine of warmheartedness, could be a wary and distant friend; but the carefree geniality and the unthrusting, undemanding ways of the 'Wilkses', as he called them, seem to have allowed him to relax his guard, open up, and so be at his most vibrant and convivial. The Wilkses for their part warmed to both Lawrence and Frieda. After two months of frequent meetings they recorded in their diary: 'Our new neighbours have added to the interest and enjoyment of life here, and we already have a natural and very pleasant relationship with them' (Wilk 65).

It was something of a novelty for the Lawrences to have friends who held each of them in equal esteem. More often than not it was Frieda's experience to find Lawrence lionized and herself disregarded or even despised; and one of the problems of their marriage, in addition to the rivalry of wills, appears to have been Frieda's jealousy of Lawrence's share of the attention among friends that were almost always of *his* choosing. This friendship with the Wilkinsons may therefore have had a salutary effect on the Lawrences' relationship, in that it satisfied Frieda's need to have recognition of her value as a person in her own right. It also fulfilled her wish to have increased contact with other people more completely than might have been the case if social life had been confined to their twice-weekly sallies into Florence, where their closest friends were Orioli, Turner and Nelly Morrison, a Scotswoman who had once lent them her flat in Florence and had been responsible for introducing them to the Brewsters.

The Wilkinsons shared with their new neighbours a capacity for the wholehearted enjoyment of homely pleasures and amusements, such as long walks, picnics, bathing in the pools of the nearby stream, or within doors entertaining themselves with singsongs and charades. Like Lawrence, they pursued a very simple style of living, though in a manner more thoroughgoing and conventionally bohemian than did Lawrence, who drolly defined their idea of the simple life as 'nuts, vegetables, no meat, tents, fresh air, nature and niceness' (*Ph* 372).

If there was any serious incompatibility between the two families, it lay in the Wilkinsons' leanings towards Marxism, which to Lawrence and Frieda was a dreary, life-denying philosophy. No doubt, too, there was some banter concerning the Wilkinsons' cult of 'niceness', regarded by Lawrence as a negative, gutless virtue. It is testimony to the congeniality of the Wilkinsons and to the generally relaxed frame of mind that Lawrence enjoyed during the first phase of his stay at the Mirenda that 'niceness' in the way of forbearance, a quality essential in those who wished to maintain good relations with Lawrence, was not tested in the Wilkinsons for several months. Their diary for the early summer of 1926 is filled with references to good conversation, to the contentment of Lawrence and Frieda, and to merry, idyllic gatherings such as the tea the Lawrences gave them by the stream near San Polo: 'We set up the primus and made the most successful picnic possible. It was so indescribably lovely there – a fresh wind blowing – the air so translucent, the water limpid and the tea and cheese sandwiches and cakes so good. We just sat and talked and the Lawrences were very happy' (Wilk 64f.).

The general attitude of the Wilkinsons towards the outside world was one of happy-go-lucky indifference. The insouciance which Lawrence had to strive to cultivate by suppressing his intrinsic anxiety and combativeness came easily and naturally to them. Without their example and their exuberant, unintimidating companionship it is doubtful whether, even in the perfect retreat of the Tuscan countryside, Lawrence would have been able to maintain for so long the carefree serenity which by and large persisted for almost a year and enjoyed brief resurgences even beyond that period. Sagar, in his history of the relationship between Lawrence and the Wilkinsons, cited a number of works belonging to the Mirenda years whose calmness of spirit could perhaps be attributed in part to 'the golden mornings and hilarious evenings spent in the company of this unique family' (Wilk 75); and his catalogue might reasonably be expanded to include *The First Lady Chatterley*, where the tranquil pastoralism of the woodland scenes, the unembattled relations between Connie and Parkin and the predominantly mellow tones of the narrative voice all suggest a Lawrence who bears the cares of the world lightly with regard to himself, but with no lack of concern for the present state and future of society.

On the day before Lawrence's visit to the Wilkinsons to view the Mirenda, there began in Britain the longest complete stoppage in the coal industry that the country had known, the consequences of which were to sour relations in the coal industry ever afterwards. The 'coal strike', which in most parts of the country was in fact a lock-out on the part of the owners, began appropriately on May Day 1926, though the timing had been determined by the Conservative government, and it lasted until November 1926. Throughout that period it was rarely far from Lawrence's mind, and when he returned to his native Midlands in September he witnessed its social effects at first hand.

Lawrence correctly perceived (at times, at least) that the causes of the strike had little to do with revolutionary class struggle, but lay essentially in matters of finance. Lecturing Martin Secker on the coal strike in July, he told him: 'Building your life on money is worse than building your house on sand' (Sec 75). The origins of the strike sprang in part from the government's decision in 1925 to return to the gold standard, thereby raising the value of sterling abroad to a level against the dollar which made exports so costly that they were easily undersold by Britain's industrial competitors. Coal exports were hit particularly badly, and the only means of restoring coal to a competitive price in overseas markets seemed to be either for the government to subsidize the coal industry or for the industry to cut its costs: in an industry in which labour costs formed a very high proportion of its production costs this meant reducing the wages of the miners. The raising of the cost of exports through a return to the gold standard exacerbated a situation in which, already in many areas, the coal industry was in grave economic difficulties and the colliery owners had been pressing for wage-cuts.

To avoid a confrontation in 1925, the government had agreed to grant a subsidy to the industry until the following spring. It was to expire on 29 April 1926. The Owners' Association had three main objectives to be pursued after that date: a return to wage-negotiation on a district level, as opposed to the national negotiating procedures that currently existed; an immediate reduction in pay; and an increase in working-hours. In most coal-producing districts the owners gave notice that existing contracts would expire at the end of the month. Their terms were not acceptable to the Miners' Federation of Great Britain, and it was supported in its resistance by the Trades Union Congress, which gave notice of a general strike on behalf of the miners. On 4 May, three days after the miners were locked out, workers in the transport, iron and steel, building, electricity, gas and printing industries came out in response to the strike-call. The General Strike ended after eight days, having failed in its object of paralysing the country and bringing the government to heel. The General Council of the TUC claimed to have received assurances that a settlement of the mining dispute could be achieved, but the claim was false: the only assurance secured was a vague promise from the Prime Minister, Stanley Baldwin, to 'use every endeavour to ensure a just and lasting settlement'. No such settlement was reached: the miners, further embittered by what seemed a betrayal on the part of their trades union fellows, remained locked out.[5]

As a rule Lawrence did not read newspapers, and the letters written before the strike give no inkling of his being aware of what was about to happen. But from the moment he learned of the dispute he seems to have followed the news of it in the Italian press, and he was later kept informed of the progress of events in letters from his sisters. For all his weariness with the outside world and his repudiation of his native country, this was an issue which made indifference impossible: it lay too close to the heart of a man who had spent more than half his life in a mining community.

The coal dispute and the General Strike may have come as no great surprise to Lawrence. He had, after all, foretold some such crisis as long ago as 1915, at the time of a week-long strike by the South Wales miners. Would the present industrial disputes entail the revolution and 'ghastly chaos of destruction' (*Let 2* 366) that in 1915 he believed would be inevitable at some time in the course of the following ten years? Lawrence, by now more temperate in his political opinions and more mature of judgement, was uncertain about the outcome of the General Strike, and withheld any rash predictions while it lasted. Afterwards, when the General Strike was over and he had the impression that the miners' strike had ended with it, he wrote to Kot confessing the fears which the strike had engendered. These fears lie at the heart of all versions of *Lady Chatterley* and especially inform the first draft, begun when the miners' strike was still unresolved: 'Myself, I'm scared of a class war in England. It would be the beginning of the end of all things' (*Zyt* 286). As the months of the strike dragged on without hope of any conclusion, and depressing news of its effects on the North Midlands came in regularly from his sisters, who were both losing a great deal of money as shopkeepers in places in or near the impoverished mining towns, Lawrence returned to the theme of class conflict. To Ada he complained: 'Really it's too bad they let it come to a strike: very dangerous too because it may start a real class war, and England is the one country where that is most dangerous' (*Ada* 109). 'Coal', he told his niece Peggy, 'was the making of England, and it looks as if coal were to be the breaking of her' (*CL* 921).

Even before Lawrence witnessed for himself the miseries of the colliery districts on his return to the North Midlands his broad sympathies seem to have been with the miners. He felt that a return to the eight-hour day would do them good, perhaps because he believed they wasted their leisure hours in cinemas, dancehalls and the like, but he nonetheless thought they had understandable cause for grievance.[6] This willingness to see the strike from the miners' point of view – something he endeavoured to get across to the

Wilkinsons on their first visit to the Lawrences at the Villa Mirenda[7] – suggests that he may already have been moving away from a long-held antipathy towards labour, which he had once wished to see conquered and disenfranchised. A more compassionate and wiser Lawrence seemed to be emerging. He had read in the Italian press at the time of the General Strike that the British government would maintain an iron resistance. Commenting on this to Nancy Pearn, he wrote: 'Since the war, I've no belief in iron resistances. Flesh and blood and a bit of wisdom can do quite enough resisting and a bit of adjusting into the bargain – and with iron one only hurts oneself and everybody. Damn iron!' (Hux 658).

While democratic England seemed in danger of collapse under the strain of the coal dispute, Italy was in the grip of Mussolini's fascist dictatorship, a political system close to the kind Lawrence had advocated in the past. He had experienced fascism in action in Italy before, had seen its processions and witnessed some of the faction fights between socialists and fascists which preceded Mussolini's coming to power in 1922. But fascist government was a new experience for Lawrence, and perhaps one that he only really became aware of, having spent his first months in a village community, when he reached Florence, one of the country's fascist strongholds.

Although an odious and oppressive totalitarian state, fascist Italy was not as systematically efficient or as brutal in its persecutions as Nazi Germany was to be. Italian individualism was not cowed by institutionalized terrorism such as the Nazis practised, nor was the ideology of Italian fascism founded on race hatred. As Sybille Bedford, Aldous Huxley's biographer, observed, it was possible for a foreigner to live in Mussolini's Italy without compromise to his conscience.[8] This was in some measure due to the fact that the apparatus of fascist rule was not glaringly obtrusive, except in small matters. 'One can ignore Fascism in Italy for a time', Lawrence wrote in 1928. 'But after a while, the sense of false power forced against life is very depressing. And one can't escape – except by the trick of abstraction, which is no good' (Hux 705). His first reaction, like that of other foreign residents and a large number of the native population, was a sense of irritation with the tiresomeness of a government which in its zeal for law and order had instituted countless petty-fogging rules and regulations.[9] He had no liking for the regime, which at that period he thought of as alien to the Italian temperament rather than to the human spirit in general.[10] Nor did he have much respect for the country's dictator, whom he referred to sarcastically as 'dear heroic Mussolini' (*CL* 902). In April, shortly after Lawrence returned to Spotorno, an English woman had shot the bull-headed dictator through the nose in a botched assassination attempt: 'Put a ring through it!' (Nehls 3 24) Lawrence advised the Tenente Ravagli. If Mussolini's example played no special part in the decline of Lawrence's faith in the idea of charismatic leadership, it certainly did nothing to ensure its survival.

In the first weeks of his stay at the Villa Mirenda Lawrence had to struggle to maintain a steady good humour. This was due far more to the depressing effects of the weather than to any consideration of the political situation in England or Italy. The late spring of 1926 in Southern Europe was one of the most atrocious in living memory, with long spells of wintry cold and almost unremitting rain. Lawrence's moving into the Villa Mirenda was followed by three weeks of such weather, which affected his chest and kept him indoors for much of the time. Outside, under the rain, the countryside turned 'green, green, over-green, to set your teeth on edge' (*CL* 914). 'I never knew a spring so impotent, as if it couldn't emerge' (Hux 660), he commented to Brett, with a bland lack of self-consciousness which nevertheless betrayed what dominated his thinking whenever he addressed himself to the subject of Brett.

By the end of May there came warm, sunny days, forerunners of a hot and summery June and July. The Mirenda estate began to yield its harvests. There were strawberries and basketfuls of cherries in June, and in early July the wheat was brought in, together with an abundance of fruit that had profited from the spring rains – 'big apricots, great big figs that they call *fiori*, peaches, plums, the first sweet little pears' (*CL* 925). And Lawrence mellowed into a lazy, languid contentment as he eased into the enjoyment of 'actual living', which he defined as a relationship of 'direct sensuous contact' (*Ph* 2 534) with the phenomena of the physical world – with the morning sun which conferred lordship of life, with the moon and the night which gave comforting prescience of death, with the natural features of the landscape, and with the flora and fauna and people of the earth. In his description of June at the Villa Mirenda Lawrence writes as if replete with the pleasure of consummation with the universe:

> I am always so glad when the real summer comes, and one can go about with light clothes on, and feet in sandals and not bother about anything. Here everybody gets up about 4.30, and then, from 1.0 till

about 3.30 in the afternoon the whole countryside goes to sleep, not a
peasant anywhere in the corn or among the vines, all deep asleep. We
take a *siesta* too. Then the evening becomes cooler, and the nightingale
starts singing again. There are many nightingales, in every little wood
you can hear half a dozen singing away all day long, except in the hot
hours, very lively. The wheat is very fine, and just turning yellow
under the olive trees.

Today is San Giovanni, the Saint of Florence, and a great *festa*. So
we shall go in to town this evening and stay for the fireworks. They
will illuminate the town, and everybody will be in full holiday rig.

(*CL* 921)

The singing of the nightingales and the *festa* of San Giovanni
provided him with material for two short essays – 'The Nightingale'
and 'Fireworks in Florence' which he sent off to his agent three days
after writing this letter. There was profit as well as enjoyment to be
had from such light endeavours. One such piece, a short story dashed
off in one evening, brought in seventy pounds – almost enough to pay
the annual rent on the Mirenda three times over. [11] It was probably
short stories and essays that Lawrence had in mind when he wrote to
Earl Brewster of the need to placate Mammon: 'I'm going to try
throwing a few sops to Cerberus myself – things like *The Plumed
Serpent* have no profit in them, as far as Mammon goes' (*CL* 913).

The more demanding commercial venture of a travel-book on
Etruscan sites had not been abandoned with the decision to take a
house in Tuscany rather than Umbria. The Villa Mirenda had been
rented for its convenience as a centre from which to visit Etruscan
places; and during the first month at the Mirenda his principal task,
which he set about with scholarly care, was to study the works of the
major authorities on Etruscan archaeology and civilization, in
English, Italian and German. But, to Lawrence's exasperation, none
of the works he consulted seemed to penetrate the mystery of the
Etruscans. He was to discover that, really, all that was known in the
way of fact about the Etruscans came from sparse and fragmentary
Greek and Roman sources and from what they told of themselves in
the paintings, carvings and grave-goods of the necropolises. And by
early June he had decided that in the absence of scientific fact he
would bring to bear upon the subject the imagination of a poet. [12]

Through May, June and July Lawrence continued to declare, as he
had in Spotorno, a lack of interest in writing, and an unwillingness to
yield to the pressures from Secker and from Knopf in America to
produce another novel. According to some of his letters he spent his

time either doing very little or not working at all. Even Frieda described his state as one of healthy, contented indolence. A few days after leaving the Mirenda he wrote to Catherine Carswell from Baden-Baden: 'As for literature and publishing, I loathe the thought of it all, and wish I could afford never to appear in print again. Anyhow, I am doing nothing at all now, and have no idea of beginning again' (*PL* 528f.). This was true enough of the moment, but over the past twelve weeks he had, in fact, often been quite 'busy with bits of things' (*CL* 925). In May he had completed 'Two Blue Birds' and quickly penned an introduction to Siebenhaar's translation of *Max Havelaar*. June was an especially productive month, during which he wrote three essays, typed out and reworked Frieda's translation of his play *David*, and almost completed a short story, probably 'The Man Who Loved Islands', which he despatched to London a couple of days before leaving for Germany in July. Nevertheless, by his own standards his output was small. He had, from the first, regarded his stay at the Mirenda as 'a sort of interval' (Hux 659) and he remained faithful to that idea, with very considerable benefit to his health.

Catherine Carswell was not taken in by Lawrence's protestations of having no thought of writing again, and she recalled that, in the past, periods of leisure in Lawrence's life had usually been the prelude to his launching himself into some major new undertaking.[13] Quite possibly he had nothing in mind other than the completion of his Etruscan essays. But by July the idea of a story which developed into his next novel may have been turning over in his mind. In the first fortnight in June there had occurred events which, perhaps for no other reason than their association in time, came ultimately to be linked to form elements in the creation of character and perhaps also in the fabric of the plot in *Lady Chatterley*.

Towards the end of May, Lawrence and Frieda were invited to have lunch with Sir George and Lady Ida Sitwell at the Castello Montegufoni in the Chianti country. How they came by this invitation is a mystery: it involved none of the literary trio of Sitwell children; Lady Ida had no interest in or knowledge of the world of the arts; Sir George, though a man of letters, was not by nature the kind of man to ask strangers to come and dine with him, and since his tastes were determinedly antiquarian, the name D. H. Lawrence would probably have meant as little to him as to his wife. However, Sir George was unpredictable. If his antiquarian interests took him to Orioli's bookshop, [14] and if Lawrence was introduced to him as the genius of modern English letters, then it could well have occurred to him that Lawrence's presence at lunch could serve him well in the inscrutable game of one-upmanship that he liked to play with his son Osbert.

On Wednesday 2 June Lawrence set out with Frieda for the unlikely rendezvous which some believe furnished him with the strange story out of which *Lady Chatterley* began. Probably the Lawrences were driven to Montegufoni, since a journey by public transport in the summer heat would have left neither of them in a fit state to lunch with a baronet. If the Sitwells sent their car for them – a second-hand lorry rebuilt to Sir George's specifications and known in Florence as 'The Ark' – they would by all accounts have travelled in little greater comfort. It took a full hour to travel the fourteen miles from Florence over rough, hilly country along the old road to Volterra to the Val di Pesa, where the castello was situated. As one descended the last steep hill, between stone heraldic beasts that supported the arms of the Italian Dukes of Athens, the former owners of Montegufoni, there came into full view the house which a previous visitor, Aldous Huxley, had described as the strangest place he had ever seen. Spreading itself like a village on a small hilltop, high above its buttress-like stone terraces, and surmounted by an imposing bell-tower, it appeared more nearly to resemble some ancient, inaccessible monastery than a private house. With five courtyards and over a hundred rooms, many of them uninhabitable, having not yet been touched by Sir George's zeal for architectural improvement, Montegufoni could aptly have been described, like the Chatterleys' Wragby, as a 'warren of a place without much distinction' (*LCL* 13), except, perhaps, in the realms of the bizarre, where it matched the character of its owner perfectly.

'Queer couple' (Zyt 289), Lawrence remarked after meeting the Sitwells, who appear to have found the Lawrences no less strange. Sir George was an eccentric, fussy, deeply serious, unworldly scholar, a victim of hypochondria and an acute anxiety neurosis, who had fled the tensions of real life into a private world that was bounded in time by the twelfth and eighteenth centuries. He and Lady Ida had in common, apart from their tall, strikingly attractive appearances, only a ruthless selfishness and an impulse towards lavish expenditure which Sir George strove to suppress in everyone but himself. Lady Ida was empty-headed, high-spirited, frivolous and mundane, a gregarious extrovert whose ideal world was the one she had been brought up to as the daughter of Lord Londesborough – the social and sporting gatherings of free-spending, hedonistic magnates and their families.

About the house, whose forlorn grandeur had been carefully preserved and nurtured, was an atmosphere of melancholy which accorded with the spirits of its occupants. In Sir George pathos was both a cultivated pose and a legacy of a miserable childhood. In Lady Ida it was a late acquisition which ran counter to her innate vivacity. It followed from the scandal of her trial in 1915, where she was sentenced to three months' imprisonment for fraud. She had placed herself in this situation through irresponsible folly rather than criminal intent. When, during Sir George's long absences abroad in the years before the First World War, she found herself free of the curbs he imposed, she returned to her society friends. She began to drink, gambled heavily and hugely exceeded her personal allowance. In a foolish attempt to conceal this from Sir George she fell into the clutches of a money-lender, Field, who succeeded in implicating her in his fraudulent activities, while at the same time multiplying her debts. The tragedy for Lady Ida was not only that she suffered public disgrace, but also that afterwards Sir George saw to it that she should have no further opportunity for extravagance and high-living, or for the kind of companions she most desired.

Aldous Huxley had once planned as a sequel to his novel *Crome Yellow* (in which Sir George and Lady Ida had contributed to the characters of Priscilla and Henry Wimbush) a comedy set in a large castle in Italy resembling Montegufoni, which would be 'occupied . . . by the most improbable people of every species and nationality', thereby providing 'the essential Peacockian datum – a houseful of oddities'.[15] The meeting of the Sitwells and the Lawrences seemed designed for a scene in such a comedy: two sets of ill-matched couples given to tempestuous rows; the womenfolk, disreputable daughters, respectively, of a German baron and an English viscount; the male characters comprising a coalminer's son, author of scandalous novels, and a coal-owning baronet, chronicler of *The History of the Fork*, the one being hard of hearing and the other tending to mumble as if his mouth were filled with dust newly arisen from his latest architectural improvement.

True to form, the encounter did not fail to generate humour. At the end of the month Osbert Sitwell received a letter from his mother telling him of the visit:

A Mr. D. H. Lawrence came over the other day, a funny little petit-maître of a man with flat features and a beard. He says he is a writer, and seems to know all of you. His wife is a large German. She went round the house with your father, and when he showed her anything, would look at him, lean against one of the gilded beds, and breathe heavily. [16]

Sir George's conducted tours of the frescoed rooms of his labyrinthine castello, which held his collections of antique furniture and armour, usually lasted a full hour. Frieda's heavy breathing may have owed more to exhaustion than to a passion for antique beds.

Collecting monster seventeenth-century four-posters was one of Sir George's hobbies. To Lawrence it seemed to reveal a dispiriting side of Sir George's character, and the trail from room to room and bed to bed left him feeling somewhat disconsolate. The beds were not even for sleeping in, but were there simply to be gazed on as objects of antiquity. Turning to a gilded Venetian chair, he tried it for comfort and was informed in tones of polite dismay that it was not for sitting in. On getting up, Lawrence yielded to a boyish impulse to wriggle his rump in the hope that the chair would disintegrate beneath him. [17] These lapses apart, the Lawrences seem to have shown themselves to advantage and to have behaved in a manner in keeping with Frieda's wish to present herself as the social equal of the English baronetage – an intention which may be surmised from her entry in the visitors' book, which read 'Frieda Lawrence, *geborene* Richthofen.' [18] The Sitwells, too, appear to have practised the art of keeping up appearances, in that they convinced Lawrence that theirs was an ideal, loving marriage-partnership. [19] So successful was the encounter at Montegufoni that the Lawrences were invited to call at Renishaw Hall, the Sitwells' Derbyshire seat, during the coming August, when by tradition all the Sitwells forgathered at their ancestral home. [20]

The key to the success of the meeting may well have been a good rapport between Lawrence and Lady Ida, an intelligent, unaffected and often entertaining conversationalist who, like Lawrence, was a gifted mimic. Perhaps it was his own attraction to Lady Ida that he attributed to Connie in the cruelly percipient portrait of Lady Ida as Lady Eva Rolleston, Clifford's aunt, in *The First Lady Chatterley*:

She had the remains of the *grande dame* about her, being daughter of one of the really big families. But she had rather got into disrepute, what with gambling and brandy. Still there she was, a widow now, tall and slim and unobtrusive, a bit *distraite*, her blue eyes rather vacant and her fine nose a little reddened. And still she was the *grande dame*. She was so very simple, for one thing, and in her rather blank unobtrusiveness there was still a power of commanding deference. She sipped her brandy with a noble *sang-froid*, indifferent to all the comment in the world.

Constance liked her and at the same time was depressed by her. Lady Eva was somehow like a ghost, in her black clothes and her curious naïveté, which was almost girlish and winning. Yet the odd, straightforward girlishness rested upon a very hard determination never to yield an inch, essentially, to anybody on earth. A hard imperviousness and isolation, like the Matterhorn, was the bleak centre of Lady Eva.

(FLC 30)

In *John Thomas and Lady Jane* the portrait is essentially the same, though amplified. It has moments of great poignancy, delicacy and sympathy, and perhaps gets to the heart of the problem in Lady Ida's relations with Sir George and the cause of her waywardness. Lady Eva confides to Connie: 'It's awful to be growing into an old woman, and feel no safety anywhere round you. And feel you've never had the right man's arms around you, you know, to make you feel safe, really safe!' (*JTLJ* 77). Lady Ida had been a girl of 17 when she married Sir George, at an emotional stage when she was still dependent on her strong and indulgent father. Sir George, whose upbringing as an orphan under Victorian discipline had bred a sense of living under perpetual threat of calamity, was desperately ill-qualified to offer her the security she needed.

One bulwark of reassurance in the Sitwell household, despite a penchant for roistering which he sometimes indulged to excess, was Henry Moat, the butler. A spirited raconteur and conversationalist, with an irreverent sense of humour for which the whimsies and self-importance of Sir George provided a ready butt, he was the beloved companion of every member of the family, whom he served for over forty years. His huge, portly frame with its genial, ruddy face – Edith compared him to a benevolent hippopotamus – presided over Lady Ida's lunch-parties at Montegufoni. Lawrence evidently struck up an acquaintance with Moat, was attracted to his engaging character and intrigued by his curiously close, brotherly relationship with Lady Ida. To anyone who has read Osbert Sitwell's auto-biography *Left Hand, Right Hand!*, where Moat appears as one of the dominant and best-loved figures of his early life, Henry Moat is instantly recognizable as Collingwood, butler to Lady Eva in *John Thomas and Lady Jane*. In the final version Collingwood disappears, along with many of the other attributes which identify Lady Eva with Lady Ida.

In *Lady Chatterley's Lover* the Chatterley family group was made closely to resemble the Sitwells: Osbert and Edith became Clifford and Emma Chatterley, brother and sister; Lady Ida's family background as daughter to a viscount was given to Clifford's mother; and Sir George's character was for the first time attributed to the father, Sir Geoffrey. In this version, too, the Chatterleys' Wragby took on more of the features of the Sitwells' Renishaw Hall. Lawrence seems to have decided that it was therefore expedient that the harsh portrait of Lady Eva, the only Chatterley of the original version to be self-evidently modelled on one of the Sitwells, should be softened and made less revealing. Only if one has followed her pedigree through the evolution of the novel is Lady Ida discernible behind Lady Eva Bennerley in *Lady Chatterley's Lover*. Motives other than expediency may have influenced this decision. By the time he wrote the final version, Lawrence had met Osbert Sitwell and had been able to observe, as others before him had done, how extremely sensitive he was on the subject of his mother, whom he loved and admired as deeply as he hated and scorned Sir George.

According to one theory, which appears to be gaining currency, and whose progenitor is Reresby Sitwell, grandson of Sir George and the present owner of Renishaw Hall, it was during this visit to Montegufoni that Lawrence heard the strange history of a near-neighbour of the Sitwells which furnished him with an idea for a story that developed into *Lady Chatterley*. If this is true, then one explanation for the presence of the Sitwells and their house in the novel could be the family's association with the source-story.

William Arkwright, a descendant of the inventor, Sir Richard Arkwright, lived at Sutton Scarsdale Hall, six or seven miles from Renishaw. He was a contemporary of Sir George's and they had been at Eton together. In the year before his coming of age he had set out from the hall on horse-back to race his sister through the park. He failed to return and was later found lying in a nearby lane, where he had been thrown after his horse failed to jump a fence. According to the story, his almost lifeless body, which had suffered severe injuries to the head and a frightful emasculation, was carried to a nearby barn where Arkwright remained for six weeks before it was possible to move him. A trepanning operation was performed and a silver plate inserted in his skull; thereafter he wore headgear with inner crowns of steel as a protection.

When Arkwright later married, it was against his mother's advice, and the marriage did not turn out to be a happy one. The Arkwrights had another residence in Thorne, Devon, and for much of their married life they lived apart, moving separately between the two houses. Although the emasculation had left Arkwright impotent, he was in no other way impaired, and he lived an active, energetic life as businessman, coal-owner, sportsman, world-traveller, author and classical scholar.

There is material here to excite the interest of any story-writer who heard it, and for Lawrence there would have been the attraction of self-identification with the impotent husband, the difficult marriage and the Derbyshire setting. Had he also heard of an unfaithful wife, the identification would have been that much the greater. No true account of the Arkwrights could have given Lawrence this aspect of the plot of *Lady Chatterley*: Arkwright's wife was a devout Catholic whose character would not have disposed her to have affairs with estate-workers. But the truth of the matter is less important than what Lawrence might have heard of the Arkwrights. The situation of a woman living apart from a husband known to be impotent would inevitably have generated innuendo and mendacious rumour on the part of the prurient-minded. And it is not impossible that Lady Ida had heard some such story, which she relayed to Lawrence. The fact that gossip formed part of their conversation may perhaps be surmised from an observation Lawrence made in his portrait of Lady Ida in *John Thomas and Lady Jane*, where Lady Eva 'sat so often very still, just murmuring her gossip' (*JTLJ* 73).

There are no special links with Arkwright's story in *Lady Chatterley*, nor would one necessarily expect there to be. But what this means is that there must be other good reasons for supposing that the idea for *Lady Chatterley* had the Arkwright story as its source: the action of the novel, after all, resembles a common story-pattern in Lawrence's fiction – one that he had used in 'Sun' and *The Virgin and the Gipsy* for instance; the principal source for that story-pattern of the lady drawn to the low-class outsider was Lawrence's own affair with Frieda.

It is at least possible to provide credible justification for supposing that the subject of William Arkwright could have been raised in the course of conversation at Montegufoni; and the character of Lady Ida, and Lawrence's capacity to elicit confidences from women, provide an appropriate context of personalities for intimate tittle-tattle.

The county of Derbyshire, its places and people, would have provided common ground for conversation, and talk of the great houses of Derbyshire could have introduced the subject of Arkwright. Reresby Sitwell's theory is that the topic arose through mention of Osbert's interests in Sutton Scarsdale Hall, which years later he bought as a ruin. As a spectacular single instance of the fate that had befallen the English country house in the years immediately following the end of the First World War, Arkwright's Sutton Scardsale would be hard to rival. An act of gross philistinism on the part of a group of property speculators, who had bought the house from Arkwright, caused the pillage and destruction of an interior that contained Venetian Rococo stuccowork of superlative beauty, whose richness exceeded anything that the palaces of Venice had to offer.

There is a possibility that Lawrence visited Sutton Scarsdale Hall when he toured the Chesterfield area by car in September 1926; and he may have conflated the site of Sutton Scarsdale and features of the appearance and setting of Shipley Hall near Eastwood to create the 'Shipley Hall' of *Lady Chatterley*. This could mean that he had heard of Sutton Scarsdale, and therefore, possibly, of the history of its owner, when he dined at Montegufoni. But there is no certain proof that Lawrence visited the hall or used it in the novel. Equally, there could be alternative explanations for any such putative visit (see further, pp. 156–60).

One of those alternative explanations could also be used to provide another appropriate scenario for talk of William Arkwright. Since 1919, the name William Arkwright of Sutton Scarsdale had very probably been known to Lawrence through his former friend, Norman Douglas. For a number of years Douglas had been in correspondence with Arkwright, an admirer of his work whom he had never met and with whom he shared interests in travel and in classical antiquity. Arkwright had heard that Douglas was in financial difficulties and offered to help. At Douglas's request he agreed to forward monthly sums of £20 to him until work on his novel, *They Went*, was complete.[21] This arrangement had been made not long before the meeting between Lawrence and Douglas in Florence in November 1919 – their first since the outbreak of war. It is almost inconceivable that Douglas, who was a boaster and a tease, would not have taunted Lawrence with the windfall that had been put his way by someone from Lawrence's neck of the woods. No less certain, given Lawrence's envy of the fortunes of other writers, is the fact that, once heard, the name of Douglas's benefactor would never have been forgotten. Since he knew Derbyshire well enough to be aware of the proximity of the Sitwells' Renishaw and Arkwright's Sutton Scarsdale, Lawrence might well himself have introduced the topic of Arkwright and Sutton Scarsdale. He might even have hoped that talk of Douglas's patron might lead on to the subject of patronage of the arts, for which the Sitwell children already had a reputation. Having no realistic notion of the wealth of the Sitwells, Lawrence might have had some slender expectation that the invitation to Montegufoni could be a sign that they were contemplating taking him up as a writer deserving of their assistance.

It is thus possible to imagine plausible circumstances that would favour gossip about William Arkwright. Actual evidence within the text for Arkwright's story as the source is not strong. The Arkwright theory depends crucially upon Lawrence's sources for and his treatment of the fictional 'Shipley Hall', discussed in chapter 8. Here there is enough, perhaps, which tallies with Lawrence's associative habits of mind, to arouse at least strong suspicions that Reresby Sitwell's theory of the genesis of *Lady Chatterley* could be well-founded. It is interesting, in regard to these habits of association, that shortly after visiting Montegufoni Lawrence received news for the first time in several years of a friend, Rosalind Thornycroft, who was to contribute a great deal to the making of the novel. He also, at about that time, had a letter from Mabel Luhan containing a section of her autobiography entitled 'Constance'.[22]

Looking southwards from the Mirenda across the plains of the Arno river, Lawrence could see part of the city of Florence and beyond it the hills of the suburb of Fiesole. On the first bluff of hill up from the city, just below Fiesole, was the Villa Canovaia, where Lawrence had stayed in September 1920. The poet Eleanor Farjeon, who got to know the villa in December of the same year, wrote that in all Italy she had never seen such a romantic house, which seemed to her like the palace of the Sleeping Princess.[23] As it happens, a story-pattern which Harry Moore named after this fairy-tale, one in which a passionately dormant or repressed woman is aroused and brought to fulfilment, is common in Lawrence's fiction and is embodied in *Lady*

Chatterley. And a former resident of the Villa Canovaia, Rosalind Thornycroft, became, with Cynthia Asquith and Frieda, one of the models for Constance, the Sleeping Princess of *Lady Chatterley*.

Rosalind Thornycroft was arguably the most perfect, in terms of a sweet harmony of beauty of character, mind and appearance, of all the women of Lawrence's acquaintance. Cecily Lambert, a friend of Lawrence's who met her several times in his company, remembered the touching gentleness of her personality.[24] David Garnett, a lifelong friend of hers, described her as 'a lovely creature – a russetted apple in face, cool, delicate and critical in spirit', whose 'beauty was cool and flower-like'.[25] To Garnett she was the epitome of womanly perfection, 'almost too perfect' for her first husband, whom Garnett came to regard as 'an old bumble-puppy'.[26] Constance Chatterley has the same 'golden-ruddy' (*JTLJ* 79) skin tones; she has the softly flowing, unfashionably long, nut-brown hair of Rosalind Thornycroft; her beauty is described in the terms of coolness and images of flowers which it had evoked in Garnett;[27] and the keen critical faculties praised by Garnett are mentioned in the portrait of Constance in the second version of the novel.[28] The Constance of *The First Lady Chatterley*, 'a woman with a gentle, warm soul' (*FLC* 120), more perfect in being than her successors, who need to be educated out of snobbery, wilfulness and the desire to dominate, perhaps most closely resembles Rosalind Thornycroft in personality.

Within a few days of visiting the Sitwells, Lawrence seems to have heard news of Rosalind Thornycroft, which he passed on to his sister, Emily King, who had met her at Pangbourne, Berkshire, in 1919: 'By the way, Rosalind . . . is married again . . . I'm glad she's settled down again' (*CL* 919). The paternalistic solicitude of the last remark reflects an attitude that surfaces elsewhere in matters pertaining to Rosalind Thornycroft, of whose marriage Lawrence most probably learnt in a letter from Richard Aldington, written in reply to Lawrence's letter of April: Aldington, also mentioned in the letter to Emily, had taken a cottage near Pangbourne, where Rosalind Thornycroft had lived.

Her house, 'The Myrtles', had been loaned to Lawrence for a time in August 1919, while she herself moved to a nearby cottage vacated by her sister and brother-in-law, Joan and Herbert Farjeon. It was an unhappy period in Rosalind Thornycroft's life, alleviated a little by the joyous and exciting company of the Lawrences, with whom she sang Mozart arias at the spinet in 'The Myrtles' (the source, perhaps, for Constance's liking for Mozart and for the presence of a spinet in her sitting-room),[29] walked and picnicked on the downs, and went out on bicycle rides and excursions by pony-trap. She was preparing to leave 'The Myrtles' for good and to depart for Italy with her family of three small girls to escape the scandal of the divorce her husband was threatening.

One of Lawrence's tasks when he departed for Italy in November 1919 was to investigate, as a possible temporary home for Rosalind Thornycroft and her children, a house belonging to Orazio Cervi, who had modelled for her father, the sculptor Sir Hamo Thornycroft RA; and through his meeting with Lawrence, Cervi also became the unwitting model for Pancrazio in Lawrence's *The Lost Girl*. Lawrence found the house, high in the Abruzzi mountains, 'staggeringly primitive' (*Let* 3 431) and quite unsuitable for young children. When, therefore, Rosalind Thornycroft arrived in Italy in January 1920, she followed Lawrence's recommendations and settled in Florence, where she rented the Villa Canovaia.

In August of that year Lawrence and Frieda, who were staying at Taormina, Sicily, travelled northwards through Italy to Milan, where they separated. Frieda set off for Germany to see her relatives; and Lawrence made for Lake Como for a walking tour which was to be followed by visits to Venice and Florence. When Frieda last visited Germany alone in the late autumn of 1919, Lawrence had given Aldington the impression that he would not care if he never saw her again. Perhaps nothing had changed to alter his attitude in the ensuing months, for he found himself in an odd frame of mind, as if he had somehow slipped his moorings: 'I feel all unstuck, as if I might drift off anywhere' (*Let* 3 585), he told Rosalind Thornycroft, shortly before he and Frieda split up.

The windows of the Canovaia had been blown out by an explosion at a nearby ammunition dump, and Rosalind Thornycroft had had to move up to a house in Fiesole. On reaching Florence at the beginning of September, Lawrence moved into the Canovaia for a stay that lasted almost the whole month. It was a beautiful, decaying old house of great character, not only in its appearance but in the population of cats, puppies, goats, chickens and children which wandered in and out of its large rooms. The exterior had a courtyard where a fountain played; there was a turret overlooking Florence, a shaded balcony decked with vines, and a terraced garden with

persimmon trees and a fascinating world of animal and insect life –
lizards, tortoises, cicadas and fireflies.

The house and gardens of the Canovaia were an inspiration to
Lawrence, as also, apparently, was the pleasure of the company of
Rosalind Thornycroft and the children, whom he frequently joined in
Fiesole, taking the track beneath the walls of the ancient Etruscan
hill-city, armed sometimes with presents from the Canovaia for the
girls, such as a yellow duckling or a salamander. There were walks
together in the hills above Fiesole, Sunday roasts cooked by Lawrence, tea parties, and in the evenings simple suppers of cheese and
wine on the terrace overlooking the city.[30]

It was an idyllic period for Lawrence, during which he seems
finally to have thrown off the nightmare memories of the war years, to
experience a sweet morning-awakening to feelings of warm, reposeful
sensuousness. Out of his holiday of September in Florence came some
of the finest of all his poems, combining delicacy, humour, and
precision of observation and statement with outstanding technical
achievement. These verses, which formed part of the anthology
Birds, Beasts and Flowers, include the set of six poems, 'Tortoises',
inspired by the tortoises of the Canovaia gardens, which traces with
wry, self-critical humour the development from birth to maturity of
tortoise, man and Lawrence. Other poems dating from this period are
inhabited by a 'subtly-smiling' (*Poems* 296) eroticism that Lawrence
attributed to the Etruscan race beneath whose city-walls he passed on
the way to Fiesole: such are 'Pomegranate', 'Peach', 'Figs' and
'Cypresses'. Quite different in spirit are 'Grapes' and 'Medlars and
Sorb Apples', which pass through the 'dusky and tendrilled' (*Poems*
286) avenues of underworlds and antediluvian otherworlds, suggesting, perhaps, in their Orphic and Dionysan attributes, a purging of
the Titan inheritance of sensuality and an ascetic cultivation of the
divine nature in the form of 'ecstatic subtly-intellectual' being.[31]

Rosalind Thornycroft was present when some of these poems, such
as 'Grapes' and 'Medlars and Sorb Apples' were first conceived; and
'Figs' may have a play on her name and a reference to the daring she
showed in taking off alone with three children to Italy: '*Here's to the
thorn in flower! Here is to Utterance!/* The brave adventurous rosaceae'
(*Poems* 283). The poems hint at a strong, spiritual attraction on
Lawrence's part and a possible 'flow in the air' (*CL* 914), as Lawrence
would have described it, between Rosalind Thornycroft and himself.

The letters to her are matter-of-fact, shortish and often concerned in a fussy, paternalistic way with travel arrangements. On occasion a warm casualness enters into them, but even these letters have an oddly withdrawn quality, a neglect of the exuberant expression of ideas or feelings that is typical of his letters to intimate women friends. It has often been observed that Lawrence tended to fit the tone and content of his letters to the personality and views of their recipients; and perhaps he tempered these letters to a cool, objective mind which would not have welcomed the sort of passionate outpourings bestowed on Cynthia Asquith. Rosalind Thornycroft's association with Cynthia Asquith in the portrait of Constance Chatterley, and her role in the making of the Canovaia poems, might suggest that she shared with her the status of muse and dream-woman to be admired from afar. If that was so, then his letters to her seem to point up the distance which perhaps both parties wished to preserve between them.

From almost the moment of his first meeting with Rosalind Thornycroft, Lawrence was attracted by the literary potential of her life-history. He had planned in 1919 to collaborate with her brother-in-law, Herbert Farjeon, in the writing of a play. The project was abandoned when Lawrence proposed that its subject should be Rosalind.[32] Seven years were to pass before Lawrence returned to the subject in *Lady Chatterley*.

Elements of biographical fact that make possible an identification of Rosalind Thornycroft as one of the models for Constance Chatterley are distributed over the three versions of the novel. In all of them Constance is the daughter of a Royal Academician, Sir Malcolm Reid, who has another daughter Hilda, with whom Connie enjoys a specially close relationship. These bare facts, paralleling the relationship between Rosalind, her sister Joan and their father, Sir Hamo Thornycroft RA, were sufficient to alert Joan Farjeon, after a reading of *Lady Chatterley's Lover*, to the likelihood that Lawrence had made use of her family in the novel.[33]

Rosalind Thornycroft had had the cultured, unconventional upbringing under a mother with Fabian leanings that is attributed to Constance Chatterley in the last two versions of the novel, having been educated at a famous, progressive co-educational school – King Alfred's, Hampstead. And in her youth she had, like the Constance of *Lady Chatterley's Lover*, fallen in love with a Dresden student who was 'musical': her first husband had for a while trained as an opera-singer in Dresden. In this version, too, Connie and Clifford had been part of a Cambridge set closely resembling one to which David Garnett, Rosalind Thornycroft and her first and second husbands had belonged – a group 'that stood for "freedom" and flannel trousers, and flannel shirts open at the neck, and a well-bred sort of emotional anarchy, and a whispering, murmuring sort of voice, and an ultra-sensitive sort of manner' (*LCL* 10).

All these correspondences between the life-histories and physical appearances of Constance Chatterley and Rosalind Thornycroft could conceivably have been entirely coincidental. What makes it absolutely certain that Rosalind Thornycroft was one of the women Lawrence had in mind when composing his portrait of Lady Chatterley is a detail which he introduced in *John Thomas and Lady Jane* and suppressed, no doubt for the reason that it betrayed the identity of his subject, in the version intended for publication. Rosalind Thornycroft sometimes undertook commissions for the illustration of books. Often, as in the case of Eleanor Farjeon's book of verse and stories for children, *Nuts and May* (with some beautiful illustrations of the Canovaia and its tortoises), the commissions were provided by members of her family. Lawrence comments in the novel: 'Constance too made quaint drawings and illustrations for old books. Sometimes her illustrations were published; she had a little name for her work' (*JTLJ* 14). In a later passage Lawrence returns to the subject of her work as illustrator: 'If it hadn't been for Hilda or her father, who got her commissions for illustrating some children's book or some quaint little volume of verse, she would have let her drawing and painting lapse, like the rest, though she really had a certain gift' (*JTLJ* 41).

Constance Chatterley is not the only character in the novel to whom Rosalind Thornycroft lent details of her biography. In all versions, details proper to her life have been shifted over to Connie's sister Hilda, who took her appearance from Rosalind Thornycroft's sister, Joan. As a result, as is not infrequently the case with Lawrence's treatment of real people and places in this and other novels, Rosalind Thornycroft appears in two distinct manifestations. It was she, not her sister Joan, who, like Hilda, 'suddenly married a man ten years older than herself, an elder member of the same Cambridge group';[34] and it seems to have been of Rosalind Thornycroft's move to Italy with her three girls that Lawrence was thinking when he had Hilda leave her husband and depart 'bag and baggage with her two children' (*FLC* 34f.) for Scotland. Like Hilda, she clearly 'wove a lot of importance round her little girls, round herself as mother', and 'took her duties terribly seriously' (*JTLJ* 55). By the final version Hilda's marriage has reached precisely the same sequel as that of Rosalind Thornycroft: her 'husband was now divorcing her . . . she even made it easy for him to do that'.[35]

Four weeks after Lawrence had written to Emily of Rosalind Thornycroft's marriage, the time came for him to set out with Frieda on their planned visits to Germany, to attend the baroness's 75th birthday celebrations, and then to England. The early summer days at the Mirenda had been so lovely that neither of them wished to leave and risk losing the contentment that had made for an unusually easy life together. For Lawrence the prospect of long train-journeys in the sweltering heat was discouraging, and as the time of his visit to England approached, his heart sank more and more at the thought of it. Characteristically, he began to dither over whether to go at all: 'Of course the thought of England, as it draws near, depresses me with infinite depression. But perhaps we may manage a month. Perhaps we may shirk it after all' (Zyt 288).

Where the visit to Baden-Baden was concerned, the appeal of the coolness and freshness of the air up in the Black Forest began to exert itself as July in Tuscany turned heavy and thundery. And on the 12th of the month 'Lorenzo', as he was known in Italy, set off to assume again his German title 'Fritzl', which was the baroness's pet-name for him.

Following the usual pattern of his stays in Baden-Baden, Lawrence sampled the mineral waters, ate heartily, attended tea-parties with old ladies and gentlemen of the aristocracy and strolled through the woods. A short walk through the forest took one to the entrance of the funicular railway that ground its way up to the summit of Merkur, the highest hill in the region, where there were magnificent views of the Rhine Valley and the rounded, wooded hills of the Schwartzwald. The hill became the subject and the principal character in the allegorical essay 'Mercury', written at this period. And it may have been that the thunder-storm which terrified the holiday-makers who gathered on the summit of 'Mercury' on a hot, summer Sunday, steamy after prolonged rainfall, belonged to Lawrence's own experiences of 25 July.

The hot weather had broken in torrential rain a week after Lawrence's arrival, flooding the valley of the Rhine; and it was still pouring on the day the Lawrences set out on a twenty-hour journey through the night to London, which they reached on the evening of the 30th. The arduousness of such an unbroken journey left Lawrence in no mood to discern liveliness in a city and a country which he had long regarded as moribund.

6

'Something of an Odyssey'

On arriving in London, the Lawrences moved into the studio flat which Millie Beveridge had arranged for them to rent in Rossetti Garden Mansions, a Chelsea apartment-block in Flood Street, which ran between the King's Road and the riverside London Embankment. Lawrence probably knew the building well from an earlier period; during the First World War it had been the home of a former friend, the composer Philip Heseltine, who was the model for Halliday in *Women in Love*.

Already waiting for Lawrence was a note from Kot, whose bone-crunching handshake, when they met next day, put the seal on the friendship which in the course of the year had been pieced together again by letter. In the opinion of Beatrice Campbell, a mutual friend of Kot and Lawrence, Kot was a man of the highest moral integrity, who in his whole life never acted or spoke dishonourably in any matter.[1] Though she confessed that some thought her opinions exaggeratedly high, it must be said that his conduct in regard to Lawrence, both during and after his friend's lifetime, gives every support to her claims on his behalf. It is one of the most solid testaments to the sincerity and integrity of Lawrence that he retained the regard and affection of a man who was supremely intolerant of any want of such virtues in others.

Lawrence had for two years been corresponding with an earnest young Cambridge graduate, Rolf Gardiner, with whom he arranged a lunch-time meeting at Rossetti Gardens during his first days in London. Gardiner had become acquainted with Lawrence's work in his adolescence; and as an undergraduate he had seized upon Lawrence as the prophet he needed to articulate the disjoint strands of Christian mysticism, romanticism and Spenglerian historicism that filled his head. He became a Lawrentian of the extremes, contemptuous of democracy, of rational thought and of 'intellectuals', and dedicated to the establishment of a natural aristocracy led by a charismatic priest-king;[2] more worthy of sympathy among the causes

Gardiner espoused under the inspiration of Lawrence was the preservation of rural England. He was attempting the practical application of Lawrentian ideals and looked to Lawrence as the potential leader of a younger generation devoted to the cause of reactionary social and political change. In July 1926 he had summoned up the courage to sound Lawrence out on the possibility of joining him in the pan-Nordic youth movement he had founded, the aims of which were wholeness with one's fellows, with the soil and with one's soul; hiking, camping and agricultural labour were its main activities, and special importance was attached to the roles of song and dance.[3]

Two or three years earlier Lawrence might have wished for such an eager disciple. But by the summer of 1926 he had lost interest in collecting disciples and in male fellowship. The 'Rananim' ideal of a community of like-minded individuals remained dear; but it no longer burned in him. As for Gardiner's beliefs in charismatic leadership and in an oligarchy of natural aristocrats, here, too, the meeting may have come too late for him to be able to share them any longer with his adopted mentor. Later that year he wrote to Lawrence: 'I take it you meant *The Plumed Serpent* absolutely seriously' (Nehls 3 122). Lawrence neglected to comment on this assumption in his reply, though a year earlier he had affirmed to Secker: 'I *do* mean what Ramon [*sic*] [in *The Plumed Serpent*] means – for all of us' (Sec 65). Not until March 1928 did Lawrence write an explicit personal rejection of the leader-hero ideal: 'The hero is obsolete, and the leader of men is a back-number' (*CL* 1045). But its rejection by the autumn of 1926 is implicit in the words of Duncan Forbes, the Lawrence-figure in *The First Lady Chatterley*: 'No, I've hated democracy since the war. But now I see I'm wrong in calling for an aristocracy. What we want is a flow of life from one to another' (*FLC* 243).

Gardiner's interests were in mass-movements, and Lawrence balked at the idea of associating himself with anything that smacked of institutional organization. In proposing a meeting with Gardiner he had expressed himself frankly and considerately, preparing Gardiner for the fact that he intended keeping him at arm's length with a warning that Gardiner would find him 'wary beyond words' (*CL* 928) of committing himself to anything.

In the same letter he confessed: 'I believe we are mutually a bit scared. I of weird movements, and you of me.' Perhaps Lawrence was also a little afraid of Gardiner as the kind of person who founded weird movements and as someone whose long, intense, blustering letters he found disturbing. It would have been reasonable for him even to have feared that he might be about to confront some strange travesty of his past self, for Gardiner had not only taken on Lawrence's system of ideas, but in his writings had adopted features of the diction and incantatory rhythms of the Lawrentian style.

A portrait of Gardiner in 1928 shows a man of athletic build and noble, clean-cut countenance, very much the picture of the contemporary Germanic hero, with a determined jaw-line and a hint of ruthlessness in the set of the mouth and the intensity of the gaze. The Gardiner Lawrence met was a slightly gauche, uncertain, self-conscious young man who was rather overawed by the occasion. Lawrence was also ill at ease; and Gardiner left with the impression that the meeting had been a rather tense, artificial occasion.

In a letter from the Mirenda in October, Lawrence told Gardiner: 'part of yourself, the fighting and the passionate part, never issues . . . from its shell' (*CL* 941). Gardiner formed a similar impression of Lawrence. The man he met was not the impassioned demagogue of the novels, whom he venerated, but a frail and vulnerable figure for whom he formed a gentle affection. Though Lawrence had given enthusiastic support to Gardiner's plan to found English centres for social and spiritual renewal,[4] it nevertheless became clear to Gardiner that even if Lawrence had the will to join in any group-venture, he had not the physical stamina for such a task.

When Gardiner next contacted Lawrence with an invitation to join a gathering in a country house in Yorkshire that summer, he declined.[5] Gardiner was 'nice', he told Brett in 1928, but, 'not much in my line' (*CL* 1038), a judgement not without a touch of comic irony, considering Gardiner's endeavours to follow the Lawrentian philosophy. Nevertheless, Lawrence was right about their differences: Lawrence's line was ideas, Gardiner's was practical action.

Lawrence remained sympathetic to the idea of setting up some kind of centre for social renewal, and continued to write to Gardiner, offering encouragement and advice. For a time he even came close to committing himself to throwing in his lot with Gardiner; but he proffered his help in the language of 'if', 'one day', 'might', and 'no use rushing' (*CL* 940f., 951). When next they met, at Les Diablerets in Switzerland in February 1928, Gardiner's projected centre was close to becoming a reality. He had acquired Gore Farm in Dorset, which was to become the Springhead Estate, where students and the unemployed were educated in farming and animal husbandry; and from this 'centre for rural restoration' Gardiner engaged in pioneering work in the fields of conservation and ecology. In founding Springhead he had faithfully carried out Lawrence's suggestions that he should find 'some place with a big barn and a bit of land' (*CL* 951) where there might be established 'a holy centre' (*CL* 1031) from which to rekindle the religious sense of at-one-ness among the English.

Perhaps Lawrence was in turn influenced in some small ways by Gardiner, whose imprint has been detected in the importance accorded to song and dance in Lawrence's vision of a better life for working people, as expressed, for instance, in Mellors's letter to Connie at the end of *Lady Chatterley's Lover*.[6] If Gardiner affected Lawrence's thinking in other respects, it seems more likely to have been as an informant rather than as a communicator of ideas.[7] The term 'suburbian' (*sic*) was to Gardiner what 'mechanical' was to Lawrence: it was the key-word of his obsessions, an epithet to be applied to the root of all the ills of society; it was a word for a habit of mind, a way of living and a political creed, as well as an architectural and geographical term. Gardiner had observed, as Lawrence by virtue of his absences could only have done discontinuously, 'the swamping of the traditional England by suburbia', a 'process which had begun like a creeping paralysis to emasculate the England of the 'twenties and to obliterate the Home Counties with a bungaloid octopus' (Nehls 3 76). In Gardiner's opinion it was 'suburbia', too, which in its political guise had begun 'to empty, by taxation, the halls and mansions which had for so long been the centres of English rural government and the repositories of English culture'. The spread of estates of desirable semi-detached villas is a minor motif in *Lady Chatterley*, where it is linked to the major theme of the fall of the English country house and the departure of the landed gentry. Neither the disfigurement of the countryside by random housing developments nor the flight of the gentry was a new element in Lawrence's fiction. But the suburban character of the housing estate in *Lady Chatterley* is topical and innovatory, and the theme of the departure of the gentry had only been lightly touched on in the past. Since these topics were among Gardiner's major obsessions, it is not unlikely that it was he who alerted Lawrence to or revived his concern for what was happening in the English countryside of the 1920s.

While Lawrence was in Spotorno he had written to Aldous Huxley, saying how much he had liked his *Along the Road*, a collection of essays on travel in Italy, and suggesting that they should meet sometime.[8] This suggestion was taken up during the first week of Lawrence's return to England, when Huxley called at the flat one evening. Though they may have met at Pangbourne in 1919,[9] the only certain previous occasion when they had spent some time together had been in 1915 in Hampstead. Huxley had then called to take tea with Lawrence at the suggestion of Lady Ottoline Morrell, and on that occasion he had been so startled and enthralled by Lawrence that when he proposed that he should join the colony he intended to found in Florida, Huxley instantly agreed. Lawrence, he told his brother Julian, was a genius, 'a great man' and 'a good man, who impresses me as a good man more than most'.[10] It perhaps says as much for the impressionability of the young Aldous as for Lawrence's personal magnetism that he could reach such conclusions after a single encounter. Lawrence, for his part, also took to Huxley; but the Florida plan fell through, and there was no follow-up meeting. In the years that followed, Huxley's initial enchantment with Lawrence declined, or so it would appear from a letter to his father in 1920, in which Lawrence became the target of the clever, malicious, supercilious wit for which Huxley became celebrated as a young man:

> I heard a pleasing tale about the effects of analysis the other day; told of D. H. Lawrence, the slightly insane novelist, who was analysed for his complexes, dark and tufty ones, tangled in his mind. The complexes were discovered, and it is said that Lawrence has now lost, along with his slight sexual mania, all his talent as a writer and produces mild little murmurings in the style of Michael Fairlees.[11]

Lawrence's and Huxley's reunion in 1926 marked the beginning of a close and, on the face of it, unlikely liaison between men whom Robert Graves somewhat crudely labelled the novelists, respectively, 'of emotional sexuality' and 'of intellectual sexuality'.[12]

Having met one future biographer in Huxley, who wrote the introduction to and edited Lawrence's collected letters, Lawrence went on at the end of the week to spend a day or two with another – Richard Aldington – and his companion Dorothy 'Arabella' Yorke. They had kept in touch through an irregular correspondence during the years when Lawrence had been away, but they had not met for seven years when Lawrence paid a visit to the Aldingtons' cottage at Padworth in Berkshire. Though it was a county he had once loved, he felt alien to the spirit of the place: the cottage, though bright and with a colourful flower garden, struck him as 'sinister';[13] in summer sunshine they walked through lush meadows beside the Kennet Canal, starred with white and yellow waterlilies; but to Lawrence the sleepy tranquillity and changelessness of the English country scene smacked only of inertia, making him more determined than ever not to make his home in England.[14] His negative reactions were not extended to his hosts, however. The Aldingtons found him on his best form, filling them with laughter at stories of his recent reacquaintance with the angelic idiocy of his compatriots, and bringing to life for them all the experiences of his travels since they last met. Aldington had thoughtfully arranged for a number of illustrated books on the Etruscans to be sent down for Lawrence from the London Library; and a good deal of time was spent working through them and discussing the Etruscan civilization.

On the Sunday, Lawrence returned to Rossetti Garden Mansions before setting off next morning to Edinburgh on the first leg of a journey to Invernessshire. There he was to stay with Millicent Beveridge and her sister Mary at Newtonmore, a Highland village in the upper reaches of the Spey valley. Already, Newtonmore had become a tourist centre and a place of summer residences, like the substantial old house Millie Beveridge owned on the edge of the village.

For all but the grouse-hunter, August is not the best of months to visit the Highlands: it is the wettest, most midge-ridden, albeit usually also the warmest season of the year. Scotland was 'a bit too damp for human habitation' (Wilk 66), Lawrence concluded. But the country was not without allure; there were quick, singular qualities in the Highland landscape which he valued: 'the shadows and lights on the low hills are queer and northern and alive' (Zyt 292), he wrote to Kot on 'The Glorious Twelfth', the beginning of the grouse-shooting season – 'an event for those who shoot, and a still bigger one for those that get shot' (*CL* 930).

The modern age had begun to invade the Highlands. New roads were being driven through the remote valleys, making them accessible to the motorists, whose cars were everywhere. Only on an excursion to Skye for a couple of days did Lawrence find a pristine landscape of wild places that had scarcely been altered since the time of the first human settlement:

It rains and rains, and the white wet clouds blot over the mountains.
But we had one perfect day, blue and iridescent, with the bare
northern hills sloping green and sad and velvety to the silky blue sea.
There is still something of an Odyssey up there, in among the islands
and the silent lochs: like the twilight morning of the world, the herons
fishing undisturbed by the water, and the sea running far in, for miles,
between the wet, trickling hills, where the cottages are low and almost
invisible, built into the earth. It is still out of the world, and like the
very beginning of Europe.

(CL 931)

The Highlands had suited Lawrence, despite the damp climate,
and the end of his holiday at Newtonmore found him in fine spirits
and good health, better disposed to discern life in the people and
places around him. On Saturday 21 August he crossed the border into
England on a train to Nottingham, where he was to spend the night
at Emily King's house, before travelling by car next day to the
Lincolnshire coast.[15]

Emily and Ada had already begun their holidays at Mablethorpe,
and Lawrence was met at the station by his niece, Emily's daughter
Peggy. Their drive together from Victoria Station to the Kings'
house, like the excursions through Derbyshire in the previous year,
appears to have been influential in the shaping of Lawrence's fiction.
In *Lady Chatterley* Nottingham figures under its own name and also as
'Sheffield'. Off Nottingham's St Ann's Well Road, which passed
through a slum area that was notorious throughout the country,
Lawrence placed the 'Sheffield' home of Parkin's friends, the
Tewsons. Lawrence would have passed the road in the car after King
Edward Street ('King Alfred' in the first two versions of the novel), on
the way to the Kings' house off Sneinton Hill. And it was probably of
this drive on a late afternoon in August at the time of the coal dispute
that Lawrence was thinking when he described Connie's journey to
meet Parkin at the Tewsons in *John Thomas and Lady Jane*:

The taxi ran on through the grey August dismalness of the town,
past huge hoardings and chocolate-coloured chapels and miserable
black dwellings. Driving slowly round a corner, Connie saw on a
church notice-board the huge words: *No Reduction In Wages!* In view of
the strike that was then on, startled that a church should make such an
announcement, she looked closer, and saw underneath the first words,
in smaller letters: *The Wages of Sin is Death*. There it was, the Midlands
in one breath!

(JTLJ 348)

Lawrence's visit to the Midlands on this occasion was too brief for him to succumb to its dismalness. Next morning, when he set off early for the coast that had given him his first experience of the sea, he was in exuberant form, chatting in French for much of the journey to help improve his niece's command of a language which, by her account, he spoke with confident imperfection. Like the previous evening's drive through the streets of Nottingham, the journey from the city to the coast on the early Sunday morning seems to have left him with impressions and fragments of experience that he drew on later when writing his novel:

> The car sped along the narrow lanes through the still, fast asleep villages of South Notts. It was all tall hedges and trees and old houses and cornsticks, the threshing machine standing silent in the stack yard because it was Sunday. A quiet little backwater of England.
>
> (*FLC* 226)

Some ten miles from Nottingham, on the road to Lincoln, Lawrence's car began the long descent of the hill down to Southwell. Below in the hollow stood Southwell Minster. Fifteen years had passed since Lawrence last visited the church, whose rounded, Norman arches 'repeating themselves' and seeming to travel ever onward, had symbolized for him 'the dogged leaping forward of the persistent human soul' (*SL* 219). Lawrence stopped off to explore the minster again, giving his niece a lively and memorable commentary on its art and architecture. It was a scene Lawrence recalled in *The First Lady Chatterley*, where Duncan Forbes is discovered 'absorbed in some of the old Norman ornament of the church' (*FLC* 226) at Southwell.

From Southwell the car continued eastwards, across the Trent and into Lincolnshire along the Foss Way, the old Roman road to Lincoln. From Lincoln the best route to Mablethorpe would have taken Lawrence to a village where the road divided, posing the question whether to drive via Louth or Horncastle to the coast. Perhaps for this reason, the name stuck in his mind, and the village of Wragby had its name applied to the hall that was the seat of the Chatterley family. It was probably later, on his return by train to Nottingham, that Lawrence read the name Coningsby on one of the stations he passed through. In *Lady Chatterley* it was used to create the name of a dukedom and the name of a public house in the area of the fictional Wragby Hall. The conjunction of the place-names Wragby and Coningsby in the novel had later repercussions in that corner of Lincolnshire, where a lady from one of the local halls had given birth to a child by one of the estate-workers. A myth was born, according to which Lawrence had not only based his novel on the incident, but had even stayed at the house in question.

The young Paul Morel of *Sons and Lovers* talked endlessly to Miriam of his love for horizontal planes, such as those of 'the great levels of sky and land in Lincolnshire' that signified 'the eternality of the will' (*SL* 219); and Lawrence remained passionately attached to the coast where, during the month of his first stay, in 1902, health and strength had slowly returned to him after an attack of pneumonia which had brought him close to death. On that occasion he had stayed at Skegness, south of Mablethorpe where he had also holidayed in the past, with his family and Jessie Chambers, in a solitary cottage beside the sea-meadows, a good way outside the town. Even by that date Mablethorpe was a burgeoning resort which, like Skegness, drew most of its large summer population from the working classes and lower middle classes of the industrial Midlands.

The bungalow where Ada and Emily were staying was in the heart of Mablethorpe, which was perhaps not to Lawrence's taste, and the house was crowded, with four adults and four children under the same roof. But if there were drawbacks to life *en famille* in a seaside town, Lawrence's pleasure on returning to the Lincolnshire coast was undiminished by them. After his first few days in Mablethorpe he wrote to Brett:

> It's rather nice – quite common seaside place, not very big, with great sweeping sands that take the light, and little people that somehow seem lost in the light, and green sandhills. I'd paint if I'd got paints, and could do it. I like it here, for a bit.
>
> (Hux 668)

On the Saturday following his arrival, Lawrence moved a couple of miles down the long promenade that linked Mablethorpe to Sutton-on-Sea, where he and Frieda occupied a small bungalow, 'one field away from the sea and sandhills' (Sec 75). Frieda had arrived the previous evening; Ada had left for Ripley a few hours earlier. At the end of their holiday Frieda went directly to London, leaving Lawrence to journey alone to Ada's house in Ripley. Clearly the daggers drawn at Spotorno had not been sheathed.

As he walked in fine weather on the wide expanse of sands, with 'a big sky over-head, and a low sea growling in the wind' (Wilk 66), Lawrence was overtaken by a sense of satisfaction and well-being that rather surprised him: 'For the first time for years, I am rather glad to be at home in England' (Zyt 295), he confessed to Kot. For a time there were dank days, when the sea looked like 'a grey slop' (Sec 77) and the deserted shore seemed 'queer and forlorn . . . as if still expecting the Vikings and sea-roving Danes' (CL 934); and on such days he found his thoughts straying southwards towards the warmth, like the swifts that were already beginning their migration. The sea air, at least, was always invigorating – 'so very bracing' (CL 933, Wilk 66) he called it in letters to Brewster and the Wilkinsons, suggesting the subliminal impact of John Hassall's famous 'Jolly Fisherman' seaside poster of 1908, with its slogan 'Skegness is so bracing'.

With Lawrence's discovery that it was still possible to feel contentedly at home in England went a sympathetic response to the people around him, most of them from the towns and cities of the Midlands:

> There seems a queer, odd sort of potentiality in the people, especially the common people. One feels in them some odd, unaccustomed sort of plasm twinkling and nascent. They are not finished. And they have a funny sort of purity and gentleness, and at the same time unbreakableness, that attracts me.
>
> (CL 933)

It was during this period that Lawrence's resolve never to write another novel showed its first signs of weakening. In his first letter to Kot from the coast he reiterated the cynical, word-weary attitude towards writing that had found its way into so many of the letters of 1926: 'I'm so bored by the thoughts of all things literary – why not sell cigarettes!' (Zyt 294). But at the same time he was becoming very conscious of the need to produce something substantial in the near future:[16] eighteen months had passed since he had last completed a major work, and he had a reputation to sustain as well as a living to earn. He had confidence of new life and health for himself, and he projected those feelings into his view of the world around him. His sense of the vivacity in himself and in the people of the Midlands, the latter proclaimed in many of the cards and letters sent from Sutton-on-Sea, appears to have been the principal factor in bringing about the beginnings of a change of heart expressed in a letter to

Secker, written within a few days of the letter to Kot: 'I feel if ever I were going to do an English novel, I'd have to come to England to do it. Perhaps this neighbourhood. But not now' (Sec 76).

The holiday came to an end in a spell of glorious September sunlight. On his forty-first birthday, and on the day following, Lawrence wrote three letters whose contents are especially pertinent to the sources, subject matter and characters of *Lady Chatterley*. In a letter to Orioli he mentioned the Sitwells and their Derbyshire seat, Renishaw Hall, which subsequently lent some features of its setting and appearance to the Chatterleys' Wragby Hall.[17] To Millie Beveridge he wrote of Frank Harris's notorious *My Life and Loves*, first published in 1923, whose pages he had flicked through in spring or early summer in Florence.[18] It had come to the attention of the English press as a result of actions taken by the French government to suppress the book. Considering the fierce disgust and abhorrence Lawrence had felt for Casanova or Joyce's *Ulysses*, his reactions to Harris's book were mild and almost favourable. Though in Lawrence's view some of its scenes were described in a distasteful and degrading manner, he respected what seemed to him – mistakenly, perhaps, in terms of every detail – to be evidence of autobiographical truth and forthright honesty. His assessment of the book may have been a little partisan: as he was probably aware, he had been much indebted to Harris at the start of his literary career.[19] But, even had he felt no personal bias in Harris's favour, he would probably have been disposed to sympathize with his situation as the victim of governmental suppression. As far as Lawrence was concerned, Harris had made a stand for the right to express the truth of matters pertaining to human sexuality. He did not see why Harris should not be allowed to expose his raw inner self to the reading public if he so wished, and he believed Harris's treatment of sex might have a cleansing effect on the public mind, like a spoonful of purgative medicine.

Lady Chatterley was intended to have the same effects on the public consciousness that Lawrence discerned in *My Life and Loves*. And Lawrence's novel also parallels Harris's autobiography in that in an oblique manner, principally through the gamekeeper, Lawrence exposed, to a degree unprecedented in his writings, sexual experiences, obsessions, fears, fetishes and minor perversions that can reasonably be assumed to have been for the most part his own. Every Lawrence novel is in some sense his own *My Life and Loves*, and it is

unlikely that Harris's book had a singular influence in determining
the frank treatment of sexual topics in Lawrence's last novel. Nevertheless, Lawrence's awareness of Harris's book, and of the problems
Harris faced in France, may well have been extremely influential in a
more general way. It served to remind him, at a time when he was
thinking of returning to novel-writing, of an aim and a challenge
which it had always been his ambition to fulfil.

During his holiday at Sutton, Lawrence had come to detect life in
his native regions; and over in the coalfields of the Midlands there
was also struggle, which was alarming, new and, for a writer,
alluring. The strike was continuing, and the situation in the East
Midlands was growing uglier now that some of the owners had
reopened the pits with offers of pre-stoppage wages, thereby induc-
ing some of the men to break ranks and return to work. What
Lawrence learnt from reports in the newspapers, and probably also in
letters from Ada after her return, suggested that the bubbling force
manifest in the vivaciousness of the people might be a magma
which, under the conditions of welling class-consciousness and
repression, could burst forth in violent, eruptive destruction. These
fears of a long-term prospect of revolution, which inform all versions
of *Lady Chatterley*, the first draft especially, had been defined in a
letter to his sister-in-law, Else Jaffe, towards the end of August.[20]
His letter of 12 September to Arthur Wilkinson also foretells of
revolution, and summarizes perfectly the thoughts and feelings of his
three weeks' holiday in Lincolnshire:

> We leave here tomorrow – and I'm rather sorry. I've got quite into
> touch with my native land again, here – and feel at home. It's a lovely
> September morning, with bright sun and a wind, and nearly high
> tide, and long, thin waves uncurling down the long, long sands. I
> think perhaps next year we may come here for five or six months. The
> sea-side is such a good place for doing nothing in. One has a hut on
> the sands, and the sea does all the shuffling about that is necessary . . .
> The coal strike continues – and in the coal areas it's a serious business
> . . . This will be the beginning of a slow revolution here in England
> . . . I do hope, in the fresh autumn we'll have some walks and picnics
> – and really discover the place a bit. I ought to do some work – I don't
> touch a pen all this time – but the Lord sends the wet with the fine.
> Tell Mrs Wilkinson to tie a string to her ankle, when she goes off into
> the 4th dimension, so that she can be pulled safely back when she's
> got beyond recall. Four is a dangerous number, as you realise when
> you're forty.'

(Wilk 66)

These were Lawrence's major preoccupations and his prevailing moods as he prepared to return next day to his native district – pessimistic apprehension over the future of English society, personal optimism, buoyancy and well-being, a new sense of belonging, and a feeling that it was high time he got on with some serious writing.

7

Return to Eastwood

On 13 September 1926 the Lawrences left Sutton and went their separate ways, Frieda to London, and Lawrence to Derbyshire. There he exchanged the tonic sea air and wide horizons of the Lincolnshire coast for the polluted atmosphere of a cramped, grimy, red-brick townlet that was hemmed around with collieries and iron-works. Ripley, about six miles from Eastwood and just to the west of the Erewash river border that divides Nottinghamshire and Derbyshire, had been 'home' to Lawrence on visits to his native Midlands ever since his sister Ada's marriage in 1913 to Eddie Clarke, who ran a tailoring business in the town. The business had prospered and the Clarkes now had a substantial detached villa, newly-built in the 1920s suburban style with wide mock-tudor gables and with large, carefully tended gardens, complete with tennis court, to the rear of the house. Lawrence's sister's fulfilment of their mother's dream of 'getting on' in the world was 'much more concrete' (*Ph 2* 261) than his own, but it had not taken her so very far from the rows of mean colliers' dwellings of their childhood. The house sat in the heart of Ripley town, and 'the black-slate roofs beyond the wind-worn young trees at the end of the garden [were] the same thick layers of black roofs of blackened brick houses, as ever '(*Ph 2* 262).

As Parkin the gamekeeper remarks in *John Thomas and Lady Jane*, 'a sister's home isn't like your own' (*JTLJ* 369), and Lawrence, no less than his gamekeeper, may often have preferred the idea of a night in 'a dry ditch' to 'a bed in people's houses'. As he set out on the train journey across Lincolnshire and Nottinghamshire, Lawrence probably had a number of reasons for dreading what might lie ahead. Visits to the people and the country of his early life had generally left him in a state of depressive exhaustion, brought on by distressing feelings of proximity to his past and a sense of alienation from everyone and everything in the Midlands of the present. On his last stay at Ada's, less than a year ago, he had felt himself smothered by painful memories of childhood, while in the smoke-laden atmosphere of the town he literally gasped for breath between coughing fits. Living with Ada was Gertie Cooper, a dear friend from the days at Lynn Croft in Eastwood. In other circumstances this would have been a happy encounter, but she was now suffering from what Lawrence feared was an advanced state of consumption, so that meeting her would be saddening on her account and might bring to consciousness an acknowledgement of the truth of his own condition.

Possibly with anxious thoughts such as these in mind, Lawrence had determined that this visit should be a short one, with the result that effectively he had only two days in which to meet old friends and tour the surrounding countryside before boarding the train for London on 16 September. Nonetheless, his experiences and impressions during this brief stay seem to have provided him with a conjunction of locations and themes that were to play a considerable part in the making of *Lady Chatterley* – Eastwood and the countryside round about it, Renishaw Hall and his car journey to and from the hall, the visible evidence of the destruction of 'Old England', and signs in the mining dispute of an impending class war. Although it cannot be proven, there is much in Lawrence's actions on those two days to suggest that he could already have had in mind a new Midlands story, and that he might have been purposely seeking out material for it.

On Tuesday 14 September 1926 Lawrence paid his last visit to his home town and to the neighbouring fields and woods that he later named 'the country of my heart'.[1] On that day a group of nine men and three women from Ripley were tried at Heanor, a Derbyshire mining town three or four miles away, on charges concerning the intimidation of a miner who had returned to work. Lawrence evidently witnessed the send-off the women received when a motor coach arrived at the market place to take them to the court. He described the incident in 'Return to Bestwood', where he gave the impression that it happened in Eastwood ('Bestwood') and that he knew some of the women involved:

> There was a scene in the market-place yesterday, a Mrs Hufton and a Mrs Rowley being taken off to court to be tried for insulting and obstructing the police. The police had been escorting the black-legs from the mines, after a so-called day's work, and the women had made the usual row. They were two women from decent homes. In the past they would have died of shame, at having to go to court. But now, not at all.
>
> They had a little gang of women with them in the market-place,

waving red flags and laughing loudly and using occasional bad language. There was one, the decent wife of the post-man. I had known her and played with her as a girl. But she was waving her red flag, and cheering as the motor-bus rolled up.

(*Ph* 2 259)

Ripley market-place was the terminus of the tram-line that ran between Nottingham and Ripley via Eastwood, and Lawrence probably observed the women's demonstration while waiting for one of the 'green and creamy coloured' tram-cars of whose 'reckless swoops' and 'breathless slithering'[2] he had written in the comic short story, 'Tickets Please'. The adventure of the journey by tram to Eastwood was to be the first of many experiences that would make the day seem like an excursion through the scenes of almost the whole corpus of his Midland stories and novels.

One of Lawrence's purposes in visiting Eastwood was to meet an old friend, William Hopkin, without whose aid *Lady Chatterley's Lover* might never have been written. Hopkin, then approaching his mid-60s, had known Lawrence since the day when, as a young man of 23, he had bumped into Lawrence's mother as she emerged into Nottingham Road from Victoria Street, wheeling a pram in which lay a sickly child that she despaired of ever rearing. He observed his development through boyhood and youth and was quick to recognize the promise of distinction. He was also saddened by seeing him often cold-shouldered and squashed in the tough, normative mining community where he was known as 'Soppy Lawrence'; and he determined to repair the damage to Lawrence's ego by providing him with the encouragement and the environment which would enable his personality and his talents to flourish.

Hopkin and his wife Sallie, to whom Lawrence became especially attached, were uniquely in a position, as far as Eastwood society was concerned, to confer these benefits by inviting him into their circle. They were free-thinking, radical intellectuals, whose local eminence in movements for social reform had led to friendships with socialists and suffragettes of national repute. Men and women of the stature of Ramsay MacDonald, Philip Snowden, Sydney and Beatrice Webb, Charlotte Despard and Annie Kenny had been visitors to the Hopkins' Sunday evening open-house sessions at Devonshire Drive, where there would be music, readings, discussions, or simple amusements and free-wheeling chatter.[3] Lawrence, who regularly

103

attended these gatherings, later acknowledged the Hopkins' contribution to his intellectual development: 'You two led me over several frontiers',[4] he told Willie in a letter written on the occasion of Sallie Hopkin's death.

Over the years Lawrence had cause to be grateful for several other acts of kindness. Hopkin had, for example, been the first of Lawrence's seniors to encourage him to become a writer, and when a local man, White Holdich, threatened a law-suit over the harmless portrayal of his wife as 'Alice Gall' in *The White Peacock*, Willie had intervened to dissuade him.

So far as is known, Lawrence had not been back to Eastwood since November 1918. Now, nearly eight years later, Sallie Hopkin was dead, Willie had married again and moved to a new bungalow on Nottingham Road, and Lawrence was returning to a changed world to seek another favour. In Willie's version of events, from which the mundane detail of a previous telephone call has probably been omitted, Lawrence walked into his house one morning exclaiming breezily, 'Come along Willie, I want you to go for a walk with me.'[5]

The walk seems to have had a twofold purpose for Lawrence. It was to be a sentimental journey on which he sought to reacquaint himself with scenes of his past life, perhaps in the knowledge that he would never return to them again; and it also gives the impression of having been undertaken in order to refresh his knowledge of the area. On the route he proposed to take there would be Will o' the Wisp revenants from his early life eddying forth from almost every glade; and though Lawrence was never lacking in most brands of courage, it is doubtful whether he would have had the spirit to confront those ghosts of memory alone. He needed companionship, and Willie, solid, cheery and sympathetic in character, a man who shared Lawrence's knowledge of and delight in the natural world, and who had enjoyed many a long walk with Lawrence in the past, was in many respects admirably qualified to accompany him.

One suspects, however, that it was not just for old times' sake or for the pleasure of his company that Lawrence sought out Willie Hopkin. Part of the woodland walk he wished to follow lay off the public footpaths. The permission of the gamekeepers would therefore be required if he was to enter those parts of the woods. For Willie, a well-known and respected public figure, a member of the urban district council and a former Nottinghamshire county councillor, it would be an easy matter to get the keepers' consent, which he had frequently obtained on past occasions. There were other respects, too, in which Willie could be of service to Lawrence. If Lawrence was considering a work of fiction or an essay that centred on modern Eastwood, Willie was in a special position to give a detailed account of the local history of the coal dispute, in which, as a socialist, he had been actively involved on behalf of the miners. And he could also furnish, as he had done in the past, a store of 'good old crusty Eastwood gossip' (*Let 2* 122) that Lawrence might later draw on.

Fortunately for the present-day biographer, writing was one of Willie Hopkin's many leisure activities. It is thus possible from the several reminiscences of Lawrence which he composed for radio and for local newspapers to put together a very full account of their last walk together which, as it turns out, provided Lawrence with a great deal of material for the physical description of woodland scenes and walks in *Lady Chatterley*.

Hitherto, details of their walk in 1926 have been known only from the text of a BBC Third Programme broadcast in 1949, which Hopkin submitted to Nehls for inclusion in his composite biography of Lawrence. The part of this text which describes their last meeting was, in fact, a revised and much abbreviated version of a more ample account which he published in the *Nottingham Journal* in 1942.[6] This newspaper article, supplemented by details from the Nehls text and from another reminiscence of Lawrence, published in 1936,[7] is the source of my reconstruction of Lawrence's walk. I have also profited enormously from information and advice given to me by Hopkin's widow, Olive Hopkin, who still resides at the Nottingham Road bungalow that Lawrence visited.

At the outset of their walk Lawrence and his companion made their way towards Lawrence's old home in Walker Street,[8] passing *en route* the inn on Three Tuns Lane. The Three Tuns became, in *John Thomas and Lady Jane*, the Tevershall pub which was barred to the game-keeper's wayward wife by the landlady, Mrs Anthony; and the name Lawrence gave her was the forename of Anthony Fitzpatrick, landlord of the inn in Lawrence's father's days. The inn had been one of Arthur Lawrence's favourite drinking-places, and the sight of it inevitably brought him to mind. Lawrence spoke affectionately of his father, who had died two years earlier, and he confessed to Willie that Arthur Lawrence had been unkindly treated by his family in the old days. The hard, bitter feelings towards his father which he projected into his portrayal of Walter Morel in *Sons and Lovers* had disappeared by the early 1920s and he now looked back on his family life from a different perspective, from which Arthur Lawrence and the children were seen as the damaged victims of the wilfulness and self-righteousness of his wife Lydia. Lawrence's father had come to represent sentient contact with life and continuity with the spirit of England's rural past, before mechanization and nonconformist education came to deaden and castrate the working men of the nation.

It is plain from Willie Hopkin's account of his dealings with Lawrence, which show him often to have been the butt of irascible or lordly remarks, that theirs was not always an easy relationship. Although their views of the world were not dissimilar, they differed profoundly in their notions of how society should be reformed, and each was inclined to preach and to speak his mind with awesome candour. Willie found Lawrence at times 'savage' and 'abominably rude' (Nehls 1 73), while Lawrence, for his part, thought Willie irritatingly sentimental and impudent. There were moments on the early stages of their walk, it appears, when the faults that each detected in the other surfaced and threatened to mar the day entirely.

Lawrence began the walk in a testy frame of mind, a symptom of the emotional turbulence that showed itself in more obvious ways on other occasions during the day. When they reached the Beauvale Schools, where he had spent a large part of his boyhood, Lawrence paused for a minute or two in quiet contemplation. Willie, who seems to have thought that Lawrence wished to be treated as a visiting dignitary, asked if he would like to go inside the school: '"Certainly not!" was his reply'.

The Beauvale Schools were in Dovecote Lane, which led out of the town towards the picturesque country cottages, open fields and farms of the village of Moorgreen. As they proceeded along the road they passed the Ram Inn. Willie asked a harmlessly ingenuous question about sources for the character of the 'landlord' of the inn of that name in *The White Peacock*[9] and received a rather haughty response. A little further along the road, almost opposite Renshaw's farm, where the family of Lawrence's Aunt Polly had lived, was the cottage May Chambers and her husband Will Holbrook had lived in before they emigrated to Canada. Here Willie could not resist the temptation to ask why Lawrence had not married her sister, Jessie. Lawrence swore at him, telling him to mind his own business, and marched on in silent fury for several minutes. Then he apologized and gave Willie an answer: 'It would have been a fatal step. I should have had too easy a life, nearly everything my own way, and my genius would have been destroyed' (Nehls 1 71).

Lawrence's irascibility subsided as he began to leave behind the manmade world and drew nearer to the quiet places in and around the woodlands. By the time they reached Moorgreen Corner Willie and he were happily reflecting upon 'the good old days' when Lawrence grew up in Eastwood. At the corner, opposite the Horse and Groom Inn, they turned to walk for a few yards along the main road to Watnall, possibly the 'Crosshill' of the last two versions of *Lady Chatterley*. [10] Ahead of them the grey tower of Greasley Church stood among tall beech trees, and across the road from the church, invisible to Lawrence, lay the fields where he had worked with the Chambers family – the setting for 'Love Among the Haystacks' and for scenes in *The White Peacock* and *Sons and Lovers*. Already, thoughts that were to be developed in *Lady Chatterley* were beginning to surface. Earlier he had discussed with Willie the change in the mentality of the miners since his boyhood; and on being reminded of the 'Love Among the Haystacks' fields he asked anxiously after them, fearing that they might have been destroyed by one of the housing developments that were spreading over the English countryside.

Just beyond the Horse and Groom Lawrence branched off the main road into the New Road, a narrow lane that ran out towards the edge of the woodlands and then turned sharply away towards Watnall. As they walked along the lane Lawrence mused on a picture of the Eastwood area as it might have been before the Industrial Revolution defaced the rural scene. The distant prospects from the New Road were magnificent, and still are. In the diffusion of mist, smoke and sunlight on an early September morning the distant mining settlements and the factories appear only as indistinct blotches of dull red and grey in a dark green amphitheatre that seems thick with woodland. Under such light-conditions, apparently similar to those Lawrence experienced, it is easy to imagine the mining countryside as it might have been in its rural past, or to conjure up visions of what might have been if the villages that cluster around the hills had developed like the hill-top villages of Tuscany.

Near the head of the shallow valley that lay below the New Road stood the ruin of Beauvale Priory, serving as a reminder of the lost England of medieval times. In the same valley, below the priory, the ugly present stood near at hand in the shape of the winding-gear and pit-heap of High Park Colliery, which kept its real name as one of Sir Clifford Chatterley's pits in the first two versions of the novel. In the near distance, a little further down the valley, was Moorgreen Colliery, the Tevershall pit of *Lady Chatterley*.

On the other side of the New Road ran a low, steep ridge, edged at the top with a narrow strip of oak-wood. Pointing to the ridge, Lawrence said: 'On that spot stood a forest ranger's cottage and he used to beat his wife.' What made Willie Hopkin consider this apparently inconsequential remark worth reporting? It must surely have been because, like many of the other remarks quoted in his *Nottingham Journal* article, he thought it had some relevance to Lawrence's fiction. The duties of a forest ranger – to police the woodlands and protect the game – are similar to those of a gamekeeper; and the wife-beating is reminiscent of the domestic strife between Lawrence's gamekeeper and the slatternly Bertha Coutts.[11] It seems, then, that Willie Hopkin believed that some of the inspiration for *Lady Chatterley* came from this chance sighting of the place where an old cottage had stood.

Just below the summit of the ridge that Lawrence was pointing to were the Shortwood cottages, two houses placed one in front of the other, which today are both in ruins. The one nearer to the road and more plainly visible has the air of having been abandoned in the fairly recent past. The other, smaller cottage, which can just be glimpsed from the road, could well have been derelict at the time of Lawrence's visit. It is now completely ruinous, though substantial parts of the walls remain. What is interesting about those walls, in terms of Lawrence's model for the keeper's cottage in the novels, is the dark red sandstone from which they were built. This was the only cottage in the neighbourhood of the woods that was built of stone, like the gamekeeper's, and the colouring of the stone matches perfectly the description in *Lady Chatterley's Lover*, where the stone of the cottage appears 'almost rosy, like the flesh underneath a mushroom'.[12] Like the cottage in this last version of the novel, it seems also to have had 'a pent-house scullery' (*LCL* 173) at the back. The land behind sloped up steeply, as it did in the descriptions of the cottage in all versions of the novel, and on the slope there grew orchard trees, as in *The First Lady Chatterley* and *John Thomas and Lady Jane*.

The siting of the keeper's cottage in all versions of the novel is left rather vague, but there are enough details to suggest that in the first version, at least, the site may have corresponded very roughly to that of the Shortwood cottage. Further up the New Road, along which Lawrence and Willie Hopkin were walking, the colliery railway from Moorgreen pit to Watnall ran parallel to the road. As the line reached the slopes of the woods it entered a cutting, where the railway was crossed by a bridge, over which passed a grassy track that branched off the New Road and led into the forest towards Robin Hood's Well. At dawn, as Connie of *The First Lady Chatterley* lay with the keeper at his cottage, she heard the sound of a train in the cutting.[13] Later, when making arrangements for another night together before her departure for France, she devised a system of signals for communicating her plans to Parkin: a green shawl hung from her window at Wragby would tell the keeper that instead of waiting for her at the wood-gate in the park he was to 'go back to the cottage and down to the lane end at the railway bridge, a good four miles away, because Connie would get down there, at the bridge over the cutting, and walk down the lane to the cottage' (*FLC* 133). The four miles' distance by road between the railway bridge and Wragby Hall fits only loosely that between the bridge off the New Road and Lamb Close House, home of the colliery-owning Barber family and one of the models for the Chatterleys' Wragby. There is a much closer fit in *John Thomas and Lady Jane*, where the distance between the park gates and the bridge is reduced to 'nearly three miles' (*JTLJ* 268), and here the bridge is reached by a 'side-road to Crosshill', just as the bridge off the New Road was approached by a side-road to Watnall. But in this version Lawrence began the process of rearranging and obscuring the original geography: the bridge is sited *on* the side-road, and access to the cottage is by an 'overgrown lane, that led only to the cottage, between high hedges at the wood's end' (*JTLJ* 270). From the final version the whereabouts of the original for the gamekeeper's cottage are indiscoverable: the cottage is placed on the north side of the woods, in the opposite direction to the Shortwood cottages; and the dispositions of road, bridge, railway cutting and lane entrance have been altered in a manner that seems deliberately to lay a false trail which leads, if one follows the route of Connie's sister's car from Mansfield, bypassing the village of Bolsover, to the forbidding gloom of the Barlborough Drive entrance to Renishaw Hall, the Sitwells' residence in north-east Derbyshire.

A few hundred yards up the New Road from the Shortwood cottages were the modern houses where the keepers of 1926 lived. There Lawrence and Hopkin would have called to ask permission to walk in the forest, which they probably entered via the track that branched off the New Road and passed over the railway cutting. This would have given the shortest route to their first goal, Robin Hood's Well, which figures in every version of the novel, though only in the second version does it go by its real name. [14]

In every version of the novel the well has the status of a shrine, dedicated to the spirit of the forest, a symbol of sex, life and continuity with the past, which Connie Chatterley visits on several occasions in the course of the story. According to Willie Hopkin, it was a spot where Lawrence and his schoolfriends had spent many happy hours, and perhaps it was for what it evoked of the romance of childhood that he regarded it as the holy of holies of the forest. Lawrence's behaviour at the well, which he had visited with his brother Ernest on the occasion of Ernest's last return to Eastwood not long before his death in 1901, [15] was described thus by Hopkin:

> Stooping down he drank some of the icy cold water and then sat down hugging his knees and apparently lost in thought.
> I watched his face across which smiles and sadness chased each other like the clouds and the sunlight overhead.

Judging by Lawrence's description of the well in *The First Lady Chatterley* it was then, as it is now, a rather eerie, gloomy spot, around whose banks hung 'that silence and woe of places which had lived long ago and lost their life' (*FLC* 49):

> Constance found Clifford already at the spring, a little way up the opposite dark hill, where the larch-wood bristled with a burnt appearance all round, and great leaves of the burdock shoved out into the riding. It was ghostly and sinister as ever.
> Only the spring was pretty. It bubbled up in a little, brilliantly clear well that had pebbles on the bottom which wavered and danced. Bits of eyebright and cinquefoil flowered among the grass on the bank. Then the water ran rapidly downhill in a tiny ditch.
>
> (*FLC* 109)

A little way beyond the well there had been a long, narrow, timbered building, with some brickwork and a fireplace inside. Here, when Willie Hopkin was a boy and the people had been allowed free access to the woods, they made tea for the dances held on Maid Marian's Dancing Green nearby. Only the outline of the hut now remains, and it seems to have been in a tumbledown state when

Lawrence and Hopkin saw it: in *The First Lady Chatterley* the gamekeeper describes it as a 'sort of summer house' that 'used to be . . . down against the spring' (*FLC* 48). Some believe this building was also the model for the gamekeeper's hut. It may have influenced Lawrence's descriptions, but it looks as though, in describing the hut, the clearing and the narrow path that led to it, Lawrence was drawing on memories of a furtive visit to a keeper's hut in High Park Wood that he made as a boy with one of the Chambers girls. This boyhood exploit is described in the memoirs of May Chambers:[16]

> In the rich glow of afternoon we entered the shadows of the great oaks, and followed a narrow path to the heart of the wood, then in between trees, where I signalled him to be silent. I sniffed and listened, then drew him towards a tiny clearing where stood a little pavilion of poles with the bark still on. His eyes widened with amazement as we stepped on the deep green grass.
> 'What is it?' he whispered.
> 'The keepers' hut', I whispered back.
> 'They might be around', he suggested.
> 'No, there's no smell of tobacco smoke.'
> We drew away down a path.
> 'They've never caught me here yet', I said, 'and I've been scores of times. Its like a fairy tale, 'I could make a story about it, couldn't you?'[17]

From Willie Hopkin's several accounts of Lawrence's last walk over the old ground, and from the correspondence between the fictional topography of the novels and the actual physical features of the landscape in and around the woods, it is possible to follow quite closely the route Lawrence took from Robin Hood's Well to the point where he rejoined the Alfreton–Watnall road at Willey Lane, near the tip of Moorgreen reservoir and not far from Lamb Close House which stood on a promontory on the opposite side of the road. In all versions of the novel the journey Clifford and Connie make to and from Wragby Hall and the well in the woods reflects a substantial part of Lawrence's route. What is omitted is that section of his route which comprised a walk from a point near Annesley Lodge to Annesley Kennels and back again to the lodge. This part of the walk appears only in *John Thomas and Lady Jane*, where Lawrence's return from Annesley Kennels provides the itinerary, described with real place-names, for a Sunday afternoon stroll undertaken by Connie and Parkin.

111

On leaving Robin Hood's Well, Lawrence would have descended, as Sir Clifford did, 'the damp, grassy, uneven riding' (*FLC* 110) through the larch woods towards the main riding through the woods, which seems to have changed little in its outline from the time of Lawrence's visit. There, where the track from the well joined the main riding, they reached 'the bottom of the dip [in the riding] and turned to the long slope ahead' (*FLC* 110). During Connie and Clifford's excursion to the well, Clifford's wheelchair had 'softly curved out of sight' of Connie, watching from above, 'as the riding swung round in the dip below' (*FLC* 108). The present riding still follows this downward curve, which bends to the right, as does the riding in *John Thomas and Lady Jane*. At the dip at the bottom of this slope, as Connie and Clifford were returning from the well, Clifford's motorized wheelchair failed on the steep incline and had to be manhandled back to the hall by the keeper.

Lawrence and Hopkin would have followed the long upward slope of the riding until they reached a point where five of the forest ridings met. There they seem to have joined the public footpath from Misk Hill, emerging from the dense woodland into the open, grassy cleft that rose gently towards a bare knoll between Morning Springs and Park Springs woods. Here, and on the hillside leading up to the knoll from Felley Mill, Lawrence found that the First World War had had an enduring effect on the physical landscape of England. Like many other woodlands up and down the country, parts of High Park and Morning Springs Woods had been felled for trench timber, and places 'that he remembered tree-covered and secret . . . [were] now bald and exposed' (*JTLJ* 26).

At this point, near Annesley Lodge, known locally as 'the Jacobean House',[18] the footpath from Misk Hill joined the track between Felley and Annesley. The route Lawrence gave Clifford and Connie lay to the left, down the hillside, towards Felley Mill. Lawrence and Willie Hopkin were to take that path later in their walk. First, they turned right along the track that skirted the edges of the woods and took them, after a mile or so, to the Old Kennels belonging to Annesley Hall.[19] One of the Kennels cottages Lawrence had made the home of Annable, the gamekeeper of his first novel, *The White Peacock*; and in the woods, a field away from the Kennels, was the old quarry where, in the novel, Annable's body had been discovered. In fact so many of the places Lawrence passed on his last walk in these parts had been drawn on in *The White Peacock* that it is tempting to suppose that the journey was planned with *The White Peacock* in mind, but it is probably more likely that his itinerary was intended to take in favourite spots of his youth, which inevitably coincided with the sites of scenes in the novel.

Some of Lawrence's old haunts, those closest to Haggs Farm, were deliberately avoided. 'In later years', according to Willie Hopkin, 'he would never go anywhere near Felley for the memory of the old days and the old friendships were [*sic*] too vivid to be borne'.[20] Maybe that was the reason why he did not take the expected route to Moorgreen reservoir from Annesley Kennels. This lay along a pathway that he had known well in the past and had described in *The White Peacock*: it followed Weaver's Lane, on the opposite side of the valley to the woodlands, and descended to pass Felley Mill pond and the mill farm. Instead, he evidently chose to return to the denuded knoll near the Jacobean House, because it is there that we find him next in Willie Hopkin's report of their walk.

Several months later Lawrence trod that ground yet again in his imagination when penning the conclusion to *John Thomas and Lady Jane*. At that point in the novel, in order to give the impression that the setting for the main action was far away from the area between Annesley and Felley, Lawrence shifted abruptly into the use of place-names that were real and appropriate to the locality. He was describing a Sunday afternoon walk, many miles distant from Wragby, that Connie and the gamekeeper had arranged. They met at Hucknall Torkard and walked to Annesley, where they 'took a footpath that led round past the deserted kennels, towards Felley Mill' (*JTLJ* 373).

In the woods to the right of the footpath from Annesley Hall, not far from the old quarry near the Kennels, Lawrence and some of the Chambers children had once come across a little dell that was thick with primroses:

> With cries of delight we fell upon them and gathered bunches, when suddenly we saw a young girl, very well-dressed and very prim, who passed us haughtily. As we were trooping out, a hoarse shout came, and looking around, we saw an angry keeper who waved a stick at us and called on us to stop. Threateningly he called upon my eldest brother [Alan] and Bert to stand apart and drove the rest of us off.
>
> (Nehls 3 594)

Lawrence had recalled the scene in *The White Peacock*[21] and perhaps the memory of it returned when he was walking near the spot with

Hopkin. When he was completing *John Thomas and Lady Jane*, it must have occurred to him that it would be an amusing irony if he were to use the scene again, and this time have one keeper, Parkin, caught by another. Connie and Parkin, having strolled off the path that led by the Kennels, make their way 'into a little hollow of a wood' (*JTLJ* 374), where they are discovered in the act of making love by a fat, burly, very Annable-like keeper, who warns them that 'Squire and some of 'is folks is walkin' a bit down the 'coppy' (*JTLJ* 374f.). The two lovers rejoin the path and continue through the derelict countryside in the direction of Felley. Surveying the scene, the narrator comments: 'The path, the whole hillside is a desert now, given over to rabbits and strolling colliers. In a sense it is dead. The kennels are grown deep in nettles. Dead as Nineveh!' (*JTLJ* 376). Lawrence and Hopkin, following the same path, reached the Jacobean House and the steep fields above Felley Mill. Near a fallen thorn tree Lawrence paused and stood gazing out over the country beyond, with a look of intense grief upon his face. The scene before him was the one which later marked the conclusion to *John Thomas and Lady Jane*:

> Across was Haggs Farm, and beyond, Underwood, the mining village and the mines. The old, old countryside where Byron walked so often, and Mary Chaworth. Now colliers straying with their lasses, from ugly Underwood, from Eastwood, from Hucknall. And the millponds at Felley, lying so still, abandoned, abandoned like everything that is not coal or iron, away below. The dead countryside! and the grisly live spots, the mining settlements!
>
> (*JTLJ* 376)

In the moments when his gaze turned towards the abandoned mill-ponds at Felley he was looking down upon the scene that opened *The White Peacock*:

> I stood watching the shadowy fish slide through the gloom of the mill-pond. They were grey descendants of the silvery things that had darted away from the monks, in the young days when the valley was lusty. The whole place was gathered in the musing of old age. The thick-piled trees on the far shore were too dark and sober to dally with the sun, the reeds stood crowded and motionless. Not even a little wind flickered the willows of the islets. The water lay softly, intensely still. Only the thin stream falling through the mill-race murmured to itself of the tumult of life which had once quickened the valley.
>
> (*WP* 1)

The final scene of one version of his last novel thus drew to its close with a glimpse of the scene that had opened his first novel. In the time that had elapsed between writing the two novels Lawrence had passed from ailing early manhood to mortally stricken middle age, while in the same period the country around Felley seemed to have degenerated from the languor of old age into the inertia of death.

Willie Hopkin studied Lawrence as he looked out over the countryside, and then, overcome himself by the sight of Lawrence's emotion, walked away from him, down towards the mill-pond. 'I have seen sadness on many a face', he wrote, 'but nothing like Lawrence's at that moment'. His grief was perhaps compounded of reaction to the desolation of the countryside and of memories of an intensity of joy that could never be relived. In a well-known letter to David Chambers, written some two years after his last sight of Haggs Farm, he tried to put into words the feelings that thoughts of his young days at Haggs evoked in him:

> Whatever I forget, I shall never forget the Haggs – I loved it so. I loved to come to you all, it really was a new life began in me there. The water-pippin by the door – those maiden-blush roses that Flower would lean over and eat and Trip floundering round. – And stewed figs for tea in winter, and in August green stewed apples. Do you still have them? Tell your mother I shall never forget, no matter where life carries us. – And does she still blush if somebody comes and finds her in a dirty white apron? Or doesn't she wear work-aprons any more? Oh, I'd love to be nineteen again, and coming up through the Warren and catching the first glimpse of the buildings. Then I'd sit on the sofa under the window, and we'd crowd round the little table to tea, in that tiny little kitchen I was so at home in.
>
> *Son' tempi passati, cari miei! quanto cari, non saprete mai!* – I could never tell you in English how much it all meant to me, how I still feel about it.
>
> (*CL* 1100)

Although in actuality he could no longer bear to approach the farm, he returned to it in his imagination in each of the three versions of *Lady Chatterley*, where it goes by the name of Marehay Farm, named after a farm on the western edge of Ripley. In the first version Lawrence had Constance pass by the farm and return to the hall by the route from the Haggs to Willey Lane that Lawrence had habitually taken in the past – 'through the thick fir plantation called the Warren' (*FLC* 74) and across the fields, described as 'the open park' in the novel. In the second and third versions Constance calls in at the farm, to be greeted first by the barking of 'Bell', the dog (plainly, in *Lady Chatterley's Lover*, the Chambers' white bull-terrier, Trip, which he had given the name 'Bill' in *Sons and Lovers*), and then by Mrs Flint. Mrs Flint is a former schoolteacher, described in *John Thomas and Lady Jane* as 'a rather pretty woman already beginning to fade' (*JTLJ* 131), who has a baby that is redhaired, like its father. Lawrence was thinking of May Chambers, whose husband William Holbrook had hair of that colour. Flint, the name with which he concealed her identity, was the name of the family at Willeywood Farm, a mile away from the Haggs on the opposite side of Willey Lane.

After spending several minutes in sad contemplation of the lost *locus amoenus* of his youth, Lawrence continued, like Connie and Parkin after him, 'down the tussocky hill, above the grey-green country' (*JTLJ* 376) and rejoined Willie Hopkin. For a good while they walked together in silence, following the path that ran through the woods beside Felley Brook, along by Moorgreen reservoir, and then out on to Willey Lane. When at last Lawrence spoke again, he 'went off into a lot of brilliant nonsense to hide his emotion'.

But for the fact that it was taken in an opposite direction, the route Lawrence and Hopkin had followed between Annesley Kennels and Willey Lane was identical to the one he recommended most strongly to Rolf Gardiner in the celebrated 'country of my heart' letter of December 1926:

> Go till you come to the lodge gate by the reservoir – go through the gate, and up the drive to the next gate, and continue on the *footpath* just below the drive on the left – on through the wood to Felley Mill (the *White Peacock* farm). When you've crossed the brook, turn to the right through Felley Mill gate, and go up the footpath to Annesley. Or better still, turn to the right, uphill, *before* you descend to the brook, and go on uphill, up the rough, deserted pasture – on past Annesley Kennels – long empty – on to Annesley again. That's the country of my heart.
>
> (*CL* 952)

A large section of the walk Lawrence prescribed for Gardiner is followed on several occasions by Connie or Connie and Clifford in each version of the novel. A little further up from where the pathway from Felley joined Willey Lane, just past the reservoir, and on the opposite side of the road, stood Lamb Close House. This house, the seat of the Barber family, was Wragby Hall of the novel in terms of its immediate geography of woodlands, woodland paths, a nearby coalmine and adjacent mining settlement, though the wider geography of Wragby's setting, and some features of the hall and its park, derive from the Sitwells' Renishaw Hall. In the topography of the novel, Moorgreen reservoir and Willey Lane disappear entirely, and the red gravel drive that ran from 'the lodge gate by the reservoir ... to the next gate' (*CL* 952) is extended beyond its actual beginning at the lodge as a path that led up across the park to the hall.

The correspondence between real and fictional landscapes is perhaps closest in the description of Clifford and Connie's excursion to Robin Hood's Well in *The First Lady Chatterley*. Connie follows Clifford's chair as it moves 'slowly along the red gravelled path' (*FLC* 106) across the park. When they reach the wood she opens the gate and they pass through to 'the open cleft of the riding between the silent grey trees', taking what in real geography was 'the footpath just below the drive on the left' (*CL* 952). They journey on, through a hazel copse, and 'at a cross-path [where the nearer of the two footpaths to Annesley joins the path to Felley] came to the open oak-wood, which sloped uphill in a beautiful free slope' (*FLC* 107). They climb the slope, 'where many trees had been cut during the war', until they reach the top of the hill. In real terms they had come to the clearing near the Jacobean House, and from that point they make their way down the gentle slope of the forest riding and up to Robin Hood's Well on the hillside opposite.

With the exception of Connie's walk from Marehay Farm (the Haggs), which depicts scenes that could never have grown dim in Lawrence's memory, all the country walks that are described in any detail seem to reproduce some part of Lawrence's itinerary, and many of the country scenes of *Lady Chatterley* lie on or near that route.[22] His ramble with Hopkin seems, therefore, to have had a seminal influence on the making of *Lady Chatterley*, in that it provided the material out of which was created the fictional woodland landscape which is a vital feature of the symbolism and the structure of the novel.[23] The walk was a necessary precursor to *Lady Chatterley*, not simply because it renewed Lawrence's knowledge of the lie of the land and enhanced his capacity to give detailed physical descriptions of scene, but more importantly because it provided him with fresh emotional and imaginative responses which made it possible for him to write, with immediacy and from a different point of view, of the old landscape that had figured prominently in *The White Peacock* and *Sons and Lovers*.

When Lawrence and Hopkin reached Willey Lane and began to walk up the short hill towards Engine Lane (the 'Engine Row' where Mellors was lodging at the conclusion of *Lady Chatterley's Lover*), the rural part of their walk was almost at an end. Ahead of them, already visible above the crown of the hill, were the buildings, the head-stock and pit-heap of Moorgreen Colliery. The pit, standing harshly incongruous amidst fields of wheat, had been a familiar and even attractive sight to Lawrence in the past, if the sentiments of Paul Morel in *Sons and Lovers* accurately represent those of the author:

> 'The world is a wonderful place', she said, 'and wonderfully beautiful.'
> 'And so's the pit', he said. 'Look how it heaps together, like something alive almost – a big creature that you don't know.'
> 'Yes', she said. 'Perhaps.'
> 'And all the trucks standing waiting, like a string of beasts to be fed', he said.
> 'And very thankful I am they *are* standing', she said, 'for that means they'll turn middling time this week.'
> 'But I like the feel of *men* on things, while they're alive. There's a feel of men about trucks, because they've been handled with men's hands, all of them.'
>
> (*SL* 154)

His reactions to the colliery in 1926, reported in 'A Dream of Life', were altogether different. Moorgreen pit, modernized and expanded, no longer redolent of animal life, had been deserted by man and nature:

> At Engine Lane Crossing, where I used to sit as a tiny child and watch the trucks shunting with a huge grey horse and a man with a pole, there are now no trucks. It is October and there should be hundreds
> . . .
> And the pit is fuming silently, there is no rattle of screens, and the head-stock wheels are still. That was always an ominous sign, except on Sundays: even when I was a small child. The head-stock wheels twinkling against the sky, that meant work and life, men 'earning a living', if living can be earned.
> But the pit is foreign to me anyhow, so many big buildings around it, electric plant and all the rest . . .
> It is different now: all is much more impersonal and mechanical and abstract . . . Moorgreen is no more what it was: or it is too much more. Even the rose-bay willow-herb, which seems to love collieries, no

longer showed its hairy autumn thickets and its last few spikes of rose around the pit-pond and on the banks.[24]

Like other signs of degeneration towards the impersonal and abstract cited in 'A Dream of Life', the sight of the new buildings and electrical plant was probably not a new one to Lawrence – the plant is mentioned as one of Gerald Crich's improvements to the mines in *Women in Love* – but it was nonetheless a jarring reminder, whose impact was no doubt heightened by Lawrence's years of having lived surrounded by natural beauty, of deterioration in the architectural landscape and of discontinuity with the homely past of childhood. In *Lady Chatterley* Moorgreen Colliery may have played a dual role. It was certainly the model for Tevershall pit whose chimney could be seen from Wragby Hall park and whose burning pit-bank filled the hall with its sulphurous stench. And it may also, in conjunction with other collieries that Lawrence witnessed on the following day in Derbyshire, have contributed to what would appear to have been Lawrence's only pejorative description of a coalmine, that of the monstrous colliery with 'all the astonishing and frightening overhead erections of a really modern mine' (*JTLJ* 157, *LCL* 160) at Stacks Gate, which is partly Eastwood in another guise (see below, Chapter 8).

From Moorgreen Colliery Lawrence and Hopkin proceeded along Engine Lane towards Greenhill Road and the rows of miners' dwellings known as The Breach, where Lawrence had spent his earliest years. Beyond the dust-blackened hedgerows on the right of the road, and running parallel to it, was Beauvale Brook, whose course had been the site of some of the favourite spots of Lawrence's boyhood – the dam and waterfall of Annable's mill at Beggarlee, the bathing-place at the dipping-hole near the fall, and the old stone sheep-bridge not far from the Breach houses.[25] The disappearance or adulteration of each of these places is catalogued in 'A Dream of Life': the dam, a term applied in the local dialect to the stretch of water behind an embankment, had been excavated in 1913 and converted to an outdoor swimming-pool that was of concrete construction, as were parts of the bed along which the stream now flowed; the waterfall had gone with the building of the swimming-baths, and the old bathing-spot at the sheep-dip had likewise disappeared; the sheep-bridge had been replaced by a new one of iron.[26] The reminder of the passing of these features of the landscape of childhood, whose loss had probably been registered on previous visits to Eastwood, served to point up the gulf which now separated him from his past. 'That life seemed a hundred years' ago!' he remarked to Willie Hopkin as he passed The Breach without a glance in the direction of his old home – 'an end house of hideous rows of miners' dwellings' (*Ph* 261).

The ugliness of modern dwellings, the insentience of the architects who set the houses in harsh parallel lines, and the spread of housing estates over the countryside are prominent features of the 'one England blots out another' theme which is common to each version of *Lady Chatterley* and comes to the fore in the great *tour de force* which describes Connie's journey by car from Tevershall to Uthwaite and Shipley Hall.[27] The role of modern housing in the extinction of the old agricultural England of the rural past is especially prominent in the account of Connie's drive in *Lady Chatterley's Lover*, where glimpses of the 'great plasterings of brick dwellings on the hopeless countryside' (*LCL* 162) pervade the whole narrative – 'new "villas"' (*LCL* 159) on the road out of Tevershall, a 'reddish plastering of miners' dwellings, newish' (*LCL* 160) at distant Warsop, 'rows of handsome "modern" dwellings, set down like a game of dominoes' (*LCL* 160) at Stacks Gate, pink rows of new houses 'plastering the valley' (*LCL* 162) of Uthwaite, and 'an array of red-brick semi-detached "villas" in new streets' (*LCL* 165) which would in the future constitute the Shipley Hall Estate.

This motif, like many of the others in *Lady Chatterley*, was not a new element in Lawrence's fiction. It had, for example, been emphatically stated, with even greater rhetorical force than in *Lady Chatterley's Lover*, at the conclusion of *The Rainbow*, where the image of advancing disease, (merely hinted at in *Lady Chatterley's Lover*) is made explicit.[28] In *Lady Chatterley* the spread of housing developments had a special contemporary relevance to the England of the early 1920s, the period in which the action of the novel is set. Under a Ministry of Health scheme set up in 1919, local authorities had been required for the first time to provide decent housing for people who could not themselves afford it, and the effect of these measures was to stimulate a building boom which lasted until the downward turn in the fortunes of the economy in 1921. Later, in an attempt to regenerate the building industry, the Conservative government of 1923 introduced a new bill by which government subsidies, to be administered by local authorities, were to be paid on each new house that was built. Preference was given to private rather than local-authority building, thus giving free reign and encouragement to the speculative builder. New plots of small houses, such as those Lawrence described on the Shipley Hall Estate, began to mushroom throughout the land. Eastwood itself had not, however, been substantially affected by these waves of building. Such building as there was seems to have been on a relatively small scale: under the 1923 scheme, for example, the urban district council planned to have a hundred houses built by September 1926.

There was a measure of hyperbole in Lawrence's claim in 'Return to Bestwood' that the place was all built up and that he was never quite sure where he was in Nottingham Road, Eastwood's main thoroughfare.[29] Closer to the truth was his account of the town in 'A Dream of Life', where he confessed that though 'Newthorpe' (Eastwood) had changed in character over the last twenty years, it had not grown by all that much.[30] One change in the way of new building that had occurred since his last visit, and which he noted in 'Return to Bestwood', was the extension to Gabes Lane, now renamed Wood Street. Leading off from Nottingham Road and curving downhill towards The Breach, where there had once been open ground and allotment gardens, was a street of red-brick, semi-detached villas of the kind he no doubt had in mind when, later, he wrote of the new streets of the Shipley Hall Estate in *Lady Chatterley*.

The new houses may have first come into view as Lawrence passed by The Breach, which is the point where Willie Hopkin's narrative comes to an end. They must have walked from The Breach to Nottingham Road, because it was just off this main street where Lawrence met Charles Leeming, a former pupil of his at the British School, Eastwood, where Lawrence had spent four purgatorial years practising the 'savage teaching of collier lads' (*Ph 2* 593) during his period of teacher training. Leeming had a keen eye for detail and a good memory:

> I stood against Clarke's tailor's shop at the top of Alexandra Street – Bert's younger sister married Eddie. Somehow I felt something warm behind me. I turned round and I saw Mr Hopkin and Bert Lawrence. Mr Hopkin shouted to me 'Charles, come across here.' I did. He said 'Do you know who this is?' 'Yes.' 'Who is it?' I said 'Bert Lawrence', and Bert was looking down Alexandra Street and slanting sun in his eyes. It would be about half-past four. He giggled, I think, kind of giggled and said 'Yes, you're right.' But he looked miserable, I

thought, yes, miserable – his eyes seemed to be glazed somehow – and afterwards Mr Hopkin said he was most miserable. You see it would be the last time he'd come to Eastwood distressed him. He'd seen so much of it – strikes, misery, poverty. Really there was not much poverty in Eastwood [in the past], because there were not many people when I was a boy in Eastwood, and everybody knew one another and helped one another.[31]

Lawrence felt that the colliers of his native district were the only people who moved him strongly, and with whom he sensed a connection 'in deeper destiny'. 'It is they', he wrote, 'who are, in some peculiar way, "home" to me' (*Ph 2* 264). And yet, as he acknowledged, he was no more at home with the working classes than with the middle classes, with whom he felt no such human flow. His behaviour on meeting Charles Leeming – the shy giggle of embarrassment and the disinclination or incapacity to relate to him, implied by his staring down the street and by the glazed eyes – seems to bear out part of what Lawrence said of his relations with the colliers in 'Return to Bestwood': 'I shrink away from them, and I have an acute nostalgia for them' (*Ph 2* 264).

Alexandra Street, where Lawrence met Charles Leeming, led down to Devonshire Drive, where Willie Hopkin and his wife Sallie had lived; and at the end of the short drive the new Devonshire Drive Schools had been built. It looks as though Hopkin took Lawrence to see the new school and that they were on their way to or from Devonshire Drive when Willie hailed Charles Leeming, because the school provided one of the models for the school buildings of Tevershall, described in the context of Connie's drive through the town in the final version of the novel: 'Just beyond [the Congregational chapel] were the new school buildings, expensive pink brick, and gravelled playground inside iron railings, all very imposing, and mixing the impression of a chapel and a prison.'[32]

Alexandra Street is one certain point on Lawrence's walk through Eastwood after leaving The Breach. For the rest one can at least be sure that they walked up the long hill of Eastwood to Willie Hopkin's bungalow near Hill Top, and it was perhaps this walk through the long straggle of Eastwood that furnished the impressions for Connie's drive through Tevershall. The uphill journey that she makes through the village of *The First Lady Chatterley* plainly corresponds (with the exception of the siting of the church at the top of the hill) to one that climbs Eastwood's Nottingham Road, with the chapels of the various sects properly named after their Eastwood counterparts and placed in the appropriate order. In the book, however, they are presented as if each one were visible from the road – the Wesleyan chapel, the Methodist chapel, the Congregational chapel and the Christadelphian chapel (this last being on Dovecote Lane at Hill Top).

In *John Thomas and Lady Jane* the same journey through Tevershall draws on real geography in a different way. It begins as one that passes up Nottingham Road, with the chapels now decked out in accurate detail: 'The Wesleyan Chapel stood behind iron railings. It was of blackened red brick, with stone facings, and black notice boards. The Methodist Chapel, higher up, was newer, still rather pinky, red in comparison with the other buildings, and like a large cinema building, with a big slate roof' (*JTLJ* 155). The cinema image prompts the narrative vision to shift to Tevershall's concrete picture-palace, which was Eastwood's 'Empire' on the corner of King Street, further up Nottingham Road. But there follow, next, views of the Congregational chapel with its sandstone walls and its steeple, of the school behind it, and of the Sun Inn, whose landlord, Sam Black, was a former schoolteacher. It becomes clear that what Connie sees on her drive up through Tevershall corresponds to what might have been seen, had one wandered off the main road on occasion, on a journey that went up Eastwood hill as far as the cinema and then descended again to the Market Place where stood the Sun Inn, managed by Sam Wood, who had taught at the Beauvale Schools when Lawrence was a boy. In the novel, Connie's car, having reached the Sun Inn, with the old church on the left, 'began to slip greasily downhill, past the Mechanics' Hall and its much more modern successor, the Miners' Welfare, on towards Stacks Gate' (*JTLJ* 156). Translated into Eastwood geography, this means that the car turned at Eastwood Market Place down Mansfield Road, past the building that in Lawrence's day had housed the Mechanics' Hall and by 1926 had become the premises of the Miners' Welfare Club.

In *Lady Chatterley's Lover* the narrator's eye takes in all the places mentioned in the second draft, but now the drive *uphill* through Tevershall corresponds to a journey *downhill* through Eastwood, with the Wesleyan chapel therefore deceptively placed higher up the hill than the chapel of the Primitive Methodists. But these are perfunctory attempts at disguise, and Eastwood emerges all the more clearly from the picture of Tevershall as a result of the added list of public houses, all bearing their real names: 'the Wellington, the Nelson, the Three Tuns, . . . the Sun . . . the Miners' Arms' (*LCL* 156). To this version of Tevershall has also been added a garage where the chauffeur fills Connie's car with petrol. This was Leivers' Garage, the latter-day descendant of the Star Livery Stables of Lawrence's youth and of *Sons and Lovers*.

When Hopkin and Lawrence parted company at the end of the day, Willie asked when Lawrence would be coming over to Eastwood again: '"Never. I hate the damned place!", was his bitter reply.' Such unalloyed hatred did not reveal itself in those writings that followed closely upon his last visit. 'Return to Bestwood' registers depression, a sense of alienation, and opposing emotions of 'devouring nostalgia and an infinite repulsion' (*Ph 2* 257). Connie in *The First Lady Chatterley* reacts to Tevershall in similar fashion:

> It was the hopeless, dismal ugliness that so depressed her. She had been used to Sussex, and a lovely old house in the fold of the downs. She could never get used to this awful colliery region of the north Midlands. And yet she liked it too: it gave her a certain feeling of blind virility, a certain blind, pathetic forcefulness of life. If only it could realise how ugly it was and change a bit.
>
> (*FLC* 60)

In the sentiments attributed here to Connie Chatterley, there is continuity with those of Alvina Houghton in *The Lost Girl*, the last of Lawrence's previous 'Midland' novels to deal at length with the Eastwood district. The impressions of Tevershall in *The First Lady Chatterley* accord with Connie Chatterley's emotional reaction to the place. There is pathos in its universal paltriness and drabness, instanced by Connie's fleeting glimpses from the passing car of 'small dwellings with glistening black slate roofs like lids: and poky shops with stacks of soap, or turnips and pink rhubarb, or huddled drapery' (*FLC* 59). Like its chapels, the village is 'dreary and ugly to a degree', but the degree is not extreme, as it is in subsequent versions.[33]

A change of mood from the tranquil contentment of the period when he began the first draft of the novel made for a very different portrait of Tevershall in *John Thomas and Lady Jane*, which shows a reversion to the position in regard to the Eastwood area that Lawrence had held in *The Rainbow* and in *Women in Love*. The 'long, dark-red straggle' (*FLC* 59) of Tevershall in the original draft gives way in this version to a 'long, sordid straggle' (*JTLJ* 155), which picks up an epithet that had been prominent in the description of Beldover (Eastwood) in *Women in Love*. Gudrun, returning from her new life in Chelsea and Sussex, compared the coalmining country to an underworld: 'The colliers bring it above ground with them, shovel it up' (*WL* 11). Connie, 'accustomed to Scotch hills, Kensington, or Sussex' (*JTLJ* 156), is struck by the same image: 'transplanted into these Midlands, she seemed to have left England altogether, to have entered some weird and unnatural country where everything came from underground' (*JTLJ* 156). As in *Women in Love*, the subterranean nature of the place is suggested by the blackness that pervades it; but here, in *John Thomas and Lady Jane*, the touches of red amid the black add a lurid, infernal quality to the appearance of the village: to the 'black slate roofs' of the first version are appended 'black-red miners' dwellings', 'black earth', 'blackened red brick', 'black notice-boards', 'black trees' (*JTLJ* 155f.). Sympathy for the people of Tevershall, implicit in Connie's liking for the place and her sense of its virility in *The First Lady Chatterley*, has begun to be withdrawn. The men face a hopeless position with desperate courage, but, like the people of Beldover in *Women in Love*, they have an outward ugliness that reflects their environment, and an inner being that is likewise determined: 'men with weird, incomprehensible, underground natures, like trolls' (*JTLJ* 156). The voice that in manner and tone seemed in *The First Lady Chatterley* to be authentically Connie's begins to yield to the rhetoric and generalizing commentary of the author: 'It was as if the dismalness of the climate had penetrated into every human expression and all was dismal, dismal, dismal, fatally and fundamentally so' (*JTLJ* 155).

'It is just a nightmare.' With these words Lawrence concludes his reflections on Tevershall in *Lady Chatterley's Lover*. Blackness settles yet more densely over the landscape, the pejoratives ('squalid', 'awful', 'appalling', 'terrible', 'ugly', 'weary-looking', 'forlorn', 'distorted', 'dead') multiply, and the visual images are made more repellent: 'the black earth' of *John Thomas and Lady Jane* is transformed into 'mud black with coal-dust', 'the cinema . . . built of concrete' becomes 'the plaster-and-gilt horror of the cinema' (*JTLJ* 155, *LCL* 158). But the real nightmare of Tevershall lies not so much in its ostensible frightfulness as in the responses of the mind that contemplates the sights and sounds of the village. And in this version there is no attempt to create the illusion that the mind into which one sees is Connie's: the insistent, incantatory rhythms and repetitions of the expression of reflections on Tevershall are the characteristics of Lawrence's own 'passionate drive of willed purpose'.[34] 'The utter hopeless absence of any beauty, any cheer at all' (*JTLJ* 155) of *John Thomas and Lady Jane*, which is just about credible as one of Connie Chatterley's thoughts, is expanded and intensified to 'the utter negation of natural beauty, the utter negation of the gladness of life, the utter absence of the instinct for shapely beauty which every bird and beast has, the utter death of the human intuitive faculty was appalling' (*LCL* 158).

'The horror of that creeping disease!' Aldous Huxley wrote when he was preparing his edition of Lawrence's correspondence. 'Its progress is painfully visible between the lines of the letters when one sees them all in the mass.'[35] The decline in spirits attested through the successive stages of the evolution of *Lady Chatterley*, and epitomized in the three portraits of Tevershall, might equally be regarded as symptomatic of Lawrence's physical degeneration, though it is in the transition from second to final draft that the change of authorial mood can be most convincingly linked to physical causes. The bout of haemorrhages that preceded the writing of the final version was unquestionably the determining factor in the shift of outlook towards an unqualified, despairing revulsion for modern man and his works that was without precedent in any previous writings. The intrusive self, the raging misanthropy and the tendency to overstatement that distinguish *Lady Chatterley's Lover* emerge clearly from a comparison of the responses to the awful singing of the Tevershall schoolchildren. In *John Thomas and Lady Jane* Connie, who overhears them, thinks to herself: 'How could they call that noise singing? It had as much relation to song, spontaneous song, as the squeaking on the brake of the coal-cart coming down the hill' (*JTLJ* 155). In the final version, what they conveyed implicitly through the simple, concrete image of the squeaking brake, is made explicit in a long-winded misanthropic tirade which is almost absurdly overstated:

> Anything more unlike song, spontaneous song, would be impossible to imagine: a strange bawling yell that followed the outlines of a tune. It was not like savages: savages have subtle rhythms. It was not like animals: animals *mean* something when they yell. It was like nothing on earth, and it was called singing. Connie sat and listened with her heart in her boots as Field was filling petrol. What could possible become of such a people, a people in whom the living intuitive faculty was dead as nails, and only queer mechanical yells and uncanny will-power remained?
>
> (*LCL* 158)

The nightmare of despair which had descended upon Lawrence by the time he began his final revision of the novel was the misanthropic dejection of a sick man who regarded himself as an outcast from society and viewed his own position as exemplary of the isolation of every individual in the modern industrialized world. 'There can be no fellowship anymore' (*LCL* 159), Lawrence lamented at the close of his description of Tevershall in *Lady Chatterley's Lover*. Little more than a year earlier, when he passed wearily through the streets of Eastwood at the conclusion of his walk with Willie Hopkin, he had also been touched by despair, but it was a despair born of sympathy for a people with whom he felt linked in a common destiny. The mood of depression which habitually attended a return to his native regions was deepened by the sight of the striking miners, standing idly at street-corners, 'white as cheap wax chandles, spectral, as if they had no selves anymore . . . with not a tuppence to rattle in their pockets' (*Ph* 818). It was not simply their desperate poverty that moved Lawrence: it was the fact that they were 'poor with a hopeless outlook'. In September 1926, it must indeed have seemed to a miner on strike that his position was a hopeless one. With the strike beginning to break up in the Eastwood area, the men still on strike were faced with a choice from two equally unacceptable alternatives: to accept a humiliating defeat and return to work, having achieved nothing by their months of sacrifice; or to stay out at the risk of being victimized and denied the possibility of ever working again at any of the pits in the Eastwood area.

It had been a cheerless day for Lawrence, relieved only by the beauty of the woodlands and by bitter-sweet moments such as he experienced on returning to Robin Hood's Well. The visit ended in the late afternoon when Willie and he boarded the tram for Ripley, where they were to have dinner at Ada's house. When Lawrence neared the Hill Top area of Eastwood on the way to Willie Hopkin's new bungalow, he found there no September Wakes fair in which to immerse himself and shed his cares in the way Harry T. Moore envisaged in *The Priest of Love*.[36] The Wakes had ended more than a week before Lawrence arrived, and the experiences Moore described had belonged to a previous visit to Eastwood.

At dinner that evening, Lawrence sat at the head of the table, with Ada at the foot. Eddie Clarke, a withdrawn and timorous man in company, had little to say for himself. Olive Hopkin, sandwiched between Lawrence and Willie, who between them did most of the talking that night, had little opportunity to join in the conversation, which was mainly anecdotal talk of Eastwood folk, past and present, and of Eastwood in the old days. Lawrence had valued Willie as a fount of Eastwood gossip in the past, and he may have sought him out partly for what he could provide in the way of source material. It may not have been a fact that all of the Eastwood people who figured as minor characters or gave their names to characters in *Lady Chatterley* were discussed that evening over dinner, or even during the day. But there is a fair certainty that some, at least, would inevitably have been mentioned in any talk of the old days. Significantly, perhaps, a number of the Eastwood characters in *Lady Chatterley* had in one way or another been associated with Willie Hopkin. Indeed, it seems very likely that the gossip of Mrs Bolton, Clifford's nurse, is that of Willie Hopkin dressed up in feminine style, for those of her attributes set out in this passage from *John Thomas and Lady Jane* are plainly Willie's:

> Clifford would ask Mrs Bolton for all the local news, and she, a born talker, fascinated all her life by the psychology of other people, having lived the lives of the colliers and colliers' wives vicariously for many years, would tell him all the news. The figures he had known as a boy, when the world still seemed safe, and which he had almost forgotten, she created for him again.
>
> (*JTLJ* 109)

Lawrence and Willie had a common foe in Henry Saxton. Lawrence remembered him bitterly as the bullying Sunday School superintendent of his boyhood who had been his mother's idol as Eastwood's finest example of the 'getting on' ethic which she tried to inculcate in her children. He was Willie's political enemy on the urban district council, whose chairmanship he had managed to abrogate to himself in perpetuity. In Mrs Bolton's chit-chat about Tevershall in the early 1920s, his name appears only slightly altered, while that of his daughter, Camilla, is changed to Cassandra:

> There was Henry Paxton, the burly self-made grocer who had been so loud upon the parish council and the urban district council: he was over eighty now, and paralysed, but still a tyrant. His daughter Cassandra, still an old maid, now fifty years old – how Clifford remembered the tall, wild, raw-boned, rather simple young woman – waited on him hand and foot.
>
> (*JTLJ* 109)

Willie's father, from whom he had acquired the shoe shop which he ran on Nottingham Road, was still alive in 1926, and was recalled in Ivy Bolton's conversation as 'old James Allsop, the boot-and-shoe Allsop, also over eighty, but nimble as a boy' (*JTLJ* 109). Miss Tattie Allsopp, the 53-year-old daughter of James Allsopp, mentioned in *Lady Chatterley's Lover*, was Willie's spinster sister Louie, given an altered form of the name of his other sister, Hattie. Kitty Allcock, daughter of Edward Allcock of the local building firm of Allcock and Sissons, had been a close friend of Willie's daughter Enid. She became, in *John Thomas and Lady Jane*, Cassie Allcock, whose father had built 'those new houses in Chat'ley road' (*JTLJ* 198).

Willie's old house in Devonshire Drive had belonged to the widow of the colliery manager, as Lawrence recalls in *The Rainbow*, where it figures as the house the Brangwens occupied when they moved to Beldover. Edward Lindley, general manager of the Barber, Walker collieries in Lawrence's day, appears as Mr Linley, 'a thin, red-faced, quiet man from the north' (*JTLJ* 123), manager of Clifford's collieries in each version of the novel. His wife, 'a blonde, over-dressed woman out of a country vicarage, very obsequious and toadying' (*JTLJ* 123), whom Connie could not stand, is Willie's former landlady, whose queenly airs and graces made her an unpopular figure in Lawrence's Eastwood.

Duncan Forbes, who was enamoured of Constance Chatterley, derives his profession and appearance from the artist, Duncan Grant, whom Lawrence met through David Garnett in an unhappy encounter in 1915. But his name is that of Willie Hopkin's old friend, the local GP, Dr Duncan McDonald Forbes, who had married into the Barber family. Perhaps because he attended the birth, Dr Forbes's names had been given to Duncan McDonald Forbes Meakin, a son of the horse-trading family of Lawrence's short story, 'The Horse-Dealer's Daughter'. When Lawrence attended Nottingham High School, he travelled on the same train as Meakin and Constance Chatterley, daughter of the secretary and estate agent of the colliery company;[37] and it seems to have been this association which led Lawrence to link the names of Duncan Forbes and Constance Chatterley in the novel.

As a young man Willie Hopkin had worked as a clerk in the offices of the Shipley Colliery Company, near Heanor. The company's owner, Alfred Edward Miller Mundy, 'Squire Mundy', a dapper and diminutive figure, was a well-known character in Eastwood and the surrounding district, where he had a reputation as a just and benevolent employer with whom the Barber family was unfavourably compared. There is a widespread belief in Eastwood that the scandal of his wife's elopement with her lover provided Lawrence with the source story for *Lady Chatterley*. However, the event occurred six years before Lawrence was born, and the social stature of the wife's lover, the young Earl of Shrewsbury, hardly matched that of a gamekeeper.

The idea that the plot of *Lady Chatterley* was inspired by the Mundy elopement may have arisen because it was recognized that Mundy was associated with the novel. It was not, however, as a cuckolded husband that he figured in the story, but as an elderly bachelor, a friend of the Chatterleys, and a colliery owner, like Clifford. In *The First Lady Chatterley* the name of the character, 'Squire Manby', resembles Mundy's, but in subsequent versions it was changed to 'Winter'. Mundy, like the squire in *Lady Chatterley*, was a kindly, tolerant man, who allowed the local people free access to his estate, provided they kept to the drives and footpaths. Shipley Hall, the squire's residence in *Lady Chatterley*, took the name of Mundy's house, which was the principal and perhaps the sole model for the fictional Shipley.

In reality, as in fiction, the house had been visited by King Edward VII. Mundy was a friend of the King, who paid an official visit to Shipley in 1904, but whose usual practice, both as King, and earlier as Prince of Wales, was to travel there incognito during the week of the Doncaster Races. Willie had related one anecdote concerning the King's visit in the weekly column he wrote under the pseudonym 'Anglo-Saxon' for the *Eastwood and Kimberley Advertiser*;[38] and he was probably the source of the story, embodied in the account of the squire in *Lady Chatterley*, of how the King observed that if there were coal under the lawns of Sandringham, he would open a mine and consider it fine landscape gardening.

It was probably from Willie, too, that Lawrence heard of Mundy's death in 1920 and of the subsequent fate of Shipley Hall. As in the novel, Mundy's heir had other houses, and elected to abandon Shipley. From this point, however, the histories of the real and fictional Shipleys diverge. Lawrence had the novel's Shipley demolished, while, in fact, the hall was sold and served for a while as colliery offices. In 1926 it would have been a topical subject of conversation, because in that year was held a great auction, which stripped the hall of furnishings and interior and exterior fitments, leaving it an uninhabitable shell.

Willie Hopkin's most distinct contribution to *Lady Chatterley* was himself. In the past Lawrence had drawn on Willie for Willie Houghton in the play *Touch and Go* and Lewis Goddard in the novel *Mr Noon*. In *Lady Chatterley* he appears in a number of guises. He lent a little to the character and conversation of Mrs Bolton. He appeared, with strong dialect speech that was not his natural idiom, as Willie Tewson, the earnest, ingenuous, plain-speaking socialist from Sheffield, with whom the gamekeeper stayed in *The First Lady Chatterley*, and as Bill Tewson, his reflex in *John Thomas and Lady Jane*. In this version Willie was also cast as Lewie Rollings of Tevershall: 'Yes, Lewie Rollings was still alive; and married again. Yes, he still talked socialism and wrote for the *Tevershall and Stacks Gate News*. But he hadn't any influence anymore. His kind of socialism was all words and being funny about people like Henry Paxton' (*JTLJ* 110).

Ada, and Lawrence's Nottingham sister, Emily, had been his chief informants on the progress of the coal dispute. Back now in his home regions, he could observe the situation for himself and turn for an informed history of events to Willie Hopkin, whose interpretation would probably be coloured by his socialist opinions., When Lawrence returned to Eastwood, the miners' strike, for it was a strike in the Nottinghamshire area, where the owners had not posted lock-out notices, was in its twentieth week. Through the weeks of increasing gloom and tension, order and good conduct had generally prevailed in the community. When the strike first began to break up in mid-August a large crowd – called 'a mob' in the local newspaper, but described as 'a Sunday School procession' by Hopkin in a speech to the urban district council – had marched through The Breach to Moorgreen Colliery to demonstrate against the men who had returned to work. But on reaching the colliery precincts, where a large body of police was waiting to move the demonstrators on, the crowd had turned away peaceably towards Hill Top. The next morning a situation arose which could have led to arrests under the stringent prohibitions of the 1926 emergency regulations. A crowd had gathered to urge the strike-breakers not to return to work, but again a potentially ugly situation was averted when, on the advice of the local police sergeant, the crowd dispersed.[39] In fact, in all the weeks of the strike, the only lawless incident involving Eastwood men had occurred on the banks of the Erewash canal, when a small band of strikers had set upon two black-leg miners going home from work. It was a nasty little incident, though hardly the stuff of which revolutions are made; and the fracas seems to have been partly a family affair, the ring-leader of the assailants, who confessed to having been somewhat the worse for drink, being the uncle of one of the victims.[40]

The Nottinghamshire miners, like their leaders, had begun the strike with little stomach for the battle, and in the course of the dispute most of the militant voices to be heard at meetings in Eastwood came from orators from outside the area. The local men had nothing to gain and a great deal to lose from a prolonged struggle. The coal produced in the Nottinghamshire and Derbyshire coalfield was for home consumption, and the local owners, having no need to cut production costs in what had always been profitable mines, had not sought the reduction in wages that owners in other areas had demanded. The Nottinghamshire miners' strike had therefore not been prompted by local grievances but by loyalty to men in other areas, and as the weeks went by and the hardships increased, solidarity alone proved an insufficient motive to keep all the Eastwood men out. At Eastwood, as in Nottinghamshire as a whole, the commitment to trades unionism was not strong, and the notion of a strike as a weapon in a revolutionary class struggle would have seemed ludicrous to all but a handful of men.

Only half the Nottinghamshire miners were unionized, and the remaining half of the workforce had no strike pay to look forward to while they were out. As it happened, they were to be little worse off than the union men, because the Nottinghamshire Association began the strike with empty coffers. One week's strike pay came out of loans from other union sources; after that members received only a few shillings a month from donations by the Russian trades unions.

To the striking miners of Eastwood the only ways of saving themselves and their families from starvation were to draw on savings, pawn any belongings, or seek aid from the board which administered the poor laws in the district. The local body offered relief to the families of able-bodied men only as loans to be repaid with interest. By the time of Lawrence's visit the board had lent so much that an overdraft of £126,000 had been run up, and under pressure from its bankers the board was considering putting an end to all relief by the end of the week. A relief fund had been set up by the urban district council with the main aims of giving help in cases of extreme distress and ensuring that the children were fed and adequately shod. By the second week in September its monies had been almost exhausted.

In mid-August the Nottinghamshire and Derbyshire colliery owners saw that the time was ripe to throw open the pits, bypass the union officials and appeal directly to the men to return to work on roughly the same wage as before the stoppage and an extra half-hour on the day. By the end of the month thousands of Nottinghamshire miners had signed on for work and a large number had actually gone back to the pits. Men of Barber, Walker's Eastwood collieries, along with those who worked for the Bolsover Colliery Company, were the first to break ranks. In early September coal was being turned at all five of the Barber, Walker mines, where 700 underground workers had gone back. Areas like Eastwood, where the most money was made, were always difficult for the union officials to control, but the knowledge that the local leaders were in favour of a settlement must have done little to dissuade the strike-breakers. Despite appeals for solidarity there had been, according to the local paper, 'something of a rush back to work' in the week of Lawrence's visit.[41]

To prevent intimidation and quell any possible disorder hundreds of police from outside the area – 'great big strange policemen with faces like a leg of mutton' (*Ph 2* 258) – were drafted into districts where the pits had opened. The local folk were hostile to these aliens, calling them 'blue-bottles', 'blow-flies' or 'meat-flies', the last of which terms Lawrence picked up and used of the Tevershall local policeman in *The First Lady Chatterley*. Resentment of the police presence in Eastwood was by no means confined to militant socialists. And the Barber, Walker Company's owners succeeded in attracting a good deal of that resentment to themselves by publishing a pamphlet claiming responsibility for calling in the police. The cold hostility of the Tevershall community to the mine-owners in *Lady Chatterley* was closely paralleled by the general mood in Eastwood at the time of Lawrence's visit. It was universally felt to be an insult to Eastwood that a community that had been traditionally peaceable should be treated as potentially threatening to civil order; and on the day before Lawrence's visit the urban district council had carried and forwarded to the Home Office a motion protesting against the importation of police and calling for an immediate withdrawal.[42]

The strikers were hungry, but just about managing to subsist on an inadequate diet, and they were not in an overtly revolutionary mood. But the whole community was in an utterly wretched condition – divided, confused, fearful and close to despair. The miseries of the strike had been spread throughout the town: it was not only the miners who were heavily in debt; tradespeople like Willie Hopkin saw bankruptcy just around the corner. Those who had not returned to work, still a large majority of the workforce, were under enormous strain. A situation was being reached where even the tough communist leader of one of the Eastwood branches of the union would feel he had no right to impede negotiation with the owners, when men came begging him for God's sake to do something for them before they were thrown on the streets.[43]

There was anger against those who had returned to work, and in the hearts of the men who remained solid an earnest wish to do the same. Many were afraid that if they, too, did not soon break strike they would be victimized by the owners. In this event they would lose their jobs, their houses and the means of repaying monies borrowed from the Board of Guardians. Family responsibilities and pressure from wives to honour these obligations drove the men towards the open gates of the collieries; conscientious regard for their fellow-strikers held them back. Beneath clouds of depression the neurotic tensions of being driven hither and thither crackled in the air of the mining communities, and rumours spread like wildfire: one popular belief, symptomatic of the fear and mistrust which pervaded the townlets and pit villages, was that the strange police were in reality crack Grenadier guardsmen decked out in police uniform.[44]

As he walked through Eastwood, Lawrence gauged accurately the atmosphere of the place, and sensed 'a doom over the country and a shadow of despair over the hearts of men'. His experiences of the effects of the strike on the morale and circumstances of the miners and their families in Eastwood, together with scenes he witnessed on the following day when he toured the mining districts of north-east Derbyshire, were narrated in 'Return to Bestwood'. This short essay, and a previous draft, 'Getting On', were perhaps written while he was staying at Ada's, when his experiences were fresh in his mind.[45] In the essay one can see already crystallized many of the views which were to form the burden and preoccupations of *The First Lady Chatterley*.

Judging by 'Return to Bestwood', Lawrence saw in Eastwood nothing very remarkable in the way of incidents connected with the strike and little that was suggestive of strife between labour and capital. A couple of weeks after Lawrence's visit, Willie Hopkin wrote in his column that 'thanks to the coal-owners and the Government, the miners have gone definitely Red, even in this meek and mild town'.[46] To what extent his opinions corresponded to the objective truth of the situation is hard to tell. If the criterion of redness was hatred of the bosses and a stubborn resistance to strike-breaking, then Hopkin was probably not far wrong; but if he meant that the men had become political activists, dedicated to the class struggle, then his views must have better reflected his hopes than the actual state of things. This, at any rate, was Hopkin's opinion, more important than the actual truth where his influence on Lawrence is concerned: since Willie would have been his only authoritative informant regarding the history of the strike and the current state of opinion in Eastwood, he must have played a significant part in shaping Lawrence's picture of the situation.

Ada would have been Lawrence's source concerning the situation on the Derbyshire side of the coalfield, and it is possible that what she had to relate seemed to confirm the interpretation which an idealistic socialist like Willie put upon events. Unlike Willie, she would have been able to cite local incidents which lent substance to the notion of a new militant antagonism towards capital in the coalfields. Ripley during the strike was a good deal redder than Eastwood: socialist opinions were more commonly heard from platforms in the town, and the image presented by some of the events that took place was by no means that of a meek and mild township.

Early in the strike a bus full of schoolchildren had been stoned by a group of angry miners, causing some slight injuries to the passengers. By the end of August the local pits were reopened, and the buzzers summoning the men to work were heard again in the early morning for the first time since April. Those who responded to the call got an ugly reception from the rest of the community. After a noisy demonstration against a blackleg miner at the nearby Pentrich Colliery, an extra contingent of police from Birmingham was drafted into the town on the following morning. News that the man was again at work spread rapidly, and by the afternoon a huge crowd waited round the approaches to Pentrich Colliery and lined the route from there to his home. Escorted by the police, to the accompaniment of hooting, booing and tin-panning, he was allowed to reach his house without any attempt at physical violence.[47] When he was accorded the same treatment on the following day, arrests were made. It was probably news of this affair which formed the opinions Lawrence vouchsafed to Arthur Wilkinson in a September letter from Sutton-on-Sea:

> The coal-strike continues – and in the coal areas it's a serious business. For the first time, iron seems to be entering the soul – or the consciousness – of the workers. This will be the beginning of a slow revolution, here in England – but a serious one. It's a funny country – so *safe*, and so kindly. And yet, way down, a certain ruthlessness.
>
> (Wilk 66)

It is interesting that Lawrence's analysis of the collective personality of the mineworkers, expressed also in *Lady Chatterley*, should correspond quite closely to what seems to have been the personality of his father, and it is quite possible that he generalized childhood fears of the violence latent in Arthur Lawrence's character to the whole of the mining community.

The outcome of the August demonstrations was the trial of 14 September, which made for a special cause of resentment and tension in the colliery districts on the day of Lawrence's return to Eastwood. By way of protest against the court action there was to be a march from Ripley, and mass meetings were to be held throughout the day in Heanor, the place of the trial. It was the raucous send-off given by red-flag-waving women sympathizers to the female defendants which Lawrence evidently witnessed at Ripley market-place as he set out for Eastwood. This scene, the only angry, fervid demonstration pertaining to class struggle that he witnessed during his stay in the colliery districts, had a profound effect on Lawrence's assessment of the situation. It showed to him a depth of antagonism and socialist militancy that was unprecedented in his experience, exposing the alarming extent of the changes wrought in the mentality of the local people since his time. What struck him most forcefully was the fact that it should be women who were behaving in this way. The conclusion he drew, expressed in a letter next day to Kot and reiterated in *Lady Chatterley*, was that the womenfolk of the mining districts had 'turned into fierce communists' (Zyt 300). In *The First Lady Chatterley* the class hatred of the Tevershall women was epitomized in the figure of Mrs Bolton. This version portrays her as a fifth-columnist within Wragby Hall, silently hating 'the great class of owners and bosses' (FLC 40) and conspiring to bring about

Clifford's downfall by her efforts to detach Connie from him so that she might find the circumstances to meet a lover.

Lawrence's view of women's attitudes is quite contrary to that view put forward by the historian A. R. Griffin, who suggests that it was pressure from the wives which drove the men to break the strike.[48] But in Ripley, at least, there was some local justification of the realism of Lawrence's picture of feminine militancy. A sizeable body of the miners' wives was active in support of the strike: a couple of weeks before Lawrence's arrival a packed meeting of the wives had enthusiastically responded to a proposal that the women should join the fight to keep the coal strike solid.[49]

On the whole, the Derbyshire coalfield area seems to have presented Lawrence with more vivid and more deeply affecting scenes of the effects of the coal strike than did the visit to Eastwood. When he wrote from the Mirenda to Rolf Gardiner the following December, it was his car journey in the Chesterfield area that supplied him with the images of the strike: 'I was at my sister's in September, and we drove round – I saw the miners – and pickets – and policemen – it was like a spear through one's heart. I tell you, we'd better buck up and so something for the England to come, for they've pushed the spear through the side of *my* England' (*CL* 952). One such scene, possibly witnessed near one of the Bolsover Colliery Company pits, was described in detail in 'Return to Bestwood':

> It is past three. Down the path from the pit come straggling what my little nephew calls 'the dirty ones'. They are the men who have broken strike, and gone back to work. They are not many: their faces are black, they are in their pit-dirt. They linger till they have collected, a group of a dozen or so 'dirty ones', near the stile, then they trail off down the road, the policemen, the alien 'blue-bottles', escorting them. And the 'clean ones', the colliers still on strike, squat by the wayside and watch without looking. They say nothing. They neither laugh nor stare. But here they are, a picket, and with their bleached faces they see without looking, and they register with the silence of doom, squatted down in rows by the road-side.
>
> The 'dirty ones' straggle off in the lurching, almost slinking walk of colliers, swinging their heavy feet and going as if the mine-roof were still over their heads. The big blue policemen follow at a little distance. No voice is raised: nobody seems aware of anybody else. But there is the silent, hellish registering in the consciousness of all three groups, clean ones, dirty ones and blue-bottles.
>
> (*Ph 2* 263)

The confrontation seems all the more threatening for its silence and inaction. Was it their own doom, in the defeat of the strike, that Lawrence perceived in the strikers, or the impending doom of English society, torn apart by civil strife? Perhaps both, with the débâcle of society as a more long-term prospect. What Lawrence believed he witnessed was a country 'on the brink of a class war' (*Ph 2* 265). The phrase 'class war', hardly used today, did not denote the armed conflict which 'war' seems to suggest: it was synonymous with the present-day 'class conflict'. What Lawrence and others thought they were observing in 1926 – mistakenly, as it happened – was the beginning of the fulfilment of Marx's prediction of an increasing polarization of society in terms of hatred between the exploiting and the exploited classes, growing exploitation of the workers, and an ever-increasing conflict between capital and labour. The culmination of this process, according to Marxist theory, would be revolution; and it is clear from Lawrence's letters, and from comments in *The First Lady Chatterley* that appear to express authorial opinions, that for a while he entertained the view that a gradual, and not necessarily excessively violent, revolution was a distinctly possible if not inevitable outcome of the social processes that were then in train.[50] Indeed, one could say that *The First Lady Chatterley*, the most overtly political of the three versions of the novel, sets out the Marxist thesis in presenting the separation of Tevershall society into 'haves' and 'have-nots', revealing an intensification of the class struggle and prophesying revolution or some cataclysmic social upheaval.

Lawrence was probably aware – as many others were at that period, including Willie Hopkin,[51] who might have spoken to Lawrence in this vein – that defeat of the miners' strike, an increasingly likely outcome in Nottinghamshire and Derbyshire, would not mean an end to the prospect of class warfare. Rather the contrary: if the miners were crushed, it would instil a bitter opposition to the coal-owners that would last for generations. Furthermore, the government intended to force down wages in every sector of industry in order to make exports competitive: it seemed very likely that if the Miners' Federation was beaten, there would be further industrial struggles as the government turned to take on other unions.[52] Lawrence's fears of a class war were therefore well founded, and were by no means the lone anxieties of a poetical eccentric. Though Lawrence's prophecies in 'Return to Bestwood' and *The First Lady Chatterley* never came to pass, this was mainly because he had not foreseen that mass unemployment would intervene to weaken the power of organized labour.

If there was a single dominant factor which impelled Lawrence to break his vows never to write another novel, it was the strike of 1926, and what Lawrence saw of its effects on the mining communities, what he heard of its history, and what he feared as its consequences. He did not, however, elect to set *Lady Chatterley* within the period of the 1926 strike, but instead chose the years 1920–3. In this way he avoided a number of dangers which might have attended a topical novel, such as its potential for being too journalistic and too political, the possibility of it becoming quickly outmoded by too specific an association with a particular event in history, and the probability that any analysis of the situation, or any conclusions which might be drawn, would be proved mistaken by the subsequent course of events. What Lawrence did was to shift back by a few years the present picture of an increasingly polarized society on the verge of social and moral disintegration. He could safely do so, because the period in which he set the novel marked the time of the beginnings of economic decline and industrial unrest which led up to the miners' strike and the General Strike of 1926.

Another aspect of the social landscape of the England of 1926 which was a powerful influence on the shaping of *Lady Chatterley*, and which Lawrence related to the hostility of the proletariat, was the demise of the old class of landed gentry, bringing with it the fall of the country house and its estates. This, too, provided a theme and a background to the novel which could readily be translated to an earlier period, since this phenomenon of postwar England had begun in 1919. Lawrence had probably heard from Willie Hopkin or Ada of the fate of Mundy's Shipley Hall during the first couple of days of his return to the Midlands. On the day following his visit to Eastwood he appears to have witnessed at first hand the effects on the landscape of the flight of the squirearchy.

8

Renishaw

The next day, 15 September, brought a change in the weather: the soft autumnal stillness of the day of the return to Eastwood persisted, but the skies had turned grey and there was rain on the air. 'These Midlands!' (Zyt 300), Lawrence complained to Kot in a letter written that morning, letting him know of his intended arrival in London the next day. The letter went on to describe briefly the effects of the miners' strike – the misery of 'families living on bread and margarine and potatoes', the communism of the womenfolk and the unpleasant change in the atmosphere of the mining communities. There are resonances here with 'Return to Bestwood', and it seems possible that Lawrence spent much of the rest of the morning on the draft of the essay and on the first pages of the final version, where the incident of the women's demonstration in the market-place is said to have taken place 'yesterday'.

The remaining part of 'Return to Bestwood', perhaps completed the following morning before Lawrence departed for London, reveals that in the afternoon Lawrence and the Clarkes set out for a journey into the countryside, which took them in the direction of Chesterfield. This journey into the north-east corner of Derbyshire, a region of gentle hills surmounted by great halls and of valleys scarred with coalmines and blast furnaces, provided Lawrence with the wider geographical setting for *Lady Chatterley* and with a set of impressions that contributed substantially to the atmosphere which permeates Wragby Hall and the industrial landscapes of the novel.

It is tempting to suppose, in this excursion to a part of Derbyshire not noted for its scenic beauty, some motive other than sightseeing. But, according to 'Return to Bestwood' (which, as the account of the market-place scene shows, does not always faithfully record the absolute truth of Lawrence's experiences), the route he took was prescribed by a spontaneous decision as to where they should drive and by an accident of circumstance that followed from that decision:

'Where shall we go this afternoon? Shall we go to Hardwick?' Let us go
to Hardwick. I have not been for twenty years. Let us go to Hardwick:

> Hardwick Hall
> More window than wall.

Built in the days of good Queen Bess, by the other Bess, termagant
and tartar, Countess of Shrewsbury.

(Ph 2, 264)

The drive to Hardwick from Ripley took Lawrence through
Butterley, with its great iron foundry, through Alfreton and past the
old church that Paul and Miriam visited on the walk to Wingfield
Manor in *Sons and Lovers*, and then off the lorry-laden Chesterfield
road and along country lanes to Tibshelf.[1] Having passed through
Tibshelf, Lawrence reached a fork in the road, where there was a
signpost to Teversal. Lawrence later adopted the name, slightly
altered by the addition of an *h* and a final *l*, for the mining village
adjoining Wragby – 'Tevershall'. Just before the turn-off for Hardwick Hall was a lane signposted to Huthwaite. Lawrence used this
name, too, in this case dropping the *h* to give 'Uthwaite', the home
town of Wragby, which in terms of geography and appearance was
modelled on Chesterfield.

Lawrence arrived at Hardwick to find the hall shut and the park
closed for an indefinite period, no doubt, he supposed, for fear that
the miners' strike might lead to vandalism. But the 'No Admittance'
signs had failed to deter miners bent on using the park for sport and
recreation. As the Clarkes' car headed away from the hall, Lawrence
saw 'colliers slowly loafing, fishing, poaching in spite of all notices'
(*Ph* 2 262); and he seems to have recalled this scene when writing of
Shipley Hall in *John Thomas and Lady Jane*, where there were 'gangs of
colliers lounging by [Squire Winter's] ornamental water, and fur-
tively looking for a chance, maybe, to poach a bird' (*JTLJ* 160).

According to the narrative of 'Return to Bestwood', Lawrence's
objective on leaving Hardwick was Chesterfield. In this matter the
essay seems once again not to have given an entirely faithful account
of actual events. He certainly set out in the direction of Chesterfield,
as his description of the Hardwick fishponds shows, and he ultimately reached the town. But the evidence of the three versions of
Lady Chatterley, and of Lawrence's letters, leaves little doubt that his
real goal, which seems to have provided him with the broad

geographical setting of the Chatterleys' Wragby and some features of the appearance of the house and park, was the home of the Sitwell family at Renishaw.

When Lawrence met Sir George and Lady Ida at Montegufoni, he had been invited to Renishaw in August, when the whole family, including Osbert, Edith and Sacheverell, would be in residence. Shortly after his visit to Montegufoni, he wrote to Ada suggesting they should drive to Renishaw when he came over in the summer; and in a July letter to Brett from the Mirenda he mentioned Osbert and Edith among the three people (the other was Gardiner) whom he specially wished to see when he arrived in England.[2] He knew, however, that with the passing of August there was little chance of finding the Sitwells at home, and said as much in a letter to Orioli,[3] written only a couple of days before he reached Ripley. If, as seems practically certain, he *did* drive to Renishaw on 15 September, the decision to go there may have been made only on being thwarted in his plans to visit Hardwick. Since he was not very far from Renishaw, it might have seemed that it was worth taking a chance on there still being a Sitwell in residence. This was a day when, whether for literary purposes or out of simple curiosity, he seems to have taken a special interest in the English country house. Even, therefore, if there was no one at Renishaw, a visit could have seemed a not unrewarding proposition. 'Return to Bestwood' has no reference to Renishaw or to the area round about it. Perhaps it did not suit his artistic purposes to mention it in his account of his travels in the Chesterfield area; but there is a fair possibility that by the time he wrote the final part of the essay (very shortly after the excursion, according to my conjecture), he had already decided to make use of Renishaw in his fiction.

A few years later, in 1933, Frieda's daughter Barby found herself touring the same area with 'a couple of Swiss film-directors' (Nehls 3 188), looking for suitable locations for shooting *Lady Chatterley's Lover*, the film rights for which had been sold to a Swiss producer. In Barby's version of events they came by chance upon Renishaw. She concluded, from its striking parallels with Wragby and from a memory of having been told of a visit by Lawrence to the Sitwells, that the house must have been Lawrence's model for the seat of the Chatterleys. She therefore telegraphed Osbert Sitwell in London as follows: 'Discobole, Paris, propose filming Lawrence novel. May we inspect Renishaw Hall?' Osbert replied: 'If you refer banned book

Lady Chatterley's Lover your request gross as it is libellous' (Nehls 3 188).

It is clear from the raw nerve that Barby's telegram searched out in Osbert that he believed Wragby was Renishaw, and in a note to Nehls he went a little way towards acknowledging this, when he wrote: '[Lawrence] claimed, I understood, to have known the place and to have used it as a background. He certainly had never entered the house, as his descriptions of it prove. He may, of course, have trespassed in the park. Nevertheless, since Renishaw is some twenty miles from where he lived, I think it unlikely' (Nehls 3, 693, n. 312).

Reresby Sitwell, Osbert's nephew and the present owner of Renishaw Hall, came independently to the same view that Wragby was Renishaw. When Osbert turned Renishaw over to him in 1965, Maynard Hollingworth, the agent in Sir George's and in Osbert's time, was still in charge of the estate. Reresby Sitwell has a memory, which he could no longer vouch for as having a factual source, of asking Hollingworth whether Lawrence had ever visited the hall and of being told that he *had*, and that Hollingworth himself had greeted Lawrence and had taken him through the house to view the gardens behind. One or two clues from *Lady Chatterley* tend to confirm the authenticity of Mr Sitwell's recollections. Firstly, there is the name 'Collingwood', given by Lawrence to Lady Eva's butler – Lady Ida's Henry Moat. Maynard Hollingworth was a great friend of Henry Moat. He was very tall, like Moat, but spare where Moat was portly. It would have been very much in the Lawrentian manner for him to have noted some common factor between the two men and to have applied a slightly altered form of the name of one to the other, thereby producing 'Collingwood'. More significantly, there are a couple of details in the description of Wragby's interior and layout in *The First Lady Chatterley* which seem to undermine Osbert's conviction, based on a reading of the final version, that Lawrence had never been inside the house. On one clandestine excursion by night to meet the keeper in the woods, Connie walked downstairs and sat for a while, awaiting the moment when everyone in the house would have retired, 'in her own small sitting-room that had window-doors opening to the garden' (*FLC* 172), which was at the rear of the house. The way through Renishaw Hall to the gardens behind leads via just such a small sitting-room, whose French windows open onto the lawn.

143

Apart from Reresby Sitwell's memory of a conversation with Hollingworth, there is no other evidence outside the texts of *Lady Chatterley* to show that Lawrence visited Renishaw. No D. H. Lawrence appears in the visitors' book, and there is nothing in the records of the estate office; but Lawrence left a lasting calling-card in aspects of the description of Wragby and in accounts of Connie's car-journeys to and from the hall.

In *Lady Chatterley's Lover* (which in this section will be the main source of reference since in most respects it has more features pertaining to Renishaw and its environment than other versions) Connie and Clifford first arrive together at Wragby after a 'dank ride in a motor-car up a dark, damp drive, burrowing through gloomy trees, out to the slope of the park where grey damp sheep were feeding, to the knoll where the house spread its dark-brown façade' (*LCL* 14f.); it was a gated driveway, and at the top of the knoll the drive made 'a grand sweep round a lozenge of grass in front of the entrance' (*LCL* 150). This is a precise description – even down to the sheep that grazed the park – of the Barlborough Drive up to Renishaw Hall from the East Gate at Renishaw Lane End, the gate by which one would enter Renishaw Park if one were arriving from Hardwick.

If the damp is also a reminiscence of the approach to the hall, then the grey, drizzly weather of the Wednesday morning must have persisted into the afternoon and added to the cheerless appearance of Renishaw. The drive does not permit a view of the rather pretty and romantic south side of the hall or the beautiful formal gardens that stretch beyond it. Lawrence's first impression on approaching the hall would have been of the end of the east wing and the northern façade, a long screen of stone, practically without ornament save for its crenellations, with its windows shuttered for the months when there would be no residents. The only welcoming aspect of the visit may well have been, as it was for the newly-wed Chatterleys, the stammered greetings of a couple of the family's employees, 'hovering like unsure tenants on the face of the earth' (*LCL* 15). Little wonder, then, that Lawrence should perhaps have found the place 'dismal' and 'melancholy' like his Wragby Hall.

Renishaw began in 1625 as a small, compact, H-shaped house in the Jacobean style, and this early house now forms the central core of the long, rambling building that resulted from the additions made by Sir Sitwell Sitwell at the turn of the eighteenth century. On the

north side he filled in the area between the two arms of the central H
with an entrance hall with a Gothic porch. The whole house appears
from an outside view to be of three storeys, but, except in the central
portion, this is an illusion created by three tiers of windows. The
Chatterley's Wragby likewise has a three-storied central portion, at
the top of which Connie has a sitting-room. But there is little else in
the description of the hall itself that distinguishes it as Renishaw in
the final version of the novel.

The hall is described as a 'long low old house in brown stone,
begun about the middle of the eighteenth century, and added on to,
till it was a warren of a place without much distinction' (*LCL* 13).
Most country houses are old, and the collocation of 'long' and 'low' is
a cliché in the description of architecture – one that Lawrence quite
frequently draws on in the portrayal of all sorts of buildings and
rooms. Such a description could fittingly be applied to Renishaw,
and to many another country house. However, as Harry Moore
observed, Lawrence had earlier used precisely these words to describe
his most popular model for country houses – Lamb Close House,
home of the colliery-owning Barber family of Eastwood. 'Shortlands'
in *Women in Love* was 'a long, low old house, a sort of manor farm,
that spread along the top of a slope' (*WL* 23). Lamb Close is built of
brown stone, like Wragby – Renishaw's stone is grey; and a
mid-eighteenth century date would be less appropriate to Renishaw
than Lamb Close, which was converted into a shooting-box at that
period and subsequently rebuilt by the Barbers. Lamb Close is truly
'without much distinction', a comment which Renishaw's façade
hardly deserves, however grim its appearance or incongruous its
blending of the Georgian and the Gothic.

Harry Moore noted that the Chatterleys' Wragby looked very
much like Lamb Close. It is easy to see how a great deal of the
opening description of the setting and prospects of the hall rightly
gave him that impression:

> It stood on an eminence in a rather fine old park of oak trees, but alas,
> one could see in the distance the chimney of Tevershall pit, with its
> clouds of steam and smoke, and on the damp, hazy distance of the hill
> the raw straggle of Tevershall village, a village which began almost at
> the park gates, and trailed in utter hopeless ugliness for a long and
> gruesome mile . . . From the rather dismal rooms at Wragby she heard
> the rattle-rattle of the screens at the pit, the puff of the winding-
> engine, the clink-clink of shunting trucks, and the hoarse little
> whistle of the colliery locomotives. Tevershall pit-bank was burning,

had been burning for years ... On the low dark ceiling of cloud at
night red blotches burned and quavered, dappling and swelling and
contracting, like burns that give pain.

(LCL 13f.)

All the familiar sights, smells and sounds of Eastwood, as perceived
from Lamb Close, appear to be there – Moorgreen Colliery and its
railway and burning pit-bank, Eastwood perched on its hill, and the
night-time glare of the nearby Bennerley blast furnaces at casting-off
time.

But Renishaw, too, 'stood on an eminence' and had, in nearby
Eckington, a mining settlement that 'began almost at the park gates'
and straggled uphill for something like a mile. It had a nearby mine,
Renishaw Colliery, and Osbert's accounts of the hall describe distant
prospects of burning slag heaps and nights when the flares of Stavely
furnaces lit up the whole sky. It is easy to understand why Lamb
Close House and Renishaw Hall should each have supporters in the
claim to have been the model for Wragby.

The wooded hills adjoining Lamb Close supplied the woodland
scenes for the novel, and Eastwood was the model for Tevershall, the
home village of Wragby. Hence, it might be expected that on closer
examination the prospects of Wragby should turn out to be those of
Lamb Close. Both houses, like Wragby, are surrounded by wooded
hills and have a road to Mansfield running close by, but only in the
case of Lamb Close could the road be said to have 'swerved round to
the north' (*LCL* 43) of the woods. Each had a nearby mine, a pit
village on a hill, a view of a church; but only from Lamb Close park
could one take in at a glance, as Connie and Clifford could at Wragby,
a view up a shallow valley combining a mine, a hill-top village and a
church standing above it.

In *Lady Chatterley's Lover* the immediate environment of Wragby,
with the exception of the drive to the house, is thus that of Lamb
Close. Lawrence must have been aware of the superficial resemblances
which the setting of Lamb Close bore to Renishaw, and seems to have
exploited the ambivalence of reference to the real world which his
picture created, in order to make identification of his model more
difficult. The hall itself, as depicted in *Lady Chatterley's Lover*, was
built by conflating features of Lamb Close and Renishaw, which
contributed its three-storied central portion; and the drive up to the
house was Renishaw's Barlborough Drive.

Although one would have imagined that a move in a contrary

direction would have been a safer course of action, it is a curious feature of the evolution of *Lady Chatterley* that the more closely Clifford Chatterley comes to resemble Osbert Sitwell in the progress of the novel through its three stages, the greater and more obvious become the links between Wragby and Renishaw. In the first version the house has no distinctive central portion; only at the very end of the novel, almost as an afterthought, are there features such as a suggestion of Renishaw's drive and an implied three storeys to the house which show that Wragby could not have been entirely modelled on Lamb Close. In this version, where in appearance Clifford resembles Gerald Crich of *Women in Love* (himself partly modelled on Major Thomas Philip Barber, the owner of Lamb Close House), it was Barber's home, not Osbert Sitwell's, that was uppermost in Lawrence's mind when he created Wragby. Lawrence inadvertently dropped a hint to this effect with a slip of the pen that allowed the 'Wragby Hall' of the opening pages of the novel to change its title in the passage describing 'the old square tower of [Tevershall] church, of brown stone like Wragby House' (*FLC* 103).

There is no reason to suppose that Lawrence used Renishaw in order to pay off a personal grudge. He had no cause to have changed his mind about Osbert and Edith since July, when he was very much looking forward to meeting them. Nor could he have felt a piqued disappointment at finding no one in when he reached Renishaw, because he had not expected anyone to be there. One factor which influenced him must have been the grim and powerful impression made on him by Renishaw and the industrial landscapes around it on a grey, miserable afternoon. But the real reason for the presence of Renishaw in *Lady Chatterley* was most probably that he badly needed a house and a general setting that would not be transparently Lamb Close and the Eastwood area.

He had already in his writing career used Lamb Close for the colliery-owner's country house in *The White Peacock* and in *Women in Love*. Its owner, Major Barber, and tragic episodes from his family's recent history, had appeared in *Women in Love*. Barber was married, and therefore the likelihood of a successful libel action would have been considerable if the house and estate of a cuckold could have been plainly identifiable with Lamb Close and its environs. To use aspects of Renishaw and its bachelor owner in the portraits of Wragby and Clifford was a much safer proposition. If, as has been argued, the purpose of the use of Renishaw was to act as a red-herring, which would deflect attention from Lamb Close, then history has shown that plan to have been extremely successful. It has been so largely because of the fame of the Sitwells. If Lawrence had schemed in a way that appears alien to his nature, he could have foreseen either that the Sitwells' celebrity would make the family and their ancestral home recognizable and so take the spotlight off Eastwood, or that Osbert and Edith, known to be sensitive to slights on the part of their fellow authors, would make a public fuss and themselves draw attention to the use of their family and Renishaw. As it happened, only Edith took the lure, if any such was intended.

Lawrence's chief ploy, in concealing the fact that the main action of the novel centred on Lamb Close and its neighbouring woods and mining settlements, was to provide his Wragby with the wider setting of north-east Derbyshire (well away from the Lawrence country proper), calling Nottingham 'Sheffield', and in the final version naming Chesterfield several times. Simply stated, Lawrence created the landscape of his novel by transporting Lamb Close (modified by the addition of features of the hall and park at Renishaw) and the area within a three- or four-mile radius of Lamb Close House to north-east Derbyshire, which provides the wider geography. But the true picture of Lawrence's use of his sources for the creation of the world of Wragby and its environs is rather more complex. Viewed, as it was never intended to be, as a reflection of the real world of Lawrence's sources, the portrait of the Chatterley country may be compared to a witty *trompe l'oeil* painting. One can look at Wragby and its situation from one perspective and see Renishaw Hall, sited between Chesterfield and Mansfield, and from another distinguish Lamb Close House, High Park Woods and Eastwood.

In 'Return to Bestwood' Lawrence and the Clarkes ponder what to do next when they find Hardwick Hall and its park closed to them: 'Where shall we go? Back into Derbyshire, or to Sherwood Forest. Turn the car. We'll go on through Chesterfield' (*Ph 2* 262). Quite possibly this discussion either belongs to or was reiterated at the time they left Renishaw. Sherwood Forest lay in the direction of Mansfield, and it looks as though the memory of a glance at the map gave the itineraries for Connie's journey with her sister to and from the town. There are two possible routes between Renishaw and Mansfield: one, rather longer, but offering a good, straight run, just skirts the village of Bolsover; the other passes through the centre of the village. Two very similar itineraries could be chosen between

Wragby and Mansfield. On the outward journey Hilda implicitly took the road that avoided Bolsover, because when in the evening she drove Connie back to the Wragby estate to spend the night at the keeper's cottage, she took 'the other road, through Bolsover'. By the time she reached the lane to the cottage it was almost nightfall 'and the small, lit-up train that chuffed past in the cutting made it seem like real night. Hilda had calculated the turn at the bridge-end. She . . . swerved off the road . . . into the grassy, overgrown lane' (*LCL* 252). The route from Bolsover to Renishaw provides a near-perfect match in the conjunction of a lane end, and a bridge over a railway cutting that runs parallel to a road. And the point where Hilda's car turned off is no grassy lane leading to a cottage, but the East Gate to Renishaw Hall. A slight alteration to the original arrangement of features has disguised the true location of the original for the gamekeeper's cottage.

From Renishaw Lawrence appears to have driven to Chesterfield and thence towards Matlock and the Peak District. This final, 'Matlock', part of the afternoon's excursion, providing a welcome contrast to the industrial area of the north-east corner of the county, is mentioned in a letter from the Mirenda to Nancy Pearn, which tells of his travels in the Chesterfield and Matlock districts.[4] What would seem to be Lawrence's recollections of a journey from Renishaw to Chesterfield provides the weightiest evidence for linking the site of Wragby Hall with that of Renishaw in all versions of the novel.[5] This journey evidently furnished a good deal of the material and inspiration for the 'destruction of Old England' theme in *Lady Chatterley*; and for views that are by turn, or even simultaneously, uplifting and depressing, the road Lawrence appears to have taken to Chesterfield has few rivals in the whole of the county.

In *Lady Chatterley's Lover* Connie is driven by chauffeur to the nearby town of Uthwaite; and Lawrence's Uthwaite, although in name derived from a village near Hardwick, clearly denotes Chesterfield, which also figures in other parts of this version under its own name:

Uthwaite, on a damp day, was sending up a whole array of smoke plumes and steam, to whatever gods there be. Uthwaite down in the valley, with all the steel threads of the railways to Sheffield drawn through it, and the coal-mines and the steel-works sending up smoke and glare from long tubes, and the pathetic little corkscrew spire of the

149

church, that is going to tumble down, still pricking the fumes, always
affected Connie strangely. It was an old market-town, centre of the
dales.

(LCL 161)

The line engraving is so exact in all respects that the true identity of
Uthwaite would have been betrayed even without the telltale
appearance of the twisted spire that distinguishes the church of St
Mary and All Saints, Chesterfield.

At the outset of Connie's journey to Uthwaite from Wragby, her
car 'ploughed uphill through the long squalid straggle of Tevershall'
(*LCL* 158). The village of Eckington, close by Renishaw Hall, may
have been a joint contributor (with Eastwood) to the description of
the long, uphill straggle of Tevershall which began at the park gates.
If Connie's uphill journey is partly based on Lawrence's experiences
on leaving Renishaw, then he must have opted for the shorter,
upland alternative of the two possible ways to Chesterfield. Once
Eckington is left behind, the road takes a southerly direction, enters
high, open country, dips a little and then almost mounts to and
straddles the 500 ft contour. Ahead and to the left unfold broad
vistas of rolling green hills, their tops on a fine day mottled with
patches of sunlight and shadow: 'The rain was holding off, and in the
air came a queer pellucid gleam . . . The country rolled away in long
undulations, south towards the Peak, east towards Mansfield and
Nottingham' (*LCL* 160).

On the eastern skyline one can just make out from this road the
once-ruined keep of Bolsover Castle. Below it lies the old village of
Bolsover, then New Bolsover Model Village, and the colliery that in
1926 was owned by the sixth Duke of Portland, half-brother to Lady
Ottoline Morrell. In all but the first version of the novel, Bolsover
masquerades under the title of Warsop:

> As she rose on to the high country, she could see on her left, on a
> height above the rolling land, the shadowy, powerful bulk of Warsop
> Castle, dark grey, with below it the reddish plastering of miners'
> dwellings, newish, and below those the plumes of dark smoke and
> white steam from the great colliery which put so many thousand
> pounds per annum into the pockets of the Duke and the other
> shareholders. The powerful old castle was a ruin, yet it hung its bulk
> on the low sky-line, over the black plumes and the white that waved
> on the damp air below.

(LCL 160)

There is rather more here than would have met the eye of a traveller on the Chesterfield road. Lawrence was probably drawing on a closer view he had had when travelling from Hardwick to Renishaw, a journey which would have taken him through Bolsover. What had been a pretty Georgian village had expanded, in an effusion of red brick, almost to the size of a town since the sinking of the great Bolsover pit in the last decade of the nineteenth century. When Lawrence completed 'Return to Bestwood' Bolsover was no doubt high among the places he had in mind when he wrote of 'old villages . . . smothered in rows of miners' dwellings' (*Ph 2* 262). Bolsover Colliery, always in the vanguard of mechanization techniques and the exploitation of by-products, may have influenced the portrayal of the 'really modern mine' which dominates 'Stacks Gate', the next landmark on Connie's journey to Uthwaite. It may also have been aspects of the general impression of Bolsover and its model village which lent something to the monstrosity Lawrence created in 'Stacks Gate':

> Stacks Gate, as seen from the highroad, was just a huge and gorgeous new hotel, the Coningsby Arms, standing red and white and gilt in barbarous isolation off the road. But if you looked, you saw on the left rows of handsome 'modern' dwellings, set down like a game of dominoes with spaces and gardens, a queer game of dominoes that some weird 'masters' were playing on the surprised earth. And beyond these blocks of dwellings, at the back, rose all the astonishing and frightening overhead erections of a really modern mine, chemical works and long galleries, enormous, and of shapes not before known to man. The head-stock and pit-bank of the mine itself were insignificant among the huge new installations. And in front of this, the game of dominoes stood forever in a sort of surprise, waiting to be played.
> This was Stacks Gate, new on the face of the earth, since the war. But as a matter of fact, though even Connie did not know it, downhill half a mile below the 'hotel' was old Stacks Gate, with a little old colliery and blackish old brick dwellings, and a chapel or two and a shop or two and a little pub or two:
> 'But that didn't count any more. The vast plumes of smoke and vapour rose from the new works up above, and this was now Stacks Gate: no chapels, no pubs, even no shops'.
>
> (*LCL* 160)

Stacks Gate, in terms of the underlying wider geography of the novel, ought to correspond to Staveley. And Staveley is hinted at in the first letters of Stacks Gate, in its colliery and chemical works, and in its position to the left of an upland road to Uthwaite (Chesterfield), three miles south of Wragby (Renishaw). But nothing else in the carefully plotted landscape of Stacks Gate fits Staveley at all. It rather looks as though Lawrence may have taken in a distant view of the squalid clutter of furnaces, factories, chimney-stacks and mounds of industrial débris that defaced the valley of the river Rother, and continued along the highroad to Chesterfield. Consequently, when later he needed to fill that space on his canvas, and give substance to the place that had seemed so appalling from afar, he drew on his imagination and on other places he had known at close hand. Stacks Gate is everywhere and nowhere in the industrial north Midlands, a fictive conglomeration of all the worst of what was new, a frightful image of modernity, and a threatening portent of what the future might be like. In the smaller actual geography which the novel draws on – that which belongs to the Eastwood area – Stacks Gate appears, in some respects, to correspond to the village of Underwood.[6]

The picture of Stacks Gate as a modern mining community is not, in fact, an entirely new one in Lawrence's fiction. It is a development, to a greater degree of frightfulness, of a landscape he had drawn in *The Rainbow*:

> Wiggiston was only seven years old. It had been a hamlet of eleven houses on the edge of heathy, half-agricultural country. Then the great seam of coal had been opened. In a year Wiggiston appeared, a great mass of pinkish rows of thin, unreal dwellings . . . Everything was amorphous, yet everything repeated itself endlessly. Only now and then, in one of the house-windows vegetables or small groceries were displayed for sale.
>
> In the middle of the town was a large, open, shapeless place or market-place . . . surrounded by the same flat material of dwellings, new red-brick becoming grimy . . . with just, at one corner, a great and gaudy public-house, and somewhere lost on one of the sides of the square . . . the post-office.
>
> The place had the strange desolation of a ruin . . . The rigidity of the blank streets, the homogenous amorphous sterility of the whole suggested death rather than life. There was no meeting-place, no centre, no artery, no organic formation. There it lay, like the new foundations of a red-brick confusion rapidly spreading, like a skin-disease.
>
> Just outside of this, on a little hill, was Tom Brangwen's big, red-brick house . . . Further off was the great colliery that went night and day. And all round was the country, green with two winding streams, ragged with gorse, and heath, the darker woods in the distance.
>
> (*Rainbow* 392f.)

Wiggiston has been identified with Bentley, near Doncaster, where the Barber, Walker Colliery Company opened a seam in 1908. The pit had taken on for its underground workforce men who had been working the same seam of coal at High Park Colliery and Watnall Colliery. In one sense it is right to link Wiggiston with Bentley. But the landscape of Wiggiston is largely based on an imagined picture of Eastwood in the early days of its industrial expansion, as can be seen from the market-place with its post-office and 'great and gaudy public house' (Eastwood's Sun Inn) and from the description of the countryside round about. Likewise, Stacks Gate is in essence a modern version of the beginnings of industrial Eastwood.

The notion that Lawrence did not pass through Staveley tallies with the remaining parts of the description of Connie's journey to Uthwaite. Her car continues along uplands, with 'the rolling country' still in view, and she sees 'looming again and hanging on the brow of the sky-line . . . the huge and splendid bulk of Chadwick Hall, more window than wall, one of the most famous Elizabethan houses' (*LCL* 161). Hardwick Hall, Lawrence's first stopping-place on his afternoon's travels, shines out through a slight alteration to its name in a popular rhyming saw that local people had half-mockingly applied to it for centuries.

The Elizabethan house represented the past: 'The present lay below . . . The car was already turning, between little old blackened miners' cottages, to descend to Uthwaite' (*LCL* 161). There, in the first version of the novel, Connie Chatterley called at 'the old druggist's shop' and 'had a cup of tea in the clean, awkward little tea-shop' (*FLC* 62) – reminiscences, possibly, of Lawrence buying patent remedies for his troublesome bronchials in Chesterfield and indulging his addiction to tea.

In the past, as one entered the town centre of Lawrence's Uthwaite, there used to be signs with a wrought iron and wooden surround welcoming the traveller to 'Chesterfield, the heart of industrial England'. Lawrence's journey in the region of this industrial heart-land made an extremely strong impression on him: in this corner of Derbyshire the remnants of the rural and urban scenes of the past contrasted more starkly with modern industrial development than they did in the Eastwood area; the great houses were more stately than most of those in Lawrence's native district, and there was industry and squalor on a scale that was unparalleled in and around Eastwood.

The passage describing Connie's journey from Wragby to Uth-waite, embracing at the beginning Lawrence's responses to the Eastwood of 1926 in the portrait of Tevershall, is one of the few sections of any length to survive intact, albeit revised and amplified, from the first draft through to the final version. And in the last two versions the status and significance of the account of Connie's journey is enhanced by a shift from a position near the beginning in the original version to almost the exact centre of the novel. The state of the vital spirits at the heart of the central industrial region of the country become a prognostic of the condition of the life-force in the whole of England. In *The First Lady Chatterley* the sense of 'blind virility, a certain blind, pathetic forcefulness of life' (*FLC* 60) that Connie experienced is symbolized by the 'powerful-looking' castle of Bolsover, the greatness and nobility of Hardwick, the church at Uthwaite, 'whose twisted spire pricked up in the valley' (*FLC* 61). Even the 'great proud colliery' (*FLC* 60) of Stacks Gate is noble in its activity, though devilishly inspired. True, the passage closes with a sense of doom and hollow lifelessness as the destiny of Shipley Hall is contemplated, but it is a doom not yet quite at hand.

In tandem with the description of Tevershall, the portrayal of the Derbyshire coal district follows a progressive descent towards pejor-ation and the expression of authorial despair through succeeding stages in the evolution of *Lady Chatterley*. In *John Thomas and Lady Jane* the country remained 'alive, labouring under a queer, savage weight of dismalness and acquiescence' (*JTLJ* 156). But the sense of hopelessness becomes more powerful, the virility and forcefulness of life are no longer asserted, one or two of the original symbols of those qualities become lifeless or threatened, and new images of mechanized sexuality begin to take their place. By the time Lawrence came to write the final version of the novel, when he sensed his own life-force ebbing away from him, all that was left of that sense of vitality in Lawrence, as in his perception of the industrial Midlands, was a stubborn determination to survive, 'to live from one's resist-ance' (*LCL* 158). As he turned over in his mind the recollected images of his travels in the Chesterfield area, he saw in them a new meaning, already beginning to surface in *John Thomas and Lady Jane*, which was quite different from what he had discerned in his first recorded impressions: the powerful old castle was, after all, a ruin; Hardwick nothing more than a lifeless showplace; the spire, for all its phallic pointing, 'a pathetic little corkscrew . . . that is going to tumble down' (*LCL* 161). The natural stone totems of virility and continuity with the past came to be replaced by metal, mechanical contrivances – the long tubes of the steelworks chimneys, the rising 'overhead erections of a really modern mine' (*LCL* 160). And everywhere the life of the countryside, the old towns and the great estates was choking on a steady flowing haemorrhage of new red brick.

Lawrence's letter to Nancy Pearn implies that on leaving Chesterfield he made for Matlock, the gateway to the Peak District. The area between Chesterfield and Matlock presented a very different landscape from the one Lawrence had passed through on the journey from Renishaw – one which must have given some intimation of how the country east of Chesterfield might have appeared before the coal deposits were exploited. It was an area of low, steep hills and moorland pasture, dotted with patches of woodland and bleak, picturesque villages hardly touched by the modern world.

There is a direct route over the moors from Chesterfield to Matlock, but judging by the narrative in *Lady Chatterley's Lover* Lawrence seems to have ignored it. His account of Connie's drive from Chesterfield must mean that Lawrence knew the first few miles of the Derby Road out of the town:

> Upon the old crooked burgess streets hordes of oldish blackened miners' dwellings crowded, lining the roads out. And immediately after these came the newer, pinker rows of rather larger houses, plastering the valley: the homes of more modern workmen. And beyond that again, in the wide rolling regions of the castles, smoke waved against steam, and patch after patch of raw reddish brick showed the newer mining settlements, sometimes in the hollows, sometimes gruesomely ugly along the sky-line of the slopes.
>
> (*LCL* 162)

The trunk-road from Chesterfield to Derby acts almost as a boundary line dividing the countryside to the west from the mines and factories to the east. A couple of miles out of Chesterfield, plainly visible on a slope on the 'country' side of the road, Wingerworth Hall had either already been reduced to a pile of masonry or was in an advanced state of demolition. Built by Francis Smith of Warwick in 1729, its demolition had begun in 1924, and it was very probably 'Fritchley', 'a perfect old Georgian mansion . . . even now, as Connie passed in the car [on leaving Uthwaite], being demolished'.[7] Like the Fritchley Hall described in *John Thomas and Lady Jane*, Wingerworth

Hall was 'too big, and in the wrong place, next the mines which had made its wealth' (*JTLJ* 159).

It was, just possibly, shortly after passing Wingerworth that Lawrence turned off at Tupton into the Derbyshire countryside along the lanes to Ashover and thence to Matlock. At the conclusion of a digression on the destruction of old England Lawrence gives a valedictory roll-call of the names of lost and passing country houses: 'Fritchley was gone, Eastwood was gone, Shipley was going' (*LCL* 163). The Walker family had left Eastwood Hall, Nottinghamshire, before the First World War, but the house had remained in use as colliery offices, and indeed it still serves that purpose to this day. Derbyshire, which is after all 'the county' to which Lawrence had been referring in this part of the novel, also had an Eastwood Hall, which once belonged to the Reresby ancestors of the Sitwells. Eastwood Hall, however, was not destroyed by the social and economic forces that prevailed in Britain after the First World War, but by the Parliamentarians in the English Civil War. Its site was marked on the 1921 Ordnance Survey map, and its tall, ivy-covered, dilapidated walls could be clearly seen from the lane as one descended into the village of Ashover from Tupton on the Chesterfield–Derby road. It is possible, therefore, that Lawrence was playfully using the same kind of duality of reference to the real world that he used in creating Wragby and its environs.

In his portrayal of Shipley Hall, it is conceivable, but by no means certain, that Lawrence conflated a model from the Eastwood area with one from the Chesterfield area, just as in the portrait of Wragby and its environs. But the only solid reason for supposing that he could have had a model in addition to the real Shipley for his abandoned and doomed countryhouse lies in the comment in *Lady Chatterley's Lover* that Shipley was 'near enough to Uthwaite',[8] in other words, in actual geography, not far from Chesterfield.

Lawrence's account of his leaving Hardwick Hall makes it clear that the Clarkes' car must have been travelling towards the village of Heath. If, as seems beyond doubt, he then made for Renishaw, the most attractive and appropriate route for an afternoon's sightseeing would have taken him via Bolsover, which in fact is mentioned in 'Return to Bestwood'. One of the alternative routes to Bolsover from Heath would have led him to follow the signpost to Sutton Scarsdale, and thence past Sutton Scarsdale Hall which stood close to the road, clearly visible from a passing car. Being within three miles or so of

Chesterfield, it was, like Shipley in the novel, 'near enough' to Lawrence's Uthwaite.

Sutton Scarsdale Hall was the former residence of William Arkwright, of whose emasculating injuries and unhappy marriage Lawrence is thought to have heard on his visit to Sir George and Lady Ida, thus acquiring – so some believe – an idea for a story which developed into *Lady Chatterley*. If, of course, Lawrence had already heard of Arkwright and Sutton Scarsdale from the Sitwells, then the sight of it on the map, close to Hardwick, would very likely have led him to visit the hall. Alternatively, if there had never been any conversation on that topic at Montegufoni, the name Sutton Scarsdale could still have excited his curiosity, since William Arkwright of Sutton Scarsdale would very likely have been known to him as Norman Douglas's former patron.

Tradition has it that it is the architect's plan for Sutton Scarsdale Hall that the old nobleman in the periwig is pointing towards in 'Marriage à la Mode', one of the scenes in Hogarth's *The Rake's Progress*. If there is any truth in the story, and if indeed Sutton Scarsdale *was* one of the models for Lawrence's 'Shipley', then the first and last chapters in the history of the hall were depicted in bawdy satires of English society in art and literature. But there seems to be no absolute proof for either claim.

The history of Sutton Scarsdale, at its beginning and in its last days, is remarkably close to that of the Shipley Hall of the Mundy family, near Heanor, and both histories resemble (but do not entirely follow) that of the fictional Shipley. Sutton Scarsdale, designed by Francis Smith of Warwick, had been built in 1724. Like the real and the fictional Shipley it had been built on the site of an earlier dwelling, in this case a fifteenth-century hall. The original owner, for whose tastes it had been designed, was the Earl of Scarsdale, ambassador to the court of Venice. It was a building of supreme elegance, the grandest mansion of the period in the whole of the county, with an imposing Corinthian façade and a particularly impressive interior, whose stuccoed panels and ceilings had been richly decorated at lavish cost in the full Venetian Rococo style. Towards the end of the eighteenth century it was acquired by Sir Richard Arkwright, the inventor, mill-owner and pioneer of the Industrial Revolution; subsequently it had become the seat of a junior branch of the family, the Arkwrights of Sutton Scarsdale. So it remained until 1919, when William Arkwright, the hall's last resident, gave up the struggle to maintain a house that must have been enormously expensive to keep up and an estate which probably yielded a very low economic return in all but the royalties from its mineral resources, the rights to which were retained when the estate and the hall were put up for sale. Arkwright himself moved to his other, smaller house at Thorne in Devon.

The hall came on the market at a time when hundreds of country houses up and down the land were available for purchase. No buyer came forward and it was withdrawn from the sale, being later acquired by a syndicate of brothers in hopes of making a profit on a subsequent sale as an institution of some sort. The plan failed, and to cut their losses the syndicate decided that every removable part of the interior and the lead from the roof should be sold off, thus condemning a unique work of art to extinction. Although there were plans to blow it up, the hall was still standing in 1926, as it does to this day, now 'an eyeless and roofless ruin in which . . . foxes nest'.[9] Its structure is currently being fortified by the Ministry of the Environment so that it may stand – as Osbert Sitwell, who bought the ruin in 1945, intended it – as a monument to 'the greed of the native speculator'. Like the Mundys' Shipley, demolished in 1942, its park was not engulfed by the estates of desirable semi-detached villas which became the destiny of Lawrence's Shipley. In both cases the coal beneath proved a more valuable asset, and both parks were torn up by open-cast coalmining, to be subsequently grassed over again and made to resemble the 'strange bald desert' (*LCL* 165) of green that Lawrence envisaged after the trees of the Shipley estate had been felled. Sutton Scarsdale, like Bolsover Castle and Hardwick Hall, now enjoys uninterrupted views of the M1 motorway, which further south cleaves through Lawrence's 'country of my heart'.

Two details in the history of Lawrence's Shipley fit that of the real Shipley and not that of Sutton Scarsdale: unlike Sutton Scarsdale, Shipley was sold by the heirs after the death of the owner; and the house was built in the period 1740–60, which better matches the mid-eighteenth-century date that Lawrence gave Shipley in *Lady Chatterley's Lover*, and precisely fits the 1760 house of Lawrence's original draft. Some aspects of the appearance and setting of the fictional Shipley apply uniquely to the Mundys' Shipley, as, for example, the siting of the park gates near a level crossing, or 'the little lake where the house itself stood' (*JTLJ* 160) – a detail which appears only in *John Thomas and Lady Jane*.

Both the real Shipley and Sutton Scarsdale had, in common with the Shipley of *Lady Chatterley*, a deer park with ornamental ponds and a public right of way running through it, and an alley of yew trees (more impressive in Shipley's case) which had approached an older house; both parks were hedged around with nearby collieries (though only in the case of Shipley were there specifically three collieries belonging to the owner of the house, as in the Shipley of *Lady Chatterley's Lover*, and both were bordered by mining settlements (though, again, in Shipley's case the settlement was more intense and threatening, more closely paralleling the situation of the fictional Shipley). Neither house had a stuccoed exterior, like Lawrence's Shipley, but part of the rear of Sutton Scarsdale, facing the road, perhaps had stucco where the brickwork shows today: most of the house, like the Mundys' Shipley, was built of stone.

There may just possibly be an intimation of the lavishness of the interior of Sutton Scarsdale in Lawrence's Shipley: 'The rooms were panelled with creamy-painted panelling, the ceilings were touched with gilt, and everything was kept in exquisite order, all the appointments were perfect, regardless of expense' (*LCL* 163). But the décor of the Mundys' Shipley, though not comparable in beauty with Arkwright's house, could no doubt have been similarly described.

Did Lawrence visit Sutton Scarsdale, and being struck by its similarities to another derelict house and abandoned park in his native Erewash district, take the real Shipley Hall as his principal model and shift it into north-east Derbyshire? It is a possibility worth entertaining since such a process would have replicated Lawrence's treatment of Renishaw and Lamb Close. But the fact that it cannot be proven has repercussions in regard to Reresby Sitwell's theory of the source-story for *Lady Chatterley*. So, too, does the possibility that Lawrence, if indeed he saw Sutton Scarsdale, could have come across the house largely by accident, without being led there by any knowledge of the life of William Arkwright. There were no close similarities between Arkwright's life and physical condition and Clifford's. The main support for the 'Arkwright theory' was Reresby Sitwell's conviction that the novel's Shipley Hall must be Sutton Scarsdale and that it must have been through hearing of Arkwright during talk of Osbert's interest in the hall that Lawrence came to visit Sutton Scarsdale. In the light of the present evidence that theory becomes almost as empty a shell as Sutton Scarsdale or Shipley Hall was in 1926.

The Arkwright theory remains, nevertheless, an intriguing possibility which seems to fit in, at least, with the methods and associative habits of mind which Lawrence appears to have followed in the pre-literary phases of the composition of the novel. One or two scraps of evidence favour an intuitive suspicion that Arkwright's story could well have been the source for *Lady Chatterley*. In the second version of the novel, in which Clifford is partly modelled on Osbert Sitwell, the owner of the fictional Shipley is said to have been 'a friend since Eton of Clifford's father, Sir Geoffrey' (*JTLJ* 151). Sir Geoffrey, named for the first time in the textual history of the novel in this version, stands for Sir George Sitwell; and Sir George and William Arkwright had been not only close neighbours in the county, but had attended Eton together, and shared the same interests in scholarship and travel. This detail may, therefore, hint at a Sitwell source for knowledge of the relationship between Sir George and William Arkwright. There is also the curious fact that almost alone amongst the people and places portrayed in the novel, Shipley Hall retains its real name through all three versions. An explanation for this could be that Lawrence had been influenced by the Arkwright story, had also conflated the site of Sutton Scarsdale and the appearance of Mundy's Shipley, and chose to retain the Shipley name in order to cover up any Arkwright associations with the novel. Lastly, the presence of members of the Sitwell family in the novel could be explained as due to their contextual association with the source-story, and the use of Rosalind Thornycroft as one of the models for Constance Chatterley might be attributable to chronological association with Lawrence's first acquiring the idea for the story.

Lawrence's experiences on his travels through Derbyshire provided most of the material for the powerful theme of 'one England blots out another' which arises out of Connie's journey to Uthwaite. The obliteration of the landscape of a vital pre-industrial England under the deadening, dehumanized, mechanical constructs of the machine age is a central feature of the Lawrentian outlook on contemporary life at all periods in his career, but only in *The Rainbow* does the force of its expression approach that in *Lady Chatterley*. An important facet of this theme in *Lady Chatterley* is the death of the English country house, and with it the extinction of the landed gentry. The Wragbys and the Shipleys of England, together with the landowning class who inhabited them, are shown to be doomed. And it could be argued that it is Clifford's attempt to preserve himself and his house from this impending doom, by immersing himself in his efforts to make the mines pay, which in fact leads to the destruction of his personality and brings nearer the fall of his house and class by increasing the dehumanization of the mining industry and its employees, thus fostering the conditions for class war and revolution.

'Ten years more of the hard times and Gobley, with all its peers, will be deserted and decaying. Fifty years and the countryside will know the old landmarks no more. They will have vanished as the monasteries vanished before them.'[10] So Aldous Huxley had written of the future of Gobley, the country house in *Crome Yellow*. Lawrence had to an extent himself foreshadowed Huxley's picture of the decline of the country house and its estates in *The White Peacock* of 1911. And in the beginning of *The Lost Girl*, the last of the novels to have a mainly Midlands setting before *Lady Chatterley*, Lawrence had already touched on the flight of the squirearchy and on the interpretation of its motives, both of which were to be treated more fully in his last novel. In *The Lost Girl*, completed six years previously (though its prototype, 'The Insurrection of Miss Houghton', had been begun in 1912), he observed that even by 1913, 'the last calm year of plenty', 'the old "County" [had] fled from the sight of so much disembowelled coal, to flourish on mineral rights in regions still idyllic'.[11]

In 1913 there had been only the local and particular evidence of the departure of the Walker family from Eastwood Hall to substantiate a picture of the flight of 'the old "County" '. But by 1920, when Lawrence completed his revision of *The Lost Girl*, there was in progress throughout England an emigration in droves of the landed gentry and lesser aristocracy from their country houses and estates. The effect of this exodus was a transfer of land on a scale without equal since the time of the Norman Conquest.

The main factors which prompted the departure of the landowning classes, according to the historian T. O. Lloyd, were the economic effects of a six-year period of inflation coupled with increases in taxation and the low economic yield from landownership. At this period, too, political and social change had made the ownership of land no longer a source of the political power it had bestowed in the past. Under the pressure of economic and social forces such as these, the old landowning classes trimmed their sheets to the wind and sold their land to the tenants and their houses to manufacturers or to institutions. In retrenchment they sacrificed the larger house and estate and continued to reside in their smaller country houses; they held on to their unsaleable grouse moors in

161

Scotland and also to their urban real estate, which later restored them to riches. [12]

The extent of Lawrence's realism may be judged by the fact that his Manbys, the heirs to Shipley in *The First Lady Chatterley*, did much the same: they 'had a house in town, a lodge in Scotland and a villa near Nice' (*FLC* 62) and they abandoned the Shipley estate, which was, in any case, detestable to them. Lawrence's understanding of the causes of the departure of the gentry was as unsentimental as T. O. Lloyd's, but inevitably less objective. It was also more particular in so far as it applied to a specific region. For Lawrence the evacuation of the landed gentry in the Nottinghamshire and Derbyshire coalfield was precipitated by the uncontrollable growth of the industry and the mining communities that had made that class rich. The ugliness of the industrial scene and of the proliferation of the mean dwellings of the workers, the grudging resentment of an alien mushrooming proletariat made ugly by an environment that was devoid of beauty – these factors conspired in the build-up of a will that 'was against the gentleman owner' and which proved too 'hard to live up against' (*LCL* 164).

Lawrence's view of the condition of the mining country and of England as a whole is presented in all his Midlands novels in terms of the mutually determining relationship between the architectural landscape and the social landscape. [13] In *Lady Chatterley* Lawrence showed a society which was degenerating towards dissolution as a result of its lost contact with the spiritual, social and architectural ideals of the past. An entirely similar presentation of the condition of postwar England had been offered by C. F. G. Masterman in his study *England after the War*, published in 1922, and dealing primarily with the period of the early 1920s in which Lawrence set *Lady Chatterley*. The striking parallels in the pictures of English society and point of view between Lawrence and Masterman, whether coincidental or through Lawrence having read Masterman's work, bear witness to the underlying realism of *Lady Chatterley*. This remains true of the general character of the novel in all its versions, however much the progress towards melodramatic stereotyping of Clifford, or towards overstatement or mythic narrative.

Lawrence's only individual eccentricity in his analysis of English society – an important and fundamental one – was in tracing the origins of all social maladies to an imbalance of the cerebral, cognitive consciousness over the phallic, intuitive consciousness. In all other respects Lawrence's observations, diagnoses and prognoses find support in Masterman's comprehensive study of the state of England in the four years which followed the peace of 1918. Masterman showed an England in which there was a greater division of class than had existed for fifty years, and in which the struggle between capital and labour had become 'more fierce and uncompromising' than ever before.[14] Between the working and the privileged classes there was mutual fear, suspicion and antagonism which resulted from the absence of any real contact or communication either way. Like Lawrence, Masterman doubted whether, if the bad times persisted, the workers would have the patience to endure the situation without turning to direct organized action against the exploiters.

In Masterman's England, as in Lawrence's, all classes of society were wholly lacking in spiritual ideals. Everywhere there was disillusion and disenchantment; and the fruits of the peace had been callous indifference rather than tenderness. Society had become greedy and trivialized, ruled by the pursuits of material wealth and of ephemeral pleasures of the senses. 'Today', Masterman observed, 'the populace, seeking to forget, demand bread and games; other classes, money-making and accumulation of goods; others dancing or music'.[15] The public had become 'like a child which escapes from a drab reality into the fairyland of pantomime' or into the celluloid fantasies of 'the ever multiplying cinema'.[16]

The spread of the red-brick coagulations of the suburbs, the dereliction of the countryside and the fall of the country house are all chronicled in Masterman as in *Lady Chatterley*. Even Lawrence's prophecies of the imminent doom of society, expressed in the imagery of the Apocalypse, are equally or more prominent in *England after the War*. The image of the nation's present and its future, as intuitively felt by a poet informed mainly by the impressions of fleeting visits to England, thus coincides substantially with the informed, judiciously researched view of a former cabinet minister in Asquith's Liberal government, a Cambridge fellow of rational if somewhat sentimental temperament. Their portrayals of the state of the nation in the early 1920s can be considered representative of how England seemed, at the time, to men of high moral principle and conservative disposition.

While he had been holidaying in Britain Lawrence had read in *The Times Literary Supplement* that in contemporary society the ownership of property had become a religious question. It made some impression on Lawrence, for he quoted it in 'Return to Bestwood' and in all versions of *Lady Chatterley*. [17] Perhaps it was the notion that the question of property-ownership might be pertinent to his quest for a religion of life, combined with his identification with the suffering have-nots in the colliery districts, which led Lawrence towards a view of socialist aims that was sympathetic, if by no means entirely approbatory. Within the cycles of action and reaction that characterized Lawrence's life, this was not a new development. At earlier periods he had undergone similar swings towards socialism, but they had never lasted for long, and neither did the change of heart brought on by his visit to Ripley. But it remained with him while he wrote 'Return to Bestwood' and *The First Lady Chatterley*.

At the conclusion of 'Return to Bestwood', Lawrence set out an inventory of his most cherished convictions. Among these was a statement suggesting a new commitment to democracy and acceptance of socialist programmes:

> I know that we could, if we would, establish little by little a true democracy in England: we could nationalise the land and industries and means of transport, and make the whole thing work infinitely better than at present, *if we would*. It all depends on the spirit in which the thing is done.
>
> (*Ph* 2 265)

These and other solutions to the question of property-ownership were not seen as ends in themselves, but as intermediate instruments in establishing a new society in which men and women could find immortality through living for life – for 'the beauty of aliveness, imagination, awareness, and contact' (*Ph* 2 266).

Very similar views are put forward by Duncan Forbes, Lawrence's mouthpiece in *The First Lady Chatterley*. Forbes has no political opinions, but confesses that he would be a communist if he were a working man. He personally found the communists and their doctrines uninspiring but believed they had 'a sense of genuine injustice' (*FLC* 241). The triumph of communism, Forbes/Lawrence naïvely believed, might, by destroying the existing materialist culture, pave the way for the Lawrentian Utopia of a new relationship between men, based on passionate human contact and a caring for life and for 'the life-flow with one another' (*FLC* 242). In this version, as in no other, the keeper is a politically motivated working-class hero who becomes a communist determined to force the owners to give up their property, preferably with as little bloodshed as possible. Parkin, combining communism and a passion for life, has the destructive and creative impulses necessary for transforming the existing world into the new, ideal society.

At the end of 'Return to Bestwood', Lawrence wrote:

> I know we must take up the responsibility for the future, now. A great change is coming, and must come. What we need is some glimmer of a vision of a world that shall be, beyond the change. Otherwise we shall be in for a great débâcle . . . I know these things. And it is nothing very new to know these things. The only new thing would be to act on them.
>
> *(Ph 2 265)*

'Words are action, good enough, if they're the right words' (*CL* 800), Lawrence had written to Rolf Gardiner in 1925. The writing of *The First Lady Chatterley*, in which he showed 'the glimmer of a vision' of a better world, could be seen as Lawrence's personal response to the summons to action in 'Return to Bestwood'.

9

The First Drafts of *Lady Chatterley*

Lawrence left Ripley on 16 September for London, where he and Frieda were to spend the remaining few days of their stay in England at Carlingford House, Hampstead, not far from the studio of Mark Gertler, who had arranged the accommodation for them.

It was probably at the studio that Lawrence first met Gertler's friends, Professor Bonamy Dobrée and his wife Valentine. Evidently it was a warm meeting which held out the promise of a close relationship between the Lawrences and the Dobrées.[1] Lawrence and Frieda lunched with them before leaving London and were invited to visit them in Egypt, where Dobrée was Professor of English at Cairo University. Lawrence appears to have very much looked forward to getting to know the Dobrées better. Their withdrawal of this invitation, for sound family reasons (see p. 235), shortly after it had been repeated in 1927, provoked a bitter and irrational response in Lawrence, to whom it seemed yet another let-down by middle-class acquaintances, up to their hot and cold Murryish tricks. His sense of rejection seems to have played an important part in, although it could simply have been a major symptom of, the swing of his mood towards paranoia in the period leading up to the writing of *Lady Chatterley's Lover*.

Some of the postcards Lawrence sent from London in September show views of the British Museum. It was evidently the Etruscan book which was still planned as the most important task in hand when he returned to Italy. The tombs of the Etruscan city of Vulci had been rifled in the nineteenth century, and their contents – 'vases and statues, bronzes, sarcophagi and jewels' (*EP* 144) – could only be studied at the Vatican, the Florence Museum and the British Museum. *Etruscan Places* shows that Lawrence had seen the grave-goods of the 'Tomb of Isis' at the British Museum, and his letters suggest that he also spent some time in the Print Room, familiarizing himself with the drawings of Etruscan sites that were kept there.[2]

Perhaps Lawrence's mysterious need, on his last day in London, to

166

visit the National Gallery in order to re-examine a couple of pictures was connected with his plans for the Etruscan book and his search in the Museum for suitable illustrations. This last day was a hectic one. On the gallery steps he finally met, after a number of botched arrangements, the elderly Australian writer Siebenhaar for whose translation of *Max Havelaar* he had written an introduction. Lawrence allowed him only snatches of conversation as he raced down the Strand to lunch with Robert Atkins, whom the English Stage Society had appointed director of Lawrence's play *David*, then scheduled for performance in December. Lawrence promised to return to assist at rehearsals in November, though it was unlikely that he could have managed to get back so shortly after his return to Italy.

On the eve of Lawrence's departure there was a small gathering of old friends at Carlingford House, which included Kot, Catherine Carswell, her husband Don and her brother Gordon MacFarlane, none of whom would see Lawrence again. The night provided a happy finale to their acquaintanceships, with the whole company united in a harmonious spirit of gaiety and warm friendship. Next day Lawrence and Frieda took the boat-train to Folkestone and crossed the Channel in fine, breezy weather. Despite many plans to visit England during the remaining years of his life, Lawrence never brought them to fruition – a failure which does not seem ever to have caused him a moment's regret.

The Lawrences made a leisurely progress back to Florence, stopping off at Paris, Lausanne and Milan on the way. In Paris, where they stayed for two or three days, Lawrence's good humour was such that he even discerned friendliness among the Parisians. Strolling contentedly in the Luxembourg Gardens in the warm autumn sunshine, he sensed a carefree simplicity in the quality of Parisian life that came as a welcome change after the tense atmosphere of London.[3]

In *The First Lady Chatterley* Lawrence had Connie and her sister Hilda stay, as he and Frieda had done, 'in a smallish hotel opposite the Louvre palace on the left bank of the river'; and he imparted to Connie the emotions he had felt on revisiting Paris. Here Connie, too, came to like the people, and unwound emotionally as she 'felt herself settling into the historic past' (*FLC* 136). She admired the brilliance of the flowers in the Luxembourg Gardens in mid-summer – 'so purely decorative', 'fine, splendid, showy, jaunty!' – just as Lawrence had done in late September, three weeks before he began writing the novel.[4] In Paris, Connie of *John Thomas and Lady Jane* was also 'happier than in London': she felt 'a certain tenderness' descend upon her again and sensed in the people and the atmosphere of the city an accord with her own 'slowly-pulsing but vital passion' (*JTLJ* 282). But, like Tevershall and the English Midlanders, in *Lady Chatterley's Lover* Paris and the Parisians fell under a disenchanted regard. In the first drafts Connie had come to be depressed by the city after a while. In the final version this is her initial and principal response. The sensuality that Connie of the first versions had admired in the people was 'worn-out for lack of tenderness', and Paris had become, for her, 'one of the saddest of towns': 'Sometimes she was happy for a while . . . in the Luxembourg Gardens. But already Paris was full of Americans . . . and the usual dreary English that are so hopeless abroad' (*LCL* 265f.)

On 4 October the Lawrences arrived back at the Villa Mirenda. The weather was hot and sultry and the thick walls on the south side of the villa, where Lawrence had his bedroom, had stored all the fierce heat of the Tuscan summer. On his first night he suffered a sleepless return to a hard bed, and was left longing for a fresh English North Sea breeze to come gusting through the window. In the following year, confined for the best part of a month to his sick-bed in that room, he was to be so tormented by the infernal heat that the memory of his experience destroyed his love of the Mirenda and of Italy for ever. But, for the present, no amount of discomfort or lack of sleep could diminish his pleasure at reaching the villa in time for the grape harvest, the *vendemmia*:

> It is very lovely, really – not like autumn, like summer. The peasants are bringing in the grapes, in a big wagon drawn by two big white oxen. Every hour or so they roll up with a load, to go in the big vats in the ground-floor cellars. The grapes are very sweet this year – not very big – little and round and clear, and very sweet. It will be a good wine year, even if the bulk is not enormous.
>
> (Ada 110)

This scene of harvest-time on the Mirenda estate is an extract from a letter, written on the day after Lawrence's arrival, to Gertie Cooper, to whom he showed a devoted and conscientious friendship. It is one of a stream of letters and postcards sent to her after he left England and intended to bring the spirit and beauty of the places he stayed at to her room in the Mundesley Sanatorium on the Norfolk coast, where she was receiving treatment for her tuberculosis.

Two days after the Lawrences' return to the Villa Mirenda, Richard Aldington and Dorothy Yorke arrived for a short stay. Lawrence liked both of them a good deal and enjoyed their visit. In Aldington he perhaps especially relished the malicious, caustic humour with which he demolished English society and people of his acquaintance, and which he later turned against Lawrence in his biography, *Portrait of a Genius, But . . .* During Aldington's stay Lawrence made no attempt to work, and, fresh after his summer of writing practically nothing, was relaxed, cheerful, energetic and affable.

Within a fortnight of Richard Aldington leaving the Mirenda, Lawrence had begun work on *Lady Chatterley*. It has been suggested by Janice Robinson, in a biography of Hilda Doolittle, the imagist poet H.D., that Aldington and his estranged wife, H.D., were intimately connected with the novel. In Robinson's opinion Hilda Doolittle was Constance, Aldington was Clifford, and Hilda's giving birth to a child by someone other than Aldington – Lawrence according to these claims – was mirrored in the story of Mellors fathering a child by Connie.[5]

The notion of an Aldington association with the genesis of *Lady Chatterley* is not inherently improbable. Equally there is no firm evidence in the way of links between textual and biographical detail to make any of the claims stick. But in that regard Robinson's thesis is hardly more insubstantial than the Arkwright theory of the origins of the novel. Possibly H.D. formed with the other contributors a quartet of sitters for the portrait of Constance, but the only support for this view is the fact of H.D.'s child by another man and the use of her name, Hilda, for Connie's sister. H.D. was not the only possible source among women of Lawrence's acquaintance for a plot in which a child was conceived out of wedlock. But, given Lawrence's conflationary habits in the creation of his fiction, it is very possible that the history of H.D. was one of those he had in mind as he wrote the novel. Aldington had in common with Clifford the fact that he came home shattered from the war, though in his case it was his spirit that was broken. He was also complaisant in the love affairs of a wife who had a child by another man. Any other resemblances result from the fact that Clifford represents a type of man with whom in some respects Aldington might have been associated by Lawrence. Judged by his love affairs both during the period of his marriage and after its collapse – he and H.D. had an open marriage that allowed sexual freedom to either party – he could never, however, have been regarded as either sexually apathetic or masochistically reverent of women.

After Richard Aldington and 'Dorothy Yorke' left the Mirenda, Lawrence did not bother to look up his friends in Florence. The Wilkinsons were company enough and by now had become such a familiar part of Lawrence's life, and were so easy to be with, that his regular meetings with them evidently did not count as seeing anybody. Writing to Brett of his idle contentment on returning to the Mirenda, he told her: 'I feel how nice it is, in the soft, sunny days that are already none too long, to see nobody, but just leisurely drift one's way' (*CL* 943).

Just as he was finishing this letter, he received a telegram from Aldous Huxley asking the Lawrences to lunch in Florence. He had with him his Belgian wife, Maria, whom Lawrence had known as a young girl of 17, a protégée of Lady Ottoline Morrell. During the last week in October the Lawrences and the Huxleys met several times before Aldous and Maria returned to Cortina, in the Dolomites, where they rented a villa. In Florence they dined out together on a couple of occasions and visited Huxley's old friend, the poet Vernon Lee (Violet Paget) who remarked of Lawrence: 'He sees . . . more than a human being ought to see' (Hux xxxi). On the 27th the Huxleys came out to the Mirenda for the day. Reporting their visit to Secker, Lawrence wrote: 'They were quite nice today, he and Maria, we liked them. But *triste un omo finito*, to be sentimental and Italian' (Sec 78). Huxley's view of human existence, prescribed by a sense of life's betrayal that dated from his mother's death when he was a boy of 14, was wearily melancholic and cynical where Lawrence's was usually aggressively optimistic. This melancholia, combined with a dry, languid, detached manner, gave Lawrence the false impression that he was played out. Maria Huxley, more animated and emotionally responsive than Aldous, but with a serious, rather intense personality, seemed no less lacking in *joie de vivre*. 'Really people have no pep, they so easily go blank, and so young' (Ada 113), Lawrence wrote of them in a letter to Ada on the day after their visit.

Of the two Huxleys Lawrence was the more attracted to Maria, a tiny, delicate figure with large, haunting blue eyes, who reminded Lawrence of 'a *very* small edition of Ottoline: like Ottoline's Cinderella daughter – same peculiar long cheeks' (*CL* 949). Maria was a highly-strung, extremely sensitive woman, with a strong aesthetic sensibility and a loving, tenderhearted compassion and concern for others. Lawrence, who may possibly have worked some facets of her personality into the Constance of his first draft, felt there was an underlying affinity between Maria and himself: 'The things one cares about are all inside, like seeds in the ground in winter . . . Luckily the inside thing corresponds with the inside thing in just a few people. I think it is so with us. We don't fit very well outside – but the inside corresponds, which is most important' (Hux 715).

Just as, on the face of it, Lawrence might seem an odd choice of friend for a man of Huxley's outwardly phlegmatic, rational character and intellectual disposition, so Maria would appear an unlikely choice of partner: her mind was quite untrained; she had a nervous, artistic temperament; and she lived for the thrill of aesthetic enjoyment and sensuous pleasure. Where Lawrence, usually to his disadvantage, sought friends who in some degree resembled himself, Huxley may have been drawn to his opposites, perhaps in compensation for qualities he felt to be lacking in himself. The goal of those who lead the life of reason, he believed, 'should be to combine the lyrical with the critical, to be simultaneously Shelley and the *Edinburgh Review*'.[6] Lyrical feeling and expression did not come as easily or as naturally to him as critical ratiocination. And much of his admiration for Lawrence, whom he came to consider 'the most extraordinary and impressive human being'[7] he had ever known, was for his possession of an intuitive poetic genius that he would dearly have loved to share.[8] Another aspect of Lawrence's appeal lay in Huxley's lifelong preoccupation with the paranormal, and in particular with visionary or mystical experiences which transcended ordinary levels of perception. 'To be with Lawrence', he wrote, 'was a kind of adventure, a voyage of discovery into newness and otherness. For being himself of a different order, he inhabited a different universe from that of common men – a brighter and intenser world' (Hux xxx).

Such was the value Huxley placed upon the 'otherness' of Lawrence's perception of the universe that he came not to attach too much importance to the fact that in much of his ideology he seemed to pass beyond reason and commonsense. Indeed, if Huxley is to be identified with Philip Quarles in *Point Counter Point*, as Quarles's commitment to 'the cool indifferent flux of intellectual curiosity'

(*Point* 269) might suggest, he could be temporarily seduced by the power of Lawrence's vision and his rhetoric into lending some credence to otherwise unacceptable Lawrentian doctrines of 'blood-knowledge'. After spending several hours in the company of Mark Rampion (a character modelled on Lawrence), Quarles 'really believed in noble savagery; he felt convinced that the proudly conscious intellect ought to humble itself a little and admit the claims of the heart, aye and the bowels, the loins' (*Point* 270).

Rather in the way that he himself hoped to combine the lyrical and the critical, Huxley felt the need for 'an acceptable philosophical system which [would] permit ordinary human beings to give due value both to Lawrence's aspect of reality and to that other aspect, which he refused to admit the validity of – the scientific, rational aspect'.[9] Early attempts to convince Lawrence of the need to harness his vision to scientific rationality taught him that it was futile to dispute with Lawrence in matters 'in which he absolutely refused to take a rational interest' (Hux xv). In an argument on the theory of evolution, for example, whose validity Lawrence vehemently denied, Huxley had urged: '"But look at all the evidence, Lawrence."' Lawrence replied, characteristically: '"But I don't care about evidence. Evidence doesn't mean anything to me. I don't feel it *here*." And he pressed his two hands to his solar plexus' (Hux xv).

Aldington, familiar with Lawrence's rhetoric and methods of argumentation, thought he detected a caricature of Lawrence in the portrait of Kingham in Huxley's *Two or Three Graces*, published in 1926:

'I think there's something really devilish about the women of this generation', he said to me, in his intense, emphatic way, some two or three days later. 'Something really devilish.' It was a trick of his, in writing as well as in speech, to get hold of a word and, if he liked the sound of it, work it to death.

I laughed. 'Oh, come', I protested. 'Do you find Catherine, for example, so specially diabolic?'

'She isn't of this generation', Kingham answered. 'Spiritually, she doesn't belong to it.'

I laughed again; it was always difficult arguing with Kingham. You might think you had him cornered, you raised your logical cudgel to smash him. But while you were bringing it down, he darted out from beneath the stroke through some little trap-door of his own discovery, clean out of the argument. It was impossible to prove him in the wrong, for the simple reason that he never remained in any one intellectual position to be proved anything.[10]

Since even the content of Kingham's discourse seems to have Lawrence off to a tee, Aldington can be excused for what, in fact, was a case of mistaken identity. Huxley scarcely knew Lawrence when he wrote the book, and in a letter to a friend, who had reached the same conclusion as Aldington, he denied that Kingham was Lawrence, while admitting that Rampion of *Point Counter Point* was based on him:[11] their October meeting in Florence, in fact, coincided with the period when he was beginning to work on the novel.

Aldington, perhaps at the time when Lawrence came to him after seeing Huxley in London, seems to have indulged in a little mischief-making which might, had Lawrence been at all times beset with paranoia as some of his contemporaries claimed, have made friendship with Huxley impossible. It is very probable that Aldington was the 'somebody' referred to in Lawrence's letter to Secker on 27 October: 'Somebody said in his [Huxley's] book *One or Two Graces* or whatever it is, was an unflattering character of me. But what's the odds! He never knew me, anyhow!' (Sec 78).

As people, Lawrence and Huxley had in common little more than a lack of sentimentality, and indomitable courage and determination in the face of spiritual and physical suffering. As writers, they had a mutual interest in human sexuality and a shared habit of taking off friends and acquaintances in their books. It is an interesting reflection of the general prejudice against Lawrence, which cannot entirely be dissociated from class-feeling on the part of the victims, that though he often caused offence, Huxley never attracted the hatred for this practice which fell upon Lawrence, though his satires were the more deadly by virtue of being inherently more comic.

Lawrence and Huxley were also, both of them, *pasticheurs*, who often built their characters out of a conflation of the attributes of two or more live models: Priscilla Wimbush in *Crome Yellow*, for instance, had combined Lady Ida Sitwell and Lady Ottoline Morrell. In the course of their writing careers Lawrence and Huxley were to draw on a number of identical models. Lady Ottoline had appeared in *Women in Love* as Hermione Roddice, and several of the models for characters in *Lady Chatterley* – Sir George and Lady Ida Sitwell, Osbert and Edith, Middleton Murry and Frieda – appeared also in Huxley's fiction. They also took each other off. While Lawrence became Rampion in *Point Counter Point*, Huxley was to be Arnold B. Hammond in *Lady Chatterley's Lover*: 'a tall thin fellow with a wife and two children, but much more closely connected with a typewriter' (*LCL* 33). Hammond, one of the mental-lifers and acolytes of the bitch-goddess Success who gather round Clifford at Wragby, is 'rather proud of the integrity of his mind, and of his *not* being a time-server' (*LCL* 34); but his 'pure mind' is said by one of his friends to be 'going as dry as fiddlesticks' (*LCL* 35).

When the Huxleys visited the Mirenda, they rolled up 'in a grand new Italian car – 61000 Lire' (Sec 78), offering to sell Lawrence their little Citroen, in which they had made the Italian tour that Huxley had written of in *Along the Road*. When he read the book in 1926, Lawrence had become interested in the possibilities which a car might open up for him, and may have said as much in the letter he wrote to Huxley on that occasion. Faced with the real possibility of car-ownership, he understandably balked at the idea: a motor car would have ill become the enemy of the mechanical age, and a car was, in any case, incompatible with his mood of the moment. Having spent a summer journeying through Britain and Europe, he had no desire to travel: 'It is much pleasanter to go quietly into the pinewoods and sit and do there what bit of work I do. Why rush from place to place?' (*CL* 944).

On fine days the woods were Lawrence's scriptorium. His usual practice, in San Polo as elsewhere, was to work in the mornings. After breakfasting at seven, he would make his way through the olive groves to the umbrella pine-woods near the stream behind the church of San Polo Mosciano. Near the sanctuary of San Eusebio (a small cave in the rock where he sometimes rested or took refuge from the weather, using a large slab of stone as his bed and a smaller slab as his table) was his favourite writing-place – a large umbrella pine-tree. Here he would set down the cushion he took with him, and propping his back against the trunk and his exercise book on his knees he would write, with a disciplined and absorbed concentration that made for few pauses in the rapid movement of his pen, for five hours or so. Then at lunchtime he would return to the Mirenda and submit what he had written to Frieda for her approval.

Compelled to write out of doors in order to be in a full, active relationship with the natural world during the act of composition, Lawrence habitually sought out a tree to write under. Trees afforded not only the practical advantages of support and shade. For this strange, solitary man they were, as probably they had been since his lonely boyhood, silent companions which he invested with animate life. And in sensuous contact with trees he could the more readily sense and assimilate the unconscious life-power of the universe.[12] As he showed frequently in his writings they were, with the sun, the most potent symbols of the phallic consciousness.

When Lawrence began *Lady Chatterley* is not precisely known, but it was certainly begun not long before 26 October, when the dog John, who often trotted beside Lawrence on his journeys into the woods, placed a muddy paw on page 41 of the manuscript of *The First Lady Chatterley*, and Lawrence inscribed the leaf with a record of the date, provenance and authorship of the print. From a study of breaks in the writing, identifiable from changes in the shade of the ink and the character of the hand, Michael Squires concluded that four mornings' work had gone before the section begun on the 26th, and therefore conjectured that Lawrence had begun on the 22nd.[13] However, the external evidence suggests that it would not have been easy for him to manage four consecutive mornings of writing between 22 and 26 October, and that he could have begun a little earlier. The 22nd was the day he lunched with the Huxleys in Florence and was a time when the weather entered a stormy spell, with bursts of torrential rain and hail. When, on the 21st, Arthur Wilkinson called round to the Mirenda to take Lawrence to the Villa Poggi to join Frieda, he found him whistling so loud in the kitchen that he failed to hear the knocking at the door. There is a fair certainty that the whistling was a symptom of the elation and preoccupation that attended his having already set out upon a new and engrossing project.

Whatever the exact date of the start of work on *Lady Chatterley*, the writing was certainly under way at the time of Lawrence's encounters with the Huxleys, with whom he seems to have discussed his ideas for the book. 'To Clarinda', one of the poems in *Pansies*, written after he completed the final version of the novel and originally addressed to Maria Huxley, suggests that Maria gave him encouragement in the early stages of the enterprise:

> Thank you, dear Clarinda,
> for helping with Lady C.,
> It was you who gave her her first kiss
> and told her not to be
> afraid of the world, but to sally forth
> and trip it for all she was worth.

(Poems 550)

The practical help Maria had given was to type part of the MS of *Lady Chatterley's Lover* for him when they were all together at Diablerets, Switzerland, in 1928.

It is interesting, in view of the possibility of early conversations between Lawrence and the Huxleys on the matter of *Lady Chatterley*, that there should be some correspondences in title, plot, character-type, use of settings and 'depiction of class-tensions' between *Lady Chatterley* and *Lady Connie* by Mrs Humphry Ward. The author of the paper which noted these similarities and drew attention to Lawrence's 'meticulous inversion' of the plot of *Lady Connie* was not aware that Mrs Ward was Huxley's Aunt Mary.[14] There is no evidence to prove that Lawrence had ever read the novel, but Aldous Huxley certainly had, and thought it 'clap-trap':[15] hence, it could have been that Lawrence's acquaintance with *Lady Connie* (if any such existed) came secondhand via Aldous.

Throughout October Lawrence's position with regard to his writing career remained unchanged. His intention was to concentrate on the kind of work that demanded little effort from him – short stories, essays and reviews – and only three days, at most, before beginning the first draft of *Lady Chatterley* he was telling his sister-in-law, Else Jaffe: 'I feel I'll never write another novel' (*Not I* 204). At the outset *Lady Chatterley* was not conceived of as a novel at all: it grew into one as the writing progressed. It was to have been a long short story, of about the length, perhaps, of *The Virgin and the Gipsy*. In his letter to Secker of 27 October it was described simply as 'a story – shortish' (Sec 79), and not until his next letter to Secker, nearly three weeks later, did Lawrence use the term 'novel'. The first announcement of the themes of the story came in a letter from Frieda to her son, Montague Weekley, on the last day of October: 'Lawrence goes into the woods to write, he is writing a short long story, always breaking new ground, the curious class-feeling this time or rather the soul against the body, no I don't explain it well, the *animal* part.' Here Lawrence added: 'Ooray! Eureka' (*CL* 944).

According to Frieda, the class difference between herself and Lawrence provided one of the areas of conflict in their marriage.[16] Their private 'class war' as Frieda called it, re-erupted in a short skirmish in the company of the Wilkinsons on 24 October, and was perhaps sparked off by some talk of the subject matter of *Lady Chatterley*. It was the Wilkinsons' first experience of harsh words between them, and it was duly recorded in their family journal with an apparent levity that does not seem inappropriate to the dialogue:

L.   (of the upper classes) 'I've done with them: they're hard – cruel, cruel (crescendo).'
F.   'Why didn't you marry one of your own class then, you'd have been bored stiff.'
L.   (Very sad and vinegary) 'I may have my regrets.'
F.   'Well you can be off. You can go now if you like.'

(Wilk 67)

Frieda has the last word, which was probably a trump she could always play in their quarrels, because she had the advantage of being less dependent on Lawrence than he was on her. Bickerings of this sort were probably a constant feature of their life together. But the violent rows of the past had apparently ceased. For the whole of the period when Lawrence wrote the first two versions of *Lady Chatterley* (and perhaps for the rest of their lives together) a relatively harmonious atmosphere established itself in the Lawrence household. Writing to Mabel Luhan in March 1927, Frieda claimed: 'All this winter we lived so peacefully, Lawrence and I, and with one's usual forgetfulness, I can't believe that we ever quarrelled so dreadfully' (Luhan 293).

Relations between capital and labour, between the coal-owners and the miners, which provide one of the dominant motifs of *The First Lady Chatterley*, were prominent in Lawrence's thoughts, both before and during the time when he first began writing. 'I am always thinking about the strike', he wrote in a letter of 28 October to Ada, to whom he had earlier written asking whether the strike, which he likened to 'an insanity', was breaking up in Ripley. As in the first draft of the novel, he remained broadly sympathetic to the miners: 'I'm sure it's weariness beyond words, and what the miners themselves must be feeling I don't like to think. Certainly it's one of the greatest disasters that has ever happened to England' (Ada 113). It is this disaster and an ensuing greater social débâcle of class warfare which is prophesied in the first version of the novel. News that the strike had ended reached him a week or so before he finished the first draft at the end of November.

From Frieda's accounts of the genesis of *Lady Chatterley*, and from Lawrence's letters, it appears very likely that *The First Lady Chatterley* was written entirely within the woods near the Mirenda. A letter to

Brett in late November suggests that he wrote only when the weather allowed him to work out of doors: 'I am doing a little novel – laid in the Midlands, in England – I do hope to break it off quite soon, keep it quite short. But lately it's been too wet to sit out'·(*CL* 948). The environment in which the novel was composed may have contributed substantially to the pastoral, quietly lyrical treatment of the woodland scenes in the first draft and in the succeeding version, where the lyrical passages are more profuse and more intensely and evocatively realized. For Lawrence, as for Connie of *The First Lady Chatterley*, to enter into the life of the woods was 'to break through into magic once more' (*FLC* 42); and since the mystery of unseen life and invisible energy was common to all woodlands, Lawrence could project his immediate sensible awareness of the atmosphere of a Tuscan pine-wood into his realization of life in the oak-forests of the hills of Annesley.

When Lawrence finished the first draft of *Lady Chatterley* and began work on the next version is uncertain; but estimates which place the start of work on *John Thomas and Lady Jane* in December 1926 are most probably correct;[17] and it is equally likely that very little time elapsed between the completion of the first version and the start of work on the succeeding one: the detailed picture of the furnishings and décor of Connie's sitting-room, which occurs at the end of the first version, was fresh enough in Lawrence's mind for him to wish to use it in a revised version in the opening pages of *John Thomas and Lady Jane*; and Lawrence also transferred Connie's mood of half-insane revulsion from the ending of the first draft to the beginning of the next. In some respects, in fact, notably in the characters of Connie, Clifford and Parkin, *John Thomas and Lady Jane* begins almost as if it were a sequel to the original draft, a continuation from where he left off in *The First Lady Chatterley*.

Quite possibly the first version was completed in the few days of sunshine that followed the letter to Brett on 24 November, telling her that he hoped shortly to bring the novel to an end. The mood of the last pages is, for this version, untypically gloomy and doom-laden, expressed in powerful, repellent images of nausea, death and putrescence which signal Connie's rejection of Clifford and Wragby. This spirit may perhaps correlate with the immediate, depressed aftermath of a bout of malaria and cold-sickness which drove Lawrence to his bed for three days on the 22nd. During these and the preceding days the weather had turned evil:

We had such deluges of rain, and I got wet coming up from Scandicci. Everything is steamy, soggy wet, and there are great pale-brown floods out in the Arno valley. We can see them from the window. And still it thunders and lightens at times – and it is warm. We only light the stove in the evening for the damp.

This is the time of the year I dislike most in any country. I wish it could come cold and a bit crisp. The town is no better than the country, and the country isn't much better than the town. One can only grin and abide.

(Ada 143)

In addition to being dispirited by illness and by the wet, Lawrence was beginning to feel lonely and isolated. The Wilkinsons had departed to Florence for the winter and the weather prevented excursions into the city to see them or his other friends.

It was Lawrence's habit to write from the inspiration of the moment, without any preconceived coherent plan of how the action or characters would evolve.[18] This was probably most especially true of his first drafts, out of which, in the light of reassessment undertaken both before and during the subsequent rendering of the text, a more considered version would emerge. Midway through the writing of *The First Lady Chatterley* Lawrence wrote to Secker: 'I have begun a novel in the Derbyshire coal-mining districts – already rather improper. The gods alone know where it will end – if they will help me out with it' (Sec 79). The major fault with this version was that the gods remained aloof, and no notion of an ending came to him. After the Sheffield episodes, where Connie is faced with the problem of coming to terms with the narrow, stifling realities of working-class life, the novel meanders loosely towards a somewhat abrupt and unsatisfactory conclusion. At this point Lawrence seems to have been eager to have done and get on with the next version, and appears, therefore, to have decided to shelve the search for a well-rounded, resonant conclusion until he was next faced with the problem. The last paragraph of *The First Lady Chatterley* was thoughtlessly dashed off without care for its quality: it is trite and jejune to such an extent as to suggest that it was playfully intended as a parody of the cheap, pornographic novelette.[19] Connie, we learn, had never realized what a tomb Wragby was:

Till she had loved Parkin – her Op. Yes, she loved him. He was a man, if he wasn't a gentleman. Anyhow there came a breath of fresh air with him, and a breath of fresh life. My lady's fucker, as he called himself so

179

savagely! How he had hated her for not taking him fully seriously in
his manly fucking! Ah well! The future was still to hand!

(FLC 253)

Michael Squires suggests that the first day of December may have
marked the beginning of work on the revised version, *John Thomas
and Lady Jane*;[20] and this may well be accurate to within a day or so.
In between finishing the first draft and starting on its successor,
Lawrence may have hit upon the idea for an ending which had earlier
eluded him. On 28 November Rolf Gardiner wrote to Lawrence
describing a recent day's hike in the Lawrence country. Beginning at
Hucknall Torkard, he had walked to Watnall Hall and through the
meadows to the Alfreton Road. Lawrence replied on 3 December:

How well I can see Hucknall Torkard and the miners! Didn't you go
into the church to see the tablet, where Byron's heart is buried? . . .
I've gone many times down Hucknall Long Lane to Watnall . . . it's a
great Sunday morning walk.

(CL 951)

Lawrence went on to suggest as a future possibility for Gardiner the
walk from Moorgreen reservoir to Annesley referred to in Chapter 7.
Towards the close of *John Thomas and Lady Jane*, Parkin and Connie
went into Hucknall church to examine the memorial to Byron at
the outset of a Sunday stroll, but then took off in the opposite
direction to Watnall, to Annesley Hall, where they walked, in
reverse, a large section of the walk recommended to Gardiner.
Lawrence could, of course, have recalled his letter to Gardiner nearly
three months later, when he was rounding off the second version. But
it seems quite likely that he could have had this ending in view when
he began in the early days of December, thus enabling him to embark
on *John Thomas and Lady Jane* in the spirit of confidence which his
style exudes in that version.

When Lawrence wrote 'novel goes nicely' (Sec 82) at the end of his
letter of 6 December to Secker, it was very probably to the revised
version that he was referring, since the mode of expression does not
suggest nearness to a conclusion. But the most reliable evidence of a
start on *John Thomas and Lady Jane* comes in a letter of 19 December
to Brett: 'Now it's a lovely sunny day, and I sat out in the wood this
morning, working at my novel — which comes out of me slowly, and
is good, I think, but a little too deep in bits — sort of bottomless

pools' (Irv 72). The slow rate of progress is consistent with Squires's evidence of breaks in the handwriting of the MS, which shows a reduced daily output as compared with the first version.[21] It is also to be expected that a much reduced speed of writing would have been demanded by the greater attention to concrete detail and to tautness and beauty of expression which characterizes this version.[22] *John Thomas and Lady Jane* has, to a degree far in excess of any other version, passages redolent of that pool-like quality of depth and stillness that Lawrence mentioned to Brett:

> The air was soft and still, as if all the world were going to sleep. And once out in the park, in the silence and the suspended softness of the Saturday afternoon, it seemed as if the world had gone unpeopled. It was a soft, grey, deep afternoon, as it may have been before mankind became too many for the natural earth.
>
> In the wood was a great stillness. Heavy drops fell from the bare boughs, with a strange loud noise. Nothing else moved. Life had withdrawn itself, and a deep remoteness had come over the familiar places. Among the trees was depth within depth of untouched silence, as in an old, yet virgin forest.
>
> Constance walked dreamily on. She felt melancholy, but it was the soft, living melancholy of rest, of passivity.
>
> (*JTLJ* 50)

Lawrence had written the first version at great speed, having completed the equivalent of more than 250 closely printed pages in the space of less than forty days, working only, apparently, on mornings when the weather was fair. It was characteristic of him to write with such dash, especially when preparing a first draft.[23] At what stage he determined that *The First Lady Chatterley* would constitute an *esquisse* for another version that would demand a complete rewriting is impossible to determine. Perhaps the decision coincided with the realization that it was a novel rather than a long short story he was engaged on; or perhaps he began with the intention of a later complete revision. From the beginning, *The First Lady Chatterley* is generally vague, apparently deliberately so, in relation to details in the depiction of scene and in providing the background to characters and events.[24] This may have been because Lawrence was aiming at rapid completion, so that he could then patiently revise, flesh in the details and make the work more concrete at the next stage in composition. An alternative or ancillary explanation for the minimal detail of the first version is that Lawrence was aware that he was attempting a transition in his mode of writing. Earlier, when writing the first draft of what became *The Rainbow* he had attributed vagueness in the writing to a transitional phase: 'I write with everything vague – plenty of fire underneath, but, like bulbs in the ground, only shadowy flowers that must be beaten and sustained, for another spring' (*Let 2* 143).

Although there were a number of reasons why Lawrence should have been dissatisfied with the first version, it is unnecessary to seek out some special motive which caused him completely to rewrite the novel. In doing so he simply followed habitual working methods which he had employed for all his major novels. In Sicily in 1921–2 the American author James Henry Forman asked Lawrence why he no longer wrote after the manner of *Sons and Lovers*, a question which must have been posed often enough by critics and acquaintances for it to be extremely irksome. Lawrence replied patiently that his novels always passed through three versions with two stages of complete revision: the first of these versions was always like *Sons and Lovers*.[25] In its pastoralism and in the theme of love *The First Lady Chatterley* harks back to *Sons and Lovers*. But the correspondences which link the first draft with his early novel and distinguish the first version from other versions of *Lady Chatterley* are primarily the return to realism and the absence of authorial interpretation and didactic commentary. Quite possibly, then, it was Lawrence's practice, in the mature period of his career, to produce in the first instance a simple, realistic outline which would then be transformed into a more symbolistic work which also made explicit the implied authorial philosophy of the first version.[26]

Shortly after beginning *The First Lady Chatterley*, Lawrence discovered 'an orgy' of delight and a means of relaxation which sustained him throughout the *Lady Chatterley* period, in taking up painting as a hobby. Maria Huxley provided him with the means to embark on a pastime which in the space of a couple of months began to attract him as an alternative professional career. When the Huxleys visited the Mirenda, Maria left with Lawrence four canvases that her brother had daubed on; and Lawrence began making his first pictures for the purpose of brightening up the bare walls of the apartment. At the time of the Huxleys' visit, he had begun a thorough redecoration of the Mirenda, which he continued to work on through October and November, painting pieces of furniture, 'window frames by the mile, doors by the acre' (*CL* 945) in order to make the place more comfortable for the winter months, when it would be more lived in. For this purpose he had acquired several brushes and had brought in 'a little stock of oil, turps and colour in powder'. Hitherto his paintings, executed mainly in his youth, had usually been copies of the work of others. Now he decided to turn his hand to original art:

> So for the sheer fun of covering a surface . . . I sat on the floor with the canvas propped against a chair – and with my house-paint brushes and colours in little casseroles, I disappeared into that canvas. It is to me the most exciting moment – when you have a blank canvas and a big brush full of wet colour, and you plunge. It is just like diving into a pond – then you start frantically to swim. So far as I am concerned, it is like swimming in a baffling current and being rather frightened and very thrilled, gasping and striking out for all you're worth. The knowing eye watches sharp as a needle; but the picture comes clean out of instinct, intuition and sheer physical action. Once the instinct and intuition gets into the brush-tip, the picture *happens*, if it is to be a picture at all.
>
> At least, so my first picture happened – the one I have called 'A Holy Family'. In a couple of hours there it all was, man, woman, child, blue shirt, red shawl, pale room – all in the rough, but, as far as I am concerned, a picture. The struggling comes later. But the picture itself comes in the first rush, or not at all. It is only when the picture has come into being that one can struggle and make it *grow* to completion.
>
> (*Ph 2* 602f.)

His approach to art followed closely that which he employed in novel-writing, where he faced the challenge of an empty exercise book with the same thrill of being swept away into the unknown as he felt when standing before a blank canvas. Moreover, his account of the relationship between initial sketch and finished canvas – the initial rush of inspirational creativity which brings a work into being, followed by a process of struggle in which it is made to grow to completion – seems to parallel the methods of composition used in creating *Lady Chatterley* through successive stages of development.

Through art Lawrence found an alternative method of expressing his ideas and feelings. In the act of 'disappearing' into the canvas he was able to lose consciousness of the self in a way that was impossible for him in writing; and in this way the painting gave recreation after a morning's work and kept the creative spirit buoyant in him at times when he was bored or enervated through the emotional and mental demands of writing the novel. It was especially beneficial to him, no doubt, at the time when he was in the throes of the painstaking and spiritually draining process of revising the first draft and investing the novel with a depth of feeling that had to be dredged up from the inner self. 'Soul-work' (Hux 679), Lawrence called novel-writing, and there were times when, with a view to lightening the burden on the soul, he became more attracted to painting as a professional career than to literature. 'Think I'll turn into a painter', he told Kot, 'it costs one less, and probably would pay better than writing' (Zyt 304).

By 11 November his first effort in painting had been completed: 'I've already painted a picture on one of the canvases. I've hung it up in the new *salotto*. I call it the "Unholy Family", because the *bambino* – with a *nimbus* – is just watching anxiously to see the young man give the semi-nude young woman *un gros baiser*. *Molto moderno* (CL 945). Subsequently, he modified the title to 'Holy Family', turned the child's nimbus into the back of one of the Vallombrosa chairs that adorned the *salotto*, and endowed the man and the woman with a nimbus each. Perhaps the picture was designed with Parkin, Connie and their expected child half in mind: the male figure has the moustache and brown eyes of the keeper, and the blonde woman has the skin colour, blue eyes and full figure of Lady Chatterley.

The painting was on view when the Wilkinsons were invited round to celebrate the unveiling of the whitewashed, repainted and newly furnished *salotto*. They were justifiably critical, being artists themselves, of the design of the painting, but it was the subject which they found most objectionable. Their reactions show what Lawrence was up against, where his compatriots were concerned, in his endeavours in art, as in literature, 'to make the sex relation valid and precious, instead of shameful' (Hux 682). Here was a Marxist bohemian family, who in all other respects had rejected the norms of English society, but who recoiled in revulsion from the sight of a pair of full breasts and a hand clasped close to one of them:

> The room is very bright and pleasant, except for a large picture painted by Lorenzo which seemed to us a revolting blot on the wall. Uncle Roger [the Wilkinsons had a mistaken idea that the male figure was a portrait of a relative] and an imbecile fat woman with most of her clothes missing and a pert child, are bunched together in a most unpleasant group.
>
> Lorenzo explains that it is a modern painting, all in rounds and curves and colour, and we let him have his say and offered no criticism. In spite of this picture we had a quite nice party, and lots of talk and fun.
>
> (Wilk 67)

As a letter to Secker written next day shows, Lawrence was quite aware of their silent revulsion: 'I've painted a nice big picture that our vegetarian neighbours the Wilkinsons are afraid to look at, it's too "suggestive". Why do vegetarians always behave as if the world were vegetably propagated even?' (Sec 80).

The reactions of the Wilkinsons, the first people to see the picture, may have incited Lawrence towards a more daring subject for his next painting, and may even have had some little influence in determining that *John Thomas and Lady Jane* should be more 'improper' than its predecessor, both in the nature of the lovemaking of Connie and Parkin and in the explicit details which accompany the accounts of their acts. The next painting was based on a scene from Boccaccio's story of the gardener whom a group of nuns discovered asleep with his genitals unwittingly exposed. Lawrence thought the finished work 'very nice' – 'Well, not exactly *nice*!' replied Arthur Wilkinson, when he saw the picture on Boxing Day.[27]

What with his continuing enjoyment of the Mirenda and its setting, his generally good relations with the Wilkinsons, his casual approach to work, and the relaxing escape he found in painting, Lawrence had been able to write the first draft of *Lady Chatterley* without being gripped by the fraught, nervous intensity that he had shown in the past when tackling a major project. If the Wilkinsons had to learn to exercise some tolerance with Lawrence's ways, it was at this stage only in regard to his tactless pedantry. On 18 November there was a farewell gathering at the Villa Poggi before the Wilkinsons left for Florence: 'We treated Lorenzo to a concert; and he treated us to criticism as usual, telling Bim about her painting, and Pino about violin music in his superior way. We smiled' (Wilk 67). Lawrence himself had begun to feel some irritation with Mrs Wilkinson, on whose selfish femininity he laid the blame for the family's departure in a letter to Ada.[28] Writing to Brett shortly after the Wilkinsons had left, he told her: 'We are mostly alone. Our neighbours have gone into Florence because she, Mrs Wilkinson, is so tired of cooking. She did extremely little, – but no doubt you will sympathise with her' (*CL* 948).

Lawrence did not take well to this unsought-for loss of companionship. And from late November the theme of fellowship and his relations with society becomes especially prominent in his letters and in his work. It occupied his mind, on and off, for the remainder of the *Lady Chatterley* period, and found its way into the last two versions of the novel. Lawrence was a solitary man, who enjoyed his loneness and preferred it in moods when he found people tiresome and wearying; but he also loved, when it suited him, the company of compatible friends. All his life there had been an uneasy relationship between these two conflicting needs in him, and according to mood and circumstance he had swung erratically between the two. While the Wilkinsons were in residence, the two conflicting tendencies had been in a stable equilibrium. He had people, living within two minutes' walking distance, who neither imposed on him nor depressed him; and he had the sanctuary of the wooded hills in which to work, sit, take long walks and gratify his eremetic instincts.

Having lost the facility of the Wilkinsons being within close call, he felt his loneness extremely, but understated it in his letters: 'Sometimes I wish things were a little more convivial. But one has to take life as one finds it, and the kind of conviviality one *does* get doesn't help much' (*CL* 947). This complaint seems to have been directed against his Florentine acquaintances and visitors to the Mirenda rather than towards the Wilkinsons, despite their irksome embarrassment at 'Holy Family'.

In mid-December Lawrence told Kot that he had lost all interest in people and preferred his solitariness. But this was a rationalization, tailored to his present circumstances. More nearly true was the view he put to Maria Huxley – that though it might not be good for him, he was best alone unless he could choose his company 'rather squeamishly' (*CL* 954). He set about attempting to do just this as soon as the Wilkinsons had left. First he wrote to Secker, who had earlier expressed an interest in coming to Florence, but here Lawrence drew a blank. He had heard from Kot that Gertler might be in Florence for the New Year, and asked Kot to pass on an invitation to come out to the Mirenda, but Gertler had changed his plans. Lawrence was more successful with Millie Beveridge, who arranged to come with her sister and Mabel Harrison to stay at the Villa Bianca, just over the hill from the Mirenda; but they were not due until near the end of February, when the Wilkinsons would already have returned. By Christmas the Brewsters had arrived back in Europe and two days into the New Year Lawrence wrote to them of the attractions of Tuscany for the landscape painter, hoping to persuade them to take a house there. This bore one small fruit in a visit from Earl to the Mirenda for a short stay in January.

One of the visitors to the Mirenda whom Lawrence may have had

186

in mind when complaining of the quality of conviviality among those that he *did* meet was Frieda's lover, the Tenente Ravagli, now promoted to Capitano. A fortnight before his visit, the Lawrences had dined with him in a restaurant in Florence, where he had to give evidence before a court martial. The trial was postponed and he was obliged to return later to Florence, from where he journeyed out to the Mirenda to pay a surprise visit. Lawrence assumed Ravagli had fabricated the story of the postponed trial as a pretext for getting together with Frieda; and Ravagli was greeted with a cold, hostile reception and a demand to see the military travel documents authorizing his journey to Florence. Having reassured himself, Lawrence turned cordial, but got no pleasure from the company of Ravagli, who seemed to bring with him 'a dense fog of that peculiar inert Italian misery, dreariness' (Sec 79). There was an element of rivalry in his hostility to Ravagli, of course, but the major cause of offence was to Lawrence's pride. Judging by remarks made to Barby on a later occasion, he was complaisant in the Frieda–Ravagli affair;[29] but in this instance it must have seemed to him that, in invading his territory with what appeared to be a hollow excuse, Ravagli was trying to make a monkey out of him.

Though he scarcely spoke to most of the peasants on the estate, save to exchange greetings, Lawrence found some pleasure in the unspoken empathy which he felt existed between him and the *contadini*. It was they, he wrote in 'Autobiographical Sketch', composed during the period of his winter isolation, who made up his *'ambiente'*. He had, he said, no wish to share their lives in their cottages, nor was he inclined to romanticize them: 'But I want them to be there, about the place, their lives going on along with mine, and in relation to mine' (*Ph 2* 595). With two of the Pini family on the estate, a brother and sister, there was a closer contact, especially with Giulia Pini, with whom he continued to keep in touch by letter after he left the Mirenda. Giulia, 'gay and amusing and wise' ('*Not I*' 176), helped around the house. Her brother Pietro did some of the heavy work and drove the *barroccino*, a two-wheeled carriage the size of a dog-cart that took the Lawrences to and fro from the tram terminus or on shopping expeditions to Scandicci. It was Pietro, with Giulia as his accomplice, who provided the tree for the Christmas festivities Lawrence and Frieda had planned for the peasant families, stealing out in the dark hours before sunrise to cut down a pine tree from the priest's wood behind the church. The tree, set in the bright, whitewashed *salotto* and decked with candles, gold and silver paper, tinsel threads and sweets and wooden toys for the children, became the centrepiece of the party for the *contadini*, held after sunset on Christmas Eve.

On Christmas Day, to add to the north European flavour of the season, imparted by the tree and a plum-pudding, there came a light skittering of snow. And on Boxing Day there was another party, for the Wilkinsons – a night of 'singing and feasting' with all six of them 'as sympathetic and merry as could be' (Wilk 68).

In mid-January Earl Brewster arrived for a couple of days. Lawrence, as several of his friends observed, was remarkable among gifted talkers in that he would always listen with eager attentiveness to the tales and conversation of others. In the freezing-cold, wintry evenings of Earl's visit they sat before the roaring fire in the *salotto*, while Earl recounted the experiences of his visit to India. In the daytime he and Lawrence took long walks together in the hills.

By now Lawrence had completed six paintings, which with some trepidation he showed to Brewster. Though he could be confident of no prudish aversion to the subject-matter, he feared that a professional artist might find them disappointing: 'I don't imagine Earl thought much of my pictures . . . not enough "values" and colour for tone substitution' (*CL* 960f.), he told Brett after Earl had left. In fact he was wrong: it had been the values and colour, together with the design, which most appealed to Brewster.[30] In offering his pictures to the world, the fear of failure, of proving a disappointment, seems to have been felt almost as keenly as it was with his literary creations. Arguably, it is the key to Lawrence's personality – to his social malaise, his aggression, his nervous irritability, his pretence of conventional virility and perhaps his sexual problems. The fears showed themselves even in little matters, to which he nevertheless often attached inordinate importance. When, for instance, the Wilkinsons arrived for a Sunday meal at the end of January, they found Lawrence 'very unhappy' and 'over anxious', worrying himself over the success of a potato cake he was baking for them in the oven.[31] In his dreams, too, the fear of failure was sometimes a prominent feature. He gave one example of such a dream, trivial but disturbing, in a letter of 10 February to A. W. McLeod, his former colleague at the school where he taught in Croydon. Though his teaching days were long past, he still had a recurrent troubled dream in which the class had left for home when he found he had quite forgotten to mark the roll.[32] In the following month he told Achsah Brewster of a recurring nightmare concerning his brother George's child, who had been brought up in the Lawrence household. 'The child would run to meet [Lawrence], as he used to do, with his arms outstretched for Lawrence to carry him, but where the child was running was a dangerous precipice' (Brew 272).

On the last day of Earl's visit they went to Florence to meet Alberto Magnelli, the Florentine abstract painter, and to view his work. Lawrence was not so bigoted in his tastes that he could not admire the beauty of colour and form of the paintings, but an art without discernible reference to the visible world was inevitably 'a dead nothingness' as far as he was concerned. He did not take, either, to Magnelli's 'self-important' and 'arch-priesty' manner, nor did Magnelli find *him* agreeable;[33] and the visit left Lawrence in a foul temper for several days, during which he longed for a bolshevist revolution that would sweep away all the degeneracy of the modern Western world. Such attitudes were typical of his reactions to modern art and artists, whether representational or abstract. When he visited Augustus John in 1917 he had prowled around the studio muttering 'Let the dead bury the dead'.[34] And when Duncan Grant, the principal model for Duncan Forbes in *Lady Chatterley*, had shown him his work in 1915. Lawrence took it upon himself to deliver a frank lecture on the worthlessness of his efforts.[35] A memory of this scene may have come to him when he was writing *Lady Chatterley's Lover*, where Mellors, on seeing Forbes's paintings, remarks to Connie: 'It is like a pure bit of murder' (*LCL* 300). But it seems to have been fresher recollections of the visit to Magnelli that Lawrence was mainly drawing on, for the paintings and the artist's high-priestly conception of his art are Magnelli's, and the hostility between the two men was true only of the mutual dislike that arose between Lawrence and the Italian:

> His art was all tubes and valves and spirals and strange colours, ultra modern, yet with a certain power, even a certain purity of form and tone: only Mellors thought it cruel and repellent. He did not venture to say so, for Duncan was almost insane on the point of his art: it was a personal cult, a personal religion with him.[36]

A mood of discontent and rebellion set in during the winter months and found its most forceful and coherent expression in the letter written to Brewster towards the end of February, quoted in

Chapter 1, where he diagnosed his rebelliousness and his difficulties in relating to people and the modern world as due to the 'change of life' – physiologically induced changes in the psyche of the male in his 40s. Painting, and (though he did not mention it) almost certainly the indulgence of a desire to be sexually provocative in the writing of *John Thomas and Lady Jane*, helped him keep his exasperation under control by satisfying the needs to rebel and to realize passionately held beliefs:

> I try and keep the *middle* of me harmonious to *middle* of the universe. Outwardly, I know I'm in a bad temper, and let it go at that. I stick to what I told you, and put a phallus, a lingam you call it, in each one of my pictures somewhere. And I paint no picture that won't shock people's castrated social spirituality. I do this out of positive belief, that the phallus is a great sacred image: it represents a deep, deep life which has been denied in us, and still is denied. Women deny it horribly, with a grinning travesty of sex. But *pazienza! pazienza!* – One can still believe. And with the lingam, and belief in the mystery behind it, goes beauty . . . But as for life, one can only be patient – which by nature I'm not . . . And meanwhile one has to preserve one's *central* innocence, and not get bittered.
>
> (CL 967)

The Wilkinsons found Lawrence in these months more frequently angry and complaining than before, more inclined to launch into diatribes, as against America or womankind, or to be unpleasant to Frieda. But his moods were manageable, and the Wilkinsons found that, without too much effort on their part, they could jolly him out of them. They settled again into the Villa Poggi shortly after Earl Brewster left Florence, and resumed their regular meetings and walks with the Lawrences. And with their return Lawrence's concern with fellowship and his relations with others became less commonly expressed in his correspondence for a while, though in his February letter to Brewster he still felt that close encounters with people, especially new or casual acquaintances, were unbearable to him.[37]

Anger and discontent appear to have festered in Lawrence as a result of being left to turn in upon himself in the weeks when he was denied the mollifying company of the Wilkinsons. The mood could also have been fed by what Lawrence learnt of the reactions of the audience and some of the critics to the English Stage Society production of his play, *The Widowing of Mrs Holroyd* in December.[38] Rolf Gardiner, who had been to the first night, reported to Lawrence that he had overheard Shaw speak in fulsome praise of the dialogue, but hinted at a poor general audience reception. The critics lighted on the slowness of the last act as a major flaw in the play.[39] Lawrence wrote a diffident and generous letter to the director, Esmé Percy, and the cast, taking responsibility for any demerits in the play, acknowledging grudgingly that some of the criticism was probably justified and inviting the opinions of Percy and the actors.[40] This, however, was an occasion when doing the right thing triumphed over honesty. He was furious over the fate of the play and blamed the cast, director, audience and critics – everyone but himself.[41] Judging by the acclaim the play attracted when next produced in London, at the Royal Court Theatre in 1968, Lawrence was right to believe that the play deserved a better reception and better standards of direction and performance.[42] Nevertheless, the predominantly favourable tenor of the 1926 reviews suggests that Lawrence's angry disappointment was the reflection of an insecure ego that was excessively sensitive to criticism and content only with tokens of triumph.

Lawrence told Maria Huxley, among others, of the failure of the play:

> I believe they hated it, and somebody says I ought to write about the class I come from, I've no right to venture into the Peerage – people educated above their class, etc! *O tra-la-la! La gente invidioza è la bestia piu maleducata ancora. Come mai!* [The envious crowd proves itself once more to be the most ill-bred brute of all. As usual!]
>
> (*CL* 955)

The critic Lawrence referred to was Ivor Brown (see n. 38) whose meaning, not altogether clear, appears nonetheless to have become distorted in Lawrence's memory. At the end of his review, Brown had written: 'He has also suggested how well he might have written if he had stuck to the life he knows instead of plunging into the theory which is clamorously acclaimed by people who have been educated beyond their intelligence.' Lawrence's faulty recollection concerning venturing into the Peerage seems to have reflected his current preoccupation with *Lady Chatterley*.

It is probably no coincidence that shortly after he read the reviews of the play, when writing 'Autobiographical Sketch' for Insel-Verlag, Lawrence allowed a personal class-consciousness to intrude into the narrative of his life. Hitherto, he had revealed little in his literary work of what his personal feelings were in regard to his working-class origins and his relations with people of more privileged backgrounds. That they should have appeared first in this 'Autobiographical Sketch' was largely determined by the fact that the original was written for a German readership. For the majority of his English readers, revelations of personal class-consciousness would have been regarded as indelicate and tasteless – almost as unwelcome as the subject of sex. Indeed, it seems quite possible that Lawrence would not have caused half so much offence with *Lady Chatterley's Lover* had he not spliced sex with class feeling in the novel. Apparently recognizing that 'Autobiographical Sketch' might backfire on him if it were published in England, he at first left it to Nancy Pearn to decide whether he might regret submitting it to editors for acceptance.[43] Afterwards he instructed her to do nothing with it – a ban which must later have been lifted, for it appeared in 1929 in the *Sunday Dispatch*, an appropriate home in so far as the paper did not have an upper-middle-class audience.

From 1926 onwards, the subject of class-consciousness occupied Lawrence's mind a great deal and began to appear in his essays, his fiction and his poems. It was an issue of which he had always been acutely aware, but which he had sensibly chosen to exclude from his public writings. The fact that it came to greater prominence in this period appears to have been determined by no particular external cause. Probably the history of his thoughts on class was very much as he related it in 'Autobiographical Sketch' (*Ph 2* 592–5). When he returned to Europe he realized that he had been wrong in the past to attribute the alienation he felt from society to 'the oldness and worn-outness of Europe'. The continent was, as he discovered in Spotorno in 1925, very much alive; so that when next he felt strongly his isolation from most of his acquaintances he had to look for a new answer, and it seemed to him now that it was the class gulf which divided him from friends who mainly belonged to the middle class. They were 'charming and educated and good people', but for a man of working-class origins their company was stifling and repressive: they somehow prevented some vital part of him from working. He looked at other writers of common stock, like Barrie and Wells, who had been able to bridge the gulf and successfully make the transfer into the middle class. He had not been able to do so and considered himself the less successful for that reason. He *could* not, because he was unwilling to sacrifice his working-class 'passional consciousness' and 'blood-affinity' with his fellows.

Although he had overstated the position and romanticized it with talk of 'passional consciousness' and 'blood affinity', he was surely not far wrong in his conclusions. Of course, his family upbringing and genetic inheritance would have made him a misfit in any society, as he confessed through Parkin in *John Thomas and Lady Jane*. But the effeminacy and sensitivity which made life difficult for him in working-class society would not have been such handicaps in the world of fellow artists. The difficulties which he had in establishing warm relations with his friends, and the source of his inhibitions in their society, owed a great deal to differences of values and codes of behaviour between the classes, and to Lawrence's awareness of those differences. It was not within the English middle-class tradition to give passionate expression to personal feelings, whereas with the working class it was natural to do so. More importantly, perhaps, there were differences of behaviour between himself and his friends which were constrained not only by class but by the social norms operating in Lawrence's native regions.

In the Nottinghamshire–Derbyshire area and perhaps extending more widely, but not generally, over the country, there are traditions of social behaviour embraced by the working class and the lower middle class which differ significantly from those current among the same classes elsewhere and from those of other classes. This is a large and impressionistic claim which may nevertheless be found, when tested, to have some validity. Enter a shop, for instance, in Lawrence's Midlands, and one may often find oneself engaged in more than a friendly commercial transaction or phatic communion on some such topic as the weather; rather, there may be some involvement in a personal relationship in which the shopkeeper communicates some fragment from his or her personal history or daily life. It is more common in this area for people to show, even to casual acquaintances, an unguarded candour amounting almost to naïvity in regard to their personal lives, their concerns and enthusiasms. It is not because they are by nature warmer or more passionate than others. It is simply because there are no social taboos to inhibit self-revelation.

To the English middle class such behaviour is either vulgar and embarrassing in its naïvity or, to the sympathetic at least, surprising. It is not what they are used to. In Lawrence, who had this candid manner of self-presentation, it was the more disturbing to his acquaintances because heightened by his personal vitality and passion. Consider, for instance, the reactions of the young Aldous Huxley on first meeting Lawrence in 1915: 'Before tea was over he asked me if I would join the colony [Lawrence's proposed Rananim in Florida], and though I was an intellectually cautious young man, not at all inclined to enthusiasms, though Lawrence had startled and embarrassed me with sincerities of a kind to which my upbringing had not accustomed me, I answered yes' (Hux xxix). In this respect Lawrence's personality appears to have been shaped by a specifically regional class culture. And since the sincerities and innocently unwary presentation of the self are distinguishing features of his work, it seems reasonable to claim that those attributes are among those which distinguish him as a regional writer.

'One can belong absolutely to no class', Lawrence concluded in 'Autobiographical Sketch'. He could affiliate neither with the middle class nor the working class; no amount of 'blood-affinity' could tie him to a class from which he was dissociated by intellectual snobbery: working people, he believed, were 'narrow in outlook, in prejudice, and narrow in intelligence'. The lack of a sense of belonging to any definable group was central to his feeling of isolation. Though his background might be defined as working-class on socio-economic grounds, he had been brought up in terms of outlook and social mores to be, like his mother, one of the English lower middle class, an amorphous group with no sense of a collective identity. For this reason he was destined to remain for the rest of his life, as he acknowledged in a later poem, an 'in-between'.[44]

Why was Lawrence unable more thoroughly to adopt middle-class ways? Partly it was because he set great value upon the 'passional consciousness' which he felt was his inheritance from the working class. But other aspects of his personality also made him unadaptable – his stubborn nature and innate conservatism, his need to guard his individual identity, his aggression, and most importantly his equation of virility with working-class male behaviour. It is doubtful whether he was right to claim that this unwillingness to adapt socially inhered in his writing to such an extent that it made it impossible for him to 'rise in the world and become even a little popular and rich'. This is somewhat maudlin, self-pitying twaddle of the kind he would have condemned in others. Besides exposing class-conscious grudges and envy, it betrays aspirations to success and wealth which he habitually denigrated in other people.

There was another hint of rancour in 'Autobiographical Sketch' in the passage: 'In the early days they were always telling me I had got genius, as if to console me for not having their own incomparable advantages.' But, on the whole, the subject of class feelings had been handled in a controlled manner, and criticisms of the middle class had been restrained. In *John Thomas and Lady Jane* class-consciousness and the matter of the gulf between classes, though vigorously expressed and given greater emphasis than in Lawrence's first draft, is similarly dealt with without much bitterness. At the same time, class becomes more subjective an issue, largely divorced now from the theme, prominent in the first version, of political struggle for the ownership of property. The decline of this aspect of class antipathy was probably much influenced by the fact that the miners' strike had ended before Lawrence began the second version.

The original Parkin's attitudes towards the upper classes had formed part of a political philosophy, and by the end of the book he had become secretary of the works' communist league. But in *John Thomas and Lady Jane* class-consciousness becomes entirely personal and apolitical, and Parkin's hatred of the gentry is made more conspicuous by being introduced at the beginning of the book, rather than towards the close as it had been in the first draft. As with Connie and Clifford, the character and attitudes established by the end of the first version tend to be carried over to the beginning of the revised text. In relations between Connie and Parkin, too, the gulf between the classes of society receives greater emphasis. Their relationship runs less easily and is much slower in reaching fruition, not only because of the introduction of struggle between the male and female will, but because Connie's fears of contact with the lower classes, as expressed in the first version, have been replaced by feelings of class-superiority and a measure of repulsion which must be overcome before a full, warm relationship with Parkin can be achieved. The class-consciousness which separates them is highlighted by Connie's responses to Parkin's use of dialect, the emblem of his working-class status. In the first version Parkin had been given two speech-codes – the 'broad' dialect and a form of the dialect which had been influenced by the standard language. And one of the several functions of the switches between these two styles of speech had been the expression of Parkin's own class-consciousness through the use of his most strongly dialectal speech as a gesture of defiance and contempt when addressing the gentry.

In *The First Lady Chatterley* Connie recognized, from the beginning, the social meaning of Parkin's linguistic behaviour. She accepted it uncritically, and throughout their relationship was amused and enthralled by Parkin's dialect speech, which she would imitate laughingly to herself. But in *John Thomas and Lady Jane* linguistic class-consciousness exists on both sides. Parkin uses the broad regional dialect, as before, to put up a resistance which is drawn more sharply to the reader's attention by a more marked contrast with his other speech style, which is closer to Standard English than the formal style of his predecessor. Connie is in this version repelled by his use of dialect. The thought of his voice, speaking to her in dialect, makes her wince with shame, and she resents especially the 'unspeakably intimate' (*JTLJ* 241) *thou* and *thee* forms which characterize it. When, ultimately, she fully acknowledges and expresses her love for Parkin, all the elements which divided them – her female will, her fear of the power of the phallus and her class-conscious attitude towards the dialect – dissolve in the one moment, suggesting that they were interlinked. The signal of her complete acceptance of all that Parkin represents is her newly discovered love of the dialect and her playful imitation of it.[45] It is an act of homage, acknowledging her recent bodily submission to the power of the phallus. Implicitly she has recognized that the dialect is the language of the phallic consciousness, in which the most potent four-letter words are the *thou* and *thee* forms she had earlier resented. Like the erect phallus, they are the expression of Parkin's power and his tenderness. These pronouns had been lost in the history of the standard language, just as the tenderness of feeling and intimacy which they could convey had disappeared, so Lawrence believed, from the higher classes of English society.[46]

In adding a wider gulf of class-consciousness which Connie had to leap before she and Parkin could meet in full communion, Lawrence had clearly been much influenced by thoughts of the class divisions, both linguistic and cultural, which separated his father and mother – a topic he touched on in 'Autobiographical Sketch':

> My father was a collier, and only a collier, nothing praiseworthy about him . . . My mother was, I suppose, superior. She came from town, and belonged really to the lower bourgeoisie. She spoke King's English, without an accent, and never in her life could even imitate a sentence of the dialect which my father spoke, and which we children spoke out of doors.
>
> (*Ph 2* 592)

These words were echoed in the first stanzas of the comic, satirical poem 'Red-Herring':

> My father was a working man
>   and a collier was he,
> at six in the morning they turned him down
>   and they turned him up for tea.
>
> My mother was a superior soul
>   a superior soul was she,
> cut out to play a superior rôle
>   in the god-damn bougeoisie.
>
> We children were the in-betweens
>   little non-descripts were we,
> indoors we called each other *you*,
>   outside, it was *tha* and *thee*.
>
> (*Poems* 490)

The poem implies that *tha* and *thee* were forbidden to the Lawrence children as the most stigmatized forms of the dialect; and Constance Chatterley's hostility to these words may derive from Lydia Lawrence's linguistic prejudices.

'Autobiographical Sketch' had been written while Lawrence was still 'slowly pegging away' at the MS of *John Thomas and Lady Jane*, which he worked at 'in sudden intense whacks' (Zyt 306), interrupted by breaks when the effort of concentration diminished the will to write. By 23 January, when he wrote a long, nostalgic letter to Gertie Cooper, then facing the decision whether or not to have an operation to remove part of her diseased lung, Lawrence may have been just beyond the midway point in the novel and in the process of composing the Tevershall gossip of Mrs Bolton. There are a number of features of the letter which suggest this could have been the case.[47] Lawrence asked after Jinny Bolton, a friend of Gertie's whom he had evidently met the previous summer. His head was full of Eastwood in the old days, of life at Lynn Croft and at the Congregational Chapel with the Cooper girls and the Chambers family. 'Sometimes', he told Gertie, 'it seems so far off! And sometimes it is like yesterday' (*CL* 963). He had just heard from Ada of the death of Willie Hopkin's father, referred to in the letter and in the third version of the novel; and thoughts of Willie prompted some complaints to Gertie of his behaviour after Sallie's death, when he had begun to court one of the Swain girls. This may in turn have led him to use the name Swain when creating Mrs Bolton's tales of Bertha Coutts, who left Parkin to live with a collier of that name. He had Swain and Coutts set up house together at a site that was plainly 'The Alley', the lane leading from Brinsley level-crossing to New Brinsley church. Jem Swain, married to Lawrence's Aunt Sarah, had lived there; and since he had been sexton to the church, it must have given Lawrence some amusement to have the husband of his prim and unwelcoming aunt named as the foul-mouthed, beer-swilling braggart, not 'quite right in his head', who cohabited with a slattern.

Work on the novel apparently continued to be performed out of doors. Throughout the winter months it usually remained warm in the stillness of the pine-woods, which afforded cover when the chill *tramontana* wind blew from the north. And there was always colour in the landscape, with 'a glitter of olives and layers of deep, soft green umbrella pines, and . . . puffs of orange willow trees' (Irv 72) in the dells beside the stream. As the days began to lengthen, the first flowers emerged in the *pineta* – dull, green-coloured Christmas roses, followed in February by 'the first wild violet and purple anemone'. By the time the yellow petals of the wild crocuses had opened in late February, Lawrence was closing *John Thomas and Lady Jane* with a picture of the drab 'grey-green landscape' of his native woodlands in August. On 25 February he wrote to Nancy Pearn: 'I've done all I'm going to do of my novel for the time being.'[48] His remarks imply that he may already have been contemplating yet another version.

It was a common practice for Lawrence to set aside the draft of a novel and then return to it some time later. He could then effect substantial changes in a fresh spirit, ensuring spontaneity even in the act of revision.[49] This seems to have been his present plan for *Lady Chatterley*, which he intended 'to let . . . lie and settle down a bit' (*CL* 965), before taking it up again. In the following month he told Pearn that he had to 'go over it again' (*CL* 970). And later, in August, he wrote to Secker of his intention to write 'a continuation' (Sec 93) of the existing version at some later date. By this he probably meant a new approach to the novel as it currently stood, using 'continuation' as the most appropriate term for the process of continuing re-creation which characterized the progress of his novels from original draft to published version.

Although sometimes he thought he might publish the novel, he had no firm intention of doing so, and no great interest in its ever seeing the light of day. At this stage publication seemed, in any case, impossible, since he realized it was unprintable as it stood, and he was resolved never to cut it. In June, after Pollinger of Curtis Brown had been pressing him to sign a contract for *Lady Chatterley*, he informed Secker that it was still possible that 'that young woman' (Sec 89) might some day be flung on the fire. He could hardly have seriously contemplated such a fate for the novel, but he was certainly reluctant to see it in the hands of a publisher, and would have preferred to see it destroyed by fire than by expurgation.

Probably he had completed his second version a few days before he wrote to Nancy Pearn towards the end of February. He had told Brett on 9 February that he was nearing completion; and his letter to Pearn enclosed a review of four books and mentioned a short story ('The Lovely Lady') that he had almost finished: these may well have been written after he had set aside the novel. He had also been reading a series of Galsworthy novels that left him 'just nauseated . . . up to the nose' (*CL* 968). This reading was for a critical essay on Galsworthy which he sent to Pearn at the end of February. Galsworthy's Forsytes, as Lawrence saw them, were much like Clifford and his cronies, especially as subsequently presented in the final version – cerebral, dead, inhuman 'social beings', in whom the acquisition of wealth was 'the controlling principle' (*Ph* 540f.), and for whom no passion existed, even among those who pursued a dog-like career of fornication.

Aldous and Maria Huxley seem to have continued their timing of arrivals to coincide with significant moments in the history of *Lady Chatterley* by reaching Florence at about the time when Lawrence had just finished, or was in process of finishing, the second version of the novel. However, opportunities for meeting on this occasion were cut down by both Lawrence and Aldous succumbing to influenza, of which Lawrence had recurrent bouts for a fortnight. The Huxleys arrived at the Mirenda during one of the intervals, accompanied by Mary Hutchinson, one of Lady Ottoline's Garsington set. The after-effects of illness had increased Aldous's natural melancholia. Lawrence found him 'still absolutely gone in the grouches' (*CL* 968) and he thought Mary Hutchinson 'very faded'. Reflecting on their meeting, Lawrence felt that it had increased his dissatisfaction with human society and fostered his wish to flee the world. 'It's no good', he told Brett, 'for me the human world becomes more and more wearisome. I am really happiest when I don't see people and never go to town' (*CL* 968).

Lawrence's influenza had been milder than his attack of the previous year, and it seems not to have been accompanied by haemorrhages. But the after-effects continued for some little while, and by mid-March (shortly before he set off to join the Brewsters in Ravello, from where he was to embark on an exacting tour of Etruscan sites) he was still very feeble. His breathing had again been badly affected: walking with the Beveridge sisters and Mabel Harrison in the hills around the Mirenda, he was unable to go more than fifty yards at a stretch without stopping for breath. But the quiet ecstasy with which he responded to the Tuscan countryside was undiminished. 'Tuscany is very flowery' (Sec 85), he observed in a letter of this period to Secker, after extolling the loveliness of the wild flora of the Tuscan spring – anaemones in blue, scarlet and purple, primroses, violets, grape hyacynths and budding wild tulips. Evidently he was already thinking of the title for an essay, 'Flowery Tuscany', the first two parts of which were composed in March.[50]

'Flowery Tuscany', one of the most beautiful of all Lawrence's essays, was written with the same contemplative, lyrical sensitivity to pastoral landscape and the life of inanimate nature that characterized *John Thomas and Lady Jane*. It records Lawrence's last moments of rapture in Tuscany and seems also to have been the last piece Lawrence ever wrote in such a style and mood. When he returned from his tour of Etruria to the Mirenda, where he wrote the final part of the essay during the last week of April,[51] he found that the Tuscan countryside had gone dead for him. His new attitude showed through in this third section of the essay, where the spring blossoms are passing or have already fallen, where the wood in late April 'has lost its subtlety and its mysteriousness', and the newly opened orchids are 'lonely' – 'too aloof and individual' (*Ph* 55). At the time of writing, Lawrence believed that the change was seasonal and that summer would bring a new resurgence, in himself as in the landscape.

10

'A Strange New Shadow'

On 19 March Lawrence left the Mirenda to see the Brewsters in Ravello, breaking his journey with a two-day stay in Rome, perhaps with the aim of examining Etruscan artefacts at the Gregorian Museum in the Vatican. The Brewsters were renting the Palazzo Cimbrone, Lord Grimthorpe's imposing mansion, with a large, wooded estate surrounding formal, terraced gardens crowded with statuary. A year earlier, when Lawrence and Brett were in Ravello, they had walked through the grounds where he had begun his career as an original artist with his 'Blue Venus', a voluptuous rendering of a blue-green bronze statue near the entrance to the woods. During his stay with the Brewsters he began a crucifixion scene in the gardens, which under the influence of the Cimbrone statues transformed itself into 'Fauns and Nymphs'.

After a week at the Palazzo, where Lawrence made a full recovery from the after-effects of influenza, he drove by carriage with the Brewsters to Sorrento for a weekend. Walking back with Earl from a drive to the edge of the peninsula, Lawrence spoke for the first time of his new novel:

> The joy of creation was still upon him: but he was in doubt regarding publication . . . he spoke of its tenderness, and emphatically declared that to his mind it was not an improper book. He reiterated, as in the past, that the only unforgivable sin is to deny life: that there are no words which should not be spoken, no thoughts which should not be expressed: in the darkness of suppression and secrecy poison is engendered: when the hidden words and thoughts are brought into the clear daylight the poison departs: the author renders this service when he writes with reverence for life.
>
> (Brew 120)

Addressing himself to the apparent paradox of Lawrence's obsession with the subject of sex and his puritanical abhorrence of what he called 'sex in the head', Brewster implied that Lawrence's 'possession' with sex was dispassionate and objective: he compared it to that of the physician who wishes to heal. Brewster thought of Lawrence's distinction between the pure, intuitive, phallic consciousness and the impure, cerebral consciousness as similar to the meaning of the Fall in *Genesis*, 'when physical purity vanished with the coming of mental curiosity'.[1] And it is quite possible that Lawrence's beliefs in phallic innocence and cerebral corruption had their origins, like much of his thought and sayings, in the Bible studies of his nonconformist upbringing.

Lawrence's exploration of the remains of Etruscan civilization, already perceived by him as the embodiment of the old, pre-lapsarian phallic consciousness, began with a journey in early April to Rome, where he and Earl examined the treasures of Cerveteri at the National Museum, the Villa Giulia. Next day, 'a sunny April morning' (*EP* 14), they set out for the pillaged tombs of Cerveteri, crossing by train the twenty miles of the Campagna Romana plain, the meeting place of the Italic populations and the Greek and Etruscan civilizations.

Nothing remained of the high citadel of Cerveteri. Only the great necropolis told of the former Etruscan presence, which Lawrence felt to be powerfully alive still as he passed the phallic *cippi* standing by the entrances to the passages and penetrated what he called the *arx*, the dark womb within. Even the shapes and proportions of the underground walls and spaces seemed to have 'a simplicity, combined with a most peculiar, free-breasted naturalness and spontaneity' (*EP* 28). The architecture of the cities of the dead, like the artefacts that the tombs had once housed, appeared to express 'ease, naturalness, and an abundance of life' (*EP* 28) – qualities which Lawrence regarded as the essence of the Etruscan spirit. The ascetic simplicity of the tombs suggested 'the natural beauty of proportion of the phallic consciousness, contrasted with the more studied or ecstatic proportion of the mental and spiritual Consciousness' (*EP* 25f.). The conquering Romans, who thought the Etruscans vicious and under whose influence Etruscan civilization withered into extinction, were for Lawrence the exemplars of the mechanical, mental consciousness: like Clifford's set or Galsworthy's Forsytes, they hated the yoni and the phallus, 'because they wanted empire and dominion and, above all, riches: social gain' (*EP* 31).

Next morning Lawrence and Brewster travelled on by train to Tarquinia, where they spent two days exploring the attractive little local museum and the celebrated painted tombs of the necropolis. In their 'vigorous, strong-bodied liveliness' the murals seemed to transcend art. 'You cannot think of art', Lawrence wrote, 'but only of life itself, as if this were the very life of the Etruscans, dancing in their coloured wraps with massive yet exuberant naked limbs, ruddy from the air and the sea-light, dancing and fluting along, through the little olive trees out in the fresh day' (*EP* 65). There was a sympathetic, easy flow of touch that united the paired men and women on the friezes. There was the Lawrentian male–female dualism, too, in the paintings – violence and gentleness, day and night, fire and water, destruction and creation. Many of the themes, major and minor, of *Lady Chatterley* (and indeed of the whole corpus of his works) were reiterated within the travelogue form of his Etruscan sketches.

In the sketches of Cerveteri and Tarquinia there is a special joy, not only in the Etruscan sites themselves, but in the spring flowers growing around the graves and tumuli, symbolizing perhaps eternal life in the midst of death, and showing continuity with 'Flowery Tuscany'. In his account of their Etruscan travels, Earl Brewster recalled: 'My first impression of Lawrence as the botanist, deeply loving nature, still seems to me to contain the essential truth of his character. I think of him as close to those Hindu worshippers of *Shakti*, – life, vitality, power' (Brew 121f.). Lawrence's American friend Witter Bynner had once sent him some of his verses, in one of which he had written 'My single constancy is love of life!' (*CL* 885). Lawrence queried its appropriateness to Bynner, but it is a line that Lawrence could fittingly have written of himself.

After Tarquinia Lawrence's mood seems to have begun to change: his vitality and enthusiasm appear to flag; and his fascination with the landscape, the flora and the Etruscan sites, as attested in the first four essays, tailed off. He had seen the best of the sites at the beginning of his tour, and the remainder appear to have offered mainly disappointment.

On 9 April Lawrence and Brewster travelled the dozen miles from Tarquinia to Vulci. The journey took them through the Maremma, once a swamp that had been a notorious breeding ground for the malaria mosquito, and now, for the most part, drained and planted with fields of wheat. But the last five miles to Vulci, by horse and gig, took Lawrence and Brewster through unreclaimed heathland that was one of the wildest and most desolate parts of Italy. The loneliness of the place struck a cord with the two men, both of whom were inclined towards the hermit's life; but Vulci itself was unremarkable. The tombs, rifled in 1828 and their contents dispersed to the Vatican, to Florence and to the British Museum, were damp and gloomy, and many were difficult or impossible to enter.

Volterra was the last site to be visited, and the subject of Lawrence's last essay in the incomplete series that was posthumously published as *Etruscan Places*. It was one of the hill citadels, parts of whose Etruscan walls still remained. They were 'not much to look at' (*EP* 151), Lawrence observed. On the chilly, grey Sunday and Monday when Lawrence visited Volterra, the town seemed a bleak, sombre spot. He did not bother to visit the tombs there; and on the Monday morning, when he entered the museum to study the ornament of the unique alabaster urns of Volterra, Lawrence felt, so he remarked in the essay, as close to his own tomb as he had ever done.

After a five-hour bus journey from Volterra over mountain roads, followed by a dash to catch the last tram to Vingone, Lawrence arrived back at the Mirenda. Next day, Barby Weekley arrived for a holiday of three weeks, in the midst of which Lawrence wrote to Ada that he and Frieda had made an irrevocable compact never again to have relations to stay unless one or other of them was alone in the house.[2] Barby's presence disrupted his routine and some of his plans, adding to the unsettled, irritable feelings which oppressed him on his return. Exhaustion and the onset of illness were the main contributors to his discontent. There would never again be periods of resurgence of strength and vigour in Lawrence's life. His health was entering a phase of unrelenting decline.

Two days after arriving back, Lawrence caught a cold from Frieda, which affected his chest and plunged him into a state of depressed inertia, which he had difficulty throwing off. As far as Lawrence was concerned, the source of these afflictions was menopausal. To Mabel Luhan he wrote: 'I feel for the time a sort of soreness, physical, mental and spiritual, which is no doubt change of life, and I wish it would pass off. I think it is passing off . . . but till it heals up, I don't feel like making much effort in any direction' (Luhan 295). But these feelings hung over him for more than a month. In early May he fell ill again, for almost a fortnight, with what he diagnosed as a bronchial cold combined with malaria.[3] Writing to Ada, he referred the origins of his ill-health to middle age, rather than to the diseased condition of his lungs:

When one turns forty it seems as if one's old ailments attack one with a double fury. I never seem to get really free. And then one gets sort of disillusioned. I feel like turning hermit and hiding away the rest of my days from everybody. But I suppose it is a phase, a sort of psychic change of life many men go through after forty. I wish it would hurry up and get over and leave me feeling more or less myself.

(Ada 123f.)

Lawrence had got back to find Tuscany as beautiful as ever it had been. The spring was fine and warm; there were tulips still shining red in the cornfields, and on the estate the apple trees were in flower and the peach blossom was out; the nightingales had begun their spring chorusing, which, even in his own melancholy, Lawrence could never regard as anything but joyous. But although there were times when some of the old thrill to the life and beauty of the Tuscan hills returned, often Lawrence now viewed the countryside only with loathing.[4] He had already begun to feel the weariness with Italy and alienation from it that is usually held to postdate his illness of July.

The lease on the Mirenda was due for renewal in early May; and Lawrence now found that he had no real wish to stay on. Having no idea of where else he might go, he took the house for another year, but with no enthusiasm. 'One goes a bit soddened in Italy', he told Brewster. 'I believe I could never stay in this country longer than two years on end' (*CL* 981). As Lawrence realized, the fault lay mainly in himself: he could probably never have endured any country for a longer period. His illness and present state of disorientation and low spirits played some part in his rejection of Italy and the Mirenda, as also did his generally malcontent, dissatisfied character. But perhaps a more important factor was his lifelong quest for novel experiences. The known cycle of fruiting, decay and flowering was about to begin again at the Mirenda. There was no prospect of anything new in the way of sense-experience to look forward to.

April and May were for the most part difficult months, when it proved hard for Lawrence to break out of his inertia and find the will and energy to get on with things; and he found more difficulty than usual in making decisions and sticking to them. 'Anything I *say* I'll do, I seem never to do' (Zyt 311), he told Kot: it was a remark he not infrequently made in his correspondence. He had said he would go over to England to assist in the production of his play *David*, now scheduled to be performed on 22 and 23 May. In March he decided he would not go, and felt the same when he returned to the Mirenda. By the end of April he had reluctantly decided that he should go, and by early May he was changing his mind once more. He fell ill for ten days and wrote regretting that he could not attend. When he recovered he thought he might set off for London after all, but never did.

Lawrence was in a similar state of uncertainty as to what to do about *Lady Chatterley*, as he told Nancy Pearn in a letter of 12 April:

> I am in a quandary about my novel, *Lady Chatterley's Lover*. It's what the world would call very improper. But you know it's not really improper – I always labour at the same thing, to make the sex relation valid and precious, instead of shameful. And this novel is the furthest I've gone. To me it is beautiful and tender and frail as the naked self is, and I shrink very much even from having it typed.
>
> (*CL* 972)

It occurred to him, with a foresight borne out by subsequent events, that the typist might rebel at the text. Though Secker and Knopf were pressing him for the MS, he was 'inclined to do just nothing' (*CL* 972): writing novels seemed, in any case, 'a waste of time'. Next day he told Secker he had decided to let the MS lie at the Mirenda; but a fortnight later he informed Secker that he had decided he would have the novel typed, in London, and would send it to him 'before long . . . so that you can see how possible or impossible he is. But there is much more latitude these days, and a man dare possibly possess a penis' (Sec 87).

In the weeks of ditheriness and lethargy, necessary chores, domestic and literary, began to pile up worryingly. He had wanted to write up his Etruscan sketches while the experiences of his travels with Earl were fresh in his memory. But it was the end of April before he was able to make a start, and the writing seems not to have really been approached in earnest until the end of May. Nevertheless, Lawrence had worked diligently, when he was able, on smaller things during these months. He produced four new short stories – 'The Escaped Cock', 'The Man Who Was Through with the World', 'None of That' and 'Things'; he wrote a number of essays, including the final section of 'Flowery Tuscany', 'Making Love to Music', and probably 'Germans and Latins' and 'Germans and English' (two versions of the same essay); and in addition he wrote a new introduction to his translation of Verga's *Mastro-don Gesualdo* and reviewed two books.

'The Escaped Cock' had been inspired at Volterra on Palm Sunday by the sight of an Easter toy in a shop window – a cockerel being pursued by a man.[5] The resplendent cock in the story, which breaks loose from the cord that tethers it, parallels Christ's emerging from the tomb. Lawrence identifies with the bird and with the Saviour, and both represent Lawrence freeing himself from the oppression of authority, from the constraints of old relationships, and from old patterns of behaviour and thought, to emerge in free, isolate individuality.

The strength which Christ draws on to revive and break open the tomb derives from 'revulsion' and 'unspeakable disillusion' (EC 105) with regard to humanity. These moods reflect those which persisted in Lawrence from this period up to and beyond the time when he completed *Lady Chatterley's Lover*. The Christ who rose from the dead in the story was middle-aged and disenchanted; the 'enthusiasm and burning purity was gone' (EC 113). Probably Lawrence was feeling, too, that like the cock, his voice 'had lost the full gold of its clangor' (EC 104), for after *John Thomas and Lady Jane* – itself somewhat subdued and spare in style by comparison with *The Plumed Serpent* – his prose style in fiction never again showed the tonal riches of the past. In one respect, Lawrence's position in 'The Escaped Cock' was dissimilar from that of *Lady Chatterley's Lover* and harked back to the insouciance of his first months in Italy. Christ felt that he had now outlived his mission, and that the preacher, the teacher and saviour had died in him at the crucifixion. He could now go forward into his own separate life, free, and immortal by virtue of 'having discovered the inner world of insouciance' (EC 117).

The theme of resurrection occupied Lawrence, too, in his painting, when he returned to the Mirenda; and the correspondence between this and his fiction is further illustrated by the figure in his 'Resurrection' painting: the painted Christ has the same black beard and 'wide-open, black sombre eyes' (EC 106) as the Christ of 'The Escaped Cock'.

In the low spirits and enervated disillusionment of the time of Lawrence's return to the Mirenda, the warm, carefree 'old, young insouciance' had given way to the cold, jaded indifference of the resurrected former Messiah in his story. Only the unwillingness to take on the messianic role remained from the insouciant period. The mood had to be combated. In 'The Man Who Was Through with the World' Lawrence made fun of his eremetical inclinations towards withdrawal from society into the loneness of his individuality in a satirical portrait of Henry the Hermit, which caricatured himself and Earl Brewster, who was similarly inclined.

'Time we all did a bit of resurrecting' (*CL* 976) he told Earl. His remedy for himself was not to return to an insouciant approach to life, but to channel and draw on the rebellious instincts of the early months of 1926. 'If the leopard can't change his spots, perhaps I can mine' (*CL* 974) Lawrence had declared. But, in shedding one of his past selves, he adopted no new identity or position but simply re-emerged as another of his former selves, the pre-insouciant Lawrence, the prophet and warrior-priest. It is as if in spurning Italy he repudiated the insouciant spirit he had always associated with the country. He had had enough of the carefree life, which left one gutless and soddened in docile passivity. He wished now to get away as soon as possible to Bavaria for the summer, where he could be among a fighting race that was more congenial to his desire to assert his pugnacious virility.[6]

Lawrence's first intimation of a wish to come out fighting appeared in a letter of 3 May to Brewster – another 'change of life' letter: 'We have been too repressed and too "spiritual" all our lives: and too much insisted on the sympathetic flow, without a balance of the combative: now the hour-glass turns over' (*CL* 974). By the end of the month he had become resolute in his fighting purpose, his resolve strengthened by the poor reviews of his play *David*:[7]

> It's no good my thinking of retreat: I rouse up, and I feel I don't want to. My business is a fight, and I've got to keep it up. I'm reminded of the fact by the impudent reviews of the production of *David*. They say it was just dull. I say they are eunuchs, and have no balls. It is a fight, the same old one. *Caro*, don't ask me to pray for peace. I don't want it. I want subtly, but tremendously, to kick the backsides of the ball-less.
>
> (*CL* 980)

America, like Germany, seemed to Lawrence 'a good fighting country' (*CL* 980), and for that reason he felt a half-hearted inclination to get back to the ranch. Shortly before the lease on the Mirenda was due for renewal, Mabel Luhan and Brett had formed a temporary alliance to get Lawrence back where they wanted him, and they had sent a telegram urging the Lawrences to come to Taos and bring the Brewsters with them. Lawrence's reluctance to commit himself brought forth a furious letter from Brett, accusing him of 'inertia' and threatening to shake him till his ears rattled in order to get him out of it. The resurgence of his old fighting self brought with it Lawrence's former relish for the battle of the sexes. Brett's fury, far from irritating him, made her suddenly more alluring: 'Very tempting that kind of female rage!' (*CL* 976), he observed to Earl.

At about the time when he began to think of taking up the cudgels against the lily-livered and mealy-mouthed, Lawrence resolved to make peace with an adversary who was one of his natural allies in that fight. For a year now he had refused to speak or nod to Norman Douglas whenever their paths happened to cross in Florence. Their enmity, after several years' friendship dating back to *The White Peacock* days, had begun, perhaps, when Douglas read or heard of his portrayal as Argyle in *Aaron's Rod*. But open warfare only broke out after the publication of Maurice Magnus's *Memoirs of the Foreign Legion*, with an introduction by Lawrence. Magnus was a sad scoundrel and sponger, with a chequered history that included service as a legionnaire and as Isadora Duncan's manager. He was one of Douglas's homosexual friends, to whom Lawrence had been introduced by Douglas in November 1919. In 1920, harassed by the police, he killed himself in Malta. A note that he left appointed Douglas as his literary executor. But Magnus's Maltese creditors, whom Lawrence had met on a visit to Magnus, refused to allow the MSS to pass to Douglas, and instead handed them over to Lawrence. Lawrence consented to prepare the *Memoirs* for publication, having first sought Douglas's agreement.

After the book appeared in 1924, Douglas attacked Lawrence in a pamphlet – *D. H. Lawrence and Maurice Magnus: A Plea for Better Manners* – complaining of the way he and Magnus had been portrayed in the introduction to the book, and claiming that Lawrence had made out of the book money that properly belonged to the literary executor – Douglas. Douglas did quite well financially out of this salvo against Lawrence, probably a good deal better than Lawrence had done from the *Memoirs*: the first edition, advertised in *The Times Literary Supplement* and privately published at five shillings a copy, sold 500 copies in the first fortnight and went into two further reprints.

Lawrence first heard of the pamphlet in 1925 and was hurt, but did nothing about it. Only when it reappeared in Douglas's anthology, *Experiments*, when Lawrence was back in Europe, did he write a public defence of his actions. And he did so, in a letter published in the *New*

Statesman on 20 February 1926, only as a result of promptings from Secker, his publisher and the publisher of the *Memoirs*, who appreciated the harm Douglas had done to Lawrence among a public always ready to believe the worst of him. Lawrence's reply was simple, temperate and devastating. But it was Douglas's own words, more than Lawrence's honest eloquence, that condemned him and left him looking petty and dishonest. Lawrence had kept a letter from Douglas, telling him to pocket whatever was left over from publication of the *Memoirs* after the creditors had been paid off, and giving permission to Lawrence to refer to Douglas in the introduction.

It was certainly not the question of money that had caused Douglas to act so outrageously. Aldington believed that a rich woman who loathed Lawrence (Moore implies it was Nancy Cunard) had put him up to it and contributed money towards publication.[8] Another possibility is that it was a mean act of personal malice conceived in the fever of a few days of physical agony: the idea for the pamphlet seems to have come to him at a time when he was tormented by an abscess the size of a coconut on his jaw. Whatever prompted Douglas to write, the real source of his anger was the caricature of him that appeared in the introduction to the *Memoirs*. Douglas was a malicious prankster, who enjoyed playing tricks on other people, including Lawrence, whom he tended to make fun of for his earnestness and penny-pinching. It must have been galling to find the tables turned and himself made a cheese-paring figure of fun by a man he considered to have no sense of humour.[9]

As those who knew Lawrence well have vouchsafed, Lawrence was a splendid comedian who could easily reduce his companions to helpless states of hysterical laughter. What Lawrence lacked was wit; and this is one of the reasons why he was rarely able to provoke laughter in print. His humour was that of the *farceur* and mimic: without the gestures, the facial mannerisms and the voice, all he was able to produce in his writings were rather droll, but not strikingly amusing caricatures. Only when presented with Douglas's larger-than-life posturings, his roaring energy and intrinsically farcical behaviour, was Lawrence able to do justice in ink to his comic talents:

> 'Look here', said D——. 'Didn't you say there was a turkey for dinner? What? Have you been to the kitchen to see what they're doing to it?'
> 'Yes,' said M—— testily. 'I forced them to prepare it to roast.'
> 'With chestnuts – stuffed with chestnuts?' said D——.
> 'They *said* so', said M——.

'Oh, but go down and see that they're doing it. Yes, you've got to keep your eye on them, got to. The most awful howlers if you don't. You go now and see what they're up to.' D— used his most irresistible grand manner.

'It's too late', persisted M—, testy.

'It's *never* too late. You just run down and absolutely prevent them from boiling that bird in the old soup-water', said D—. 'If you need force, fetch me.'

M— went . . . He came back to say the turkey was being roasted, but without chestnuts.

'What did I tell you! What did I tell you!' cried D—. 'They are absolute ——! If you don't hold them by the neck while they peel the chestnuts, they'll stuff the bird with old boots, to save themselves trouble. Of course you should have gone down sooner, M—.'

(*Ph 2* 306)

The title of Douglas's pamphlet – *D. H. Lawrence and Maurice Magnus: A Plea for Better Manners* – suggests something of the manner and attitude of its contents. It was the lofty, restrained rebuke of the gentleman to the lowborn cad. The maliciousness of the piece was covert. Lawrence was described as a characteristic phenomenon of the age of 'personality-mongering', an age in which it had become a popular sport for writers to caricature their friends: it gave encouragement to the 'squeaky suburban chuckle' and bred a school of 'cerebral hermaphrodites': writing of that sort was 'not only bad literature but bad breeding'.[10] It required no great sensitivity on Lawrence's part to see that Douglas was telling him he was an ill-bred, effeminate hack.

Probably it was Orioli, the mutual friend of Douglas and Lawrence, who wrought from Lawrence the promise to be reconciled to Douglas which he referred to in a letter to Secker of 29 April, a day when he had evidently visited Florence for the first time since his return from his Etruscan travels.[11] It was in Orioli's shop, probably on Lawrence's next visit to Florence, three weeks later, that Lawrence and Douglas first exchanged friendly greetings again. Lawrence and Frieda were in the shop, talking to Orioli, when Douglas marched in. It was Douglas who held out the olive branch in the shape of a proffered pinch of snuff. Lawrence accepted, remarking, '"Isn't it curious" – *sniff* – "only Norman and my father" – *sniff* – "ever give me snuff?"'[12]

This was not the only occasion when Lawrence commented upon similarities between Douglas and Arthur Lawrence. It suggests that he may have seen Douglas, with his avuncular manner, his strong,

211

virile face and physique, as an admired father-figure. In 1928, when taking a drive with the Brewsters through the Black Forest, Lawrence roused himself from silent communion with the peace of the woods to discourse on 'X', plainly Douglas. His father and Douglas had been 'the only people he had known who always followed joy' (Brew 295). He and his father had both been hedonists – they were like sunflowers in their brightness and in the self-regarding resoluteness with which they instinctively followed the sun of their pleasures and ignored the shadows. Douglas had courage, too, a Lawrentian courage to face up to reality and vicissitude and live beyond them, preserving his spirit unbroken and remaining true to himself.

There were other qualities in Douglas that Lawrence may have found admirable. He had Lawrence's love of the natural world and a scientist's knowledge of botany and zoology, for which Lawrence's own considerable expertise was no match. And Lawrence could well have grudgingly envied him his gruff masculinity, self-assurance, and gentlemanly manner and appearance. Professionally, too, Lawrence had a high regard for Douglas, which he maintained even while at odds with him. Douglas's position *vis-à-vis* Lawrence was rather similar. Though inevitably he wrote of Lawrence patronizingly and generally dismissively in his memoirs, *Looking Back*, there was at the heart of his essay on Lawrence a paragraph of almost unqualified praise for the man. There were few plaudits, though, for his work, other than the remark that 'his genius was pictorial and contemplative'.[13] Douglas's biographer, Mark Holloway, suggested that Douglas might have regarded Lawrence's work with a sort of nostalgic envy for its lyrical spontaneity – a quality which he could have felt himself to have been once capable of achieving, had his own work not taken a different direction.[14]

Though some of their regard for each other survived their quarrel, and though they remained superficially on good terms after their reconciliation, neither Lawrence nor Douglas was able completely to pardon the other. In June 1928 Douglas took Bennett Cerf, a young American publisher, out to the Mirenda to visit Lawrence. Despite the fact that Douglas had spent the previous day reviling Lawrence, the two of them met with theatrical embraces and declarations of affection. When Frieda led Douglas off to walk round the gardens, Cerf (who had been expected alone) was given a dressing-down for having brought 'that man' to Lawrence's house; and Lawrence proceeded to castigate Douglas in much the same way as Douglas had

done Lawrence. Then, when Douglas returned, the joyful cama-
raderie between them was resumed. [15] Cerf was not unreasonably
disappointed by what must have seemed gross hypocrisy on both
sides. But it is not impossible that when the two of them were
together the old affection and delight in each other's company
temporarily swept away all grudges and mistrust.

As Lawrence was aware, Douglas's pamphlet had been privately
published in Florence, as had many of his works since 1924, and it
was Douglas's precedent that Lawrence followed in publishing *Lady
Chatterley's Lover*. When, in November 1927, Lawrence determined
on private publication in Florence, he often cited Douglas's example
in letters declaring his intentions; and the letters also implied that
the intended quantity, price and manner of distribution – 700 copies
(later 1,000) at two guineas or ten dollars each, half the number to be
sent to the USA and half to Britain – were in imitation of Norman
Douglas. He seems, too, to have borrowed from Douglas in other
aspects of publication: he used the same printer's shop, the Typografia Giuntina, and he used Orioli to take care of affairs relating to
printing and distribution as Douglas had done; and it may be that the
decision to bring out the first two copies on blue paper was influenced
by Douglas, who in 1922 had revived this old custom of limited
blue-paper editions. [16]

Douglas was the model, then, in the formulation of Lawrence's
plans for publishing *Lady Chatterley's Lover*. He may also have had a
hand in bringing Lawrence to a decision to publish. This decision
followed immediately on Lawrence's excursion into Florence on 17
November, his first since returning to the Mirenda after holidays in
Austria and Germany. It was 'friends in Florence' who on that
November visit urged him to publish the novel himself, and one of
the friends he encountered briefly was a 'stuttering and fading'
Douglas (Luhan 303). [17]

Douglas would have approved enthusiastically of the idea of
bringing out *Lady Chatterley*: he had himself for several years been
planning a scandalous venture into print with a book of smutty
limericks, and emboldened by Lawrence he had the book printed in
Florence, six months after *Lady Chatterley's Lover*. Lawrence's respect
for Douglas would have inclined him to be more influenced by his
advice than by that of any of his other Florentine acquaintances, and
Douglas was a very persuasive talker. However, all that one can know
for certain of Douglas's personal association with *Lady Chatterley* is

that at some time Lawrence gave a reading from the MS of one of the last two versions of the novel to a small gathering that comprised Douglas, Orioli, Reggie Turner and Collingwood Gee, who five or six years later painted from memory a picture of the occasion. [18]

On the conjectured day of reconciliation between Lawrence and Douglas, in the middle of May, Lawrence made one of his increasingly infrequent trips into Florence, attended an exhibition of modern Florentine art and lunched with Nelly Morrison, who was to be the first typist of *Lady Chatterley's Lover*. The city's usual atmosphere of nervous irritability seems to have communicated itself to its visitor. The paintings Lawrence saw struck him as mostly piffling and lacking in guts. Lunch had been an irksome affair of 'high-browish, spiritual up-soaring' (Brew 132) conversation. And the unsatisfactory nature of the day may not have been improved by the news that Osbert and Edith Sitwell were in Tuscany and were hoping to be able to call out to see him. [19] The inclination towards a solitary life had not yet been exorcised in the satire of Henry the Hermit, and what little Lawrence knew of the Sitwells may have led him to expect an extended diet of highbrow and pretentious talk. There were good diplomatic reasons, too, for not meeting the Sitwells. If *Lady Chatterley* were ever to be published in a version corresponding closely to his latest, second draft, the Sitwells would certainly have been outraged by what they saw of Renishaw in Wragby, of their mother in Lady Eva and of Osbert in Clifford.

In the first version Clifford had resembled Gerard Crich in *Women in Love*, and hence had presumably taken his physical appearance from Major Thomas Philip Barber of Lamb Close House, Eastwood. But in the second draft elements of Osbert Sitwell had been incorporated into the portrait. Lawrence made this new Clifford share with Osbert 'some extremely "titled" relatives on his mother's side' (*JTLJ* 13); and his appearance seems to match Osbert's quite closely in the 'ruddy face', the 'broad and strong' shoulders, 'the watchful look, the intangible vacancy' in the face, the expensive tailoring and the 'handsome neckties from Bond Street' (*JTLJ* 10). Apart from the detail of Clifford's 'bright, challenging blue eyes' – Osbert's were pale and lustreless – the description seems to fit Osbert Sitwell admirably, especially in the watchful, bland countenance that was characteristic of some of the photographic portraits of him. But all these physical resemblances between Clifford and Osbert could have been quite coincidental: the portrait of Gerard Crich in *Women in Love* shows similar features – a solid build, sun-tanned complexion, elegant dress, and a 'strange, guarded look . . . as if he did not belong to the same creation as the people about him' (*WL* 61).

The fact that Lawrence and Osbert had not met might suggest that any resemblances between Osbert and Clifford were indeed fortuitous, although it is not impossible that Lawrence became familiar with Osbert's appearance from the photographs and accounts of him which frequently appeared in newspapers and magazines. Lawrence also had an excellent source of information in Aldous Huxley, who had once been closely associated with the Sitwells. It must have been largely Huxley's judgement and knowledge of Osbert that Lawrence drew on in a short passage in the first pages of the second draft. This describes, with an accuracy that leaves little doubt that Osbert had become one of the models for Sir Clifford, Osbert's character, the nature of his early writings, the kind of reaction he inspired among his peers and his 'extremely "titled" relatives', and the hollowness of his personal brand of gilded socialism:

> Clifford was not popular, he was only to be pitied. He had always been too high-brow, too flippant, thought himself too clever and behaved in too democratic a fashion, to please the county. They knew he made a mock of them all. He had even pretended to be a sort of socialist, besides having written those pacifist poems and newspaper articles. There was no *real* danger in him, of course. The marrow of him was just as conservative as the Duke's own. But he pranced about in that Labour-Party sort of way, and therefore you had to leave him to his prancing.
>
> (*JTLJ* 13)

To take no steps to meet the Sitwells may have seemed attractive to Lawrence; but since word would probably get back that Lawrence knew of the Sitwells' wish to visit him, failure to respond would seem ungracious in view of the hospitality he had enjoyed at Montegufoni. It was an awkward situation, and perhaps for that reason Lawrence took a little time to deliberate before making arrangements for Osbert and Edith to visit the Mirenda.

On meeting the Sitwells, Lawrence was agreeably surprised to find that the impression created by their writings and public posturings was a false one. 'They were really very nice, not a bit affected or bouncing' (*Zyt* 314), he told Kot. The emotional insecurity that fed the Sitwells' public façade of exhibitionism, arrogance and aggressive behaviour betrayed itself in private in a quite contrary manner. They were shy, diffident, guileless and vulnerable – qualities Lawrence found appealing and at the same time disturbing.

The success of their meeting may have owed something to the fact that Osbert did not come as a writer who regarded himself as an equal or a competitor, but as an admirer who wished to pay his respects to a man of genius. His admiration was for Lawrence, the poet of delicate sensibilities, not for the strident, sententious prophet; and he had no time for the Lawrentian creeds of violence, dark gods and blood-wisdom. But he was extremely sympathetic to several other facets of Lawrence's thought: insentience, materialism, modern democracy, the middle class and the Common Man were as odious to him as to Lawrence. Osbert's character, attitude and agreeability provided a climate which favoured repose and affability in Lawrence, who proved a courteous, hospitable and attentive host.

That the two hours spent in Lawrence's company were 'extremely delightful' was all that Osbert vouchsafed in the way of comment on his relations with Lawrence when, four years later, after Lawrence's death, he wrote a brief 'Portrait of Lawrence'. It is a portrait which never attempts to approach the character of the man. It declares only visual impressions of 'the fragile and goatish little saint' who greeted him at the Mirenda:

> In his flattish face, with its hollow, wan cheeks, and rather red beard, was to be discerned a curious but happy mingling of satyr and ascetic . . . It was, certainly, a remarkable appearance. Unlike the faces of most geniuses, it was the face of a genius.[20]

Osbert's opinions on Lawrence's personality could perhaps have been implicit in his silence on the subject. By then he would certainly have read *Lady Chatterley's Lover* and could not, perhaps, write honestly on what he thought of Lawrence the man without casting aside the Sitwellian mask of aloof detachment, and appearing both uncharitable and cowardly in reserving his attack until such time as he would be safe from a return blow.

No one would describe Edith's portrait of Lawrence in 'A Man with Red Hair'[21] as detached in its point of view. But a span of almost forty years separated their meeting from her account – years during which bottled-up resentment grew into an obsession. Lawrence had passed into her personal mythology as a red-haired beastly ogre who combined the appearances of a garden gnome and an ill-executed self-portrait by Van Gogh. The images are so inapposite as to lose their force as invective; and there are several errors of fact in her essay. She does, however, seem to have kept fresh some memories of the topics of conversation on her visit to the Mirenda.

Lawrence was indelicate enough to raise the matter of the gulf between the classes in English society, a subject with which he had already associated the Sitwells in *John Thomas and Lady Jane*. Edith recalled:

> He was determined to impress upon us that he was a son of toil . . . and he seemed to be trying to make us uncomfortable by references to the contrast between his childhood and ours. But this was not our fault. Our childhood was hell, and we refused to be discomfited.[22]

Perhaps Edith told Lawrence, at the time, of her tortured and neglected upbringing: there are signs in his accounts of the Chatterley family in *Lady Chatterley's Lover* that he knew something of the lives of the Sitwell children.

Lawrence, Edith reported, also talked at length on the subject of Sir George and Lady Ida, whose characters and relationship he was eager to explain to their children. It could have been Edith, not Lawrence, who raised the matter. The idiosyncracies of 'the Gingers', Osbert and Edith's name for their parents, provided the staple fare of Edith's small-talk. Her indiscretions and Osbert's uncomfortable reticence seem to have been reproduced in an interlude between Emma Chatterley and her brother Clifford in *Lady Chatterley's Lover*: 'She was very witty in a quiet way about Sir Geoffrey and his determined patriotism . . . But Clifford only smiled a little uneasily. Everything was ridiculous, quite true. But when it came too close and oneself became ridiculous too . . .?' (*LCL* 11).

The behaviour of the Gingers provided Edith and Osbert with an endless store of comic stories, giving opportunities for impressive displays of wit and raconteurship. The telling of these stories also reflected their joint obsessions with their parents and perhaps expressed a desire to be avenged. Edith bore a profound grudge against both parents, while Osbert, who worshipped his mother, reserved his contemptuous resentment for Sir George. Reporting the meeting with the Sitwells to Kot a few days later, Lawrence wrote:

> They were . . . absorbed in themselves and in their parents. I never in my life saw such a strong, strange *family* complex: as if they were marooned on a desert island and nobody in the world but their lost selves. Queer!
>
> (Zyt 314)

The Sitwell family may have been the more intriguing because, despite the gulf in status, it was not so very different – especially in terms of the despised and isolated father – from Lawrence's own family with which he had been as much obsessed as Osbert and Edith were with theirs.

At this period in his life Osbert was in the throes of a profound emotional crisis. He and his brother Sacheverell had for several years lived and travelled together as inseparable companions, and Osbert had never conceived of any end to this relationship. But in 1925 Sacheverell had married, depriving Osbert of a confidant and collaborator who, with his greater emotional stability, had provided strength, support and temperate advice. The loss of Sachie left Osbert in a state of extreme malaise and lonely isolation, and, in the search for someone who might replace him, Osbert's homosexuality had begun to declare itself in romantic and as yet unrequited attachments to handsome young men. His reactions to the world, and to real and imagined enemies in literary society, during the years that immediately followed Sachie's marriage, showed an angry inner turmoil and intimations of paranoia. [23]

The anxiety and depression that Osbert experienced in the crisis years of his early 30s did not escape Lawrence's notice. To Richard Aldington, who knew Osbert, Lawrence wrote of his guest: 'He . . . makes me feel sort of upset and worried. Of him the same I want to ask: But what ails thee then, tha's got nowt amiss as much as a' that!' (*CL* 978). The switch from Standard English to dialect and the *tha* and *thee* forms had, for Lawrence as for his gamekeeper, a number of possible significations, which varied according to mood and circumstance. One of its uses for Lawrence was as a put-down whenever he detected snobbery and pretentiousness. But dialect was also the language of virility and tenderness, and here, in imagined address to Osbert, it seems to represent both affectionate concern and a patronizing assertion of his own superior strength of character.

Frieda later told how, after the Sitwells had taken leave of them, Lawrence and she, disturbed and overwhelmed by their encounter with Osbert and Edith, set out on a long walk together to talk over the impressions the Sitwells had made on them:

> They moved us strangely. They seemed so oversensitive, as if something had hurt them too much, as if they had to keep up a brave front to the world, to pretend they didn't care and yet they only cared much too much.
>
> ('*Not I*' 183)

Lady Chatterley's Lover was written four months after these conversations, by which time any concern for the Sitwells' hypersensitivity had apparently come to be outweighed by an irresistible fascination with Osbert and with the strangeness and isolation of the Sitwell family complex. The Sitwell contribution to the novel was increased to such an extent that a large section of the readership of the novel would unquestionably have recognized the Chatterleys as Sitwells:

> The Chatterleys, two brothers and a sister, had lived curiously isolated, shut in with one another at Wragby in spite of all connexions. A sense of isolation intensified the family tie, a sense of weakness of their position, a sense of defencelessness, in spite of, or because of, the title and the land. They were cut off from those industrial Midlands in which they passed their lives. And they were cut off from their own class by the brooding, obstinate, shut-up nature of Sir Geoffrey, their father, whom they ridiculed, but whom they were so sensitive about.
>
> (*LCL* 12)

Though some of the comment and interpretation is Lawrence's, the burden of the passage accurately represents the life of the Sitwell children at Renishaw as Osbert and Edith often described it; and the character of Sir Geoffrey is that of Sir George, as his children perceived it.

Edith became Clifford's sister, Emma, 'with her aristocratic thin face' (*LCL* 18), who collaborated with Clifford in his literary endeavours. She plays only a minor role in the book, as opponent and critic of Clifford's marriage to Connie: 'She was ten years older than Clifford, and she felt his marrying would be a desertion and a betrayal of what the young ones of the family had stood for' (*LCL* 13). Later the narrator comments that: 'She would never forgive Connie for ousting her from her union in consciousness with her brother' (*LCL* 18). The source for this element in the story was probably an indiscretion of Edith's regarding her attitude, and Osbert's, to the marriage of Sacheverell, who was ten years younger than herself, as Clifford was to Emma in the novel. Both Osbert and Edith had set their faces against the match, possibly because they believed that Sachie's marriage would loosen the bonds which held them together as a family trinity of writers. Since childhood they had stood together against their parents and against the world in general, and Osbert and Edith may also have feared that the loss of their brother might weaken their collective defence.

219

The nervous anxiety and loss of self-confidence which befell Osbert when Sachie passed out of his life, and which had disturbed Lawrence when they met, were introduced into the character of Clifford, who in the final version of the novel was given a more perfect resemblance to Osbert:

> He had never been one of the modern lady-like young men: rather bucolic even, with his ruddy face and broad shoulders. But his very quiet, hesitating voice, and his eyes, at the same time bold and frightened, assured and uncertain, revealed his nature. His manner was often offensively supercilious, and then again modest and self-effacing, almost tremulous.
>
> (*LCL* 16)

The character of Clifford, as it declares itself in his talk and in his behaviour, owes hardly anything to Osbert Sitwell; and the debt of the artist to his model is apparent mainly in authorial definitions of facets of Clifford's personality that are never developed as integral or persistent features of his character. Among those numerous but rather superficial traits for which Osbert was the source are Clifford's 'extremely shy and self-conscious disposition', his 'wincing sense of the ridiculousness of everything' and his fears that he might himself appear an object of ridicule, his sensitivity to criticism of his work and his 'sound publicity instinct' in attracting attention to himself and his writing (*LCL* 16, 12, 22). Likewise borrowed from Osbert Sitwell is Clifford's attitude of rebellion against authority which, in Osbert as in Clifford, was of shallow motivation and hence lacking in vigour.

Lawrence had only a general knowledge of Osbert's work as a poet and journalist before their meeting. Afterwards he must have read *Triple Fugue and Other Stories* which he might have been given when Osbert called. A short and perceptive critique of the book, not altogether uncharitable in its observations, was used as an assessment of Clifford's work as a writer:

> He had taken to writing stories; curious, very personal stories about people he had known. Clever, rather spiteful, and yet in some mysterious way, meaningless. The observation was extraordinary and peculiar. But there was no touch, no actual contact. It was as if the whole thing took place in a vacuum. And since the field of life is largely an artificially-lighted stage today, the stories were curiously true to modern life, to the modern psychology, that is.
>
> (*LCL* 17)

Later, the clever emptiness of Clifford's writing is taken up again:

> Clifford was really clever at that slightly humorous analysis of people and motives that leaves everything in bits at the end. But it was rather like puppies tearing the sofa cushions to bits; except that it was not young and playful, but curiously old, and rather obstinately conceited. It was weird and it was nothing.
>
> (LCL 53)

No less perceptive than Lawrence's appraisal of Osbert's writing is his analysis of the man. 'But what ails thee then?' – the question he would have liked to ask of Osbert when they met – is answered in a definition of Clifford's character. In the opinion of Pearson, Osbert's biographer, Lawrence correctly searched out in the following passage the acute sense of fear which was the essential source of Osbert's current malaise:[24]

> Clifford, while he was better bred than Connie, and more 'society', was in his own way more provincial and more timid. He was at his ease in the narrow 'great world', that is, landed aristocracy society, but he was shy and nervous of all that other big world which consists of the vast hordes of the middle and lower classes, and of foreigners not of his own class. He was, in some paralysing way, conscious of his own defencelessness, though he had all the defence of privilege.
>
> (LCL 10)

Osbert, who had taken grave offence in the past when he found himself lampooned by other writers, was curiously magnanimous, at least in his public utterances, in regard to Lawrence's misdemeanour. Even his satire of Lawrence as T. L. Enfelon in *Miracle on Sinai* is largely charitable, and sometimes generous in its praise. His tolerance may perhaps have come from some knowledge of the history of *Lady Chatterley's Lover*. In September 1928 he was visited by Richard Aldington,[25] who may have assured him from his own knowledge that a draft of the novel existed before his meeting with Lawrence. If Osbert Sitwell had been of a superstitious nature he might in his last years have felt that, in portraying him as Clifford, Lawrence had laid a curse upon him. The onset of Parkinson's Disease confined him to a wheelchair, like Clifford, whose example he also followed in that he allowed his life to become trivialized under the dominion of his nurse, Frank Magro.

Lawrence seems to have made one concession to the sensitivities of

Osbert and Edith in making the Lady Eva of *Lady Chatterley's Lover* unrecognizable as Lady Ida. The subject of their parents was an extremely delicate one: Osbert and Edith laughed at the antics of the Gingers and shared their family anecdotes with acquaintances, but it was always tacitly made plain that anyone outside the family circle was required to show respect by keeping silent on the topic. Lawrence had trodden on dangerous ground when he expressed opinions, albeit sympathetic ones, on the relationship between Sir George and Lady Ida; and he seems, judging by his observations on Clifford and Emma, to have registered the disapproval he met with in talking of their father 'whom they ridiculed, but whom they were so sensitive about' (*LCL* 12).

If the camouflaging of Lady Ida in *Lady Chatterley's Lover* was done in deference to the feelings of Osbert and Edith, it was not a gesture that they were in any position to appreciate. All they saw were portraits of themselves and their home in an outrageous and angry novel; and as far as Edith was concerned, Lawrence's use of those models was maliciously inspired: it was his way of paying them back for some imagined slight at the Villa Mirenda:

> We did not see Mr. and Mrs. Lawrence again, for although there had not been time for us to fall in love with them, the fact that we had not done so turned us, automatically, into textbook cases, and our relations became strained, to say the least of it.[26]

Anyone in Edith's position, however much less thin-skinned, might have been similarly disposed to suspect in Lawrence's behaviour an irrational personal antipathy. Nevertheless, this appears not to have been the case. The letters written shortly after the Sitwells' visit show only warm regard and concern, and there is no hint in later correspondence of any subsequent event or report that turned Lawrence against them. Such references as there are in his writings suggest that Lawrence continued to regard the Sitwells favourably. He included their names in a list of authors capable of providing interesting material for an anthology that Kot was hoping to publish. And a review of *The Station: Athos, Treasures and Men* by Robert Byron, whom Lawrence compared to the Sitwells, implies that he found their work 'honest' and 'charming', if also 'ephemeral' (*Ph* 283).

In the few months between meeting the Sitwells and the beginning of *Lady Chatterley's Lover*, the warmth Lawrence had felt towards them may have evaporated. Perhaps they came to be regarded impersonally as representatives of the moneyed classes and so undeserving of the sympathy he had once accorded them. Not long after the Sitwells' visit, Lawrence met another rich aristocrat, a friend of the Huxleys – Barone Luigi Franchetti. Relating this encounter to Kot, Lawrence wrote: 'I agree entirely – I have absolutely no basic sympathy with people of "assured incomes". All words become a lie in their mouth, in their ears also. I *loathe* rich people' (Zyt 316). This was Lawrence's usual position regarding the wealthy, which the diffident charms of the Sitwells had caused him to set aside.

Luigi Franchetti, a professional concert pianist, had been driven to the Mirenda with his wife Yvonne by Maria Huxley. Lawrence had to acknowledge that he was rather nice, despite the handicap of being 'as rich as Croesus', a saying that was a favourite of Douglas's, which suggests renewed contact between him and Lawrence. Lawrence was probably to see more of the Franchettis in Forte dei Marmi, where they spent part of the summer and where the Lawrences stayed with the Huxleys for a few days between 14 and 21 June. Aldous and Maria had just moved into a small villa there for the summer season.

Situated on the sea about twenty miles from Pisa, Forte had been chosen by the Huxleys for its cool breezes from the sea and from the mountains, which moderated the heat of the Italian summer. Forte's setting was an attractive one: there were sandy bathing beaches that stretched for miles in either direction, and behind the village pleasant country for rambling, either among the water meadows and copses of the narrow coastal strip or in the marble mountains of Carrara that rose above the plain. But in recent years the village itself had become crowded and built-up. Lawrence thought it 'beastly': 'flat, dead sea, jelly fishy and millions of villas' (CL 986). Nonetheless he passed his holiday in an easygoing, gentle and sociable frame of mind, talking eagerly with everyone and making special friends with the Huxleys' young son Matthew and their maid Rina. Aldous and Maria were kind and welcoming, and that summer there were pleasant evenings to be had listening to Beethoven trios performed by first-rate artistes at a neighbouring villa.

When Lawrence returned to the Mirenda, he set about writing the last of his essays on his Etruscan travels, at which he had been working hard during late May and June. He now had plans for a large volume with perhaps a hundred illustrations, consisting of twelve essays that were possibly intended to mirror the twelve city-states of

Etruria. He was now half-way through, and intended in early July to head south to Umbria with Frieda to gather material for the remainder of the book. After this volume, he intended to write a second on the 'little' Etruscan sites. None of these plans bore fruit.

On 25 June Lawrence wrote to Earl Brewster complaining: 'I had a sore chest again this week and felt "low". It's not really better yet. What have the gods got against us. I feel really *sfortunato* sometimes' (*CL* 987). He had been bathing in the sea at Forte with near-fatal consequences.

A week or so later, on a hot afternoon at the Mirenda, Lawrence had been gathering peaches in the garden. He came in with a basketful of fruit and retired to his room. Frieda recalled what occurred next: 'A very little while after he called from his room in a strange, gurgling voice; I ran and found him lying on his bed; he looked at me with shocked eyes while a slow stream of blood came from his mouth' (*'Not I'* 182).

He was attended by Dr Giglioli, a specialist from Florence, who administered coagulin to heal the cavity in the lungs, but the haemorrhages kept returning. By 18 July they appeared to have ceased, and Lawrence felt well enough to get up and take a short walk to the woods. But there was a fresh bout of bleeding next morning, eliciting a flood of tears from Frieda and bitter feelings of martyrdom in Lawrence.[27] He remained in bed for nearly four weeks. By the end of July the haemorrhaging had stopped and he was 'up and creeping round a bit' (Brew 142).

He was well looked after. Giglioli arrived every evening to examine him, cheer him up and calm Frieda. Orioli called, and also Reggie Turner and several other English friends from Florence. Aldous and Maria Huxley arrived, Maria bearing a bouquet of lotus flowers, the emblem of Isis, healer and lover of the god Osiris.

With the Huxleys was J. W. N. Sullivan, a writer on scientific subjects, especially physics and astronomy, who was staying with them at Forte. Lawrence seems to have met him at one of Brett's soirées at her studio, and had been sorry that they could not have been at Forte together. At the Mirenda Lawrence found him a little disappointing: 'He was nice, but sad – I thought he would be rather bouncing – not a bit' (*CL* 992). It evidently did not occur to Lawrence that Sullivan might not have thought effervescence was appropriate around his sick-bed. Sullivan, and perhaps parts of the conversation at the Mirenda, appeared in the gathering of Clifford's cronies in *Lady Chatterley's Lover*. He became Charles May, taking his name from Edna May, 'the Belle of New York', an actress whom Lawrence had also met at Brett's studio. Charles May was 'an Irishman, who wrote scientifically about stars', 'pale and rather fat' (*LCL* 32f.), with a satirical sense of humour. He was an apostle of promiscuous sex, whose flirtatious ways with women piqued Arnold B. Hammond (Huxley) when directed towards his wife. Connie, though she found something likeable in him, thought him 'distasteful and messy, in spite of his stars' (*LCL* 37).

On the day of the Huxleys' visit, Lawrence had been a model patient. Commenting on him in a letter to his father, Huxley wrote: 'He is a very extraordinary man, for whom I have a great admiration and liking – but difficult to get on with, passionate, queer, violent. However, age is improving him and now his illness has cured him of his violences and left him touchingly gentle.'[28] Huxley should have known Lawrence better than to suppose that Lawrence's mood of the moment might ever prove enduring. As he later came to realize, the effect of illness on Lawrence, as he summoned the energies to fight off death, was quite contrary to Huxley's predictions. It intensified the violence, anger and sense of bitter revulsion with human society that had been welling up in him before the haemorrhage attack. Some weeks later, recounting his illness to Aldington, he wrote: 'I saw the end of my days, and my only or chief regret was, I couldn't spit in the face of the narrow-gutted world and put its eye out' (*CL* 1023). One of the motives, arguably, behind the writing of the final version of the novel was a desire to avenge himself while he still had life and strength to do so.

Giglioli had tried to reassure him that there was nothing to worry about provided the bleedings did not continue, and so long as he rested, gave up work and guarded his health. But Lawrence could no longer ignore the possibility that his days were numbered and that at any moment another violent attack of bleeding might bring on sudden death. The primary cause of his illness, he told Else Jaffe and Dr Trigant Burrow, was psychosomatic. It was 'due, radically, to chagrin' (*CL* 994) he told Burrow, an American psychoanalyst with whom he was corresponding. It was a chagrin into which he had been born, he wrote; but he no doubt believed that it was nourished by his sufferings at the hands of the critics, as representatives of the authority of the eunuchs and the middle classes. Several months later he wrote to Lady Ottoline Morrell, who had herself been very ill:

> You ask me, do I feel things very much: – and I do. And that's why I too am ill. The hurts and the bitterness sink in, however much one may reject them with one's spirit. They sink in, and there they lie, inside one, wasting one . . . Then the microbes pounce.
>
> (*CL* 1063)

Lawrence could well have associated the outbreak of haemorrhaging with the wounds inflicted on him by reviews of *David* a month or so beforehand.

After the first few days of illness, when briefly he was well enough to write, he told Burrow that he was lying in bed 'furious' (*CL* 990) at his stricken state. This seems to have been more typical of his moods while he lay tormented by flies and mosquitoes on a burning bed within the baking walls of his room. The Wilkinsons had been regular visitors, and Mrs Wilkinson sat at his bedside, playing cards with him to keep him amused. Though he later wrote touchingly of his everlasting gratitude for their kindness, their solicitude often went unrewarded at the time, and exasperation with the trials of caring for Lawrence soon came to override the sympathy the Wilkinsons felt for him. When they drove him down to Florence on 3 August to take a train for Villach in Austria, just over the Italian border, they regarded his departure with 'real Relief'. Their summary judgement on the Lawrences, recorded in their diary for that day, expressed a fair-minded appraisal of the flaws which made prolonged contact with Lawrence and Frieda irksome even to the most well-disposed and charitable of their acquaintances: 'We came back pretty critical of their ways of doing and thinking – she's too vague and unconsidering for anything – and he's too precise in some ways and dreadfully scatter minded in others and has such a way of jumping to conclusions and just making things up' (Wilk 69).

It was an enormous relief to Lawrence, too, to get away from Tuscany to the fresh air of Villach, a trim little town beside a cool, glacial river in a region of mountain lakes and forests. Within three or four days he began to feel 'a different creature' (Wilk 70). He found himself able to manage short walks into the country, and after a fortnight reported to Brewster: 'I am better, but not bouncing, and the cough is a nuisance, and I wish I could get a new breathing apparatus' (Brew 145). The social and political climate also seemed more favourable than that of Italy, with its bossy fascism and tensions. Though Austria stood on the brink of civil war, the breakdown of government and the collapse of the currency seemed to have bred a carefree anarchy and a lack of interest in money among the ordinary people.

The Lawrences spent most of August in Villach, where they met Frieda's younger sister Johanna – 'Nusch' – and her husband, who were holidaying nearby. Near the end of the month they left to join Frieda's other sister, Else Jaffe, at her chalet on the edge of the forest in Irschenhausen, Bavaria. Lawrence had last stayed there in 1913, towards the end of his elopement to the Continent with Frieda. He had always liked and respected Frieda's sisters, who for a time were all together at the chalet. Else he admired for her beauty and her intellect, while Nusch – beautiful, supremely elegant and vivacious, though currently a malcontent with a new husband who bored her – was the only woman Barbara Weekley ever heard Lawrence refer to as 'desirable'.

A number of German writers called at the chalet to pay homage to a man whose works were already coming to be more venerated on the Continent than in his own country. Among them were two men with whom Lawrence formed warm friendships – Franz Schoenberner, editor of *Jugend*, and the playwright Max Mohr, for whom Lawrence and Frieda felt a special affection.

The holiday at Irschenhausen was one of the last occasions in Lawrence's life when for any length of time fear, anger and bitterness were largely banished from his thoughts. The company was good; the weather was often bright and languidly autumnal; the landscape was beautiful and held a rich variety of plant and animal life; and under the compelling influence of a cook who was determined that he should eat, he regained some weight and strength on a diet of trout, partridge and venison, supplemented by swallowings of malt beer and goat's milk. The docile quietude of the mood of Irschenhausen, expressed in a letter to Earl Brewster, is reminiscent of that of his first spring and autumn on the now repellent Mirenda estate:

> Myself I am glad to be here, in this little wooden house with the forest round the back, and in front the wide open valley going to the blue mountains. I like the dark fir trees, and the clearings where we see the red deer. I like the deep, matted wet grass where the harebells are now so dark blue, and the chicory heavenly. I love above all the stillness of the innumerable trees that are none the less silently growing, and

pressing themselves on the air so softly yet so indomitably. I am glad not to be in Italy for a while. I don't mind if it rains some days, and is dark. I like it. I don't mind that it is rather cold, I like it. I find Italy has almost withered me. Here something softens out again.

(Brew 149)

In fair contentment he faced the prospect of his demise with stoical calm. In the same letter Lawrence referred to the collapse of the 'old order' in Earl's life (apparently brought on by the altered mental state of middle age and by a change in circumstances which left the Brewsters temporarily without a home). Addressing himself to and identifying with Earl's uncertain future, Lawrence wrote of the need to adapt to a 'new shadow of destiny'. Thinking perhaps of his own destiny, he gave this shadow the attributes of life after death: 'It is time to know earnestly that there has been a change, that the wings of the archangels have snapped at last, that there are no sheltering wings, only a strange new shadow which after all will have many mansions.'

Fatalism did not imply passive resignation. 'So now the thing *must* heal up' (Irv 76), Lawrence told Brett, as if commanding his lungs to improve. The haemorrhages had so alarmed him that for the moment he was willing to 'try all the things to see what can be done'. What he remained unwilling to sample was a sanatorium cure. Giglioli had told him, perhaps with some knowledge of Lawrence's character and of the incurability of his condition, that a sanatorium was unnecessary. The doctor at the *Kurhaus* in Baden-Baden recommended a sanatorium for two months, but Lawrence would not consider it: doctors and sanatoria depressed him, he told his sister Emily.[29] When, in her next letter, Emily pressed him to attend a sanatorium, he affected in his reply an agreeable inquisitiveness which nevertheless implied a stubborn resistance to the prospect of a want of personal attention and a surfeit of institutional food and discipline.[30]

In Irschenhausen Lawrence agreed to be examined by Hans Carossa from Munich, a poet and a specialist in tubercular disease: 'If a poet who is a doctor can't tell me what to do with myself, then who can?' (*CL* 1003) Lawrence wrote. Reporting the visit to Else, who presumably knew the truth of Lawrence's condition from Frieda, Lawrence tacitly acknowledged that his haemorrhages – 'bronchial' to every other correspondent – had been from pulmonary cavities:

Yes, we saw Hans Carossa, a nice man, mild like mashed potatoes. He listened to my lung passages, he could not hear my lungs, thinks they must be healed, only the bronchi, and doctors are not interested in bronchi. But he says not to take more inhalations with hot air: it might bring the hemorrhage back.

(CL 1005)

Lawrence paid heed to his poet-doctor, and when he moved on to Baden-Baden in early October took an inhalation cure at the cold radium springs of the *Kurhaus*. Carossa had withheld his prognosis from Lawrence, but confided it to Franz Schoenberner as they walked to the station from the chalet: 'An average man with those lungs would have died long ago. But with a real artist no normal prognosis is ever sure. There are other forces involved. Maybe Lawrence can live two or even three years more. But no medical treatment can really save him.[31]

Life in Baden-Baden was, as ever, comfortable and tedious. But the spirit of the place, striking a chord with his own sense of lost vigour, seems to have been felt as more oppressive than usual and a good deal less conducive to feelings of well-being. 'We are very fortunate here', he told Else, 'but the world seems dark to me again. That scares me and I want to go south' (CL 1006). On 18 October he left the 'wintry darkness' (PL 548) of Baden, with its 'funny sort of stillness of a threatening winter' (Wilk 71), momentarily eager for the bright sun of the Mirenda.

Giglioli, the Florentine specialist, had warned Lawrence, perhaps only for the period of his convalescence, not to attempt any work. He had not been entirely heedful of this advice during the months in Austria and Germany. Although he had put no great effort into the task, he had nevertheless completed a translation, with introduction, of Verga's *Cavalleria Rusticana*. And within days of leaving the Mirenda in August, he had reviewed Trigant Burrow's *The Social Basis of Consciousness*. Lawrence had been reading Burrow's reprints since 1920, and they had begun a correspondence in 1925 while Lawrence was at the ranch. Lawrence had read Burrow's articles with great sympathy, as he did the book, which he received shortly before setting out for Villach. There was much in Burrow's conception of the psyche of modern man that chimed with Lawrence's own views, and which seemed to relate to his own personality. Burrow's notion of a pre-conscious state that had been mastered by cognitive consciousness paralleled and perhaps informed Lawrence's doctrine of the antagonism between phallic consciousness and cerebral consciousness. And Burrow's remedy for the problems of the individual and of society – expression of the societal instinct for togetherness – was analogous to Lawrence's idea of the need to establish a warm, human flow of communion between man and man, and man and woman.[32]

At the conclusion of his review, Lawrence observed that Burrow's book was helpful to 'a man in his own inward life' (*Ph* 382). Regrettably, he did not succeed in applying to himself aspects of Burrow's examination of 'normality', which in the review he described as the most interesting part of the book. When man became self-aware, Burrow had argued, he formed a picture of himself and proceeded to live according to that picture, which constituted normality, repressing instincts which did not conform. Lawrence had made a picture of himself as a 'normal', tough, virile, heterosexual male, and his whole life was a tense struggle to match up to that image.

Although Lawrence had done a little work on holiday, he had nonetheless returned to his earlier resolution never again to apply himself seriously to writing, having once more come to recognize that in the intensity of his efforts he had dissipated his energies and ruined his health. Perhaps because of its close association in time with his illness, he had lost all enthusiasm for the Etruscan book: 'I don't care very much whether I finish the thing or not' (*CL* 1008), he told Knopf on 9 October, when he wrote asking whether Lawrence had any new manuscript to offer. Nevertheless, within a day or two of telling Emily that he would no longer damage his health by writing, and while still in a very feeble state, he promised Knopf that, if he had a keen interest in the Etruscan book, he would be willing to 'sweat around Arezzo and Chiusi and Orvieto and those places, and do the other six sketches this autumn' (*CL* 1009). In regard to the MS of *Lady Chatterley*, Knopf was told that it was not for publication.

While he was in Austria and Germany, Lawrence's perennial financial worries reached a new intensity, which continued through the remainder of the year.[33] He was spending more than he earned, he told Arthur Wilkinson. He faced diminished earnings as a result of declining output brought about by ill-health, and increased expenditure on doctors, health cures and recuperative holidays. And in September he learned that he was to lose a fifth of his income from Britain. In July a new act had come into force, which imposed a 20 per cent tax deduction on all royalties earned by persons living abroad. This event, combined with an urgent need to make money, was one of the factors that led Lawrence to publish *Lady Chatterley* privately in Florence. Through such a venture, if properly managed, he stood to gain very considerably over regular methods of publication. He could pocket the publisher's profits, and his 10 per cent agent's fee, together with the money that would have been paid in tax. Having played some part in Lawrence's decision to publish abroad, the British government might be said to have indirectly influenced the scandalous content of the novel: the intention to bring the book out privately in Florence freed Lawrence from the need to tone down the final revision in order to satisfy Secker and Knopf.

11

The Wart-Hog

The period during and leading up to the writing of the third version of the novel, *Lady Chatterley's Lover*, was for Lawrence one of physical invalidity, anxiety, insecurity, depression, irrational instability, diminished judgement, acute feelings of isolation, and paranoia. These states of physical and mental health pitched him into a nightmare abyss more frightful, perhaps, than that which he had known during the war years, because there seemed no way out. They had a profound and detrimental effect on Lawrence's final revision of the novel.

In September at Irschenhausen, Lawrence had had no wish to return to the Mirenda. In October, in the cold and gloom of the Black Forest, the desire to get back had grown strong in him. When he arrived on 19 October he found that Tuscany and Italy in general meant as little to him as when he had left the Mirenda in August. Though he blamed his revulsion on his sufferings of July, the association of the Mirenda with his haemorrhages had merely served to fortify a desire to leave that was already upon him in April.

The warmth and stillness of the place in October were comforting, but they failed to overcome the feeling that he was only there because he was constrained to be. He had returned to the Mirenda because he had paid a year's rent, because he was not really fit enough to contemplate or manage a move, and because of Frieda's wish to remain in Italy, which was perhaps not unconnected with her continuing relationship with Ravagli.

The long drought of the summer had dried up the vegetation and all the streams on the estate. In the afternoons the sun still shone too fiercely and the flies continued to be bothersome. In a conversation with the Wilkinsons, Lawrence seemed to project not only his personal feelings of lifelessness onto the landscape, but also his emaciated physical appearance: 'He says there's no life in Italy – you feel the want of something. The woods are thin – no depth to them – they are thin and scraggly – the olives are scraggly, the vines are scraggly – the PEOPLE are scraggly – that's it – everything is scraggly. Poor chap – what a nightmare he does suffer' (Wilk 72).

As October at the Mirenda progressed, Lawrence sank into a grey depression. The Wilkinsons found him, on his arrival, 'a very sick man' (Wilk 71), and his health had since shown no real or continuous improvement. At the end of the month Lawrence wrote Kot a letter, one paragraph of which reads as one of the most despairing he ever wrote – sadder in its understated expression of his predicament than the rhetorical expressions of anguish that were evoked in his blackest periods during the war:

> Altogether the world is depressing – and I feel rather depressed. My bronchials are such a nuisance, and I don't feel myself at all. I'm not very happy here, and don't know where else to go, and have not much money to go anywhere with – I feel I don't want to work – don't want to do a thing – all the life gone out of me. Yet how can I sit in this empty place and see nobody and do nothing? It's a limit! I'll have to make a change somehow or other – but don't know how.
>
> (*CL* 1015)

In the first weeks back at the Mirenda, he set about planning where to go the following year. Towards the end of October he felt an urge to get back to England: 'Time to go home, I feel' (*CL* 1014), he observed to the Huxleys, his mind on Devon or somewhere nearer the Midlands. A round-the-world voyage, he thought, would have been an attractive preliminary to his return, had he the money to do it. But he hadn't any money beyond a bare minimum, he told Aldous and Maria. Later, in November, he tried to persuade the Brewsters to join him in a return to the ranch in the spring. However, Lawrence's first inclinations on arriving back at the Mirenda were for a stay in Egypt, which he felt he could not really afford, followed by a year in Ireland. Both were ideas that had earlier crossed his mind during his holidays; and the later histories of his correspondence regarding the Egyptian and Irish projects were instrumental in the growth of feelings that the world shunned him as a pariah.

A couple of days after returning to the Mirenda, Lawrence wrote to Gordon and Beatrice Campbell, the future Lord and Lady Glenavy, for advice on the feasibility of a stay in Ireland. Lawrence had been introduced to Campbell by Murry in 1913, and the Lawrences had become good friends with the Campbells, whose house in London they stayed at when they returned to England to be married in 1914.

Campbell had been a witness to the ceremony, and at one time Lawrence had thought of him as a candidate for a 'Rananim' that was to be founded in Italy after the war. The Campbells were now back in their native Ireland, where Campbell had an important post as Secretary to the Department of Trade and Industry.

Lawrence had a 'hunch', he told Campbell, that Ireland might mean more to him than Tuscany. This was a case where Lawrence's intuition might have proved an extremely unreliable guide. 'Ireland is to my mind something like the bottom of an aquarium, with little people in crannies like prawns' (*CL* 1013), he told the Campbells, implying some contrary impulse to his hunch: the aquarium image was one he habitually used of places for which he felt the deepest repugnance. He must surely have appreciated that the climate, even on the east coast (and he seems to have had the west principally in mind) was not well suited to his consumptive condition. Furthermore, it was hardly two years since he had been infuriated by the revisions he had had to make when preparing an edition of his *Movements in European History* for use in Irish schools.[1] He had every reason to be aware of the roles of dogma and authority in Irish life and to have some awareness of a deep moral puritanism that was in many respects entirely different from his own. Perhaps he should have realized, too, from his knowledge of Anglo-Irish literature, that life in the Irish countryside could give rise to feelings of isolation more complete and overwhelming than any he had experienced in Tuscany.

At the conclusion of his letter to the Campbells, Lawrence invited them to write and put an end to his plans if they felt he ought to be discouraged. Lawrence described Gordon Campbell's reply as 'cautious but encouraging' (*CL* 1021). But though he had invited words of caution he was evidently nettled by them, and assumed that he and Frieda were personally unwelcome to the Campbells. When he wrote back he told them: 'I think, you know, most probably we'll come. Won't you dread it!' (*CL* 1022). Lawrence perhaps suspected that self-interest – a wish to protect themselves and their social position in Ireland from association with the Lawrences – was the motive behind this failure to respond enthusiastically to his proposal.

It was true that Beatrice Campbell had in the past dreaded being left alone with the Lawrences, because they were so frequently embroiled in some violent quarrel between themselves; and she had not liked the close grilling concerning her private life which she had had to suffer from Lawrence and Frieda.[2] But these matters had little to do with the Campbells' response: after all the Lawrences were not asking to live either with them or even near them. On receiving the first letter from Florence, Beatrice Campbell's anxieties had to do with the heavy responsibility she felt towards Lawrence. In her memoirs she recalled the problem of finding some place that she could be sure the Lawrences would like, and mentioned also her concern for Lawrence's health in the damp Irish climate.[3]

Gordon Campbell had evidently also given very proper consideration to Lawrence's personality in relation to Irish ways and attitudes. 'Was I a monster of impatience?' (*CL* 1021) Lawrence wrote to Campbell, seemingly echoing Campbell's words in his reply to Lawrence's inquiry. In this and in many other respects Lawrence was temperamentally unsuited to life in Ireland, and Gordon Campbell, it seems, was trying as gently as possible to convey a message of this kind to him. The interpretation Lawrence chose to put on Campbell's letter, which merely responded to a request for informed discouragement, appears to corroborate the Wilkinsons' comment on Lawrence's habit of jumping to conclusions (which, they seem to imply, were always of the worst).

A fortnight before Lawrence heard from the Campbells, he had received from Valentine Dobrée, Bonamy Dobrée's wife, a letter which, in time, came to elicit an even more irrational response. When the Lawrences had met the Dobrées in London, in the early autumn of 1926, there had been talk of the Lawrences visiting them in Cairo. In the sporadic correspondence that followed this idea continued to be aired; and in early October at Baden-Baden Lawrence had received a definite invitation to come out and stay with them. To the Dobrées, as to many of his friends, Lawrence had expressed his delight at the prospect of seeing Egypt, and serious doubts as to whether he could find the money for the trip.

Within a month of being invited to the Dobrées, he had another letter, from Valentine Dobrée, withdrawing the invitation. Mrs Dobrée's father had fallen seriously ill while she was in London; she had had to stay to look after him, and then had decided that he must return with her to be nursed at their house in Cairo.[4] This now made it impossible for her to entertain the Lawrences.[5]

Lawrence responded sympathetically and courteously, and suggested that he and Frieda might come out later and stay somewhere in the neighbourhood. If he was instantly put out by the cancellation of the Dobrées' offer, he did not let on to his friends. It seems to have

235

been during the ensuing weeks, alone and brooding at the Villa Mirenda (where he remained for a month before summoning the energy and will to visit Florence), that Lawrence began to harbour resentment and suspicion over the Dobrées' behaviour. There had been no reply to his suggestion that he might come out later. Furthermore – and it was this that especially rankled in him – he had had no letter from Bonamy Dobrée, who had been the author of the invitation he received in Baden-Baden. No doubt he was right, in terms of strict etiquette, to expect to hear from Dobrée, though Lawrence's attitude suggests an excessive punctiliousness with regard to social niceties, which seems to testify to another of the Wilkinsons' observations on his character – the tendency towards fussy extremes of preciseness. Where Lawrence showed himself a little unhinged was in the importance he attached to a letter from Dobrée and in the way he construed Dobrée's silence.

The rational conclusion to draw was that Dobrée had issued an invitation on behalf of himself and his wife, and had therefore judged it unnecessary for him to explain why they could not accommodate the Lawrences, when his wife had already done so. Lawrence assumed that the real reason behind Dobrée's failure to write was a sudden dread of a visit from him. Later, reflecting on why Dobrée had had second thoughts, he deduced that someone must have warned him (or his wife) that the Lawrences could be difficult and embarrassing guests. In a letter of 8 December to Kot, Lawrence showed that the extent of his paranoid suspicions had caused him altogether to disregard the good reasons Valentine Dobrée had given for putting him off: he had also evidently forgotten that, in reply to Bonamy Dobrée's offer, he had in any case half-declined the invitation on the grounds that he would probably be unable to afford the fares to Egypt:

> Can you get from Gertler any explanation of Dobrées [*sic*] curious behaviour? He wrote very warmly in Sept. asking us to go to Egypt. I replied we'd like to, if we could. And since then, not a word from him – only a note from her, saying she hadn't been able to think of journeys – and evidently not badly wanting us. – She's a perfect right not to want us – but then in mere politeness he should answer my letter, and say, do we mind putting the thing off. – I'm surprised at his lack of manners. But I suppose there was some mischief made somewhere.
> (Zyt 332f.)

A day or two after hearing from Valentine Dobrée at the beginning of November, at a time when he was extremely depressed (as his 31

October letter to Kot shows), Lawrence received a letter from Secker. Its contents served also to nourish his view of himself as an outcast, hated and persecuted by the world. His story, 'The Man Who Loved Islands', had recently appeared in the *London Mercury*, to the annoyance of Compton Mackenzie. When he got wind of Lawrence's intention to republish the story in the anthology he was preparing for Secker, Mackenzie threatened an injunction if the story was included in the book.

Mackenzie's anger should have come as no great surprise to Lawrence. He knew that Faith Mackenzie had been offended by 'Two Blue Birds'; and in August he had begun to have qualms about Mackenzie's possible reactions to 'The Man Who Loved Islands', having told Secker: 'I do hope Mackenzie wouldn't mind, the thing isn't personal at all' (Sec 93). Secker, in a difficult position as friend and publisher to both men, had the task of communicating Mackenzie's intentions to Lawrence. In his reply to Secker, Lawrence scorned the cretinous self-esteem underlying Mackenzie's actions, and stubbornly refused to withdraw the story from the anthology: he preferred the book never to be published than to have its contents determined for him.[6] Secker had to write again, stressing the advisability of leaving out the story. His letter seems to have arrived on the same day as Campbell's 'cautious' reply on the matter of the visit to Ireland.

Lawrence had been very angry when he first heard from Secker about the Mackenzie affair. On receiving Secker's next letter, he went off like a bombshell, showering Mackenzie with a shrapnel burst of deadly invective: the hero of 'The Man Who Loved Islands' had been morally far superior to the absurd, conceited, self-dramatizing charlatan and show-off who had chosen to see himself in the character. Lawrence was the more angry because Secker had plainly called his bluff regarding the threat not to publish the book at all, and he had to accede to the omission of the story. He felt Secker had acted timorously, and may have suspected partiality. Secker was told that he could leave out 'The Man Who Loved Islands' if he wished, but was warned that in doing so he forfeited a measure of Lawrence's respect for him.[7]

Although he had begun to succumb to depression in Baden-Baden, Lawrence had for most of his time in Austria and Germany been contented and cheerful. One cause of these feelings of well-being may have been that he was cosseted by dutiful servants and hotel staff, with most of the daily chores of life taken from him. Back at the Mirenda with Frieda, he may have felt neither safe nor rested. He had, as usual, either to do most things himself, despite his feeble condition, or to face the alternative of resigning himself to the inadequacies of Frieda's household management. At the back of his mind, too, may have been the fear of more haemorrhages that would place him in Frieda's incompetent care. If relations were tense at this period between him and Frieda, the only glimpse of it fell to the Wilkinsons: at tea at the Mirenda on the day after the Lawrences' return, they witnessed some intense irritability on Lawrence's side, countered by 'dreadfully sharp' (Wilk 72) rejoinders from Frieda. Discussing the two of them after they had left, the Wilkinsons agreed that, though they were glad to see them back, having Lawrence on their doorstep had become 'rather an embarrassing problem' (Wilk 72). It is not unlikely that Lawrence picked up this sense of embarrassment and that recognition of it contributed to the development of feelings of rejection.

Lawrence had no reason to suppose that he was utterly without friends, however. The Huxleys had written with a warm invitation to come and stay at Forte as soon as possible; but he could not find the energy to contemplate the journey. Richard Aldington had heard of Lawrence's troubles and financial worries, and wrote offering a loan, earning himself heartfelt thanks and an affectionate rebuke: 'You shouldn't offer your hard-earned savings – my goodness, I damn well ought to have enough to live on – so I have, by living like a wad-sweeper' (*CL* 1023). When he wrote to Aldington on 18 November, the letters from Secker and Campbell were fresh in his mind, and his anger with Dobrée was still festering. He told Aldington: 'I find most people look on me as if I was a queer sort of animal in a cage – or should be in a cage – sort of wart-hog: *sin amor y sin disprecis*, as my dear song says.' Dobrée, he supposed, must have been gripped by a 'sudden scare of the wart-hog and his grunts' (*CL* 1024).

In October Lawrence had been in no mood to write and had little enthusiasm for painting. Though he made some perfunctory attempts at both, he was unable to bring to completion either the picture to which he returned – 'The Finding of Moses' – or the two short stories that he began. The stories, both of which could be said to be concerned with immortality of a sort, were never taken up again. One was 'The Undying Man', Lawrence's rewriting of one of two Jewish stories Kot had translated and sent to Lawrence at

Irschenhausen. It concerned Rabbi Moses Maimonides and a Christian, called Aristotle, who together discovered a method of creating an immortal being by removing a vein from a man's body and nurturing it in a jar: the man who was to become immortal had first to die, through the removal of his vein. The other story, 'A Dream of Life', also had connections with Kot: it was intended to be Lawrence's contribution to the collection of intimate confessions by well-known authors that would mark the beginning of Kot's venture into publishing. Like 'The Undying Man' the story concerned a kind of death and renewal. This was the fantasy tale, set in Eastwood, in which Lawrence imagined himself passing through deathly sleep to reawaken a thousand years later to an Eastwood that had become the New Jerusalem. It seemed to be shaping well, as a strange, compelling, mystical vision, unlike anything he had ever written before; but it was also promising to become very long. Lawrence grew weary with the effort of writing, and feelings of exhaustion and despair overcame him. Abandoning his attempt to provide an intimate confession, he concluded with a thought too private to be plainly acknowledged to anyone except, perhaps, to Frieda: 'It is true, I am like a butterfly, and I shall only live a little while. That is why I don't want to eat' (*Ph* 836).

In no other surviving letter or literary work had Lawrence ever directly acknowledged the fact of imminent death. That he did so at all, even in a manuscript never intended to be seen, is testimony to the fear and the hopeless mood of depression that took hold of him at this period – probably the last days of October, near the time when he sent his desperate *cri de coeur* to Kot. The sense of dark foreboding was still upon him in mid-November when he wrote to Else, to whom he had expressed similar, milder feelings from Baden-Baden: 'There's a queer sort of unease in the air – as if the wrong sort of spirits were flying abroad in the unseen ether – but it may be my imagination' ('*Not I*' 221). The painting of a jaguar leaping on a man, which he worked on in early November, may possibly have symbolized his fears.

When he wrote to Else, Lawrence had begun to shake off some of the torpor of depression, and was 'dabbing' at his poems which he was revising for an edition of his collected poems to be published by Secker. A couple of days later Lawrence felt something of his old vitality returning, and with it the will to get on with the business of living and working.[8] This was on the day before his visit to Florence on 17 November, a significant date in the history of *Lady Chatterley* for it was then that he was persuaded to publish the novel privately in Florence. He had found he was able to climb one of the hills surrounding the Mirenda to look on Florence in the sunshine and quite relish the prospect of visiting it. More importantly, he had that day begun writing zestfully again and was probably rather pleased with the way his satirical short story – 'Rawdon's Roof' – was progressing. He was beginning the process of resurrection; and it seems to have been angry revulsion, like that of his Christ in 'The Escaped Cock', which was the energy source for his renewal.

The writing of 'Rawdon's Roof' coincided with the anger unleashed by the arrival of the letters from Secker and Campbell on or just before 16 November. And with the writing of his satire Lawrence appears to have made a discovery that could have had an important influence on the subsequent course of *Lady Chatterley*. He seems to have found that by hitting back at the sources of his anger, by giving expression to his one potent desire of the time – to 'curse *almost* everybody' (*CL* 1015) – he could regain a large measure of physical and mental vigour. In terms of daily living he had discovered this a week or so earlier, when he remarked in a letter to Brewster: 'I'm feeling really better – I'm better when I grumble' (*CL* 1018).

There is not much doubt that revenge was the impulse behind 'Rawdon's Roof'; and although there are no strong identifying features, it seems very likely that the Campbells were the principal models for Alec and Jane Drummond in the story. Drummond himself is a rather vague figure who does not appear in the action; he is an improvident spendthrift, 'in diplomatic service or something like that' (*LAH* 70). Jane Drummond – very much a lady, with an aura of mystery about her which stems from her quiet reserve, especially in matters pertaining to her private life – has the attributes of Beatrice Campbell, as they might have been perceived by Lawrence; and the Drummonds have two children, like the Campbells.

The Drummonds are very friendly with Rawdon, who is having an affair, which may or may not have a physical aspect, with Jane Drummond. Rawdon, 'refined and handsome and subtle' (*LAH* 72), separated from his witty, scornful wife, has sworn that no woman shall ever again sleep beneath his roof. When Jane Drummond arrives seeking shelter from the husband from whose demands she has fled, Rawdon remains firm in his vow, but proves himself a flabby and cowardly figure in returning her to her violent-tempered husband and begging the help of his friend to bail him out of and sustain him through his difficulties.

Rawdon is very probably the Campbells' friend, Murry, made eligible for satire, perhaps, by the false rumour, which Lawrence heard from Kot in November, that his wife Violet had been cured of consumption. Lawrence, it seems, had returned to his old subject of Murry's affair with Frieda; and by fusing this element with Murry's friendship with the Campbells had shifted the direction of Murry's passions in the story towards Beatrice: he had, in fact, been deeply in love with Gordon Campbell.

Lawrence's purpose in visiting Florence on 17 November – his first excursion to the city since arriving back at the Mirenda – was to have lunch with Reggie Turner, whom a few days earlier he had entertained at the Mirenda, along with Orioli, the novelist Scott Moncrieff, and the young poet Harold Acton. 'I poured the tea, they poured the rest' (*CL* 1023), quipped Lawrence, who in Acton's recollection was on this occasion, as often with his Florentine acquaintances, extremely reserved, saying very little.[9]

Lawrence set off to the city in an energetic frame of mind. He felt ready to rouse himself to action. He was inwardly bitterly angry with the way the world had treated him, and probably already saw himself as the kind of figure he described to Aldington next day – the wart-hog whose unpopularity left him practically friendless and in penury. He was furious with his publisher, Secker, and inclined to have nothing more to do with him. The desire to strike back at his tormentors was strong in him, as he showed in 'Rawdon's Roof'. There were good reasons, therefore, for Lawrence to respond to the challenge when he was urged to publish *Lady Chatterley* privately in Florence.

Some of Lawrence's motives in embarking on the project were frankly set out in a letter he wrote on the following day to his agent, Curtis Brown:

> I wrote a novel last winter that the world would call improper and all that. But it is a tender and sensitive work, and, I think, proper and necessary, and I have it, so to speak, in my arms. It is . . . no use thinking of publishing it publicly – as it stands: and I won't cut it. I thought of letting it lie by indefinitely. But friends in Florence urge me to print it privately, here in Florence . . . I should make . . . a few hundred pounds . . . And no 20% tax . . .
> So if this is a simple and decent way of putting the book into the

world – and mind, one day I intend to put it into the world, as it
stands – and also, of earning money to go on with, then I don't see why
I shouldn't do it. Later, I could perhaps cut out parts . . . But I doubt
if I should. Why should I? I'm sick of cutting myself down to fit the
world's shoddy cloth.

(Brown 70f.)

The desires to preserve his own and the novel's artistic integrity and
to 'take in the badly-needed shekels' (Luhan 229) were of more or less
equal status. Mercenary as the latter motive was, and at odds with the
novel's teachings against money-lust, which are given greater prominence in the final version, it seems unreasonable to find fault with
Lawrence in this; though it must also be acknowledged that in the
importance he attached to the money-making aspect of private
publication he fell short of his own high-minded principles. In his
position, an invalid with prospects of further deterioration in his
health, to find a sizeable sum of money to cover himself was a
responsible obligation; and the use to which he eventually decided to
put some of his income from the novel was at least compatible with
his philosophy of life. 'You can give me just as much "gold" as you
can easily spare, and I'll turn it into sun some way or other' (*CL*
1041), Lawrence wrote to Harry Crosby, an American publisher who
offered him a hundred dollars in gold coins for any manuscript of
his.[10] Lawrence's plan, which illness never allowed him to fulfil, was
to use the profits from *Lady Chatterley's Lover* in pursuit of sunshine,
freedom and the grail of truly religious experience around the globe,
taking a world cruise that would end at San Francisco, from where he
would retire to the ranch.

The other motives that Lawrence made known to Curtis Brown
were his sense of duty – it was 'necessary' both to himself and society
– and his wish finally to assert himself in opposition to a world he
despised. What he did not tell his agent, since it might have alarmed
him even further, was another important ancillary consideration
which he later divulged to Harold Mason: 'The reason is, I'm tired of
never getting anything from the publishers – I'd like to be responsible to myself' (*Cent* 31). Private publication was thus an expression
of his discontent with publishers, and a means by which a man who
loved and needed to take full charge of every facet of his life could
make a very personal document truly his own in every way.

Lawrence was fully aware that to publish the novel unexpurgated
would be a rash act, which would bring down more hatred upon him.

But in a state of mind in which he saw himself already as abused, hated and ostracized, his liability to further attack was no great discouragement where the protection of his ego was concerned. He had to take more seriously Miss Pearn's earlier warnings that the notoriety which would attach to him, if he published the novel, might make it very difficult for her to place his magazine articles and stories.[11] For the last two years he had lived mainly on his income from this source, and intended to go on doing so. He therefore took note of Miss Pearn's advice, but entertained the naïve belief that by publishing privately he could bring the novel out unnoticed.[12] No copies would be sent for review to newspapers and journals; and he supposed that by this means he could escape the publicity which he was anxious to avoid at all costs: with this end in view a number of people to whom he wrote of his plans were asked to refrain from any loose talk about the 'improper' character of the forthcoming novel.[13]

Of the friends in Florence who urged publication, one seems to have been Orioli, to whom a few days later he wrote in a manner suggesting there had been recent discussion of publishing the novel: in the letter Lawrence declared a definite intention to publish, provided Orioli was willing to offer the help that would be absolutely necessary to the undertaking.[14] Turner, whom Lawrence lunched with, may have been another conspirator; and another contributing influence, as was suggested earlier, may have been the persuasive power and experience of Norman Douglas. Indeed, it is hard to imagine that anyone so cautious in matters of money as Lawrence would have risked his precious capital in such a financially hazardous enterprise without seeking Douglas's advice on the commercial viability of private publication. Quite recently Douglas had, in fact, failed to cover his expenses on his esoteric *Birds and Beasts of the Greek Anthology*. But in November he was able to commend this means of publication with sincerity and enthusiasm. Orders for his next book, *In the Beginning* (which proved to be his last novel, as Lawrence's did) had come pouring in; and he was already in pocket before the book came off the presses at the end of the month.[15] He had been driven to private publication by his hatred of publishers (and of Secker in particular), whose chief aim, he believed, was to defraud authors of their rightful dues.[16] If the matter of publication was indeed broached during their meeting, Lawrence would have found no one in Florence more vigorous in his encitement to publish privately than Norman Douglas.

On the day of his visit to Florence, by chance Lawrence met on the Lungarno an old acquaintance, Dikran Kouyoumdjian. He was a Bulgarian-born Armenian, who had adopted British citizenship and the name of Michael Arlen, which he had first used as a *nom de plume*. His example, and perhaps also his encouragement, may have helped to bring Lawrence to the decision to publish privately; and their encounter was to have considerable effect on the reshaping of *Lady Chatterley* in its final version.

For a brief period in 1915–16, when he was toying with the idea of joining Lawrence's proposed Utopian colony of Rananim, Arlen had been attracted to Lawrence, and had stayed at the Lawrences' cottage at Portcothan in Cornwall. Lawrence did not care for him, and (perhaps in reaction to his rejection) Arlen subsequently lampooned Lawrence in a satire published in *New Age* in 1916.[17] Later in the same year, Arlen was in Philip Heseltine's company at the Café Royal when Heseltine was holding up to ridicule a copy of Lawrence's poems, *Amores*. The incident was observed by Katherine Mansfield, who reported it to Lawrence. Since that time Arlen had gone on to make his name and a good deal of money as the author of satirical, romantic, society novels which captured so successfully the glitter and blithe spirit of the 1920s that they became sensational bestsellers. The most celebrated and popular of these novels was *The Green Hat*, which, both in its original novel form and as a play, had earned Arlen a fortune on both sides of the Atlantic.

Surprisingly, when they met on the Lungarno Lawrence quickly warmed to him, discovering sympathetic analogies between Arlen's position and his own. Next day Lawrence wrote to Richard Aldington:

> Imagine, I met Kouyoumdjian – Michael Arlen – on the Lungarno yesterday . . . But he too was ill – some sort of tubercular tumour – and has been curing at Davos. There's something about him I rather like – something sort of outcast, dog that people throw stones at by instinct, and who doesn't feel pious and Jesusy on the strength of it, like Cournos, but wants to bite 'em – which is good. He's one of the people I don't mind making their pile – just to spite 'em.
>
> (*CL* 1023)

Here was a pariah, like himself, except that in gaining his unpopularity among the Mayfair smart set, whom he took off in his novels, Arlen had become almost a dollar-millionaire. Lawrence learned two days after their meeting, when Arlen visited the Mirenda, that Arlen had shown considerable financial acumen by putting his American earnings into a trust which in the future would yield some £10,000 per year. It could have occurred to Lawrence that in a modest way he might emulate Arlen. He knew he could never write a bestseller, but he realized that by publishing *Lady Chatterley*, and thereby attracting to himself even greater hatred than already existed, he could make a tidy sum for himself. Arlen's example may have been influential in the emergence of the Lawrence of his last years, whom Moore styled 'Lawrence the businessman'. By 22 November, when he wrote to Kot about his intended venture into publishing, Lawrence had already done some preliminary accounting, and was reckoning that a printing of 700 copies at two guineas each would bring a profit of £600 or £700.[18] As it turned out, his estimate of a profit of a pound per copy was extremely accurate. His final gross returns on the 1,000 copies of the expensive edition and the 200 of the inexpensive one were in the region of £1,200.[19]

Lawrence seems to have been much intrigued and perhaps also charmed by Arlen, for after his first visit to the Mirenda he was invited to come out again only two days later. On this occasion Lawrence was obliged hastily to cancel the visit. Because of his tubercular condition Arlen, like Lawrence, had a great fear of catching colds, and Frieda had suddenly developed cold symptoms. There seem to have been other visits, later,[20] and the two men appear to have kept in touch for the remainder of Arlen's stay in Florence.

Lawrence's interest in Arlen could have had an uncharitable aspect, if he was already planning to use him as the model for the new character he was to introduce into the revised version of the novel; but his letters leave no doubt that he also felt a genuine, warm sympathy towards the man, which shows itself to an extent in his portrait, entirely faithful in terms of physical appearance, as the playwright Michaelis. Michaelis is an astute, practical, self-effacing and witty man, handsome, and perfectly tailored and groomed, who despite his commercial success and his eager social climbing has none of the affectation and airs of the *parvenu*. He has no illusions about upper-class society and its regard for him, and he entertains no golden opinions of his plays, which he speaks of in self-deprecating terms that show no hint of false modesty. Arlen, who regarded the writings that had brought him fame and wealth as 'rubbishy', had much the same character and sense of humour. 'I'm every other inch a gentleman', he once remarked when asked what his qualifications were for joining a London club. According to him his problem in English society was that he suffered from 'pernicious Armenia'.[21] Behind Arlen's wit there seems to have lurked a self-consciousness about his status and background; and his brand of humour hints at the masochism that informs the character of Michaelis in *Lady Chatterley's Lover*.

In letters reporting his meeting with Arlen, Lawrence commonly referred to him as 'a (sad) dog'. And in his treatment of Arlen as Michaelis he continued the canine metaphor, which principally defines Michaelis in his role as follower of the bitch goddess Success. But it is implicit, too, in his dog-like pursuit of quick copulation and in his approach to women: there is something of the lap-dog's relationship to its mistress in his seduction of Connie, before whom he kneels, buries his face in her lap, and looks up 'with that awful appeal in his full, glowing eyes' (*LCL* 27). His failings as a lover of women spring from the fact that his real love is reserved for the Jamesian bitch goddess; and his ultimate gratification is praise of his writings, which 'affected him with the last thin thrill of passion beyond any sexual orgasm' (*LCL* 54).

The flaw in Michaelis's character, then, is his inversion of the natural primacy of body over mind. Lawrence would probably have placed Arlen among this category of men. But, essentially, this aspect of Michaelis's character is dictated less by the model than by the function prescribed for Michaelis within the moral schema of the new version of *Lady Chatterley*. Michaelis is a type-figure, the principal motive for whose introduction into the novel, demanding extensive revision of the early chapters of the book, was possibly to define the phallic sex of the keeper more clearly, through setting up an antithetical relationship with active mental sexuality. In the preceding version, *John Thomas and Lady Jane*, there had been no such contrast in the sphere of sexual behaviour, because the main representatives of cerebral consciousness, Clifford and Dukes, were respectively impotent and apathetic.

Michaelis has other important functions, too. As a low-born Irishman he serves to generalize cerebral consciousness and sexual inadequacy beyond the English upper classes, thus furthering the movement, begun in *John Thomas and Lady Jane*, towards a less class-bound distribution of passionlessness and warm-heartedness. His affair with Connie has the effect of eliminating the moral problem of the keeper being the first seducer of the innocent wife of a war-wounded cripple. Necessarily, this innovation also imparts a new moral character to Connie, who, in terms of conventional morality, now becomes something of a Frieda-like harridan in her promiscuity. If Lawrence intended this aspect of change in her character, it was less important within his plan for the new Constance than the shift towards establishing her as the archetype of Lawrence's modern woman through the device of her affair with Michaelis. Her behaviour with Michaelis reveals her as wilful and egotistical in her 'selfish' insistence on clitoral orgasm: she requires Mellors's therapy to bring out the 'true' womanly passivity in her.

Lawrence probably began his revision of the novel within a few days of his first meeting with Michael Arlen. There is a lack of extant letters from Lawrence between 22 November and 5 December, which suggests that Lawrence may have entered one of those rare phases of silence in his correspondence which, when not due to grave illness, seem only to have occurred when he was intensely preoccupied with writing.[22] More importantly, there is evidence in the manuscript notebooks which argues for a starting point earlier than 3 December, which is generally held to be the day Lawrence began the process of rewriting. Squires observed that the date '3 Decem. 1927', inscribed on the fly-leaf of the second manuscript notebook of *Lady Chatterley's Lover*, is most likely to have been the date when he started on the second notebook, rather than the date when work first commenced: the ink of the inscription matches that of the first page of the second notebook, not that of the beginning of the first book.[23] By 3 December, it would thus appear, Lawrence had written 113 pages of the MS. Even if he had worked at the novel every morning of the week and maintained a high average of fourteen pages a day, he could not have begun the revision later than 26 November; and 23 November, the day his letter-writing temporarily ceased, seems a possible date for the beginning of work on the new version.

Why did Lawrence carry out a complete rewriting of the second version of the novel, which seemed to require only minor revision for the novel to qualify as one of Lawrence's most remarkable and outstanding achievements, perhaps his best novel since *The Rainbow*? Part of the answer is a simple one. In a letter to Lawrence Pollinger of Curtis Brown, Lawrence wrote of *Lady Chatterley*: 'In my usual way, I wrote the whole novel, complete, three times' (Hux 810). According to Lawrence, then, there was nothing extraordinary in his decision to write a third, final version of the novel: he simply followed his regular practice. There seems no reason to question the truth of Lawrence's statement to Pollinger, which simply echoed what he had said to Forman some seven years earlier.[24] No three complete versions of novels written before *Lady Chatterley* survive, but there is ample evidence, principally from correspondence, but also from textual evidence, that a number of the novels passed through at least three stages of composition.[25]

A more interesting question, in regard to the history of *Lady Chatterley*, is the matter of why Lawrence chose to produce a third version which differed so radically in content and mood from a second version which most critics have regarded as a work of distinction.[26] Here again, the answer seems to lie partly in habitual working methods and also in the relationship those methods bore to Lawrence's aesthetic beliefs regarding the act of composition. When he told James Henry Forman that he wrote every book three times, he added: 'By that . . . I don't mean copying and revising as I go along, but literally. After I finish the first draft I put it aside and write another. Then I put the second aside and write a third' (Nehls 2 106). It was thus his practice to write each version anew, without close reference to the antecedent version. This method determined that the content of each version would reflect the thoughts and mood of the moment, and Lawrence's habits of composition were no doubt devised to reflect his commitment to spontaneity at every stage of the creative process: the usual methods of authorial revision would have seemed too mechanical. However, it is implicit in the three versions of *Lady Chatterley* that, though Lawrence did not *copy* from the antecedent versions, modifying the text of each one as he went along, it was nevertheless not the case that he wrote either of the succeeding versions without reference to its predecessor. The MSS of both the first and second versions have interlinear revisions, which are extensive in the case of the second version:[27] such revisions would have been quite without purpose if Lawrence intended to ignore completely either of the texts when working on the succeeding version. Moreover, where a scene in the novel survives from one version to another, the verbal similarities between the two texts show that the preceding version must have been consulted during the rewriting of the novel.

One imagines that putting the antecedent version 'aside' meant, for Lawrence, having it at his side as he sat up against a tree or in bed, with his exercise book on his knees. The exemplar may on some occasions have been picked up and read closely, before being set aside while he wrote with a fresh memory of the preceding draft; on other occasions Lawrence may have glanced at the open page of the manuscript which lay beside him.

For the reasons suggested above, Lawrence's final version would tend to reflect the moods of the moment, and these, as we have seen, were anger, revulsion, a temptation towards despair, and a desire to strike back. But, clearly, the differences between *John Thomas and Lady Jane* and *Lady Chatterley's Lover* can by no means be entirely accounted for in this way. Lawrence must have begun his final draft with an overall plan for a different version of the novel, which implied dissatisfaction with the novel as it stood in its second version. The cause of Lawrence's rejection of *John Thomas and Lady Jane*, and some of the motives which inspired *Lady Chatterley's Lover*, may have been expressed by Frieda in her introduction to *The First Lady Chatterley*. But if one is to believe this, it is necessary to suppose that Frieda mistakenly applied to the first and second versions remarks that properly belong to the second and third stages in the evolution of the novel. According to Frieda, Lawrence remarked of the first version:

> 'They'll say as they said of Blake: It's mysticism, but they shan't get away with it, not this time: Blake's wasn't mysticism, neither is this. The tenderness and gentleness hadn't enough punch and fight in it, it was a bit wistful.'
>
> (*FLC* 10)

It is true that the second version shows a shift towards a more embattled position between the lovers and between the author and society. But the second version also represents a distinct movement towards Blakean qualities of lyricism and mysticism in the treatment of sex and of the woodland environment. It is also more 'wistful' than its predecessor and gives greater emphasis to the theme of tenderness. Equally, the pugnacity and the fears of dismissive critical reaction expressed in the comments quoted by Frieda seem best to fit Lawrence's moods either at the time immediately following completion of the second version or in the period shortly before he began the final version.

It seems possible that, writing seventeen or eighteen years after events, Frieda shifted onto the first version remarks made in relation to the second version of *Lady Chatterley*. This speculation finds some support in a comment in a letter to Brett which seems to refer to the second version of the novel. In this letter Lawrence had expressed some dissatisfaction with the depth he had imparted to the 'bottom-less pools' that he was creating as he patiently worked at the novel. This suggests a possible correlation with the fears expressed to Frieda over the mystical qualities of one of the early versions of the novel.

Lawrence appears to have taken steps to ensure that no charge of Blakean mysticism should be levelled at the version intended for the public. According to Frieda, the writing of *Lady Chatterley's Lover* was influenced by a special awareness of 'his contemporaries' minds' (*FLC* 10). In this version Lawrence excised or transformed scenes in *John Thomas and Lady Jane* that were of incomparable, quietly lyrical beauty. It was through scenes such as these that Lawrence had expressed the soft power of the mystery of the phallus, and it was perhaps their association with mysticism which caused them to be rejected, to the ultimate detriment of the novel. No doubt there were also other factors involved in the departure from the pastoral lyricism of the preceding drafts. When he wrote *Lady Chatterley's Lover* Lawrence appears to have wished to incline the balance of emphasis in the presentation of his case towards the negative pole. What he stood *for* had become less important than what he virulently opposed. This would tend to have the effect of diminishing the status of the phallic, natural beauty of the life of the forest.

Lawrence had described *John Thomas and Lady Jane* as 'tender and frail as the naked self is' (*CL* 972). In a letter of August 1928 he wrote to Pollinger of the second half of 'The Escaped Cock', a similarly frail and 'phallic' work:

> I feel tender about giving it out for publication – as I felt about *Lady C* . . . I can't make up my mind about having it typed and sent out. Possibly Crosby-Gaige wouldn't like it – not that I'd care a bit. Only why expose any sensitive things gratuitously? And this story is one of my thin-skinned ones.
>
> (*CL* 1081)

Lawrence's reticence with regard to *Lady Chatterley* had concerned the second, more 'thin-skinned' version, not the final version. And it may have been that the same fears of self-exposure which he felt towards 'The Escaped Cock' played no small part in determining that *Lady Chatterley's Lover* should be of a very different character from the preceding version. At the time when he wrote *Lady Chatterley's Lover*,

Lawrence was in no mood to present a frail and vulnerably naked self to a hostile world. It was now a fight between himself and the ball-less, and in preparation for the affray Lawrence clad himself in the armour of aggressive masculinity, covering those parts of the anatomy of his psyche that were tender and, to the conventional mind, feminine.

In this mood of angry pugnacity Lawrence appears to have decided that the published version should have a primary purpose quite different from that of the earlier drafts. The original intention, voiced through Tommy Dukes in *John Thomas and Lady Jane*, had been to open a chink of the tomb for the young and for future generations through the therapy of exposure to the doctrine of tenderness and touch. When he embarked on his revision this purpose had become subsidiary to the wish to shock the castrated consciousness of an older generation of middle and upper-class readers. Though he persisted in referring to the novel as 'tender' after he had completed *Lady Chatterley's Lover*, the epithet seems contradicted by the metaphor which he sometimes applied to the novel, and which appropriately expresses its new function – that of the bomb. The novel was no longer Lawrence's compassionate gift to the world, it was the instrument of the wart-hog's revenge: it was something to 'fling . . . in the face' (*CL* 1038) of a world he despised; it represented 'another blow . . . at the lily-livered host' (*CL* 1033); and the sense of public duty which inspired it was not that of the healer but of the exterminator of pests: 'We *must* put salt on the hypocritical and snaily tails' (Hux 710), Lawrence told Huxley. In 'A Propos of "Lady Chatterley's Lover"' Lawrence claimed that *Lady Chatterley* was not written in order to '*épater le bourgeois*' (*Ph 2* 514). But, while it is true that this was far from Lawrence's mind when he first began writing the novel, many of his remarks concerning the final version come very close to defining just such a purpose.

Reluctance to face charges of mysticism, fear of self-exposure and a compulsion to engage himself in a fight – these seem to have been the principal motives which led Lawrence to reject *John Thomas and Lady Jane* and to depart very considerably from its text and meaning in the final revision. They were not the kind of motives likely to bring out the best in Lawrence's writing, and they accordingly failed to do so. There was perhaps another motive, more laudable and more relevant to the novel as a work of art, which made for extensive revision – the feeling that *John Thomas and Lady Jane* was too diffuse and unstructured. Lawrence nowhere suggested this as a reason for the changes he effected, but in the revision he evidently worked hard at creating a work that was more perfectly organized. In this respect he succeeded admirably. *Lady Chatterley's Lover*, with its carefully plotted narrative structure and its network of juxtaposed antitheses, is arguably the most well-crafted of all Lawrence's novels. There remains a suspicion, however, that the ordered systems of positive and negative polarities in the novel might have been considered mechanical and contrived had Lawrence observed them in the work of a fellow-author.[28]

Lawrence's determination to follow precedent and write the novel afresh may have been personally beneficial: writing *Lady Chatterley's Lover* gave him an outlet for his anger and provided a means of escape from the stupor of depression that would have persisted in him had he remained without purpose during his months of isolated discontent at the Villa Mirenda. But as far as the novel was concerned, Lawrence's decision to carry out a thorough reworking was ill-judged. Several of the motives which his current mood dictated made for stridency of expression and rigidity of thought. More importantly, perhaps, illness had blunted his sensibilities. In a letter to Idella Purnell, editor of the poetry magazine *Palms*, Lawrence wrote of himself at the time when he was composing *Lady Chatterley's Lover*: 'Anything less uninspired or inspiring than myself just now, I wouldn't want you to see' (Bynner 331). No judgement quite so harsh could reasonably be applied to Lawrence for the whole of the period of his revision of the novel. But it seems, nevertheless, to have been true that for all that time he remained cut off from the major source of his creative inspiration. Lawrence's capacity to sense a full symbiotic relationship between himself and the life round about him had been impaired. He had grown numb to humanity and even his responses to the natural world were not those of the quick, sensitive awareness that characterized him when he was vital in health. Partly through boredom, but primarily as a result of his physical debilitation, the umbrella pine-woods where he preferred to write had meant nothing to him since April 1927. Perhaps Lawrence was in any event obliged to write at a physical remove from the natural world at this period. His letters suggest that he was often not fit enough to work out of doors and that also the weather was frequently too inclement for him to write in the open air: much of *Lady Chatterley's Lover* may have been written within the Villa Mirenda, sometimes from his bed.

On 18 December, Lawrence reported to Max Mohr that he was half-way through the revision of the novel.[29] The state of his health remained unstable. There were days when he was driven to bed, 'feeling limp' (Bynner 331); and he was troubled day and night by his persistent consumptive cough. His chest had not been favoured by the weather, which in late November and December alternated between periods of 'clammy wet warm mist' (Zyt 334) and days that were 'unspeakably cold', with 'a wind from the heart of all the icebergs' (Brew 155). His mood had changed very little from the time just before he began the rewriting, except that the act of expressing himself vehemently in the novel seems to have taken some of the edge off the anger he had earlier shown in the letters. He remained 'a bit cross' (Brew 155), he told Harwood Brewster, and the Dobrée affair still preyed on his mind. He had overcome the lethargy of depression, as far as work was concerned, but in other respects weariness and indecision kept him imprisoned in inertia: 'I feel like a pig in a garden', he told Max Mohr. 'I don't know which gate to go out of, and I am not going to be driven out. So I will sit here until I make up my mind' (Mohr 26).

Feeling himself a victim of the malignancy of disease and of a hostile world, he described himself to Kot as 'trampled almost to extinction'. Kot was himself sometimes attacked by bouts of black depression, and disappointment over his publishing plans had hit him hard. Probably it was because Lawrence saw Kot as a fellow-sufferer that he confided to him his bleakest thoughts at this period. The despairing letter of 31 October was followed by another on 23 December: 'My dear Kot, I do think this is the low-water mark of existence. I never felt so near the brink of the abyss . . . When one is in despair one can only go one worse' (Zyt 334). Lawrence nevertheless clung stubbornly, but with some desperation, to a slender bough of optimism that preserved him from the abyss of total despondency: 'In 1928 something is *bound* to begin new: must . . . we *must* have a turn soon.'

Christmas was approaching. Lawrence faced up to the season, not for the first time in his life, with 'unchristmassy' feelings of loathing. There was no longer anything novel in laying on a Christmas Eve celebration for the peasants: hence, it was not an event to look forward to. Reporting Frieda's plans for a repeat of the previous year's festivities to Harwood Brewster, Lawrence observed sardonically of the *contadini*: 'As their name is legion, with a few babies over, it's a job, and my spirit is rather faint' (Brew 155). In two letters to the baroness Lawrence described, in a similar vein of humour, Frieda's seasonable act of Christian charity to one of the children of the estate. Dino Bandelli suffered from a rupture, and Frieda, with a largesse that Lawrence would probably not have approved of in their present circumstances, decided to pay for the boy to be operated on in Florence. Subsequent events brought some amusement to Lawrence and less saintly feelings to Frieda. Terrified by the strange surroundings the boy fled the hospital and returned only when emboldened by the promise of a bicycle from Raul Mirenda.[30]

On the same day that Lawrence wrote gloomily to Kot, he found himself succumbing to the Christmas spirit. Pietro and Giulia had stolen a tree for the *salotto* again, and their evident joy in dressing the tree with candles and tinsel proved contagious. In November Lawrence had written to the Huxleys of his wish to spend Christmas somewhere in Florence where he and Frieda could 'eat turkey and be silly – not sit solitary ' (Hux 693f.) at the Mirenda. Aldous and Maria spent Christmas with friends in Florence, possibly the Franchettis, and on Christmas Day they arrived to drive the Lawrences to their villa for the traditional dinner and merrymaking that Lawrence had hoped for. On the 27th the Huxleys motored up to the Mirenda to have lunch with the Lawrences and spend the afternoon with them. The boyish thrill prompted by Pietro and Giulia was still upon Lawrence, and Huxley recorded in his diary:

> DHL in admirable form, talking wonderfully. He is one of the few people I feel real respect and admiration for. Of most other eminent people I have met I feel that at any rate I belong to the same species as they do. But this man has something different and superior in kind, not degree.
>
> (Hux xxx)

Fortified in spirit, Lawrence raced through what remained of his revision of *Lady Chatterley*. By 8 January it was complete,[31] the second half of the novel having been rewritten in the space of about three weeks, and the whole novel in just over six weeks – almost half the time it took Lawrence to complete the second version. It was an outstanding achievement by any standards, let alone for a man in Lawrence's condition. But the novel itself may have suffered from the speed of its rewriting, which could, perhaps, account for the loss of the considered, reflective aspect that distinguished the more carefully wrought second version. The driving force behind Lawrence's haste was his wish to get the novel to the printer as soon as possible. Unaware of the difficulties that lay ahead, he hoped, by completing the manuscript in early January, to have the book out by the end of March.

Like the beginning of the novel, the ending was completely transformed. The last three chapters of *John Thomas and Lady Jane* (which included Connie's call to the home of the keeper's mother in Tevershall, her visit to the Tewsons in Sheffield and her walk with Parkin towards Felley Mill) were scrapped. This was no doubt partly because the new keeper had no working-class ethos with which Connie had to come to terms. The walk to Felley with its closing view of the devastation of the mining countryside might have been preserved, with some improvements to the rather weak dialogue of the very end of the novel. But Lawrence's revision of the preceding chapters had made it hard to engineer a place for the walk. In the final version Lawrence substituted, on Connie's return to England, a number of London episodes involving herself, her father, Mellors and the artist Duncan Forbes. She and Mellors are then parted: she to take her leave of Clifford and travel to Scotland; he to work on a farm in Heanor. The novel closes with a letter from the farm to Connie. This device enables Lawrence to summarize, through Mellors, some of the teachings of the novel, especially as they pertain to the working class, principally mine-workers.

The letter warns of an impending disaster of 'death and destruction' (*LCL* 314) for the industrial masses unless people learn to reject Mammon and the money-lust, with all their attendant poisons, and begin to embrace life through acknowledgement of 'the great god Pan'. Industrial strife and the social condition of the working class, Lawrence's reactions to which had given the original impetus to writing the novel, had been largely neglected in all the pages leading up to the conclusion of *Lady Chatterley's Lover*, as indeed it had been in *John Thomas and Lady Jane*. In taking up the subject again at the end of *Lady Chatterley's Lover*, Lawrence was writing of the situation and the attitudes of the miners as they were in the last months of 1927. The coal strike had ended in the autumn of 1926, but by early autumn of the following year Lawrence had learnt of new developments which might be the forerunners of social catastrophe.

In August in Austria Lawrence read in the foreign press of a recession in British industry. Perhaps with a view to including a topical evaluation of the mood of the mine-workers in his intended revision of *Lady Chatterley*, Lawrence wrote off to Ada in September asking what the situation was like among the miners and whether they were depressed by the situation.[32] In early October he heard from Emily that the local miners were only working a two- or three-day week. He concluded that the coal industry and the colliers in Britain were finished,[33] and began to return once more to the idea of long-term revolution that he had envisaged during the coal strike.

When he was midway through *Lady Chatterley's Lover*, on 19 December, Lawrence wrote to Gertie Cooper concerning short-time working in the mines, plying her with questions that appear to have been framed with the novel in mind: 'What do [the miners] say to it? What do the young fellows say? I should like to know how they take it' (Ada 133). The substance of Gertie Cooper's reply may very well have been paraphrased in Mellors's letter to Connie. Mellors reports that the pits in the area where he is farming 'are working two days, two and a half days a week, and . . . no sign of betterment even for winter' (*LCL* 314); and of the colliers he writes:

> They grumble a lot, but they're not going to alter anything. As everybody says, the Notts–Derby miners have got their hearts in the right place . . . They talk about nationalization, nationalization of royalties, nationalization of the whole industry . . . They talk about putting coal to new uses . . . The men are very apathetic. They feel the whole damned thing is doomed . . . And they are doomed along with it. Some of the young ones spout about a Soviet, but there's not much conviction in them . . . Even under a Soviet you've still got to sell coal: and that's the difficulty.
>
> (*LCL* 314)

Appropriately, the day on which Lawrence completed his second draft of Mellors's letter, and with it his work on the novel, was also the day when he was first called upon to defend the moral and artistic integrity of the novel. While still working on the book, Lawrence had sent the first half of the MS to be typed by Nelly Morrison in Florence. In asking her to do the typing, Lawrence had warned her of the shocking content of the book;[34] and when she agreed, Lawrence invited her to let him know if ever she found it impossible to carry on.[35] From the very beginning, therefore, he had some anxieties over her suitability for the task. But his choices were very limited: no Italian commercial typist could have worked from a hand-written MS in English; and he could not send the MS to England for commercial

typing for fear of starting a public scandal before the novel was even
in print. He had to have someone who was personally known to him
whose discretion, at least, he could count on.

Near the end of December Lawrence heard from Nelly Morrison of
the distress which typing the novel was causing her, and he advised
her to leave off.[36] A few days later she reached the end of her tether.
Lawrence was prepared for and could accept her backing out. What
enraged him was that in withdrawing she also saw fit to pass moral
judgement on the book. 'Dirty bitch!' (*CL* 1033), he exclaimed in a
letter to Catherine Carswell, asking her help in finding another typist
for him. But his reply to Nelly Morrison was gracious in its
expression of apologetic thanks, and temperate but stern in its
defence of his position:

> Remember, although you are on the side of the angels and the vast
> majority, I consider mine the truly moral and religious position. You
> suggest I have pandered to the pornographic taste: I think not. To the
> Puritan all things are pure, to quote an Americanism. Not that you are
> a Puritan: nor am I impure.
>
> (*CL* 1032)

'The Puritan will want to smite me down' (*Cent* 31), Lawrence had
prophesied of the future reception of the novel. Now he was given
some intimation of how the book would alienate people who were
well-disposed towards him and were in no strict sense puritanical.

12

Phoenix

As he neared the completion of his novel, Lawrence decided that he preferred to call it *Tenderness*, an unremarkable title that seems more appropriate to the character of the second draft than to that of this last version. The ability to devise a good title for a novel was a gift Lawrence did not possess, and finding a title was always a struggle for him, and sometimes a fight between him and his publishers. *Lady Chatterley's Lover* – 'nice and old-fashioned sounding' (Sec 84) – had been the original title, which headed the MS of the first version. It was used for the published version only with reluctance. He had begun the first notebook of the final version with the inept, ambivalent title, *My Lady's Keeper*, and in the second book he had reverted to *Lady Chatterley's Lover*. The idea of *Tenderness* was aired only for a few days, after which he decided, once again, but only for want of a better title, on *Lady Chatterley's Lover*.

In early March Lawrence was supplied with the title he afterwards always preferred, and fought hard to keep, if only as a subtitle. On 21 January he and Frieda had departed to the Swiss ski-resort of Les Diablerets, where he spent six weeks recuperating in the air above the snow-line. The Huxleys were there, with Maria's sister Rose, Aldous's brother Julian and his wife Juliette, and Juliette's mother, Madame Baillot. By the end of February most of the original party had left, leaving only Lawrence, Juliette and her mother, together with the Huxley children. Lawrence lent Juliette the typed MS of the novel, which Aldous and Maria had read earlier and very much enjoyed – 'so they said' (Sec 103), Lawrence noted suspiciously.

If Lawrence gave her the book, she must have given no prior hint of prudishness. Her scandalized reactions must therefore have given further intimations of how the novel might be received even by well-wishing, sophisticated readers. With patient argument Lawrence succeeded in persuading Juliette to be reconciled to the book, and afterwards concluded that it was really a kind of envy in her that had given rise to the 'moral rage' (Sec 103) she had turned on him. In her anger she had sarcastically put it to him that he might as well call the book 'John Thomas and Lady Jane'. 'Many a true word spoken in spite' (*CL* 1043), Lawrence commented in his report of the incident, having determined there and then to make this his title.

Lawrence's occasional frivolousness in his personal life was a healthy obverse to the gravity of his other aspect. But his obdurate persistence with this title seems an aesthetically ill-considered piece of flippancy. A half-mocking title hardly became a book that advocated a due sense of reverence towards sex. This title was also at variance with another of the aims of the novel: it was inappropriate to have euphemistic terms in the title of a work that advocated restoration of the old, vulgar terms for sexual organs and functions.

The new title, *John Thomas and Lady Jane*, was a much more suitable title than *Lady Chatterley's Lover*, Lawrence told Secker.[1] During the last weeks in Diablerets he had been working on an expurgated version of the novel for Secker and Knopf. He confessed that while trying to expurgate he had become 'blind to the purple of impropriety' (*CL* 1042), finding it hard to decide which words or passages would be unacceptable. The same defective colour-vision seems to have afflicted him in respect of his choice of title. Everyone knew what 'John Thomas' stood for, and though it was a euphemism, it was not without the taint of association with its referent: it was therefore a title that would almost certainly have been considered indecent. Pressed to change it, Lawrence yielded a little by abandoning it as a main title, but was determined to keep *John Thomas and Lady Jane* as subtitle. Warned by Aldous Huxley that even subtitled in this way the book would never get through the customs, and apparently under pressure from others, too, to delete it, he toyed with the comic subterfuge of an Italianate rendering – *Giantomasso and Lady Jane*.[2] Only when correcting the last proofs did he finally agree to do away with the subtitle and publish the novel as *Lady Chatterley's Lover*.

Lawrence set off for Les Diablerets without much enthusiasm. He had no great liking for Switzerland and a thorough aversion to snow – 'It shines so cold on the bottom of one's heart' (*CL* 964f.), he had told Brett a year earlier, thinking of the ranch in winter. What he found at Diablerets was a quiet, attractive spot, with few tourists and snow that was often dry; and there were days of beauty when 'wild hot sunshine' (Sec 102) lit the snow slopes with 'a magic of brilliancy'. The Lawrences' flat in a large chalet was warm and comfortable – 'all wood, and low ceilings, just like a ship' (Brew 160). He felt that the snow scratched at his 'bronchials', and there was no improvement in his persistent tubercular cough; but in himself he became stronger and more relaxed. He liked the air and the place: 'so out of the world, as if the world didn't exist. That just suits my mood at present – when I don't want to work or think much about anything' (Brew 162). The Huxleys were only two minutes away across the snow, and there were sleigh-rides and meals taken together, with good conversation, sometimes very animated when Lawrence rounded on Julian Huxley, already an eminent biologist, as representative of professional science. After some stormy sessions, Julian Huxley learnt, like his brother, not to rise to Lawrence's bait. Towards the middle of February Rolf Gardiner joined them for three days, and just as he was leaving, Max Mohr, the Lawrences' new friend from Munich, came knocking at their chalet.

In the first fortnight at Les Diablerets Lawrence finished the revision of his collected poems, some of which he had altered almost completely from their original form. 'What a job!' Lawrence told his fellow-poet, Witter Bynner, as he was nearing the end. 'I feel like an autumn morning, a perfect maze of gossamer of rhythms and rhymes and loose lines floating in the air' (Hux 701). Having finished this task, he felt he had put behind him all the literary chores of the winter and could sit back for a while.

Maria Huxley, who had lost none of the enthusiasm for *Lady Chatterley's Lover* that had helped it on its way, had agreed to type the second half of the book – the 'phallic' part, with the 'worst' bits in it. Meanwhile, in London, Catherine Carswell had arranged the typing of the remaining chapters of the first part, from where Nelly Morrison had left off. Some of the London typing arrived in early February, some perhaps a little later; but there was a long delay in the arrival of all the chapters, due partly to Carswell's being unaware that she should impress the need for haste on the typist. By the end of February, Lawrence had still not received all the London sheets, and towards the middle of the month he had already lost patience: 'Damn them, they don't send it on' (*CL* 1039), he told Brett. On 1 March he wrote to Frieda in Baden-Baden: 'I am still waiting for the final chapters from that *woman*' ('*Not I*' 237).

The reason behind Lawrence's impatience to have a completed typed MS of the novel was that he wanted to send expurgated duplicate copies as soon as possible to his agent for the approval of

Secker and Knopf. The missing chapters finally arrived on 2 March, and three days later the duplicates were sent off. Lawrence had been through the MS, taking out passages which could be sacrificed without leaving gaps in the narrative, such as Mellors's address to his penis, and substituting weary, lack-lustre euphemisms for the words, acts and gestures that might be thought obscene. When he wrote to Secker on the day the expurgated copies were posted, he realized that he had not made a thorough job of it: 'I did a fair amount of blanding out and changing, then I sort of got colour-blind, and didn't know any more what was supposed to be proper and what not' (Sec 103). He was untypically complaisant in regard to possible violation of the novel, ceding to Secker the right to demand substantial alterations, which he would do his best to comply with.

Lawrence's agreeability in respect of large-scale cutting and alteration marked a very considerable change from the position he had held in the letter to Curtis Brown when he began writing the final version. Then, he had been uncertain as to whether he would allow an expurgated edition of any kind. The reasons for his conciliatory approach to Secker were very practical ones, which had to do with establishing the copyright of the novel. Curtis Brown had warned him that the laws of copyright offered no protection to books judged to be indecent, obscene or blasphemous. If, however, a decent, expurgated version of *Lady Chatterley's Lover* appeared *before* the unexpurgated edition, copyright would have made the novel safe from pirates. Hence Lawrence's reasonableness, and his haste to get the expurgated version to Secker, so that he could bring it out in time for Lawrence's intended publication date, which he had now shifted to the month of June. In February Secker received a letter which had an unaccustomed tone of desperation: 'The only other chance is, if you perhaps could print earlier, a copyright, say, in June, and publish in September. Then I could come out with mine in June. Is that feasible, do you know? You must manage it somehow' (Sec 101f.).

Lawrence should perhaps have recalled the copyright problem without prompting from Curtis Brown. A year earlier he had been one of the signatories to an international protest against the piracy of Samuel Roth, who was serializing James Joyce's *Ulysses* in America.[3] When, within six months of publication, *Lady Chatterley's Lover* was boarded by pirates who were to include the same Samuel Roth, Lawrence found himself sharing a common destiny with the man who may have brought the novel into being, as an antidote to the impure, mental sexuality of *Ulysses*. Lawrence had described the last part of *Ulysses* as 'the dirtiest, most indecent, most obscene thing ever written' (Brett 81). Joyce, by contrast, found only one word to express his opinions on first hearing passages from *Lady Chatterley's Lover* – 'Lush', he said. In a letter to his patroness, Miss Weaver, he was more expansive. He had 'read the first two pages of the usual sloppy English' and judged the book to be 'a piece of propaganda in favour of something which, outside of D.H.L.'s country at any rate, makes all the propaganda for itself'.[4]

While at Les Diablerets, Lawrence began planning a strategy for the advertisement, sale and distribution of the novel. He was especially concerned with how he could sell the book without drawing public attention to its existence, and with the problem of avoiding banning and seizure of the books before they reached the purchasers. He had already decided that there would be no review copies, which might initiate a scandal at an early stage in the distribution of the novel. There would also be no general advertisement. Instead he would circulate, through his acquaintances, 'a few little slips announcing the publication' (*Cent* 32). He intended to send most of the copies by post from Florence to individual subscribers. In this way they had a good chance of getting through without seizure: under the Berne International Convention, a sealed postal package could not be opened except by direct order from a Secretary of State. Though he was prepared to crate fifty copies to the Centaur Bookshop in America, he was generally reluctant to ship quantities in this way to distributors in Britain or America because he might thereby risk seizure at the ports of entry, with consequent financial loss.

The possibility of early seizure was the greater on the other side of the Atlantic, where the public office of literary censor existed; and Lawrence had heard recently from Harold Mason of the Centaur that even Rabelais had recently been placed on the banned list. Literary censorship in England operated only indirectly, through the Obscene Publications Act: for this reason censorship was more ponderous in taking effect: there was every chance of most of the books getting through before the law could act. With the American censor in mind, Lawrence decided that he would mail copies to the USA before posting the British orders. In this way there was no danger of news from Britain of the indecent character of the novel reaching the ears of the censor before the arrival of the books.

On 6 March Lawrence left Diablerets. His experiences had failed to make of him a 'snow bird' ('*Not I*' 269), but he nevertheless had favourable impressions of his stay which were to draw him back to Switzerland in early summer. 'I really think it is nicer in Switzerland: warmer even . . . I'm ten times the man, on the other side the Alps' (Brew 164) he told Earl, shortly after returning to the Mirenda. On arrival Lawrence and Frieda had a touching welcome – 'all the peasants out to meet us, with primroses and violets and scarlet and purple anemones' (Hux 706); and there was a cheerful reunion with the Wilkinsons, who found Lawrence and Frieda both looking extremely well after their holiday.

On 9 March Lawrence took his MS of the novel down to Florence, lunched with Orioli, met Douglas – 'still thinking of Jerusalem and preferring Chianti' (*CL* 1051) – then went with Orioli to the printer's, the Typografia Giuntina at 4, via del Sole – 'Sun Street' – an auspicious location for the printing of a novel which Lawrence described to Harry Crosby as 'phallic . . . but good and sunwards, truly sun-wards' (*CL* 1051). The shop was 'an old-fashioned little place' (Zyt 337), where a workforce of eighteen printers hand-set the type. The fact that none of them understood a word of English, Lawrence saw as a blessing: 'where ignorance is bliss! Where the serpent is invisible!' (Hux 709), he exclaimed in an enthusiastic report to Curtis Brown. However, Lawrence thought it right that Franceschini the master-printer should be told the contents of the book and advised not to print it if he thought it might create difficulties for him with the authorities. On hearing what the novel was about, the printer remarked nonchalantly: 'O! *ma*! but we do it every day!/like the pigeons and the other little birds!' (*Poems* 668).

Orioli's role in the enterprise was to look after some of Lawrence's affairs with the printer, to send acknowledgements of orders received and to have charge of expediting the books when they came off the press. Lawrence's principal tasks, in addition to the chores of author and copy-editor during publication, were to advertise the novel and solicit orders, to keep the accounts, and generally take charge of the business of publishing. Orioli was to get 10 per cent of the profits for what he did. The capital investment was to be entirely Lawrence's. In terms of the distribution of work and responsibility, this seems a fair apportioning of gains.

In his autobiography, *Adventures of a Bookseller*, Orioli later complained that he had been put upon and hard done by in his dealings with Lawrence.[5] But he had undertaken similar tasks for Douglas before agreeing to help Lawrence, and it is unlikely that he would have settled for less than he received from Douglas. As Aldington pointed out in *Pinorman*, Orioli's whingeing account of his dealings with Lawrence probably owed a great deal to Norman Douglas.[6] *Adventures of a Bookseller* was a joint Orioli–Douglas enterprise: Orioli's English, though colourful, was bizarre to an extent that would have made the book quite unreadable without Douglas's help. And Douglas, by nature interfering and managing, seems to have taken the opportunity of shaping the content as well as the style of the book. The description of Lawrence's phoenix design for the cover of *Lady Chatterley's Lover* – 'It suggests a pigeon having a bath in a slop-basin'[7] – is surely vintage Douglas, and worthy of the master. More demeaning and spiteful, and probably also attributable to Douglas, is the comment on Lawrence's death: 'I wonder how many of those who knew him well were really sorry when he died.'[8]

Lawrence, impatient to announce the forthcoming novel as soon as possible, was aiming to have ready, by the end of the weekend following his visit to the printer, a draft for the small leaflets he intended to circularize. These were to consist of an advertisement and a tear-off order form which was to be sent to Orioli's bookshop. The problem was that he could specify neither the title nor the intended date of publication until he heard from Secker and Knopf. He had to know whether *John Thomas and Lady Jane* was acceptable to them, and whether and when they intended to bring out the expurgated version. He was expecting to hear from Secker on Monday concerning the title, and perhaps received a disapproving cable, because his draft for the leaflets read: '*Lady Chatterley's Lover or John Thomas and Lady Jane*', with his preferred title demoted to subtitle. No letter from Secker arrived, and rightly supposing the worst from Secker's silence Lawrence must have decided to press ahead regardless and to give a publication date of 15 May, which he knew would be far too early for Secker or Knopf to do a copyright printing. *Lady Chatterley's Lover* would not have the protection of copyright, a fact which continued to worry Lawrence, though not to any great degree.

A few days after Lawrence had sent in his draft for the circular, the expected letter from Secker arrived. It seemed to Secker that there was no way in which the novel could be expurgated sufficiently for distribution to the public. He may have been playing a canny game with Lawrence, which he had decided on well in advance of receiving the expurgated MS – within a month of receiving news of the intended private publication of the novel, in fact. In a letter of 9 February to Curtis Brown, he declared that he would be very happy for the private edition to appear first: he would then be in a position to do just as he wished in expurgating the text, without interference from Lawrence.[9] As Secker probably guessed, it was safe to reject the expurgated MS that Lawrence offered, because there was little chance of it being acceptable to any other British publisher. After Secker rejected the MS, it passed to Jonathan Cape, who also refused it, remarking that it was 'a great pity' (*CL* 1053) and commending the 'large patches of sheer beauty'. Lawrence was unappeased, and in a letter to Huxley made an obscene suggestion as to where Cape might put one of his patches of sheer beauty.[10]

Lawrence received the first batch of his 2,100 leaflets within a day or two of sending in his draft to the Typografia Giuntina, whose promptness seemed to augur well for the future. Less inspiring of confidence was an error in rendering the publication date, as a result of which the circulars first sent out promised a novel that would be available from 15 May 1920.[11] It escaped Pino Orioli's notice and for a while was also overlooked by Lawrence, who afterwards blamed Pino. The date on the leaflets was subsequently altered to 1928 by hand.[12]

On receiving the leaflets on 13 March, Lawrence immediately threw himself into the task of distributing them to every contact he could think of. It was a formidable chore, even for so prodigious a correspondent as Lawrence. Between 13 and 15 March he sent off twenty-two letters to America alone;[13] and he probably continued producing something like this volume until early April. Conscience, courtesy and expediency demanded that these letters should not be merely short, formal requests. He had to make plain to his correspondents the nature and content of the novel he was asking them to advertise and/or buy. This, in turn, required some defence of the book and an explanation of its purpose. Often he was writing to old acquaintances with whom he had not been in contact for some years; and since he was asking for help as a personal favour, there had to be personal touches in the letters – reflections on old times together, accounts of his life in recent years, polite inquiries concerning his correspondent and such like. Nor was this an end to his correspondence, since he not infrequently received letters in return, to which he had to reply. In this way some correspondences that had died long ago were revived and continued thereafter, such as that between Lawrence and Lady Ottoline Morrell, who had broken with him after she found herself lampooned as Hermione Roddice in *Women in Love*. In one instance, contact was renewed at some cost to Lawrence. Montague Shearman wrote back indignant at being asked to pay for one of Lawrence's books when he had long ago lent him £10, which had never been repaid. Lawrence, who had no recollection of the loan and assumed that he must have thought of it as a gift, sent the money by return.

Typically, a letter announcing the forthcoming book would describe the tender, phallic quality of the novel and would state that it was not about sex, but about the conflict between the phallic consciousness and cerebral consciousness, the latter being the source of impure sexuality. Lawrence would ask for his leaflets to be distributed among the 'right people', and would sometimes include suggestions as to where such people might be found – in the universities in America, for example, or in Germany among the class of rich Berliners.

When writing to intimate friends, Lawrence would impress upon them his dependence on their active help in sales, without which he risked considerable financial loss. Pride, and the need to ensure action on the part of his friends, caused Lawrence to express his pleas for help in terms of statements of obligation; but his 'you must help me' (Hux 710, 713) was finely judged, suggesting desperation rather than bossiness. They were admirable letters for their purpose, revealing an aspect of business acumen beyond the clerical and accountancy skills which he is often credited with. For this reason the letters achieved a remarkable success in terms of the orders they brought in. In America, where Lawrence had fewer close contacts, sales did not go so well, and the great majority of his 1,000 copies was sold in Britain.

The manner in which Lawrence presented his book and its intended purpose was carefully attuned to the personality and tastes of the individual he was addressing. To Rolf Gardiner, who took no cognizance of the sex aspect of Lawrence's message, and for whom the language of violence held some appeal, Lawrence wrote as follows:

> Now I want you to help me a bit. I wrote . . . a phallic novel: a delicate and tender phallic novel . . . I'm publishing it here in Florence . . . I've got to sell it too: for I've got to live. So you must help me, because I know you will.

It is strictly a novel of the phallic consciousness as against the mental consciousness of today. For some things you will probably dislike it: because you are still squeamish, and scared of the phallic reality. It is perfectly wholesome and normal, and man and a woman. But I protest against it being labelled 'sex'. Sex is a mental reaction nowadays, and a hopelessly cerebral affair; and what I believe in is the true phallic consciousness. But you'll see. So I shall send you a bunch of the little order-forms, and you must get me what orders you can, because the book must be read – it's a bomb, but to the living a flood of urge – and I must sell it. And it's part of the crusade that we are both out for, and *una mano lava l'altra* – but I know you'll help me what you can. This is where I throw a straight bomb at the skull of the idealistic Mammon.

(Hux 713f.)

In between rushing out a host of letters, Lawrence designed his phoenix rising from a nest of flames which was to be printed on the cover of the book. It reproduced a design he had made on a seal symbolizing resurrection and immortality, which he had given to Murry at Christmas, 1923. By 26 March, when he visited Florence, the phoenix had been cast and printed, but there was a delay in the production of the first set of galley proofs – an intimation of the troubles that lay ahead. When he received the proofs at the end of the month, Lawrence found that, though the printer's ignorance of English left him 'unsullied', this was not the case with the proofs which resembled 'a Bach fugue' (*CL* 1052) in their endless variations on the word *didn't*.

By April Lawrence was beginning to feel that in some quarters the novel was 'rousing already a lot of gratuitous hostility' (*CL* 1055). Lawrence discerned this antipathy in the letters he received from Secker, Cape and the Curtis Brown agency. His agent seemed the main culprit. Lawrence imagined (rightly or wrongly, since it was never spelt out for him) that the agent's office was 'furious' (*CL* 1052) over his publishing the novel, and that the people there would do all they could to hinder publication. He was certainly advised that in his own interests he should do nothing to damage a reputation that had acquired a measure of respectability in recent years. Lawrence suspected that it was *their* interests and *their* pockets they were anxious to protect, and took offence at the way in which their arguments were put. To Alfred Knopf, his American publisher, Lawrence complained: 'The London people have all been trying to make me feel tremendously in the wrong, and holding up pious

267

hands afraid of touching pitch' (*CL* 1055). Knopf had handled Lawrence with more tact and consideration than Secker and Curtis Brown, expressing a liking for the novel and an interest in publishing it, provided it could be further expurgated in a way that would make it acceptable to the public.

In his letter of early April to Huxley, Lawrence reported: 'My cough is as ever: but I'm no worse: really rather well, I think. Does me good to feel furious about the novel' (*CL* 1053). Anger and preoccupation with the novelty of dabbling in so many aspects of publication kept him in reasonable health, and vital in his spirits. Although the Mirenda remained disagreeable to him, and although he grumbled on occasion about his isolation, and had a number of reasons for feeling persecuted, he evidently no longer felt anguished or depressed by events, by people or by his situation. He was finding his way towards another brief period of insouciance, which he made the title of a short essay, written at Chexbres-sur-Vevey, Switzerland, in June.

The end of March saw the final departure of the Wilkinsons, 'having packed up every old rag, pot, pan and whisker with the sanctity of pure idealists cherishing their goods' (*CL* 1050). Their journal recorded a picture of Lawrence sitting for half an hour smiling sadly amidst the débris of their goods and chattels before they set off down the hill from the Villa Poggi and out of a life they had shared for almost two years.[14] Lawrence himself was due to leave shortly after the expiry of his lease on the Mirenda in early May. Strangely, after more than a year of unrelieved discontent, and though he now had no companions nearby, he finally decided to renew the lease for six months. This was partly because he could not find the energy to pack his modest store of belongings (now increased in bulk, since he had to take a considerable number of pictures with him), and because he was touched by Frieda's sadness when they made an abortive start on packing.

The number of brief visits to the Mirenda from friends abroad or from Florence rose considerably in 1928. Frieda's sister Else and her lover, Alfred Weber, paid two visits in March and April. Barby arrived for a few days during the last week of March. In mid-April, while Frieda was away visiting Barby and Else in Alassio and Ravagli at Spotorno, Rolf Gardiner's sister Margaret arrived for the day, to find Lawrence swinging between angry misanthropy and joyousness, but nevertheless buoyant in either mood. As they walked up the track from the tram-terminus, Lawrence engineered a pause to get his breath by suggesting that they stand and look a while. Margaret Gardiner remarked how lovely the landscape was. Lawrence agreed: the world *was* lovely, but people ruined it: he hated people: they were all, the people of the modern world, corrupt and destructive.[15] His bitterness had not been diminished by the sheaf of letters he had just received from the editor of *Forum* magazine in America. They were the outraged responses of readers to the appearance of 'The Escaped Cock' in *Forum*'s February issue. In the letters Lawrence learnt that he was 'a traitor and enemy of the human race' (*CL* 1058) and that he had 'committed the unpardonable sin' (*CL* 1057), causing 'innumerable souls to be lost' (Hux 727). He was angry, too, with the editor, Helen Bramble: he felt she had failed to stand by him in the face of her readers' criticisms.

While Margaret Gardiner was with him, Lawrence had a visit from two elderly ladies whom he called 'the Virgins'. These maiden ladies, referred to as the 'Misses Smith' by Margaret Gardiner, were probably Millie and Mary Beveridge, whom Lawrence had been expecting on 13 April.[16] Lawrence showed them his paintings, of which they approved only some of the watercolours. Their objections were plainly critical rather than prudish, until Lawrence mischievously brought out his recent painting of 'Le Pisseur' ('Dandelions'), showing a man urinating. 'Really Lawrence', said one of them, 'You go too far' (Nehls 3 208). Lawrence was hurt and annoyed by their disapproval. Reporting the incident to Maria Huxley, Lawrence wrote: 'A woman who's been my friend for years told me on Saturday that my pictures were disgusting and unnecessary, and even old-fashioned. Really, I shall have to buy a weapon of some sort. Wish I had the skunk's' (Hux 724).

This visit, perhaps, and the memory of other viewings that had met with express or tacit disapproval, had the effect of depriving Lawrence of some of the pleasure he took in painting. In a letter to Earl Brewster, dated the day before Millie Beveridge's visit, but perhaps finished off later, Lawrence wrote:

> It's quite amusing to paint – if only one didn't have the feeling of other people looking on. That spoils it again. People keep coming – and they want to see one's pictures – and they don't like them . . . they stand there half-alive and make the whole thing seem like luke-warm fish soup.
>
> (Brew 168)

These experiences failed to deter Lawrence from his present plan, which was to exhibit the pictures at the Warren Gallery in London. Barby Weekley had brought news of Dorothy Warren's interest in staging an exhibition. Lawrence knew her – she was a niece of Lady Ottoline's – and wrote with a cautious pretence of little enthusiasm for the idea:[17] this was a fortnight after he had written to Earl telling him he had lost all interest in exhibiting. With Dorothy Warren's encouragement he decided to go ahead, in the knowledge that the exhibition would only add to his stock of enemies.[18]

After describing to Earl the reception given to the paintings by visitors to the Mirenda, Lawrence told him: 'I'm fed up with people. That's why I'd like to move on a bit' (Brew 168). He was currently planning his round-the-world voyage, part of the attraction of which was the idea of 'drifting out of reach of mail and malice, no letters, no literature, no publishers or agents or anything' (Brew 168). Had he been able to do so, his voyaging would have been a judicious means of keeping out of harm's way while the world reacted to the publication of *Lady Chatterley's Lover*. In the meantime he was endeavouring, with mixed success, to recapture his carefree approach to the world. On 25 April he wrote again to Earl, and also to Huxley. While the Huxley letter echoed the sentiments of his previous letter to Brewster,[19] the latest letter to Earl declared that he found he was caring less and less about the outside world: provided he could be left alone and in peace, he had little interest in moving anywhere and 'stepping out of the shade of one's bo-tree' (Brew 169). It was at this time that he decided to renew the lease on the Mirenda.

Publication of the novel had been 'a struggle' (*Ph 2* 515), Lawrence afterwards observed in his essay 'A Propos of "Lady Chatterley's Lover"'. By 25 April, when he wrote to Brewster and Huxley, the only element of struggle had been defence of publication in the face of opposition from his agent. Half of the novel was already in proof, edited and corrected, and Lawrence was expecting that by the end of the week all the type would have been set up and that the novel would be run off in time to meet the advertised publication date of 15 May. In fact, Lawrence did not receive proofs of the remainder of the novel until more than a fortnight after it was due out. The need for substantial correction, and his habit of revising texts at the proof stage, meant that Lawrence did not finish with the proofs before early June, and he began to be pestered with letters from anxious subscribers who had not received their copies.

The cause of the delay at the printers' was twofold. The printer had enough type only to print half the novel, after which he had to break up and reset the type for the second half. Had the de luxe handmade paper Lawrence ordered arrived in time, printing could have proceeded according to plan. But the paper makers failed to deliver until 16 May, and work had come to a halt at the Typografia Giuntina, where they were unable to set up the second half of the novel until the sheets of the first half had been run off.

Finally, on 7 June, all the proofs had been corrected, the sheets had been 'signed and numbered up to 1,000' (*PL* 560) and Lawrence prepared to leave for a holiday in Switzerland. His relief at having discharged all his responsibilities and finding himself free to escape was tinged with some anxiety over abandoning supervision of the final stages.

The Brewsters had arrived in Florence in June, thinking of taking up Lawrence's offer of the Mirenda for the weeks while he was in Switzerland. Towards the end of May he had been driven to bed with influenza. The Brewsters, meeting him for the first time in over a year, found him looking particularly frail and ill, and they concluded that the pleasure of Lawrence's companionship would not be available to them for very much longer. They therefore decided to accompany the Lawrences to Switzerland.

There was no planned itinerary, and the journey took on an aura of adventure. Lawrence was exhilarated. In the compartment of the train from Florence to Turin, he launched into his repertoire of salvationist hymns, remembered from his days at Eastwood's Congregational chapel. The recital ended with 'Throw out the life-line', during which he stood up to fling an imaginary rope to the drowning souls, whom he heaved back to the saving shore.[20]

From Turin, where they spent the first night, the Lawrences and Brewsters travelled to Chambéry, Aix-les-Bains, Grenoble and Nizier. Finding there a perfect old inn set among meadows of Alpine flowers, they decided to stay for the rest of the holiday. Next morning they were evicted: a local by-law forbade the innkeeper to harbour consumptives, and Lawrence's tubercular cough had made it plain that he fell under this prohibition. They left France for Switzerland, settling in a pleasant, inexpensive hotel at Chexbres-sur-Vevey, with Turneresque views of Lake Geneva below. Towards the end of June they were joined by the Huxleys, who found Lawrence looking remarkably well, all things considered.

At the start of the holiday, when staying in Turin, Lawrence and his party had found on their luncheon table a large magnolia flower which unfolded in the morning sunlight as they watched.[21] On the morning of 28 June at Chexbres, Lawrence's 'tender and phallic novel' – 'the full fine flower with pistil and stamens standing' (*CL* 1045) – lay open before him for the first time. With its leaves of hand-rolled, cream-coloured paper and its mulberry red cover, bearing the phoenix emblem, printed in black, it seemed to Lawrence 'a handsome and dignified volume' (*CL* 1065). Accompanying the book was a letter from Orioli, telling Lawrence that he had just been visited at the bookshop by Rosalind Thornycroft, whose jasmine-like beauty had inspired the portrait of Lady Chatterley.

Aldous and Maria Huxley, who had known the book and encouraged its creation from its beginnings in October 1926, left for Italy on the day *Lady Chatterley's Lover* arrived. Little more than a month after the Huxleys' departure, Lawrence wrote telling them of rumours of police seizure of the book, of a London firm of booksellers demanding the removal of copies from their shop, and of the loss of friends among subscribers who had read the book. It marked the beginning of that phase in the history of the novel which Lawrence had prophesied earlier in a letter demanding Huxley's future support – the time when the pigs would 'begin to grunt, then to squeal, then to prance their feet in the porridge' (Hux 710).

Notes

1 Cf. *CL* 851.

2 Aldington reported to Harry T. Moore (see A. Kershaw and F-J. Temple (eds), *Richard Aldington: An Intimate Portrait* [Carbondale, Ill.: Southern Illinois University Press, 1965], p. 85) that Frieda complained to intimate friends that Lawrence had been impotent since 1926. This could be a fabrication either on Aldington's part or on the part of Frieda, who might have concocted the story in order to justify her adulterous behaviour. Later, on at least two separate occasions, Frieda denied that Lawrence was impotent – once in 1932 to the sculptor Lawrence Bradshaw (see E. Delavenay, '"Making another Lawrence": Frieda and the Lawrence legend', *DHLR*, vol. 8 [Spring 1975], p. 85), and again to Harry T. Moore in the 1940s or 1950s (see Spilka 275f., n. 14). However, other evidence suggests that Lawrence was indeed impotent by 1926: in that year he failed in attempts to make love to Dorothy Brett (see below, Ch. 4); the Lawrence-figures of the three versions of *Lady Chatterley* have been or are victims of sexual apathy or impotence (see below, Ch. 4); and several of the later poems concern the death of desire (cf. 'Blank', 'Desire is Dead', 'Man Reaches a Point', 'Grasshopper', 'Basta', 'Nullus', 'Dies Irae', 'Dies Illa', 'The Death of Our Era', 'The New Word', 'Sun in Me', 'Be Still' [*Poems* 501, 504, 507–13], cited in Spilka, n. 10).

3 Middleton Murry once explained to friends that Brett's deafness was the result of a childhood refusal to listen to the conversation of members of her family. See Nehls 2 310.

4 See Hignett 146f.

5 This colony had first been planned over Christmas 1914, in reaction to a Europe embroiled in the First World War. The proposed colony took its name from the words of a Hebrew song, sung by Lawrence's friend S. S. Koteliansky ('Kot'), whom Lawrence had first met in July 1914. On the origins and meaning of 'Rananim', see Gransden 23f.

6 H. G. Wells, *The New Machiavelli* (New York: Duffield, 1910).

7 See p. 9 of Frieda Lawrence's introduction to *FLC*. Frieda uses the term 'picaresque', but it seems from the context that she intended it as a synonym for 'bawdy'.

8 Giacomo Casanova de Seingalt, whose twelve volumes of memoirs had been published in Paris between 1826 and 1838.

9 Mackenzie V 167. Lawrence's reactions to Joyce and similarities and contrasts between *Ulysses* and *LCL* are discussed in two articles which appeared in a recent anthology of writings on *Lady Chatterley*: Z. Bowen, '*Lady Chatterley's Lover* and *Ulysses*', in '*Lady*' 116–35; and J. C. Cowan, 'Epiphanies of *Lady Chatterley's Lover*', in '*Lady*' 91–115.

10   Transcript of a conversation between Mackenzie and D. E. Gerard: Central Library, Nottingham.

CHAPTER 2

1   The Saywells' fictional journey from Papplewick through a ducal park to Woodlinkin, Bolehill, Bonsall Head and Amberdale seems to correspond in actual geography to a route which begins at Cromford ('Papplewick'), passes through Chatsworth Park and Baslow ('Woodlinkin') to Monsal Head ('Bonsall Head') and thence to Bamford ('Amberdale'). Bamford can be identified from the reference to the inn at Amberdale – the 'Marquis of Grantham', which suggests Bamford's 'Marquis of Granby'. A few miles from Bamford were the huge Howden and Derwent reservoirs, constructed in 1916. It seems very likely that Lawrence visited the reservoirs with the Clarkes and that out of his visit came the idea for the finale of the novel – the devastating flood which results from 'the sudden bursting of the great reservoir, up in Papple Highdale' (*VG* 260).

For the Bolehill section of the Saywells' drive, Lawrence rearranged real geography by interpolating what, in terms of his sources, is a journey from Cromford along the Via Gellia and up to Bonsal ('Bolehill'). He was to follow similar methods of reconstituting reality when constructing the landscape of *Lady Chatterley*.

2   Pugh (261f.) correctly identifies Cromford, Bonsal and Chatsworth, but mistakenly places the Saywells' vicarage on the site of Willersley Castle, Cromford. 'The Bridge House' matches far more precisely the setting of the vicarage, and it also resembles the vicarage in its exterior appearance.

3   For a full account of Lawrence's relations with Cynthia Asquith in the period 1914–18 see Delany.

4   WWRA 163. Lawrence's analyses of Cynthia Asquith's personality appear in the character of Carlotta Fell in 'Glad Ghosts' (*WWRA* 162–202) and in the character of the heroine of 'The Thimble', who has the immaturity, the cold stoicism and separateness, and the nervous melancholia of Lady Cynthia. In the figure of Lady Daphne in the revised version of this latter story – 'The Ladybird' – Lawrence showed similar divisions of personality to those which appear in Carlotta Fell in 'Glad Ghosts'.

5   Unpub. letter of ?19 November to Cynthia Asquith: Lacy 2996.

6   Several of these points of correspondence between Lady Cynthia and Constance Chatterley are mentioned in Delany 170f.

7   Comprehensive accounts of the Lawrence–Murry relationship are to be found in the following works: E. Griffin, *John Middleton Murry* (New York: Twayne, 1969) and 'The circular and the linear: the Middleton Murry–D. H. Lawrence affair', *DHLR*, vol. 2 (Spring 1969), pp. 121–40; Lea; Delany (with reference to the period 1914–18).

8   The surviving correspondence between Murry and Frieda in the 1940s and 1950s (see *Frieda*) and a record in Murry's journal under 18 December 1955 (Lea 118) testify that Murry and Frieda did not become lovers in Lawrence's lifetime.

9   The impression of some degree of complaisancy on Lawrence's part is suggested by the absence of recrimination in references or letters to men with whom Frieda had affairs about which Lawrence appears to have known (as, for instance, Harold

Hobson and Cecil Gray). In Lawrence's last years, when he was ill and impotent, he referred with tolerant understanding to Frieda's visits to her lover, Angelo Ravagli (see Nehls 3 189).

10   The three anti-Murry stories are discussed in J. T. Cowan, *D. H. Lawrence's American Journey* (Cleveland, Ohio and London: Press of Case Western Reserve University, 1970), pp. 52–62.

11   See Lea 100, 119.

12   Murry 203.

13   Murry 119, 203.

14   Unpub. letter of 27 October 1925 to Nancy Pearn: Lacy 2974.

15   The textual history of 'Sun' also resembles that of *Lady Chatterley*. The story exists in two versions. The first version, written in 1925, was published in the *New Coterie* (Autumn 1926); the second, revised version of 1928 had a bizarre genesis. Harry Crosby, founder of the Black Sun Press (which published the story in 1928), had written offering Lawrence $100 for any MS of his. Lawrence thought of 'Sun' as especially appropriate, but could not locate the MS. At the suggestion of Nancy Pearn at his agent's office (see the passage from her letter quoted in *Calendar* 172) he therefore wrote another MS version which constituted a revision of the *New Coterie* text. The progress of the text from the *New Coterie* version to what Lawrence called the 'final' version (Hux 730) parallels especially the history of *Lady Chatterley* in its first two versions in the movements towards more explicit detail (particularly in terms of the responses and sensations of sexual organs) and towards 'elaborating more fully key symbolic patterns' in the story. For a full critical discussion of the relationship between the two versions, see M. L. Ross, 'Lawrence's second "Sun"', *DHLR*, vol. 8 (Spring 1975), pp. 1–18, from which the quotation above is taken.

The controversy over which of the two versions of 'Sun' was the original, which arises out of Lawrence's references to the Black Sun version as the 'unexpurgated' text (see B. Finney and M. L. Ross, 'The two versions of "Sun": an exchange', *DHLR*, vol. 8 [Fall 1975], pp. 371–4) would appear to have been resolved by Sagar's publication of part of the letter from Nancy Pearn and the text of the statement of copyright, obtained by Frieda in 1954, which shows that the Black Sun version was expanded from the original (*Calendar* 172).

16   Nehls 3 21.

17   Brett 260.

18   Nehls 3 21.

19   Smith 364.

CHAPTER 3

1   Murry 121.

2   *PL* 521.

3   Murry 121, 204.

4   Murry 204.

5   Lea 142.

6   *CL* 883f. The 'essay on power' refers to the title essay 'Reflections on the Death of a Porcupine'.

7   Murry 122.

8   Unpub. letter of 19 April 1926: Lacy 3115.1.
9   *The Adelphi*, vol. 4, no. 2 (August 1926).
10 *The Adelphi*, vol. 4, no. 3 (September 1926).
11 *A Midsummer Night's Dream*, II.i.250. Clifford's allusions to Keats and Shakespeare persist in subsequent versions of the novel (as do other traits which may have associations with Murry): in the second version only the quotations from 'Ode to a Grecian Urn' survive in this scene (*JTLJ* 100); and in the final version the Shakespeare quotation which appears with phrases from Keats is: 'Sweeter than the lids of Juno's eyes' (*The Winter's Tale*, IV.iv.121). On allusions to Keats and Shakespeare in the text, see Jackson 172–80.
12 Quoted in *Gossip* 60.
13 See Irv 58.

CHAPTER 4

1   Hux 652.
2   Cf. Sanders 177.
3   *Cent* 23. Professor E. D. McDonald of the Drexel Institute, Philadelphia, had compiled a bibliography of Lawrence's published works in 1924. At that time Lawrence and he began what became a regular correspondence. They met in New York in 1925, shortly before Lawrence sailed for England.
4   *CL* 889.
5   Some picture of what the state of the house might have been may be imagined from Bennet Cerf's account of a visit to the Villa Mirenda in June 1928 – a time when Lawrence was extremely unwell, but not confined to his sick-bed and able to attempt to impose some order on affairs. Cerf had been entertained in a 'slovenly room' in which there was 'an almost empty milk bottle lying in the middle of the stone floor, ignored by everybody – and a tray of half-eaten food gathering flies on a corner table' (Cerf 7f.). Frieda, replying to this article in the same journal on 10 May 1952, asserted that Cerf had never visited the Mirenda and that his account was entirely fictional. Her claim was founded on the inaccuracy of Cerf's dating (he had given Spring 1929 as the time of his visit, when the Lawrences no longer resided at the Mirenda) and on his mistaken desription of stucco walls. Cerf had, in fact, met the Lawrences at the Mirenda on 6 June 1928.
6   Information supplied by Margaret Needham.
7   'Not I' 168.
8   'Not I' 168.
9   See *CL* 868, 870.
10 H. T. Moore, *The Intelligent Heart* (London: Heinemann, 1955), p. 351.
11 *CL* 886f.
12 See Hignett 187.
13 Brett 268.
14 *More Than* 32–5. Faith Mackenzie's account does not make clear which of the two stories was specially indebted to her conversation with Lawrence: both would appear to draw on information supplied by her. Compton Mackenzie implies that it was 'Two Blue Birds' to which she took exception: see Mackenzie VI 85.
15 Unpub. letter of ?11 March 1926: Lacy 3077.

16 *PL* 284.

17 Sec 73. In fact, the title of the book was *Birds and Beasts of the Greek Anthology*.

18 Although Douglas, who had published papers on botany and zoology in scientific journals, was outstanding in his expertise, a considerable knowledge of botany seems to have united the three men (Mackenzie, Douglas and Lawrence) who contributed to the portrait of Cathcart. Lawrence's skills in plant identification are well-known; and Mackenzie appears also to have had a considerable knowledge of botany, which he put to use in a somewhat trivial criticism of 'The Man Who Loved Islands': Lawrence had strewn one of Cathcart's islands with cowslips, which preferred lime soils, not the granite of Mackenzie's Channel Islands (Mackenzie VI 131).

19 See transcript of a conversation between Mackenzie and D. E. Gerard: Central Library, Nottingham).

20 Brett 259f.

21 Hignett 187.

22 Hignett 191f. This is Hignett's transcript of Brett's own typescript. The account also exists in another version, published by John Manchester in the Epilogue to the reprint of *Lawrence and Brett* (see Brett III). This latter version, descended ultimately from the same typescript, differs mostly from the Hignett version only in minor respects. There is, however, significant variation between the two versions in the sentence which in Hignett reads: '"Your pubes are wrong."' In the Manchester version 'boobs', a modern slang term (of American provenance) for breasts, appears in place of 'pubes', a British colloquial/slang term for pubic hair. It seems most likely that 'pubes' is the correct reading and that at some stage in the transmission of the Manchester text 'boobs', a term more familiar to a modern speaker of American English, was substituted. That 'pubes' is the original reading and also an accurate reminiscence of what Lawrence said would appear to be confirmed by the evidence of an aversion to female pubic hair which Lawrence declared in his youth to George Neville. Neville had once scandalized Lawrence by adding pubic hair to a female nude that Lawrence had drawn. He refused to accept that pubic hair had any place on the female anatomy and was disgusted by the thought of it (Neville 81f.). In *JTLJ* 230f. Lawrence endowed Parkin, the gamekeeper, with a similar phobia of female pubic hair and a fetishistic preference for a shaven genital area.

23 *CL* 828f.

24 *Musical Chairs* 138. If Gray's claim to certainty was honest, it would seem that Frieda must have confided in him at the time when they were lovers. An additional source may have been the imagist poet H. D., wife of Richard Aldington, who became Gray's lover in 1918. There had been an affair, perhaps entirely cerebral, between Lawrence and Hilda Doolittle in the 1917–18 period.

25 All his deep, desirous blood had been locked, he had wanted nobody, and nothing. And it had been hard to live, so. Without desire, without any movement of passionate love, only gripped back in recoil! That was an experience to endure.

And now came his desire back. But strong, fierce as iron. Like the strength of an eagle with the lightning in its talons. Something to glory in, something overweening, the powerful male passion, arrogant, royal, Jove's thunderbolt. Aaron's black rod of power, blossoming again with red Florentine lilies and fierce thorns . . . The phoenix had risen in fire again, out of the ashes.

(Aaron's Rod [Harmondsworth:
Penguin, 1950], pp. 250f.)

26   For views which also attribute one of the causes of Lawrence's impotence to the debilitating effects of tuberculosis, see Ober 108 and Spilka's admirable account of Lawrence's impotence and its relationship to the works of his last years.

David Garnett (*Echo* 254) reported that in 1913 he noticed that a handkerchief that Lawrence had held to his mouth during a fit of coughing was 'spotted with bright arterial blood'. Ober (p. 92) comments: 'If this is taken as the first evidence of hemoptysis [spitting blood], Lawrence had a well-established pulmonary infection by that time.'

27   John Bancroft, *Human Sexuality and Its Problems* (Edinburgh: Churchill Livingstone, 1983), pp. 26f.

28   Parkin's phobia (*JTLJ* 230f.) concerns female pubic hair, while Mellors's (*LCL* 211) has to do with the clitoral area of the vagina and the physical pain associated with contact between the penis and the pubic bone.

29   Mackenzie VI 167f.

30   Alice Dax was a Liverpudlian who spoke with a pronounced Liverpool accent. Bertha Coutts was 'not a native of the [Tevershall] district, because she spoke with a queer twang that Constance did not like' (*JTLJ* 36).

31   *Musical Chairs* 138.

32   *Rainbow* 280; *WL* 413.

33   That the scene in question (*JTLJ* 270–6, *LCL* 253–9) depicts an act of buggery was first suggested by Eliseo Vivas in *D. H. Lawrence: The Failure and the Triumph of Art* (Evanston, Ill.: Northwestern University Press, 1960), pp. 130ff. The matter was first given a full and explicit public airing by John Sparrow in 'Regina v. Penguin Books: an undisclosed element in the case', *Encounter*, vol. 18, no. 35 (February 1962), pp. 35–43. Sparrow charged Lawrence with dishonesty in the covert presentation of anal intercourse, and this view has since been echoed by a number of critics, including Delavenay (60), Daleski (308) and Ober (114). The justice of this judgement is a little harsh, considering the moral climate of the time when Lawrence was writing and the outrage which Lawrence knew would be provoked even by scenes of natural intercourse. It might also be argued in Lawrence's defence that the scenes of normal intercourse in the novel are never very explicit in terms of pictorial representation of the act: this was not because Lawrence approached those scenes with a cowardly lack of integrity, but because what he wished to make explicit were the emotions and sensations of lovemaking; arguably, Lawrence is in that regard no less explicit in the presentation of buggery.

For a full bibliography of writings on the anal intercourse scene, see Widmer (310 n. 8). To the list in Widmer may be added the following works: Daleski (308–11); Delavenay (59–62); F. Kermode, *Lawrence* (London: Fontana, 1973), p. 130; M. Spilka, 'On Lawrence's hostility to wilful women: the Chatterley solution', in A. Smith (ed.), *Lawrence and Women* (London: Vision, 1978), pp. 208f.; Squires 178–80; and the papers cited in n. 36 of this chapter.

34   Ober 113.

35   William Empson, 'Lady Chatterley again', *Essays in Criticism*, vol. 13 (January 1963), p. 103 drew attention to the folkloristic belief in buggery as a means of melting a woman's frigidity and claimed that this was the intended function of the

act in Connie's case. This, however, seems to be a redundant purpose in view of the fact that what Lawrence regarded as female frigidity had already been cured in an earlier scene in which Connie yielded fully and experienced vaginal orgasm.

36 Cf. K. Millett, *Sexual Politics* (London: Sphere, 1971), p. 241; J. Meyers, 'D. H. Lawrence and homosexuality', in S. Spender (ed.), *D. H. Lawrence: Novelist, Poet, Prophet* (London: Weidenfeld & Nicolson, 1973), pp. 135ff.; and Ober 112f.

37 Mackenzie V 168.

38 Delaney 314.

39 F. Lyons, *The Hills of Annesley* (priv. publ., 1973), pp. 236–8.

40 *Frieda* 352.

41 This account of the parting of Lawrence and Brett, which differs substantially from that given in the first published version of Brett's reminiscences, derives from an unpublished MS version studied by Sean Hignett: see Hignett 192f.

42 Irv 65.

43 From an assessment of Miss Beveridge's character sent by T. B. B. Bingham.

44 Unpub. letter of ?4 April 1926: Lacy 3098.

CHAPTER 5

1 Nehls 3 57.

2 Cf. Holloway 309–11.

3 'Not I' 177.

4 Wilk 64.

5 Cf. Lloyd 141–5; Griffin 236–8.

6 Unpub. letter to Ada Clarke, ?14 June 1926: Lacy 3154.

7 Wilk 64.

8 *Aldous Huxley: A Biography*, Vol. 1 (London: Chatto & Windus, 1973), p. 139.

9 *CL* 904.

10 *CL* 927.

11 See Nehls 3 65.

12 Unpub. letter of 8 June 1926 to Millicent Beveridge: Lacy 3152.1.

13 Carswell 261.

14 Orioli knew Osbert Sitwell, and it is more than likely that Sir George also frequented Orioli's shop when he was in town.

15 Smith 202.

16 Osbert Sitwell, *Laughter in the Next Room* (London: Macmillan, 1948), p. 278.

17 Unpub. letter to Millicent Beveridge: Lacy 3152.1.

18 Pearson 225.

19 See Edith 108.

20 Unpub. letter of ?14 June 1926 to Ada Clarke: Lacy 3154.

21 *Looking Back* 426f.

22 *CL* 916.

23 Farjeon 55.

24 Nehls 1 502.

25 *Echo* 239, 167.

26 *Echo* 239,

27 Cf. *FLC* 175, *LCL* 217.

28 *JTLJ* 54.
29 Nehls 1 496; *FLC* 80, 247.
30 Nehls 2 49f.
31 *Let 3* 180. On Lawrence and the cult of Orpheus, see the discussion in Delany 333f., to which these observations are much indebted.
32 Nehls 1 460.
33 Nehls 1 461.
34 *LCL* 10. Rosalind Thornycroft's first husband was nine years her senior.
35 *LCL* 248. For a report of the divorce case (Baynes v. Baynes and Hooper) see *The Times* (27 April 1921).

CHAPTER 6

1 *Gossip* 62.
2 Gardiner's memoirs of Lawrence, written in 1929 and revised in 1956, make disturbing reading in terms of what they reveal of Gardiner's personality and political ideology. Though the revised version of the text disparages Hitler for his posturing brand of leadership, Gardiner's writings nevertheless show a number of affinities with the ideology of the Nazis, with whom he expressly sympathized in a letter to the *Observer* of 11 February 1934. This letter, a response to an *Observer* report of the previous week which had labelled Gardiner 'the English neo-Nazi' and Lawrence 'a potential fascist', led Emile Delavenay to describe Gardiner as 'pro-Nazi' (*D. H. Lawrence: L'Homme et la Genèse de son Oeuvre* [Paris: Klincksieck, 1969], p. 424). This term was described as 'inaccurate and misleading' in W. J. Keith, 'Spirit of place and *genius loci*: D. H. Lawrence and Rolf Gardiner', *DHLR*, vol. 7 (Summer 1974), pp. 127–38. Delavenay and Keith debated the matter of Gardiner's politics in the 1930s in 'Mr Rolf Gardiner, "The English Neo-Nazi": an exchange', *DHLR*, vol. 7 (Fall 1974), pp. 291–4. Delavenay, by quoting the full text of Gardiner's letter to the *Observer*, had the better of the argument.
3 Nehls 3 82.
4 Nehls 3 83.
5 Unpub. letter of 14 August 1926 to Gardiner: Lacy 3191.
6 See *Life* 207, where Sagar also cites 'A Dream of Life' and 'Nottingham and the Mining Countryside' as works influenced by Gardiner's enthusiasm for the rituals of song and dance.
7 W. J. Keith, 'Spirit of place and *genius loci*: D. H. Lawrence and Rolf Gardiner', *DHLR*, vol. 7 (Summer 1974), pp. 127–38, claims that the impact of Gardiner's thought on Lawrence was considerable. He cites, as a particular instance of Gardiner's influence, Lawrence's emphasis on man's ritual relation to the cosmos in 'A Propos of "Lady Chatterley's Lover"'; but there seems to be no great difference between the expression of this theme in 'A Propos . . . ' and in 'Pan in America' written in 1924.
8 Hux xxix.
9 See Nehls 1 501.
10 Smith 88.
11 Smith 187.
12 Robert Graves and Alan Hodge, *The Long Weekend: A Social History of Great*

Britain 1918–1939 (London: Faber, 1940), p. 19.

13 Aldington 275.

14 Unpub. letter of 8 August to Rachel Hawk: Lacy 3186.

15 This information, and other facts concerning Lawrence's stay in Nottingham and his drive to Lincolnshire next day, derive from conversations with Margaret Needham, Lawrence's niece, for whose kindness and generosity with her time I am most grateful.

16 Cf. Hux 669, Wilk 66.

17 Unpub. letter of 11 September 1926 to Orioli: Lacy 3222.

18 Unpub. letter of ?11 September 1926 to Millicent Beveridge: Lacy 3222.1.

19 As editor of *Vanity Fair*, he had allowed Richard Middleton a whole page for his review of Lawrence's first novel, *The White Peacock*, thus drawing Lawrence's name and work to the attention of the reading public: see Nehls 1 209f.

20 Unpub. letter of ?26 August 1926: Lacy 3201.2.

CHAPTER 7

1 According to the autobiographical essay 'Return to Bestwood', the two main events of Lawrence's stay with Ada – the visit to Eastwood (in most respects the 'Bestwood' of the essay) and an afternoon's drive in the Chesterfield area – occurred in that order on successive days. Monday, the day Lawrence travelled from Lincolnshire, could scarcely have been the first of those days, for when he visited Eastwood he arrived in the morning. Since he left Ripley for London on Thursday, Tuesday was the day of his visit to Eastwood if 'Return to Bestwood' faithfully records the chronology of events. Other evidence suggests that it does. The sun shone on the day of his walk in Eastwood and on Wednesday it was damp and cloudy. Wednesday afternoon would have been a more likely time than Tuesday for his excursion through Derbyshire, because it was half-day closing in Ripley and Eddie Clarke, free from the shop, would have been able to drive him.

2 *England, My England* (Harmondsworth: Penguin, 1960), p. 41.

3 Nehls 1 134.

4 *NG* 2 February 1936. Part of an unpublished letter of 25 October 1925.

5 *NJ* 11 September 1942. According to Olive Hopkin, Willie Hopkin was probably mistaken when writing that Lawrence called at the house. She believes that Lawrence must have called at Willie's shop on the Nottingham Road. This would explain the route they took to Dovecote Lane (see below).

6 *NJ* 11 September 1942. Except where otherwise stated, all quotations from Hopkin's writings and all references to events on Lawrence's walk with Hopkin derive from this article.

7 *NG* 2 February 1936.

8 Walker Street is not mentioned in any of Willie Hopkin's accounts of the itinerary; but Olive Hopkin recalls a report from a friend who observed Lawrence and Hopkin in Walker Street, which is described in 'Return to Bestwood'.

9 In the novel the inn has a landlady, not a landlord.

10 The name 'Crosshill', applied to a colliery and a mining settlement near Tevershall in the novel, was that of a hamlet near Ripley. Lawrence's choice of

'Crosshill' may have been influenced by the fact that a side-road to Watnall (the New Road along which he walked with Hopkin) led over a hill and past Crowhill Farm.

11 Bertha Coutts takes her name from Bertha Cutts, who lived beside the Lawrences in The Breach, Eastwood. See Neville 158. Lawrence's spelling was probably influenced by the name of Coutts, the famous London bankers.

12 *LCL* 88. Not all the details in the several versions of the novel fit the Shortwood cottage: its roof, for instance, was of the same red pantiles as many of the farmhouses and cottages round about, not the grey slate that Lawrence gives the keeper's cottage in *FLC* 42; and there is no sign of the stone wall that surrounded the garden in *LCL* 68. What is left of the cottage suggests that it probably did not have the dormer window of *JTLJ* 243 or the gables of *LCL* 68.

13 *FLC* 121.

14 In *FLC* the well has no name, though it is associated with Robin Hood. In *LCL* it is disguised as 'John's Well'.

15 See Neville 92.

16 On the authorship of these memoirs, see the following papers: G. T. Zytaruk, 'The Chambers memoirs of D. H. Lawrence – which Chambers?', *Renaissance and Modern Studies*, vol. 17 (1973), pp. 141–61; J. Worthen, 'The Chambers memoirs of D. H. Lawrence: a reply', *Renaissance and Modern Studies*, vol. 19 (1975), pp. 98–107; G. T. Zytaruk, 'The Chambers memoirs of D. H. Lawrence – which Chambers?": a reply to Mr John Worthen', *Renaissance and Modern Studies*, vol. 19 (1975), pp. 108–11. Zytaruk's position is that though the point of view of the narrator is that of May Chambers the real author was her sister Jessie. Worthen, whose arguments are difficult to refute, maintained that there was no substantial reason to question the original attribution of the memoirs to May.

17 Nehls 3 562. The approach to the hut along a narrow path through oak woods is identical with that described in all versions of the novel; and the 'pavilion of poles with the bark still on' closely parallels the 'hut made of rustic poles' of *LCL* 90. However, if Nehls is right to suppose that the memoirs were composed *c.* 1935, it is possible that the author's memoirs could have been influenced by a reading of *Lady Chatterley's Lover*, to which 'I could make a story about it, couldn't you?' may coyly refer.

18 The lodge has since been demolished.

19 *NG* 2 February 1936.

20 *NJ* 7 August 1934.

21 *WP* 153f.

22 Connie's meeting with the gamekeeper and his sobbing child, for instance, appears to take place at what in real geography was the footpath that ran through the wood beside the reservoir and joined the drive which led to the lodge gate.

23 Cf. M. Schorer, 'On Lady Chatterley's Lover' in M. Schorer (ed.), *Modern British Fiction* (New York: Oxford University Press, 1961), pp. 285–307 (see pp. 298f.); J. Moynahan, '*Lady Chatterley's Lover*: the deed of life', *English Literary History*, vol. 26 (1959), pp. 66–90 (see pp. 70–72); M. Squires, 'Pastoral patterns and pastoral variants in *Lady Chatterley's Lover*', *English Literary History*, vol. 39 (1972), pp. 129–46 (see pp. 131f.).

24 *Ph* 822f. This unfinished story was composed in October 1927, and Lawrence

therefore gave October rather than September as the month of his visit. I have adopted Sagar's suggestion (*Calendar* 166) of 'A Dream of Life' as a more appropriate title for a work formerly known as 'Autobiographical Fragment'.

25 The dipping-hole and the bridge are mentioned in *SL* 31.

26 *Ph* 822.

27 For an illuminating and authoritative study of Lawrence's writings on architecture and planning see J. Burke, 'The D. H. Lawrence country', *Architectural Review*, vol. 95 (May 1944), pp. 115–17.

28 *Rainbow* 547f.

29 *Ph 2* 257.

30 *Ph* 817.

31 A transcript of a recorded conversation with D. E. Gerard, part of a collection held at the Central Library, Nottingham.

32 *LCL* 158. There is no mention of a school in *FLC*. In *JTLJ* 155 only the newness of the school links it with the Devonshire Drive Schools, and it is sited *behind* the Congregational chapel, suggesting that Lawrence must have been thinking partly of the British School, where he taught Charles Leeming. In *LCL* the school is sited 'beyond' the chapel, and therefore could be either one of the two schools. Perhaps in each of these versions the fictional school, like so many of the fictive characters, places and buildings, results from a conflation of each of the schools, with the Devonshire Drive building shifted to the site of the British School and given its chapel-like appearance.

33 Both Gill and Strickland give brief critical studies of the contrasts between the portraits of Tevershall in the first and third versions.

34 F. R. Leavis, 'The orthodoxy of enlightenment', in *Anna Karenina and Other Essays* (London: Chatto & Windus, 1967), p. 238.

35 Smith 346.

36 *PL* 34.

37 Spencer 27.

38 J. C. P. Taylor, 'Boys of the Beauvale breed', *EKA* 14 April 1961, quoting an anecdote from the columns of 'Anglo-Saxon' concerning a visit by King Edward.

39 See *EKA* 27 August 1926.

40 *EKA* 27 August 1926.

41 *EKA* 17 September 1926.

42 *EKA* 17 September 1926.

43 Griffin 245.

44 Griffin 249.

45 Sagar (*Calendar* 154) suggests that 'Return to Bestwood' was not written until Lawrence returned to the Villa Mirenda. The reading 'I came home to the Midlands . . . at the end of September', the use of the present tense and the reference to an incident that occurred 'yesterday' [*Ph 2* 257, 259] point to composition while Lawrence was at Ripley; but these could be ploys to give greater immediacy to the narrative: Lawrence's first draft, 'Getting On', reads: 'I went this autumn . . . to the place of my birth'.

46 *EKA* 1 October 1926.

47 *EKA* 27 August 1926.

48 Griffin 249.

49 *EKA* 27 August 1926.
50 Cf. *FLC* 139, 146, 242.
51 *EKA* 24 September 1926.
52 Griffin 236.

CHAPTER 8

1 *Ph 2* 262.
2 *CL 929.*
3 Unpub. letter of 11 September 1926 to Orioli: Lacy 3222.
4 *CL 939.*
5 Several of the local landmarks and places alluded to in the account of Connie's journey are specified in Pugh 258f.
6 The Eastwood landmarks, mentioned as Connie's car leaves Tevershall, show that the car set off down Mansfield Road in the direction of Underwood, and the siting of the collier Swain's cottage near Stacks Gate, in an area corresponding to New Brinsley, also suggests a link between Underwood and Stacks Gate.
7 *LCL* 162. Pugh (259) mistakenly, in my view, considering the siting of the hall, identifies Fritchley with Sutton Scarsdale Hall.
8 *LCL* 165. Pugh (259) believes that the fictional Shipley is a combination of Barlborough Hall, near Renishaw, and Rufford Abbey; but there can be no doubt that Lawrence's principal model was Shipley Hall, near Heanor, Derbyshire.
9 Osbert Sitwell, *Left Hand, Right Hand!* (London: Macmillan, 1944), pp. 18f.
10 *Crome Yellow* (London: Chatto & Windus, 1922), p. 249.
11 *The Lost Girl*, ed. J. Worthen (Cambridge: Cambridge University Press, 1981), p. 1.
12 See Lloyd 101.
13 On this reciprocal relationship in Lawrence's fiction, see J. Atkins, 'Lawrence's social landscape', *Books and Bookmen*, vol. 15, pt 10 (1970), pp. 24–6.
14 *England after the War* (London: Hodder & Stoughton, 1922), p. 13.
15 ibid., p. 19.
16 ibid., p. 19.
17 *Ph 2* 264; *FLC* 104; *JTLJ* 206; *LCL* 188.

CHAPTER 9

1 Dobrée had laid the foundations for a good rapport with Lawrence in his favourable appraisal of Lawrence's works in *The Lamp and the Lute: Studies in Six Modern Authors* (Oxford: Clarendon, 1919), pp. 86–106. He had also recently written a largely favourable review of the text of the play *David* in the *Nation and Athenaeum*, vol. 39 (24 April 1926), pp. 103–4.
2 Cf. Sec 91.
3 Unpub. postcard to Ada Clarke and Gertrude Cooper, 29 September 1926: Lacy 3236.

4   See Irv 70.

5   J. S. Robinson, *H. D.: The Life and Works of an American Poet* (Boston, Mass.: Houghton Mifflin, 1982), pp. 142–80. I am grateful to Jane Thompson for drawing this extraordinary book to my attention.

The suggestion that Lawrence was the father of Hilda's child can easily be dismissed. In 1917 H. D. and Lawrence had indeed begun a love-affair which was mainly cerebral, though it could have had a physical aspect. But the child, Perdita, was born on 31 March 1919. During the period when the child must have been conceived Lawrence was at Mountain Cottage, Derbyshire. He remained there, never leaving the Notts–Derbys. area, from mid-May of 1918 to early October. In June 1918 he wrote to Amy Lowell saying he had not seen Hilda 'for some time' (*Let 3* 254) and that she was in Cornwall (where she was staying with her lover, Cecil Gray). Later in September he wrote to her again: he had not seen H. D. 'for a long time' (*Let 3* 280) and believed she had now left Cornwall. When he met H. D. in London in November for the first time in several months, she was already pregnant. Only through a 'Glad Ghosts'-style encounter in the spirit could H. D. have conceived a child by Lawrence.

6   Smith 155.

7   Smith 332.

8   Cf. Aldous Huxley, *Point* 271, where Quarles (a character based on Huxley), thinking of his friend Rampion (Lawrence), wishes dearly that he 'could capture something of his secret!'. Rampion, Charles believes, is the embodied 'proof of his [Rampion's] theories'.

9   Smith 365.

10   Aldous Huxley, *Two or Three Graces* (London: Chatto & Windus, 1926), pp. 119f.

11   Smith 339f.

12   See *Ph* 25f.

13   Squires 3.

14   V. S. Knoepflmacher, 'The rival ladies in Mrs Ward's *Lady Connie* and Lawrence's *Lady Chatterley's Lover*', *Victorian Studies*, vol. 4, no. 2 (1960), pp. 141–58. The correspondences between the two novels are perhaps not quite so striking as is claimed by the author of this paper, who acknowledges: 'Lawrence may or may not have read Mrs Ward's novel. But what seems his meticulous inversion of its plot and of the values represented by its main characters reveals not only his repudiation of an artifical outgrowth of Victorian ethical thought, but also indicates the extent of his own . . . indebtedness to the great Victorian masters.'

15   See Smith 86.

16   'Not I' vii.

17   This dating was first proposed by Keith Sagar in *The Art of D. H. Lawrence* (Cambridge: Cambridge University Press, 1966), p. 171. A later date (the spring and summer of 1927) had been proposed by E. W. Tedlock Jr in *The Frieda Lawrence Collection of D. H. Lawrence Manuscripts: A Descriptive Catalogue* (Albuquerque, N. Mex.: University of New Mexico Press, 1948), p. 23. This dating (generally accepted before the publication of Sagar's work) is mistaken: there are no references to current work on the novel in the correspondence at that period, and the activities and events of spring and summer 1927 allow no time for work on the second draft.

18   Discussing his methods of composition with Brett, Lawrence told her: 'I never know when I sit down, just what I am going to write. I make no plan; it just comes, and I don't know where it comes from. Of course I have a general sort of outline of what I want to write about, but when I go out in the mornings I have no idea what I will write. It just comes, and I really don't know where from.' (Brett 247).

19   Hinz argues that *FLC* is, unlike subsequent versions, 'an outright piece of pornography' and a masterpiece of that genre. There is much to be said for Hinz's point of view. It is the most erotic of the three versions (partly because of the realism of the presentation of the two lovers and their situation, and partly because the sparseness of explicit detail stimulates the reader's imagination). In this version, too, the four-letter words (which, contrary to some claims, including those of the author in *CL* 1167, occur in only slightly less profusion than in *JTLJ* and *LCL*) are used in ways which accord with the overall realism of the novel (see also Strickland on the use of obscenities in *FLC*). At this stage in the genesis of *Lady Chatterley* Lawrence had not yet determined to imbue these words with 'a proper reverence for sex, and a proper awe of the body's strange experience' (*Ph 2* 490). Often, in *FLC*, Parkin uses them in the expression of anger or contempt and therefore obscenely. For Hinz, *FLC* is pornographic and obscene principally because Lawrence's attitude towards his characters and their situations is 'cynical'. Perhaps the epithet is a little too strong for the degree of flippancy which Lawrence shows in this version. But it is true, as Hinz observes, that Parkin and Connie do not engage the author's sympathies as fully as in other versions; and there is also a generous measure of light comedy (described by Hinz as 'mockery') in the treatment of all the major characters – a feature of *FLC* which receives attention in Strickland and in Gill.

20   Squires 4.

21   Squires 4.

22   As Squires (176) observes, 'typically . . . [Lawrence] sketched the action in version 1' and 'developed it with lyrical intensity in version 2'.

23   The first draft of 'The Sisters' (the prototype for *The Rainbow* and *Women in Love*), for instance, had 'come rushing out' (*Let 2* 617). Squires (4) notes that the first draft of *The Plumed Serpent* was written in less than eight weeks.

24   In this version, as Hinz remarks, 'up to a point there is actually nothing much more than plot in both the literal and figurative meanings of the term'.

25   Nehls 2 106.

26   The only complete first draft of a novel other than *FLC* to survive and appear in print is *Mr Noon*, first published in full by Cambridge University Press in 1984. Because Lawrence lost interest in the novel, the usual succeeding stages of revision were neglected. The text of *Mr Noon* could be said to bear out my suggestion regarding the character of first drafts; but it is not a particularly relevant illustration: *Mr Noon* is a comedy, and its realism and lack of overt preaching are features which Lawrence almost certainly intended to retain in the projected final version. If we choose to regard *The Virgin and the Gipsy* as a first draft, which Lawrence originally intended later to expand into a full novel, the characteristics of its text (which led its first critics to assume that it belonged to an early period in Lawrence's career) could perhaps be said to support my speculation.

27   *CL* 955.

28   Unpub. letter of 20 November 1926: Lacy 3272.

29　Barbara Weekley reported that Lawrence did not reproach Frieda after she had gone off alone on a visit to Ravagli in the spring of 1928 (Nehls 3 189).

30　Brew 112.

31　Wilk 68.

32　*CL* 965f.

33　*CL 959; CL* 961.

34　C. Asquith, *Haply I May Remember* (London: Barrie, 1950), p. 106.

35　*Flowers* 35f.

36　*LCL* 299f. Squires (229 n. 14) also refers to the influence of the meeting with Magnelli on the creation of Duncan Forbes in *LCL*. Professor James T. Cowan has drawn my attention to similarities between the account of Magnelli's paintings and the portrait in *LCL* of Uthwaite (see Ch. 7): the correspondences suggest that in modern painting Lawrence discerned the same abhorrent, inhuman, mechanical power which inhered in modern industrial landscapes.

37　*CL* 967.

38　The notices (several of which are reproduced in Sklar 289–94) were generally rather favourable, viz. Ivor Brown, *Saturday Review of Literature* (18 December 1926); Desmond MacCarthy, *New Statesman* (18 December 1926); 'Omicron', *Nation and Athenaeum* (18 December 1926); James Agate, *Sunday Times* (19 December 1926); H. H., *Outlook* (24 December 1926); and Hubert Griffith ('source uncertain').

There were hostile reviews in *The Times* (14 December 1926) – 'the stilled movement of a grotesque decoration', 'stagnant and tormented, it lies like a burden on the mind' – and by St J. E. ('source unknown', 19 December 1926) – 'Insignificance was the chief feature of the piece', 'a mere exhibition'. MacCarthy's sympathetic review was not likely to have pleased the author, since it made an unflattering comparison between Lawrence's early and later works. Pointing out that the play was written in 1914, MacCarthy commented: 'Since then he has attempted to formulate directly his theory of sex relations, often to the detriment of his art, for he has taken to preaching and obscure exposition.'

39　Some (Brown, 'Omicron', H. H.) blamed the writing, but MacCarthy faulted the production, as Agate did by implication in his praise of the construction of the last act and his silence on its dramatic realization.

40　*CL* 953f.

41　See *CL* 963f.

42　The reviews of the 1968 production (see Sklar 319–21) singled out for special praise the last act, which in 1926 had been regarded as a major flaw in the writing or production of the play.

43　Hux 678.

44　'Red Herring', *Poems* 490.

45　*JTLJ* 241.

46　The significance and the realism of the gamekeepers' code-switching (particularly that of Mellors) has rarely been fully appreciated by critics of the novel. For an informed and illuminating study of Mellors's linguistic usage, see R. R. Leith, 'Dialogue and dialect in D. H. Lawrence', *Style*, vol. 14 (Summer 1980), pp. 245–58.

47　Parts of this letter were edited out of the text published in Ada 117–19 and *CL* 961–3.

48　Part of an unpub. letter (Lacy 3229.7) quoted in Squires 5.

49 See Squires 28f.

50 See Brew 277 and references to March in the first two parts of the essay.

51 The date is established by the internal evidence of reference to late April in the third part of the essay.

CHAPTER 10

1 Brew 121. Cf. Lawrence's letter to Dr Trigant Burrow, *CL* 994, which associates the Fall with loss of the pre-cognitive mode of consciousness, a state analogous to Lawrence's phallic consciousness.

2 Unpub. part of letter of 14 April 1927 to Ada Clarke: Lacy 3356.

3 Like the malaria diagnosed in Mexico in 1925, this was likely to have been, in reality, a tubercular fever.

4 See *CL* 75.

5 See *EC* 136. According to Brewster (Brew 123f.) the toy in question was 'a white rooster escaping from an egg'. But Lawrence's inscription in the holograph given to Harry Crosby describes the toy as a cock escaping from a man. Brewster mistakenly gives Easter Sunday as the day the toy was seen. Lawrence has the correct date – the Sunday before Easter. Like Lacy, I therefore take Lawrence's description of the toy to be the more accurate of the two.

6 *CL* 981.

7 In the case of the reviews of *David*, Lawrence had good cause for hurt and disappointment. No one appears to have liked it. The most scathing review was that of Richard Jennings in the *Spectator* (28 May 1927), pp. 939f. Jennings, who was puzzled as to what it was that persuaded 'a writer of such intense conviction and so little sense of humour . . . into an adventure like that of *David*', described the play as 'a series of chromolithographic "views" of scriptural scenes', 'a mere show', which 'reminded one at moments of *Ben Hur*': the audience was presented with 'a picture of familiar puppets, pulled by the hoary and gory hand of a prophet'. 'We were not convinced', he concluded, 'but that was not the fault of the actors'.

Other reviews (quoted in Sklar 296f., which does not include the Jennings article) were hostile, but a little less 'impudent' (*CL* 980). 'Omicron' in the *Nation and Athenaeum* (28 May 1927) differed from Jennings in so far as he hesitated 'to blame the author entirely for the resultant fiasco'; but the author was apportioned the blame for the play's lack of 'all dramatic movement' and for 'a tedious Wardour Street diction frequently interlarded with quotations from the most well-known book in English'. *The Times* reviewer (24 May 1927), though often 'impressed . . . by the vehemence of his impassioned words', found that what Lawrence had created was 'neither drama nor poetry'. Generally he found the play dull: 'the unending insistence on the verbal symbols of mysticism, grows wearisome long before the last of the 16 scenes'.

8 Aldington 341.

9 Faith Mackenzie (*More Than* 162) believed that what got Douglas 'on the raw' was the episode in which, after dinner at a restaurant, Douglas had the wine weighed in order to have the cost of what was left deducted from the bill.

10 Holloway 333.

11 'Germans and Latins' (*Ph* 128) mentions, and was inspired by, the sight of two

German youths on the Ponte Vecchio on 29 April.

12 Aldington 342. According to Aldington, this 'accidental' encounter was staged by Orioli.

13 *Looking Back* 350.

14 Holloway 337.

15 See Cerf.

16 Holloway 307f. The blue-paper copies of *Lady Chatterley's Lover* were presented to Orioli and Frieda. See Gransden 32.

17 Holloway 355.

18 A photograph of Gee's painting appears among the photographs following p. 250 of Holloway's biography of Douglas.

19 Unpub. letter of 19 May 1927 to Emily King: Lacy 3382.

20 Osbert 296. The essay had first appeared in *Weekend Review*, 7 February 1931.

21 Edith, Ch. 12.

22 Edith 108.

23 See Pearson 202–5, 210–12.

24 Pearson 230.

25 Pearson 200.

26 Edith 110f. There would appear to have been an altercation between Edith Sitwell and Lawrence concerning *Lady Chatterley's Lover* in Florence, perhaps in July 1929, when Lawrence returned briefly to the city to stay with Orioli: see 'To Pino', *Poems* 668.

27 Unpub. letter to Orioli, 19 July 1927: Lacy 3424.

28 Smith 288.

29 *CL* 1008.

30 Unpub. letter of ?17 October 1927: Lacy 3517.

31 F. Schoenberner, 'When D. H. Lawrence was shocked', *Saturday Review of Literature*, vol. 29, no. 8 (1946), pp. 18f.

32 On possible influences of Burrow's writings on Lawrence's thought, see E. W. Dawson, 'Lawrence's pollyanalitic esthetic for the novel', *Paunch*, vol. 26 (April 1966), pp. 60–8.

33 Wilk 71.

CHAPTER 11

1 For a detailed account of the revisions Lawrence was obliged to make for the Irish edition of his history, see F. Crumpton, 'D. H. Lawrence's "mauled history": the Irish edition of *Movements in European History*', *DHLR*, vol. 13 (Summer 1980), pp. 105–18.

2 *Gossip* 92.

3 *Gossip* 140.

4 According to his unpublished letter of 24 February 1928 to Bonamy Dobrée, Mrs Dobrée had failed to inform Lawrence of her intention to nurse her father at the Dobrees' house in Cairo.

5 Unpub. letter of 28 November 1966 from Bonamy Dobrée to Harry T. Moore, containing a transcript of Lawrence's letter of 2 November 1927 to Mrs Dobrée.

6 Unpub. letter of 3 November 1927: Lacy 3530.

7 Unpub. letter of 16 November 1927: Lacy 3540.

8 Unpub. letter of 16 November 1927 to Emily King: Lacy 3541.

9 Nehls 3 168.

10 Crosby sent Lawrence the 20-dollar gold pieces at the end of March 1928. The box containing them was handed over for delivery to a stranger who was boarding the Rome Express in Paris: it was the Duke of Argyll, who personally delivered the gold to Lawrence (Nehls 3 199f. and *CL* 1051). Later, towards the end of May, after Lawrence had sent Crosby the MS of 'Sun', Crosby sent three additional gold coins in the Queen of Naples's snuff box (*CL* 1064).

11 Brown 70.

12 Brown 70.

13 Cf. *Cent* 31, *CL* 1033.

14 *PL* 549.

15 Holloway 356.

16 See Holloway 266–70.

17 See C. Gray, *Peter Warlock* (London: Cape, 1934), p. 119.

18 Zyt 330.

19 Squires 223.

20 An unpublished letter of 8 December 1927 to Ada Clarke suggests that Arlen came out to the Mirenda on more than one occasion: Lacy 3555.

21 A. S. Frere, intro. to M. Arlen, *The Green Hat* (London: Cassell, 1968).

22 Compare, for example, the fortnight's apparent silence when Lawrence was working on 'The Sisters' in December 1913 (*Let 2* 117–19), or the week-long gap in the correspondence during December 1920, when he was writing *Mr Noon* (*Let 3* 639f.). Of course it may have been in these cases, as in the period November–December 1927, that letters which were written then have not survived.

23 See Squires 7 and 226, n. 6. Squires uses the phrase 'the *first* notebook' to refer to the first fifty-seven leaves of the MS, which were subsequently bound into the second notebook.

24 See above, Ch. 9, and Nehls 2 106.

25 There were three versions of *WP* (see *WP* xxvi); *SL* existed in at least three versions (see *Let 1* 321); *Rainbow* passed through four drafts and there were three complete drafts of *WL* (see C. L. Ross, *The Composition of 'The Rainbow' and 'Women in Love': A History* [Charlottesville, Va: University Press of Virginia, 1979], pp. 15–57, 97–123); there appear to have been three versions of *The Lost Girl*, though the first was only a twenty-page fragment, which seems to have been all that Lawrence wrote (see *The Lost Girl* [Cambridge: Cambridge University Press, 1981], pp. xix–xl).

26 See the reviews of *JTLJ* (which appeared after its first publication in English in 1972) cited and summarized in J. C. Cowan, *D. H. Lawrence: An Annotated Bibliography of Writings About Him*, Vol. 2 (De Kalb, Ill.: Northern Illinois University Press, 1985), nos. 3875, 3883, 3887, 3897, 3907, 3909, 3945, 3957, 3960, 4082, 4109, 4118, 4207, 4239, 4302, 4342, 4456.

JTLJ has received surprisingly meagre critical attention, and only in Squires is there a full analytical discussion of the text. A number of the following studies tend to be largely descriptive of differences in content between *JTLJ* and the other two versions: P. Nardi, 'Le tre redazioni dell' "Amante di Lady Chatterley"', *Le Tre Venezie* (Pardova), no. 21 (April–June 1947), pp. 135–42; E. W. Tedlock, Jr, *The*

Frieda Lawrence Collection of D. H. Lawrence Manuscripts: A Descriptive Bibliography (Albuquerque, N. Mex.: University of New Mexico Press, 1948), pp. 279–316; J. R. L. Reyner, 'The three versions of *Lady Chatterley's Lover*', *Geste* (University of Leeds), vol. 7 (1961), pp. 31–46; M. Schorer, 'On *Lady Chatterley's Lover*', in M. Schorer (ed.), *Modern British Fiction* (New York: Oxford University Press, 1961), pp. 285–307; Widmer; J. Doheny, 'Lady Chatterley and her lover', *West Coast Review*, vol. 8 (January 1974), pp. 51–6; Sanders 172–205; Delavenay; R. Beck, 'Die drei versionen von *Lady Chatterley's Lover*', *Anglia*, vol. 96 (1978), pp. 409–29; Hinz; D. Clark, *The Minoan Distance: The Symbolism of Travel in D. H. Lawrence* (Tucson, Ariz.: University of Arizona Press, 1980), pp. 360–77; J. B. Humma, 'The interpenetrating metaphor: nature and myth in *Lady Chatterley's Lover*', *Proceedings of the Modern Languages Association*, vol. 98 (1983), pp. 77–86.

Most of the writers cited above hold *JTLJ* in high regard, as also does Squires (187), who believes that a simple revision of *JTLJ*, which conserved the splendours of that version, would have made for a more satisfying final draft than the one which emerged from a complete rewriting. Exceptions to the generally favourable appraisal of *JTLJ* are to be found in the papers by Widmer and Delavenay, both of whom regard the second version as merely an imperfect draft for a novel.

27 See Squires 5.

28 Squires (182f.), commenting on 'the novel's schematic antitheses' and on its form, suggests that 'the novel approaches a diagram'. In his opinion the novel's saving grace 'is that the jabbingly incisive analysis of modern life rarely interferes with the regeneration of Connie and Mellors: the novel succeeds in forcing the diagram simply to frame the characters' sensual awakening'.

29 Mohr 26.

30 '*Not I*' 227, 229.

31 *CL* 1032.

32 Ada 133.

33 Ada 153.

34 Unpub. letter of 20 December 1927: Lacy 3561.4.

35 Unpub. letter of ?24 December 1927: Lacy 3566.1.

36 Unpub. letter of 28 December 1927: Lacy 3569.1.

CHAPTER 12

1 Sec 103.

2 *Cent* 33.

3 See Ellmann 598.

4 Ellmann 628.

5 *Adventures* 233f.

6 See *Pinorman* (London: Heinemann, 1954), pp. vii and 194f.

7 *Adventures* 234.

8 *Adventures* 234. Cecil Gray (*Musical Chairs* 139) records substantially the same observation by Douglas in a conversation with him during the Second World War: 'Do you realize that no one who knew Lawrence well, as we know him, was sorry when he died?'

9 See the text of the letter in Squires 11f.

10 *CL* 1052.

11 See Hux 715.

12 See Gransden 32.

13 A memorandum which Lawrence kept on correspondence concerning the advertisement of *LCL* (now among a collection of Lawrence's papers held by the Bancroft Library, University of California, Berkeley) records that these letters were all sent on 13 March. My dating has followed the dates on extant letters to persons named in Lawrence's note.

14 Wilk 73.

15 Nehls 3 204.

16 Unpub. letter of 13 April to Emily King: Lacy 3690.

17 *CL* 1050.

18 *CL* 1059. On 5 July 1929 the exhibition was raided by the police, following complaints to the Home Secretary and angry press reports. Thirteen paintings were removed and the owners of the gallery (Dorothy Warren and her husband, Philip Trotter) were charged under the Obscenities Act. For a full account of the exhibition, the raid and the court hearing, see Nehls 3 326–41, 342–52, 353–7, 360–75, 380–9.

19 Hux 729.

20 Brew 282.

21 Brew 282.

Index